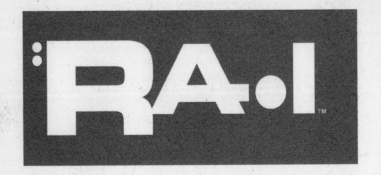

By Sanami Matoh

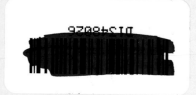

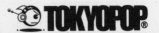

HAMBURG // LONDON // LOS ANGELES // TOKYO

RA-I
Created By Sanami Matoh

Translation - Adrienne Beck
English Adaption - Jill Freshney
Layout and Lettering - Gloria Wu
Cover Layout - James Lee

Editor - Katherine Schilling
Digital Imaging Manager - Chris Buford
Managing Editor - Vy Nguyen
Production Manager - Liz Brizzi
VP of Production - Ron Klamert
Editor-in-Chief - Rob Tokar
Publisher - Mike Kiley
President and C.O.O. - John Parker
C.E.O. and Chief Creative Officer - Stuart Levy

A [TOKYOPOP] Manga

TOKYOPOP Inc.
Wilshire Blvd. Suite 2000
Los Angeles, CA 90036

E-mail: info@TOKYOPOP.com
Come visit us online at www.TOKYOPOP.com

ISBN: 1-59816-663-8

First TOKYOPOP printing: October 2006
10 9 8 7 6 5 4 3 2 1
Printed in the USA

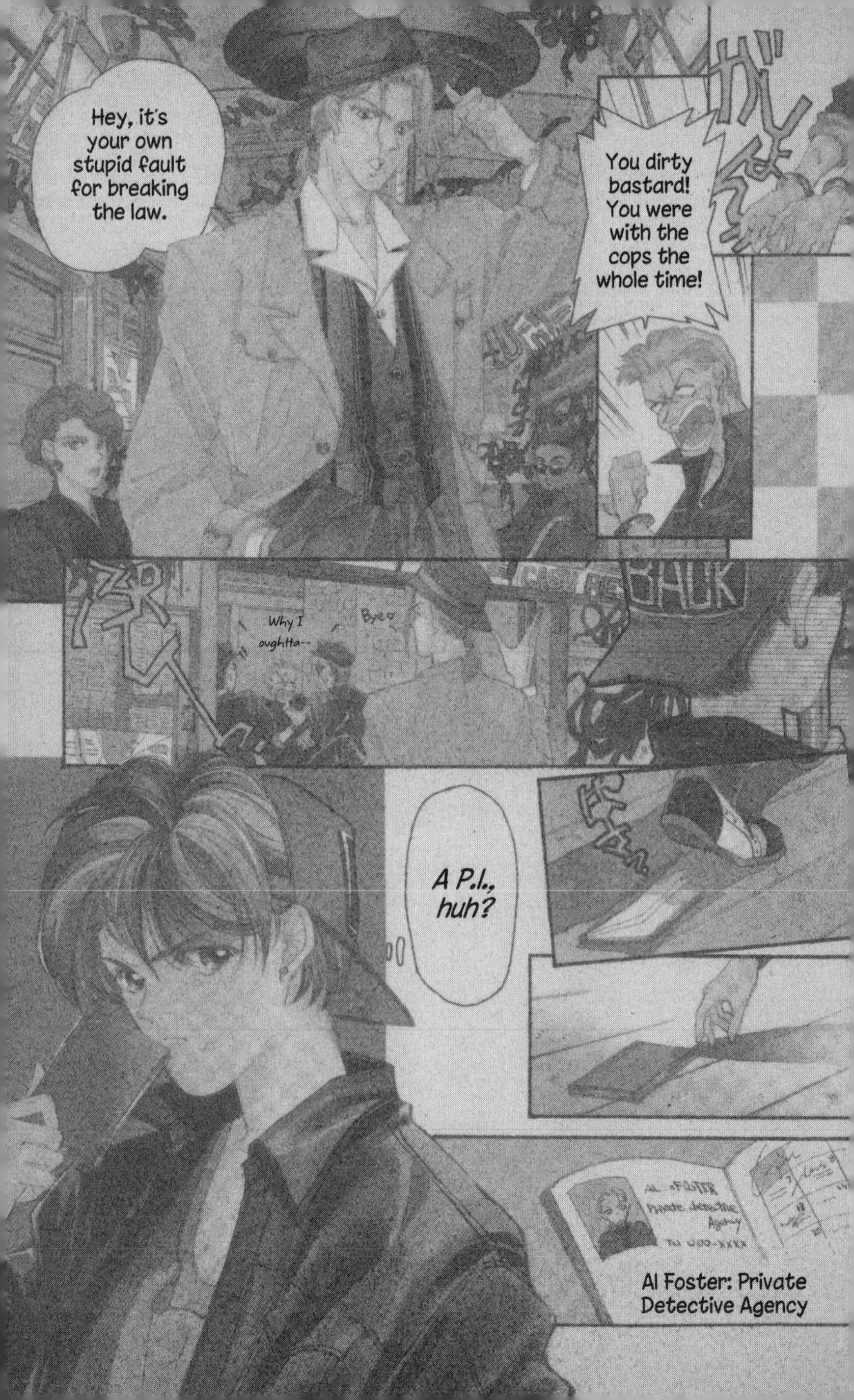
You dirty bastard! You were with the cops the whole time!
Hey, it's your own stupid fault for breaking the law.
Bye♡
Why I oughtta--
A P.I., huh?
Al Foster: Private Detective Agency

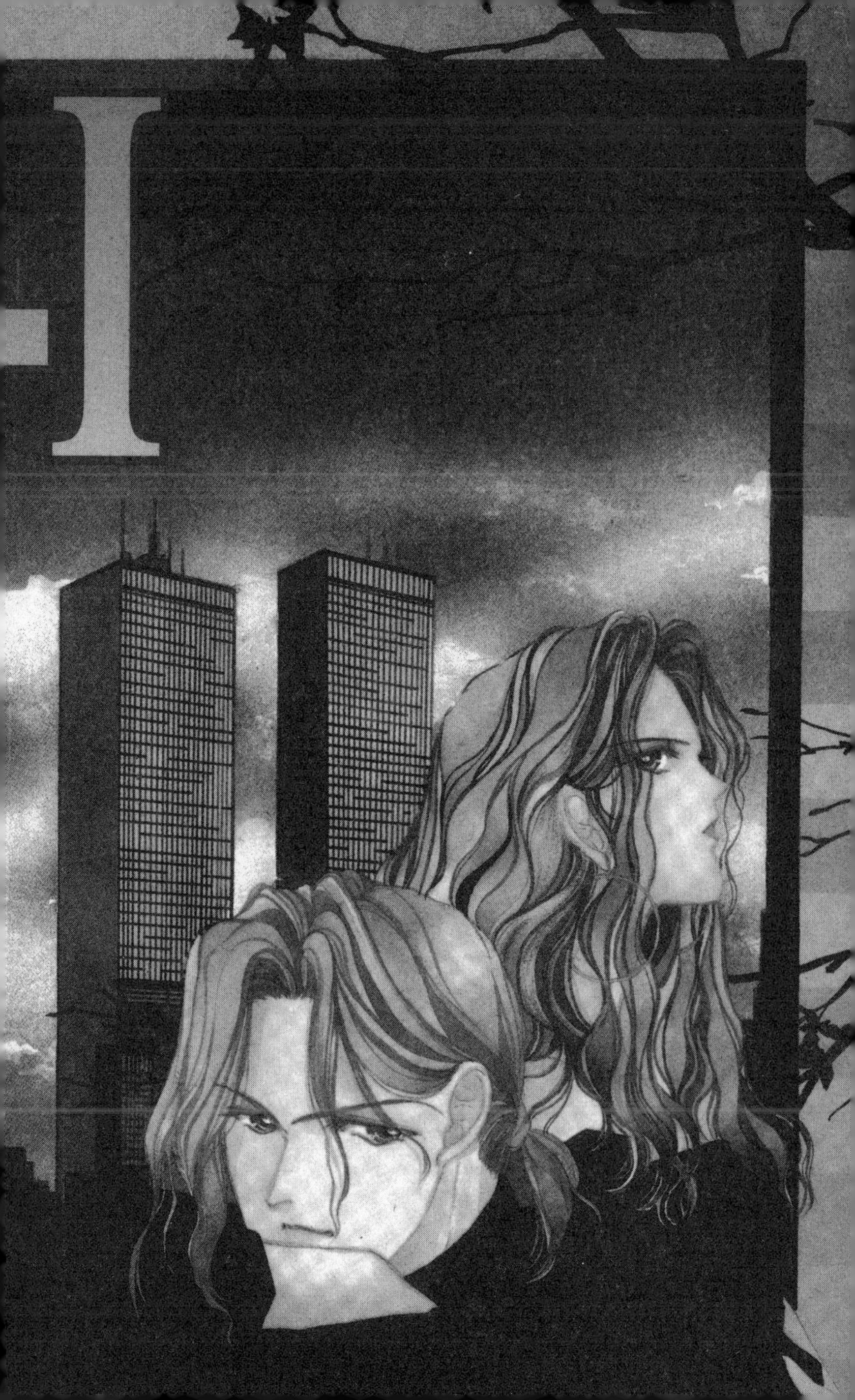
I

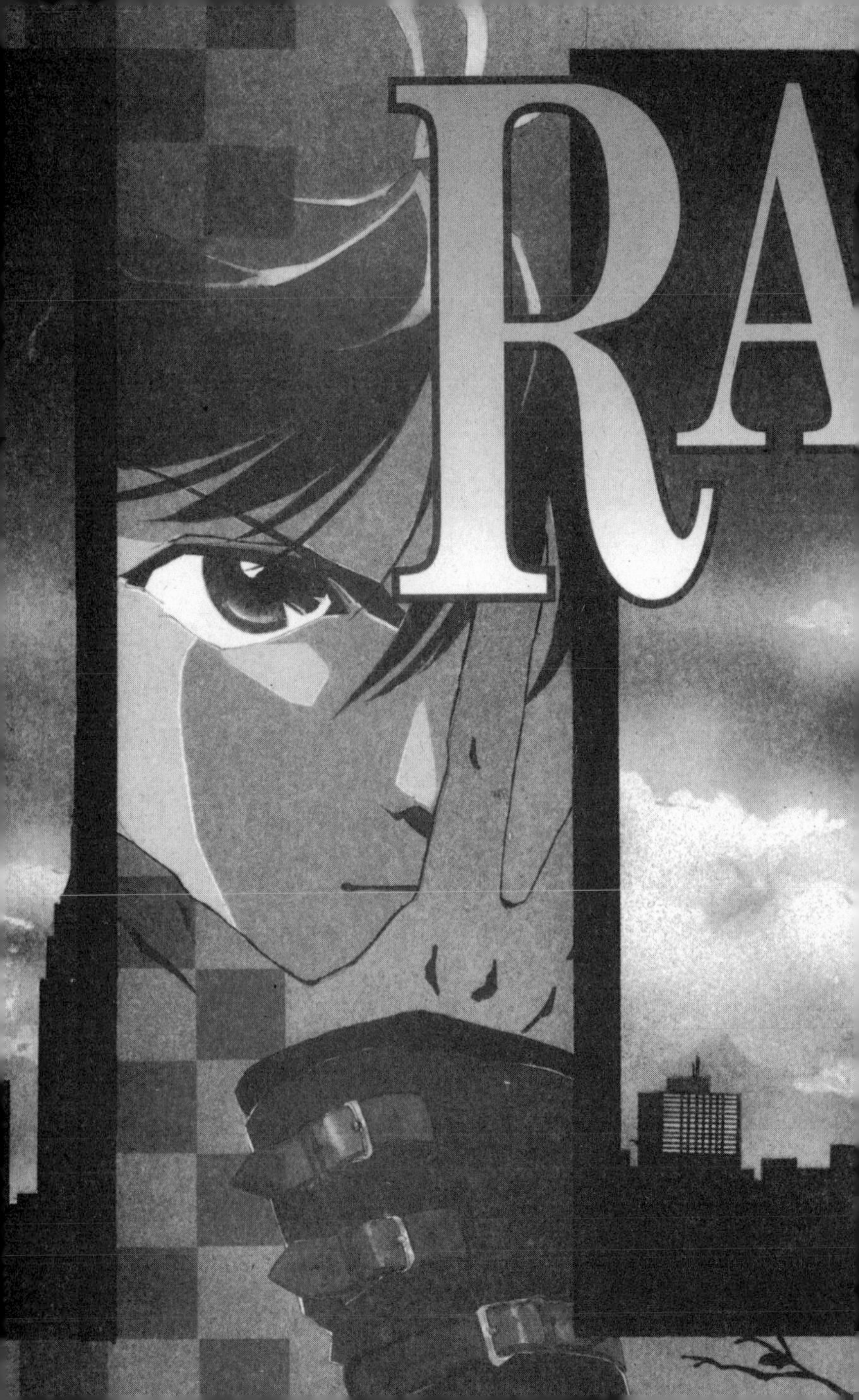
RA

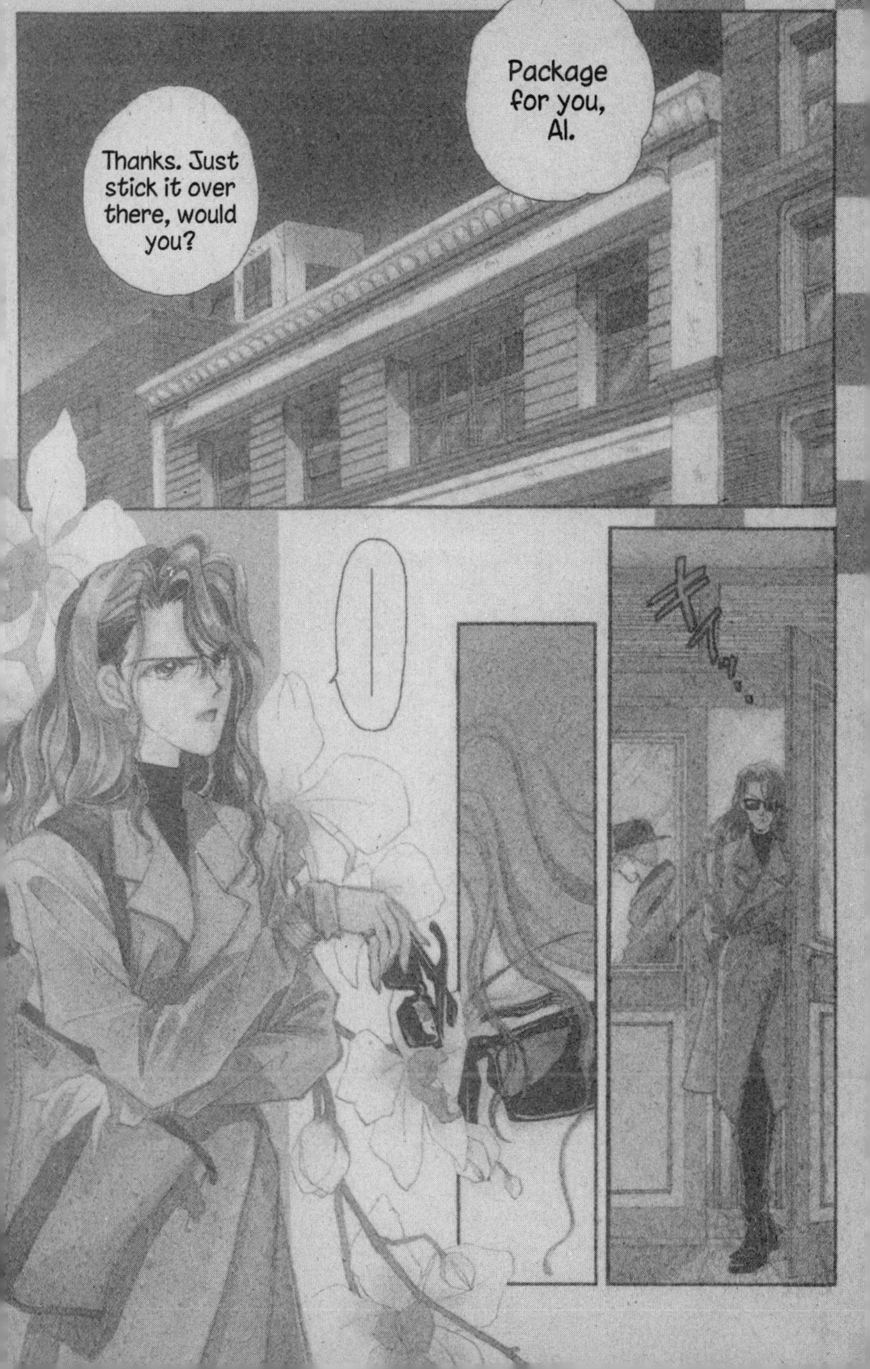
Package for you, Al.
Thanks. Just stick it over there, would you?
—

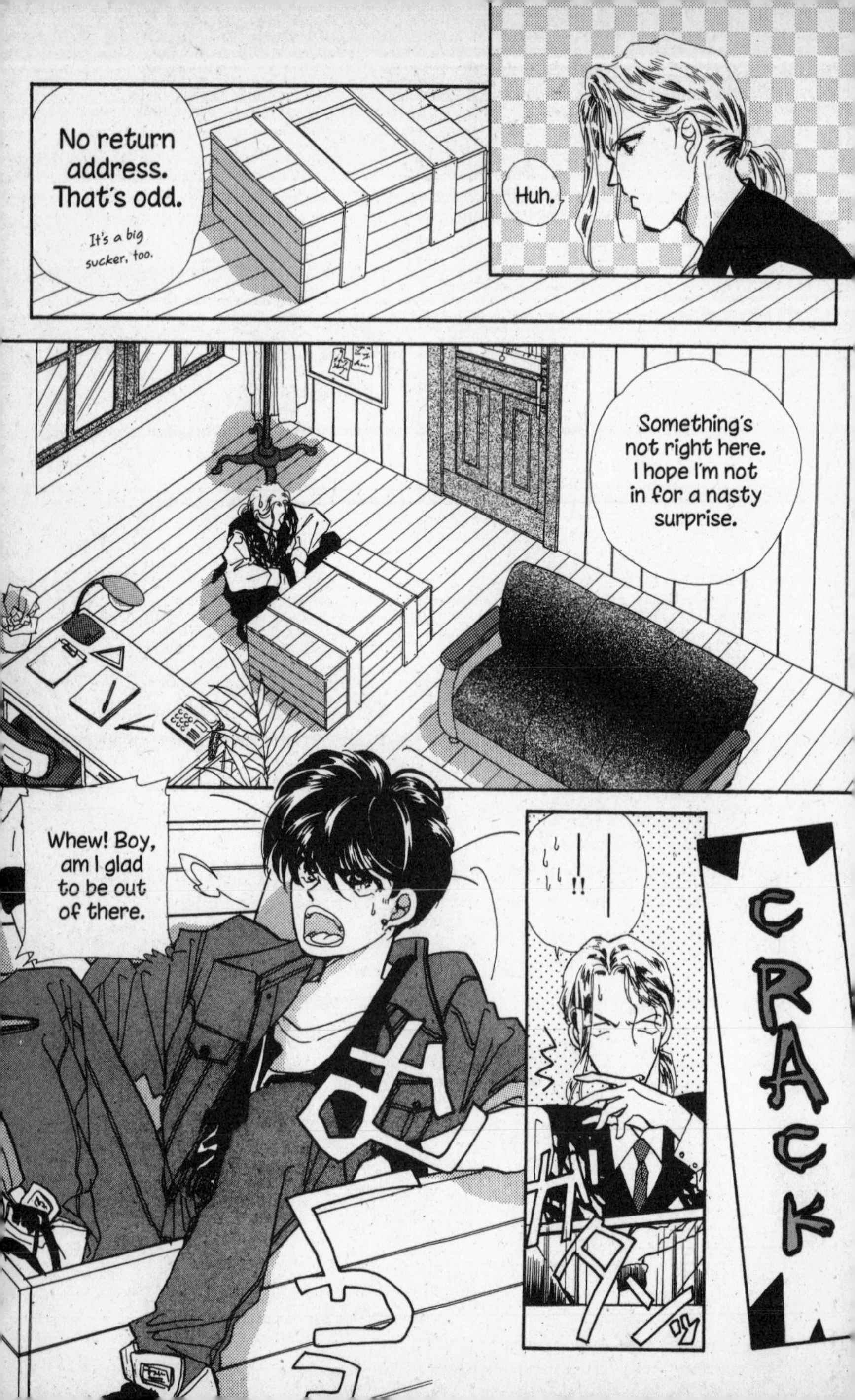
Huh.
No return address. That's odd.
It's a big sucker, too.
Something's not right here. I hope I'm not in for a nasty surprise.
CRACK
!!
Whew! Boy, am I glad to be out of there.

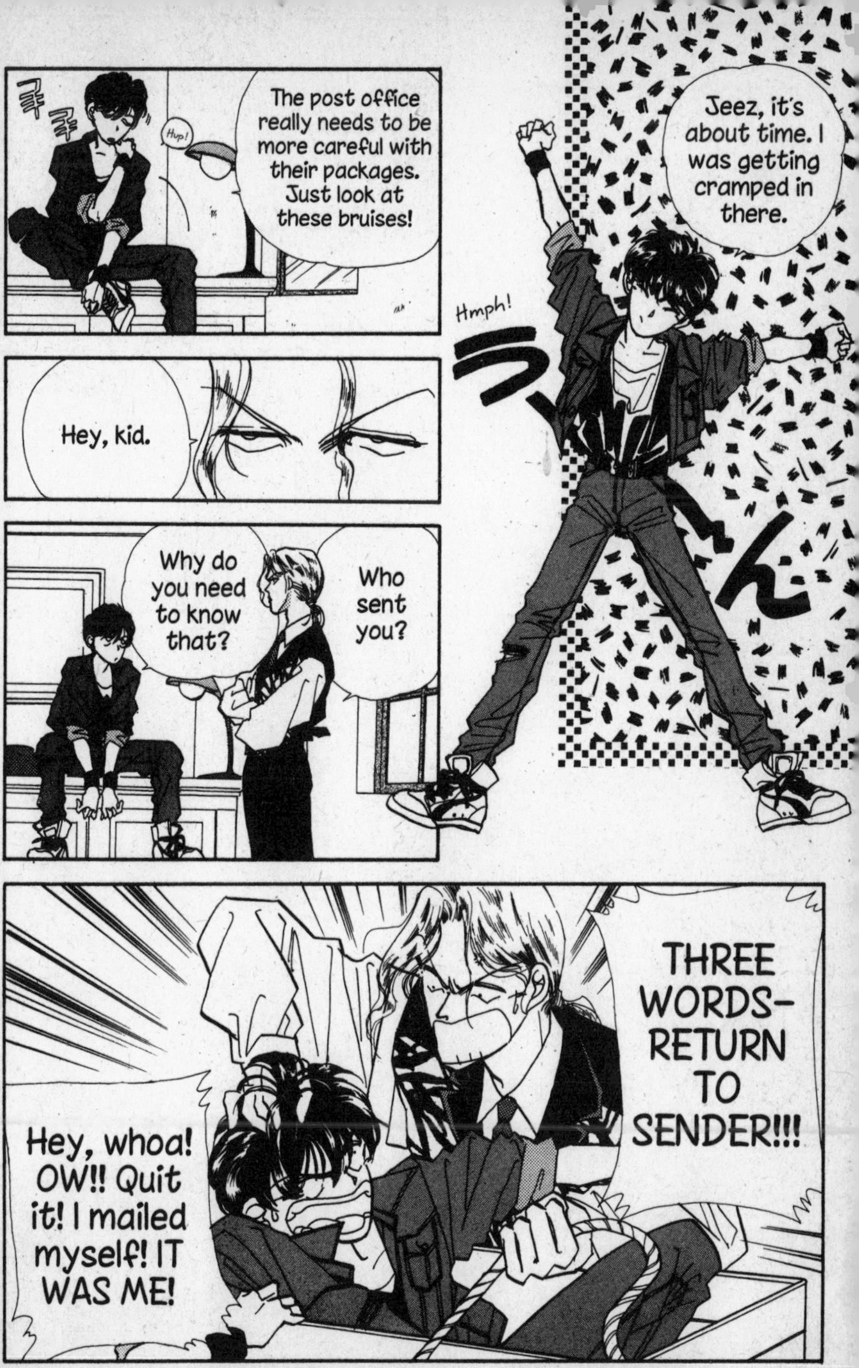
Jeez, it's about time. I was getting cramped in there.
Hmph!
Hup!
The post office really needs to be more careful with their packages. Just look at these bruises!
Hey, kid.
Who sent you?
Why do you need to know that?
THREE WORDS- RETURN TO SENDER!!!
Hey, whoa! OW!! Quit it! I mailed myself! IT WAS ME!

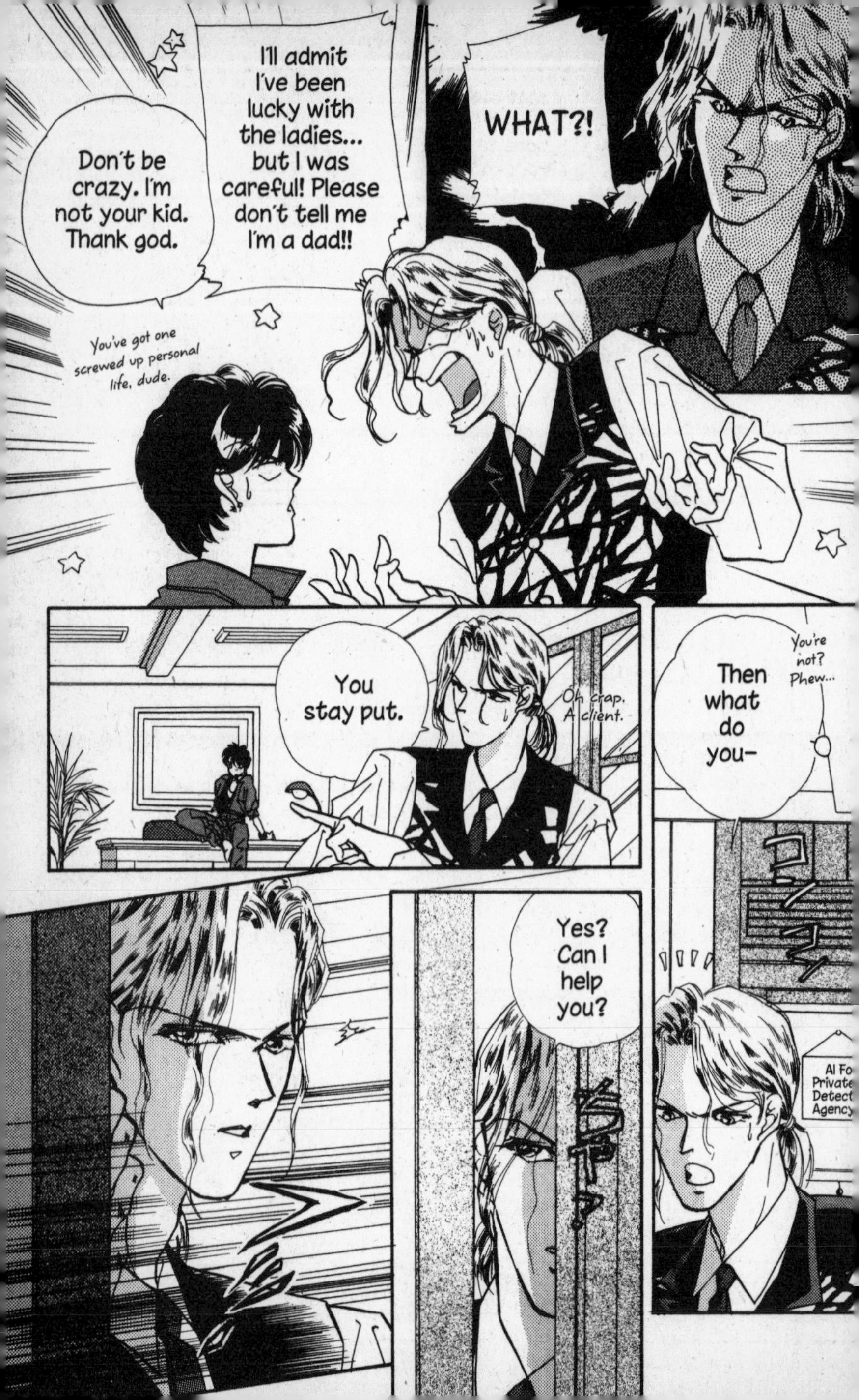
WHAT?!
I'll admit I've been lucky with the ladies... but I was careful! Please don't tell me I'm a dad!!
Don't be crazy. I'm not your kid. Thank god.
You've got one screwed up personal life, dude.
You're not? Phew...
Then what do you-
You stay put.
Oh crap. A client.
Al Fo
Private
Detect
Agency
Yes? Can I help you?

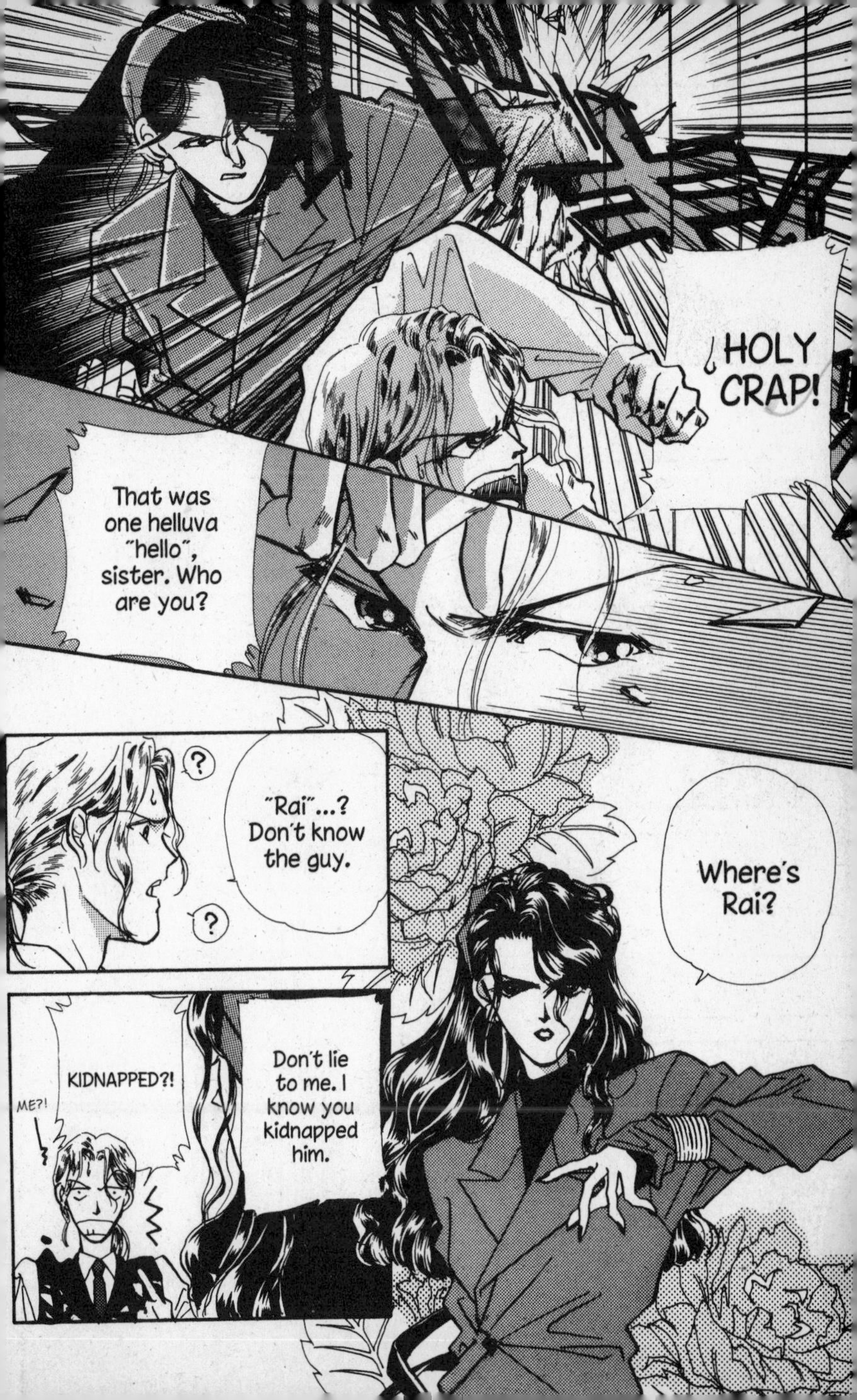

HOLY CRAP!
That was one helluva "hello", sister. Who are you?
Where's Rai?
?
"Rai"...? Don't know the guy.
?
Don't lie to me. I know you kidnapped him.
KIDNAPPED?!
ME?!

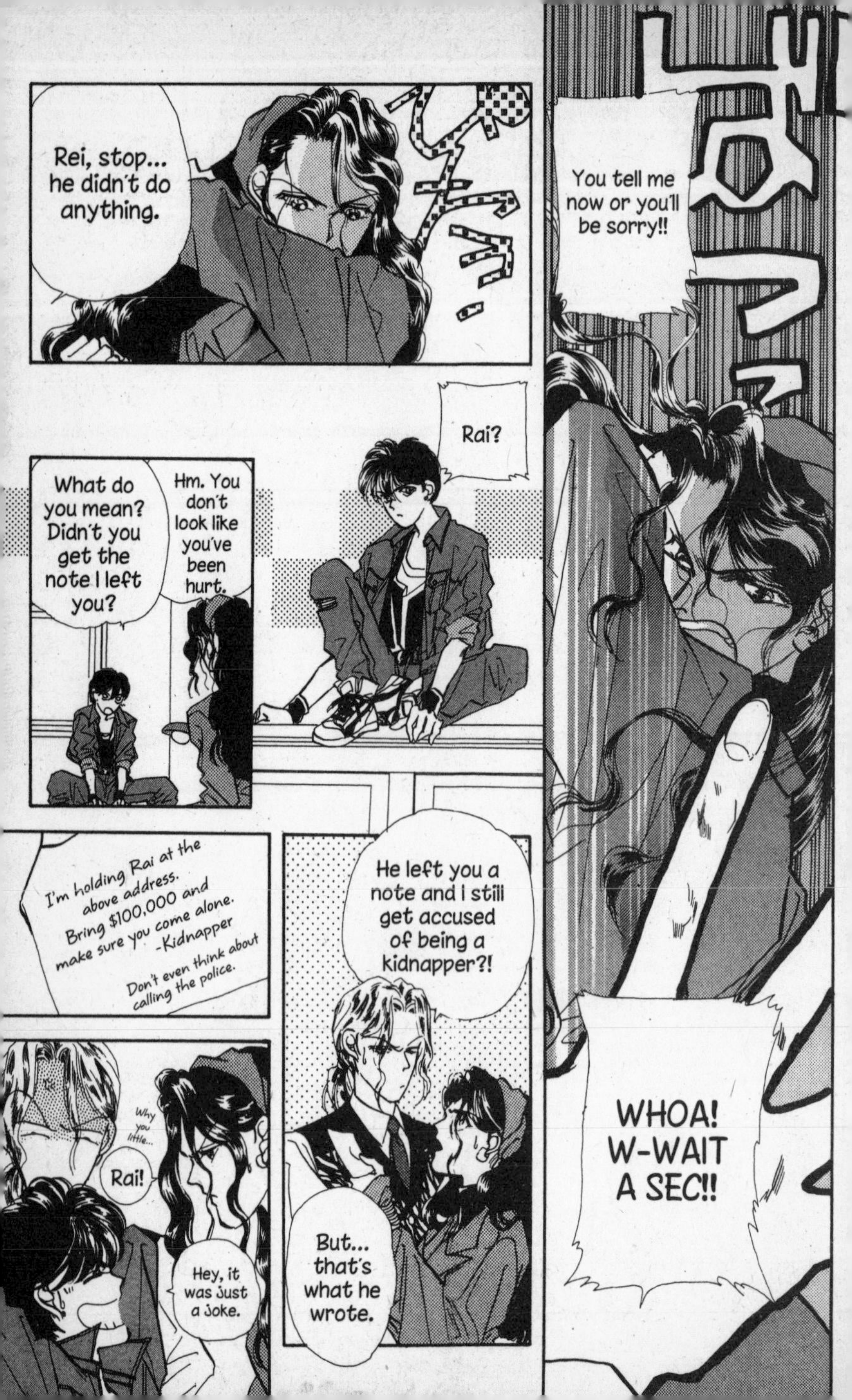
You tell me now or you'll be sorry!!
WHOA! W-WAIT A SEC!!
Rei, stop... he didn't do anything.
Rai?
Hm. You don't look like you've been hurt.
What do you mean? Didn't you get the note I left you?
He left you a note and I still get accused of being a kidnapper?!
But... that's what he wrote.
I'm holding Rai at the above address. Bring $100,000 and make sure you come alone. -Kidnapper
Don't even think about calling the police.
Why you little...
Rai!
Hey, it was just a joke.

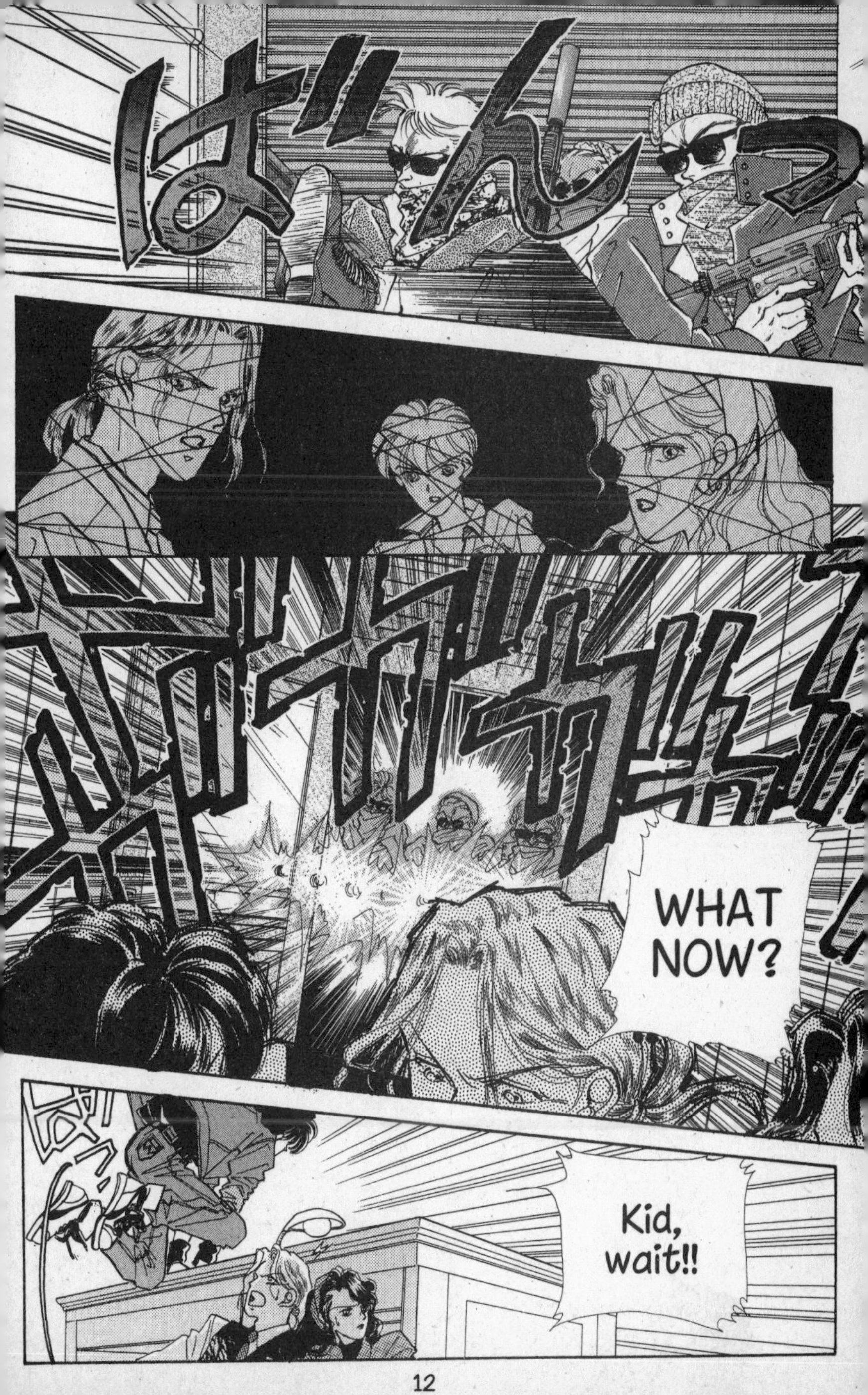
ばんっ
WHAT NOW?
Kid, wait!!

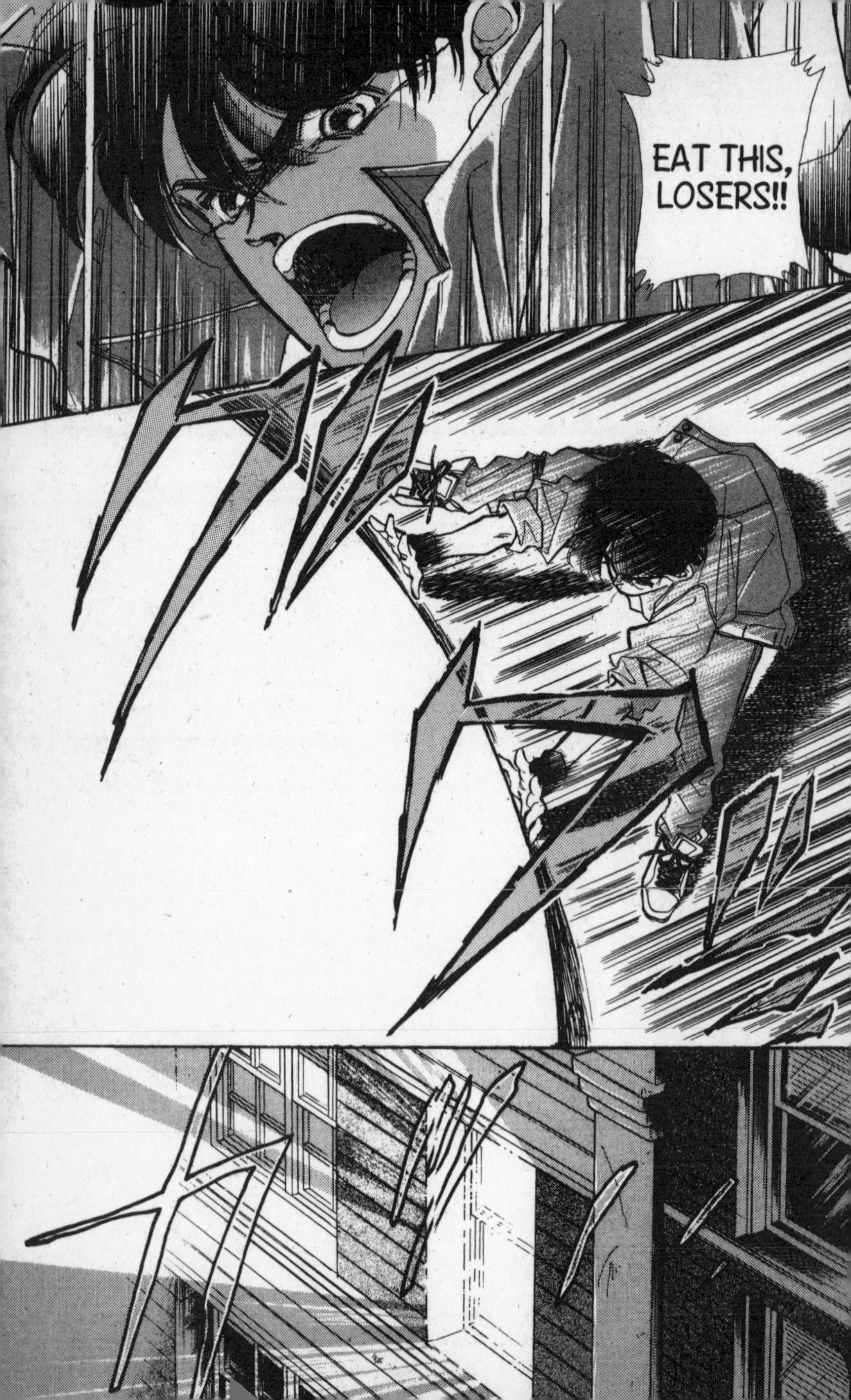
EAT THIS, LOSERS!!

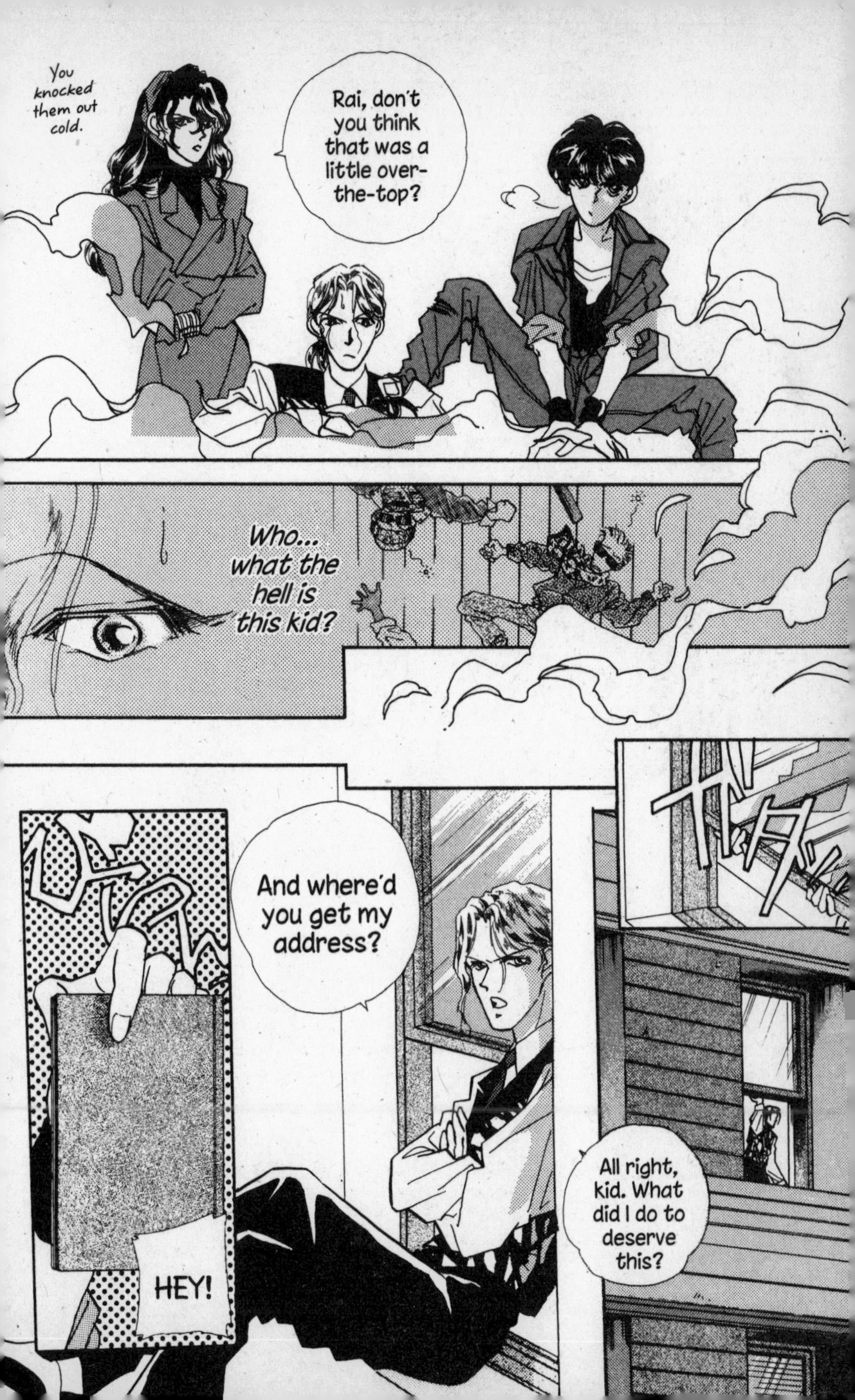
Rai, don't you think that was a little over-the-top?
You knocked them out cold.
Who... what the hell is this kid?
All right, kid. What did I do to deserve this?
And where'd you get my address?
HEY!

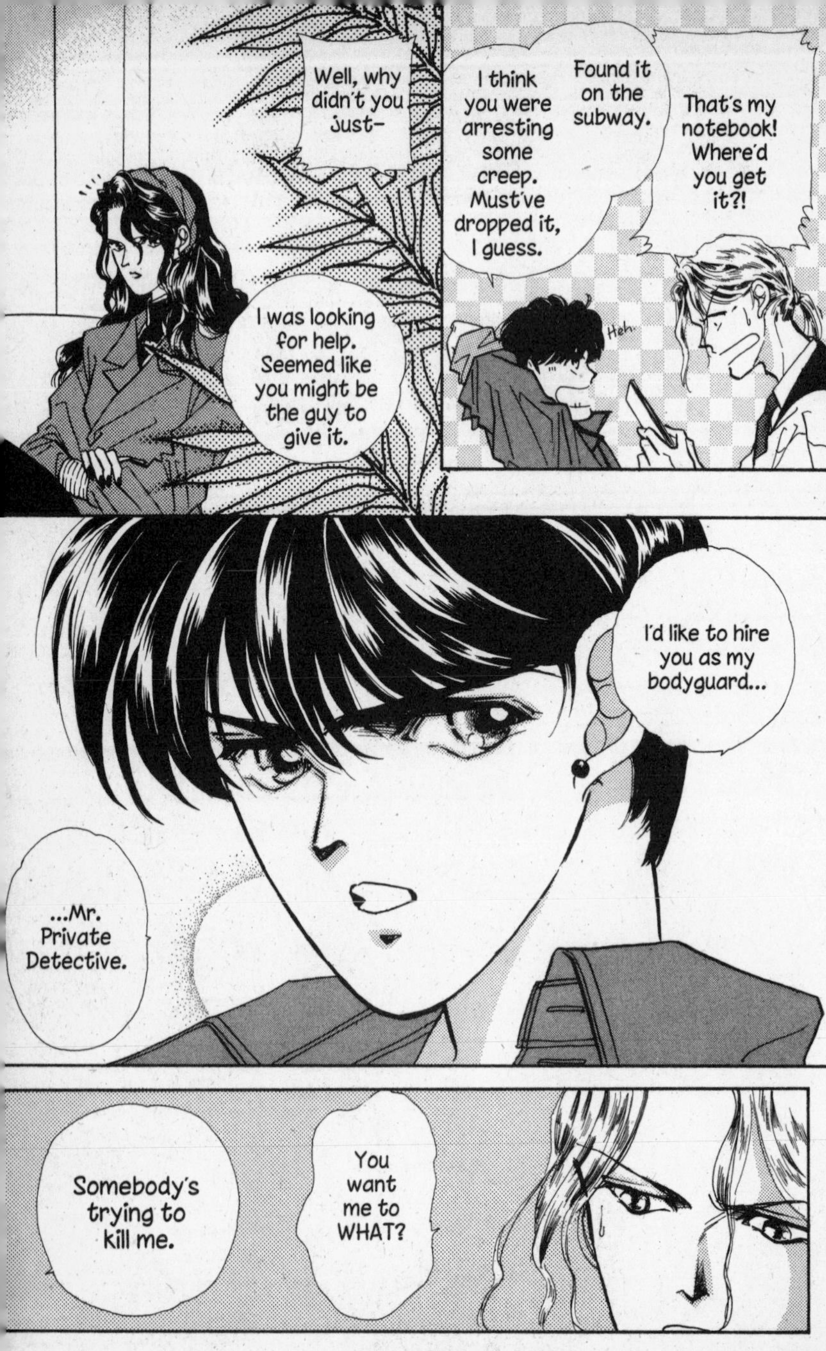
That's my notebook! Where'd you get it?!
Found it on the subway.
I think you were arresting some creep. Must've dropped it, I guess.
Heh.
Well, why didn't you just-
I was looking for help. Seemed like you might be the guy to give it.
I'd like to hire you as my bodyguard...
...Mr. Private Detective.
You want me to WHAT?
Somebody's trying to kill me.

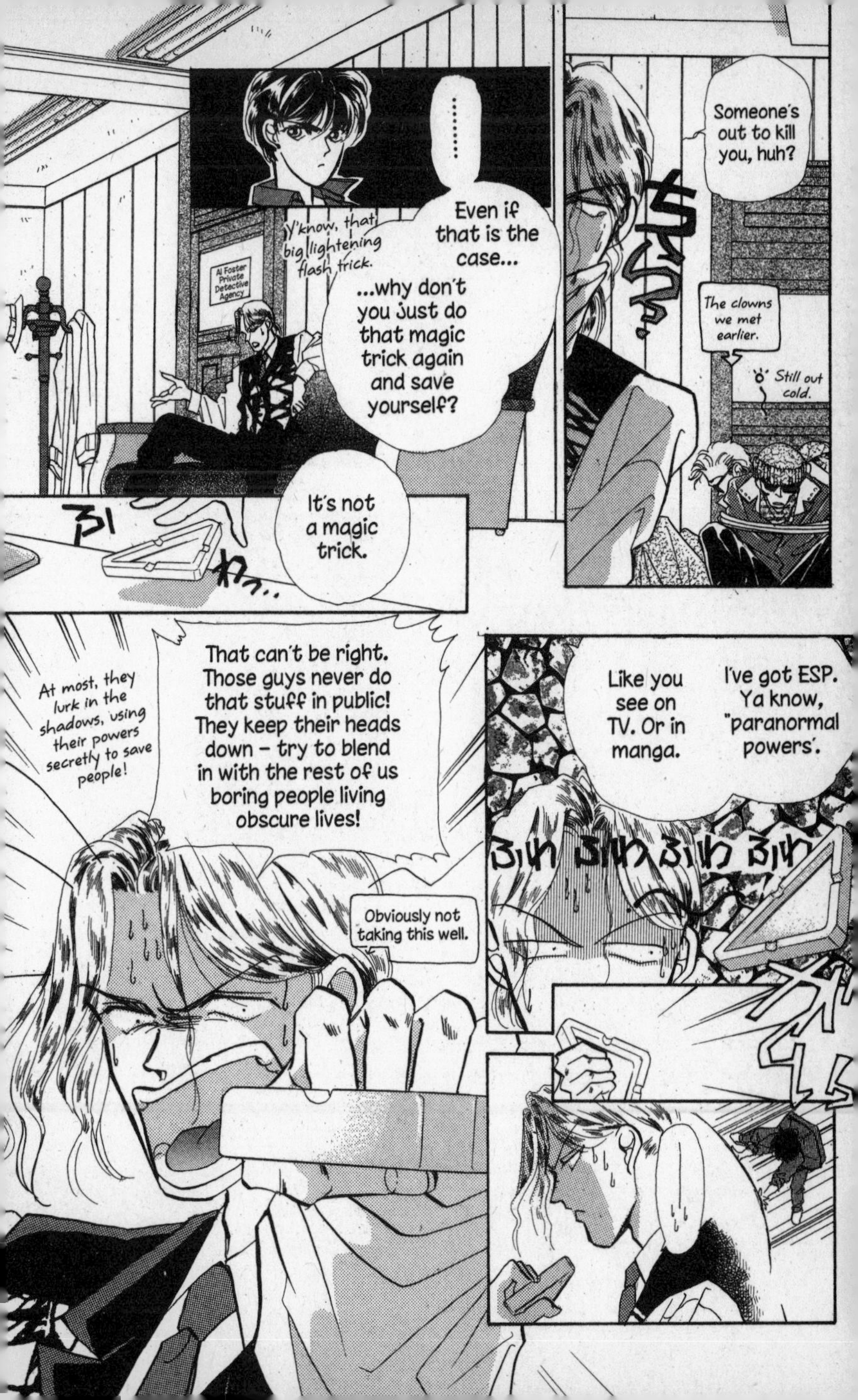
Someone's out to kill you, huh?
ちらっ
The clowns we met earlier.
Still out cold.
....
Even if that is the case...
...why don't you just do that magic trick again and save yourself?
Y'know, that big lightening flash trick.
Al Foster Private Detective Agency
It's not a magic trick.
ふ
わっ...
I've got ESP. Ya know, "paranormal powers'.
Like you see on TV. Or in manga.
ふわ ふわ ふわ ふわ
That can't be right. Those guys never do that stuff in public! They keep their heads down - try to blend in with the rest of us boring people living obscure lives!
At most, they lurk in the shadows, using their powers secretly to save people!
Obviously not taking this well.

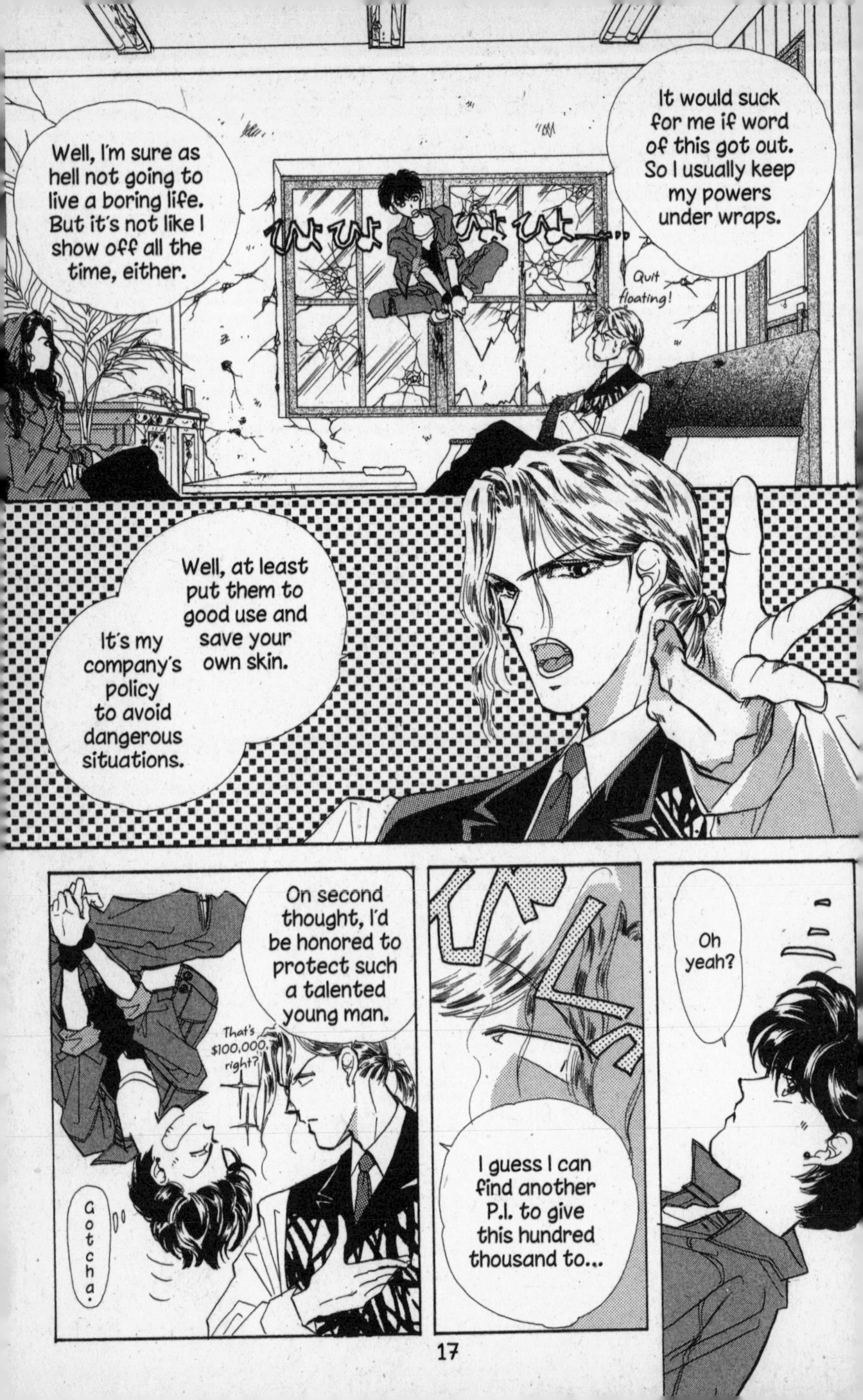

It would suck for me if word of this got out. So I usually keep my powers under wraps.
Well, I'm sure as hell not going to live a boring life. But it's not like I show off all the time, either.
ひよひよ ひよひよ……
Quit floating!
Well, at least put them to good use and save your own skin.
It's my company's policy to avoid dangerous situations.
Oh yeah?
I guess I can find another P.I. to give this hundred thousand to...
On second thought, I'd be honored to protect such a talented young man.
That's $100,000, right?
Gotcha.

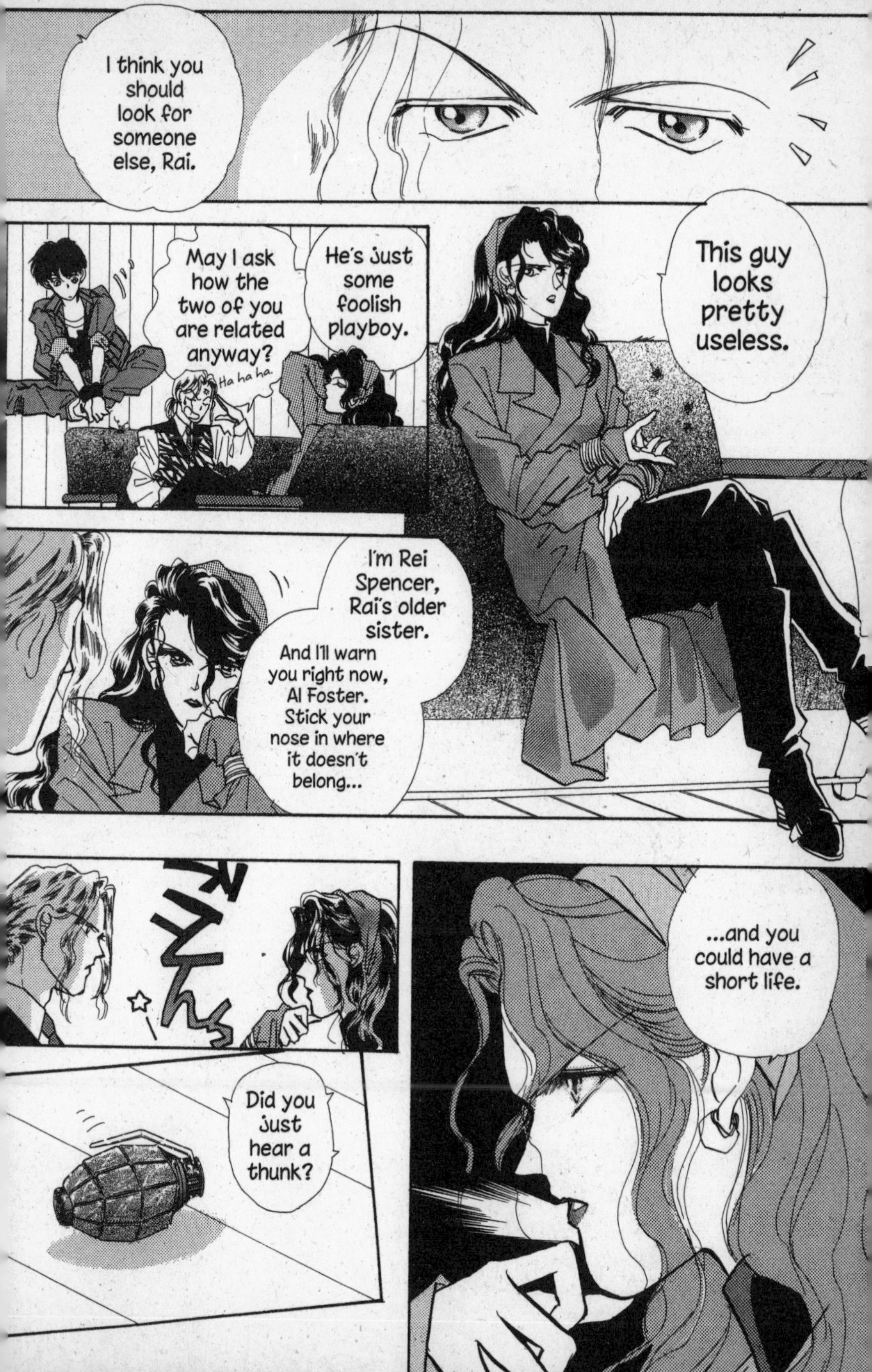
I think you should look for someone else, Rai.
This guy looks pretty useless.
He's just some foolish playboy.
May I ask how the two of you are related anyway?
Ha ha ha.
I'm Rei Spencer, Rai's older sister.
And I'll warn you right now, Al Foster. Stick your nose in where it doesn't belong...
...and you could have a short life.
Did you just hear a thunk?

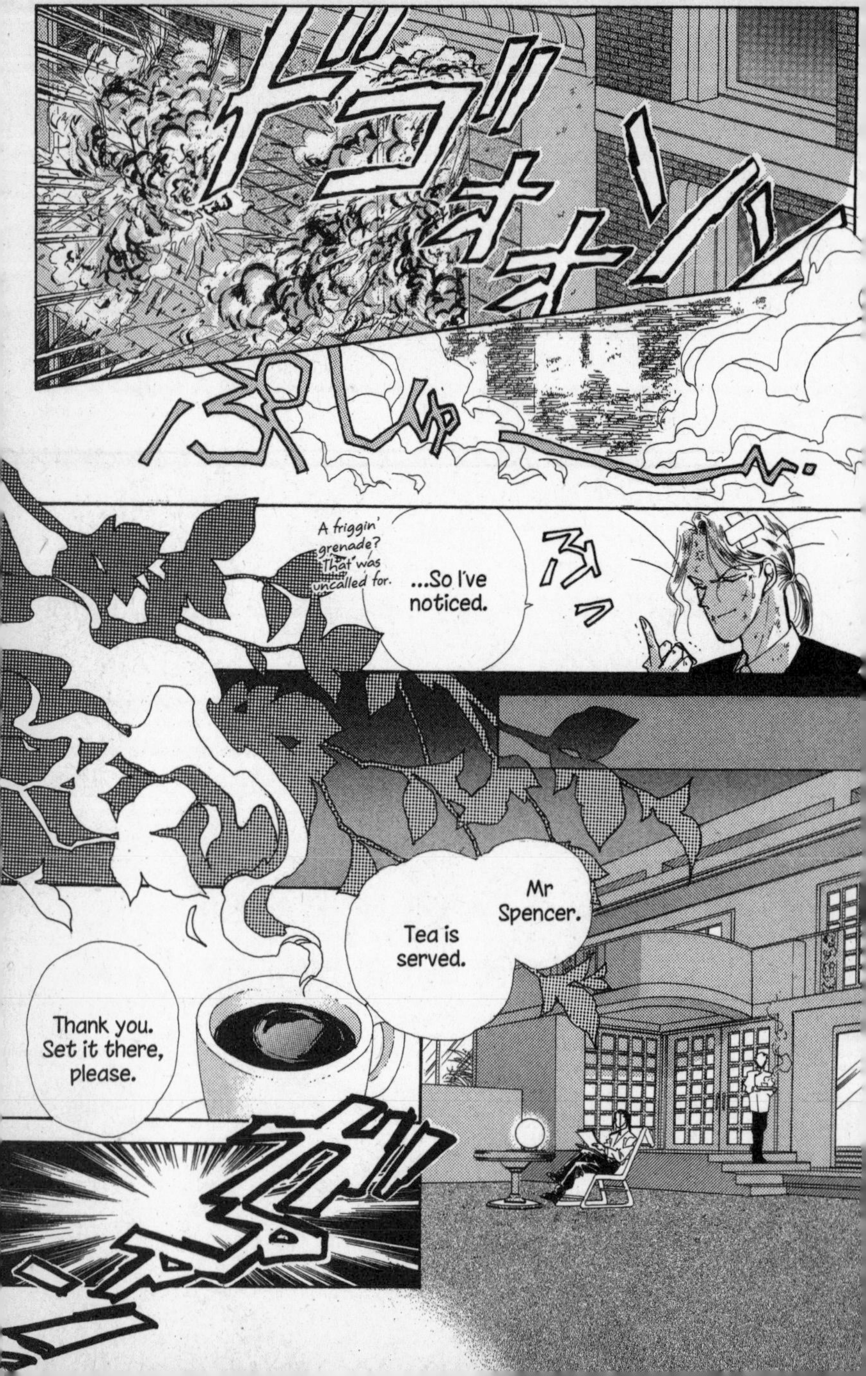
ドゴォォン
ぷしゅ~
ふっ
...So I've noticed.
A friggin' grenade? That was uncalled for.
Mr Spencer.
Tea is served.
Thank you. Set it there, please.

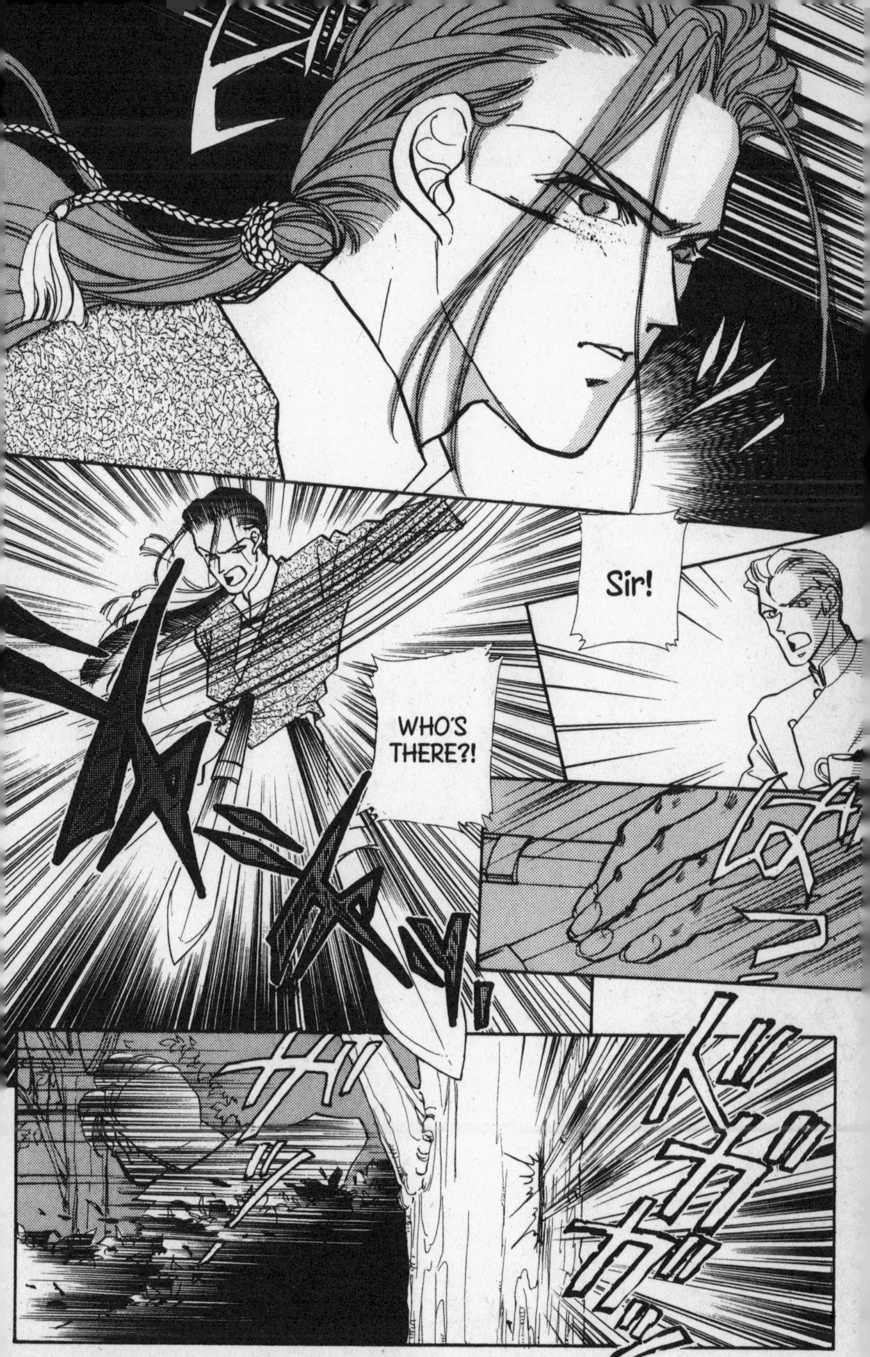
Sir!
WHO'S THERE?!

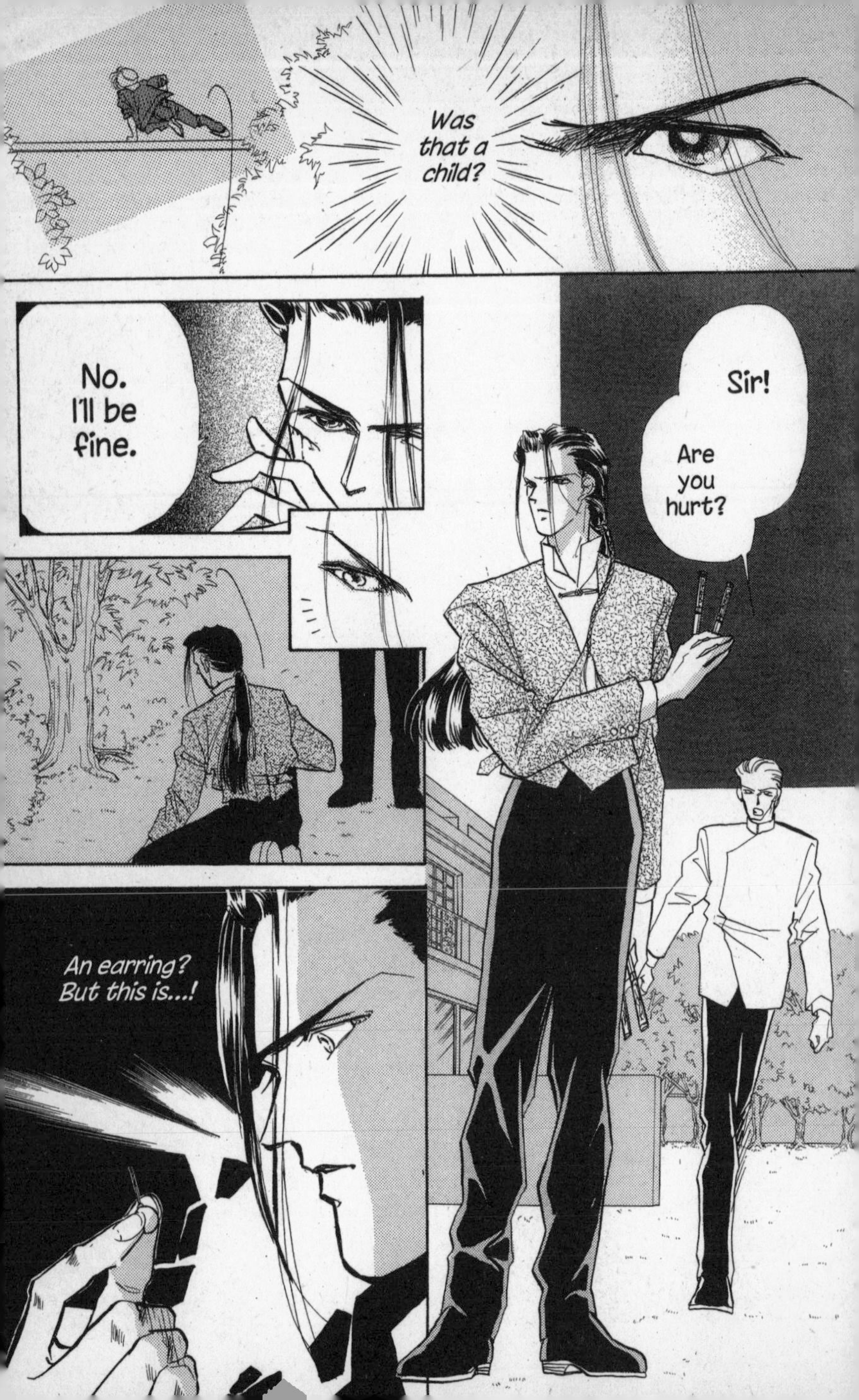
Was that a child?
Sir!
Are you hurt?
No. I'll be fine.
An earring? But this is...!

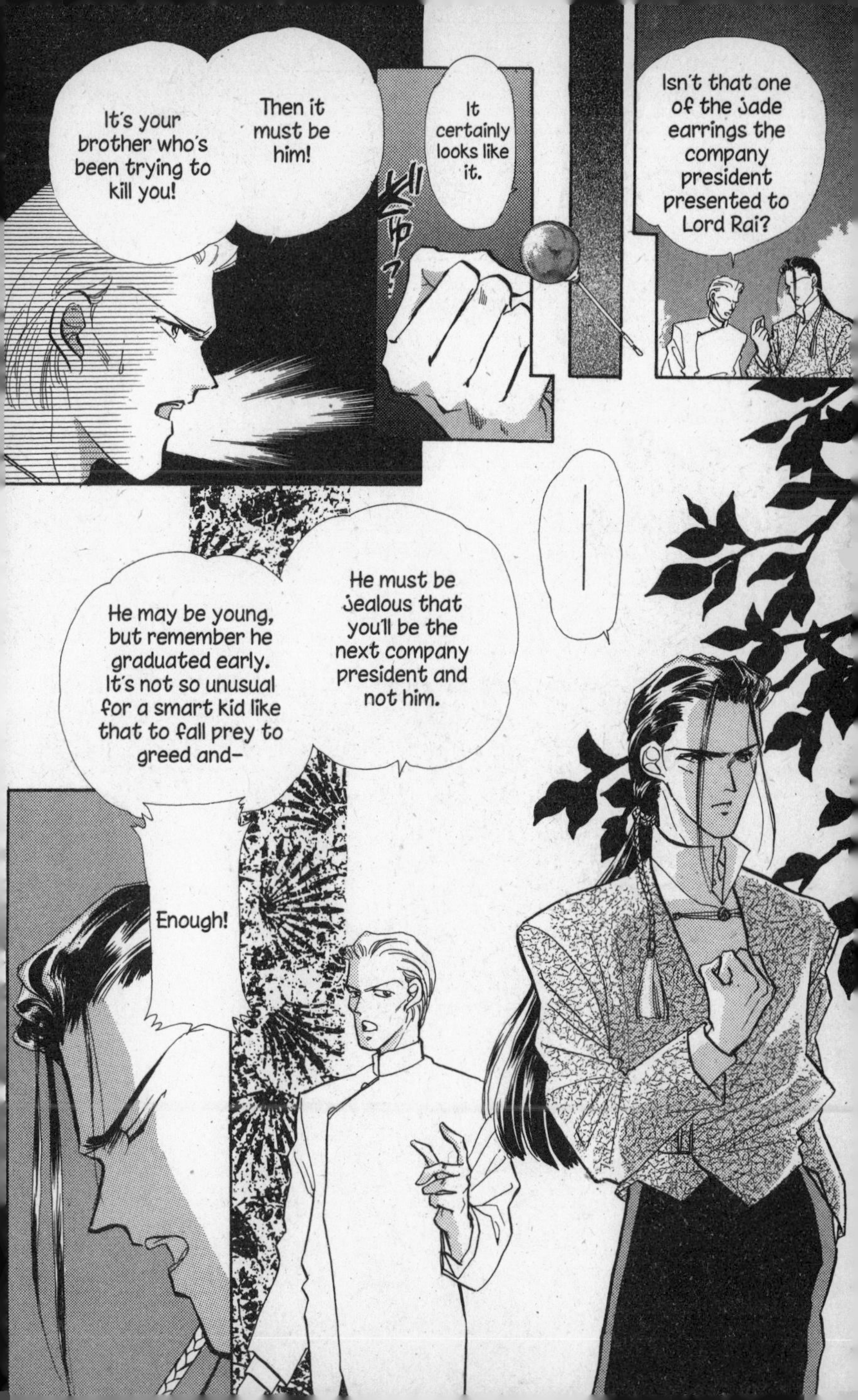
Isn't that one of the jade earrings the company president presented to Lord Rai?
It certainly looks like it.
Then it must be him!
It's your brother who's been trying to kill you!
—
He must be jealous that you'll be the next company president and not him.
He may be young, but remember he graduated early. It's not so unusual for a smart kid like that to fall prey to greed and–
Enough!

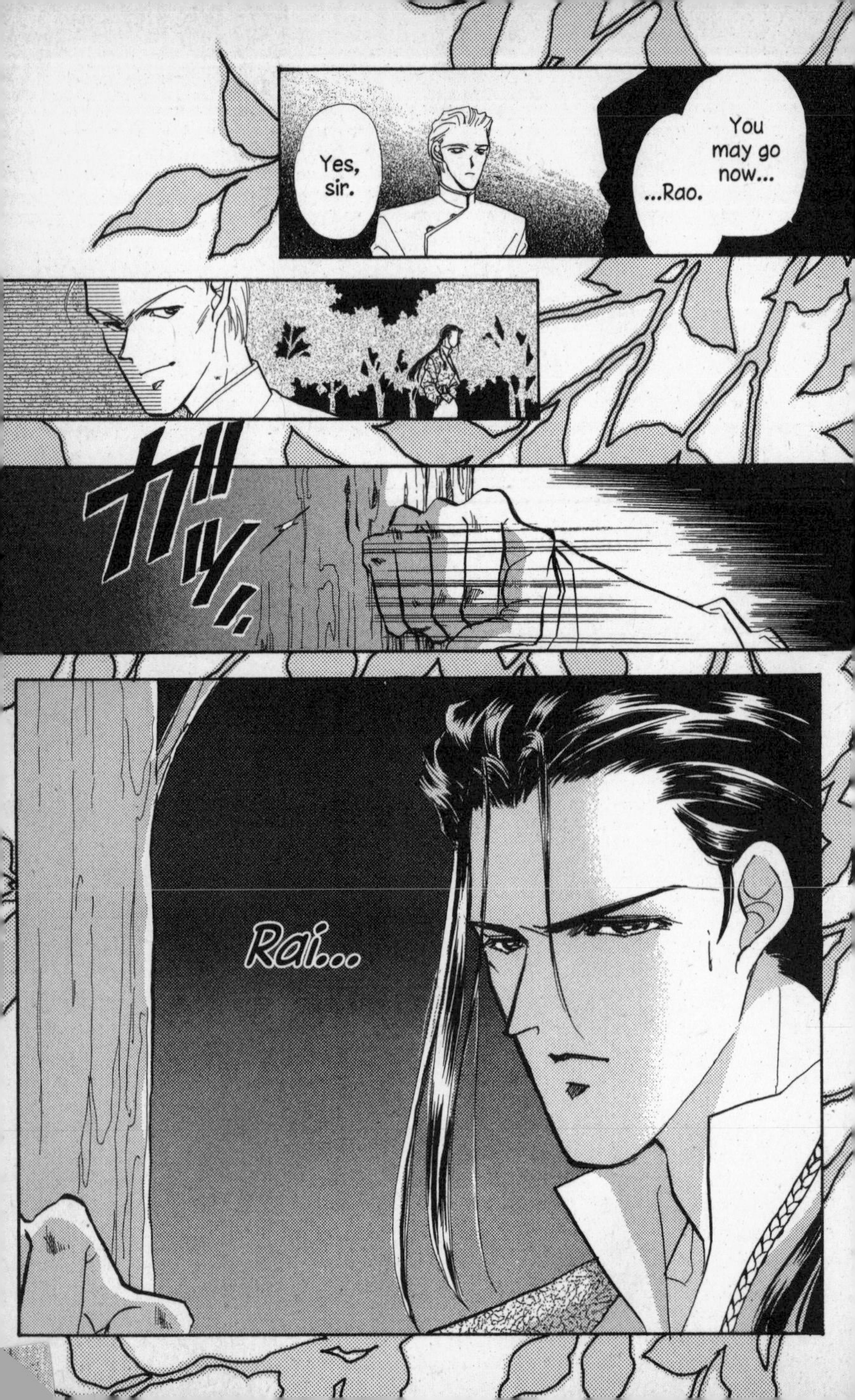
You may go now...
...Rao.
Yes, sir.
ガッ
Rai...

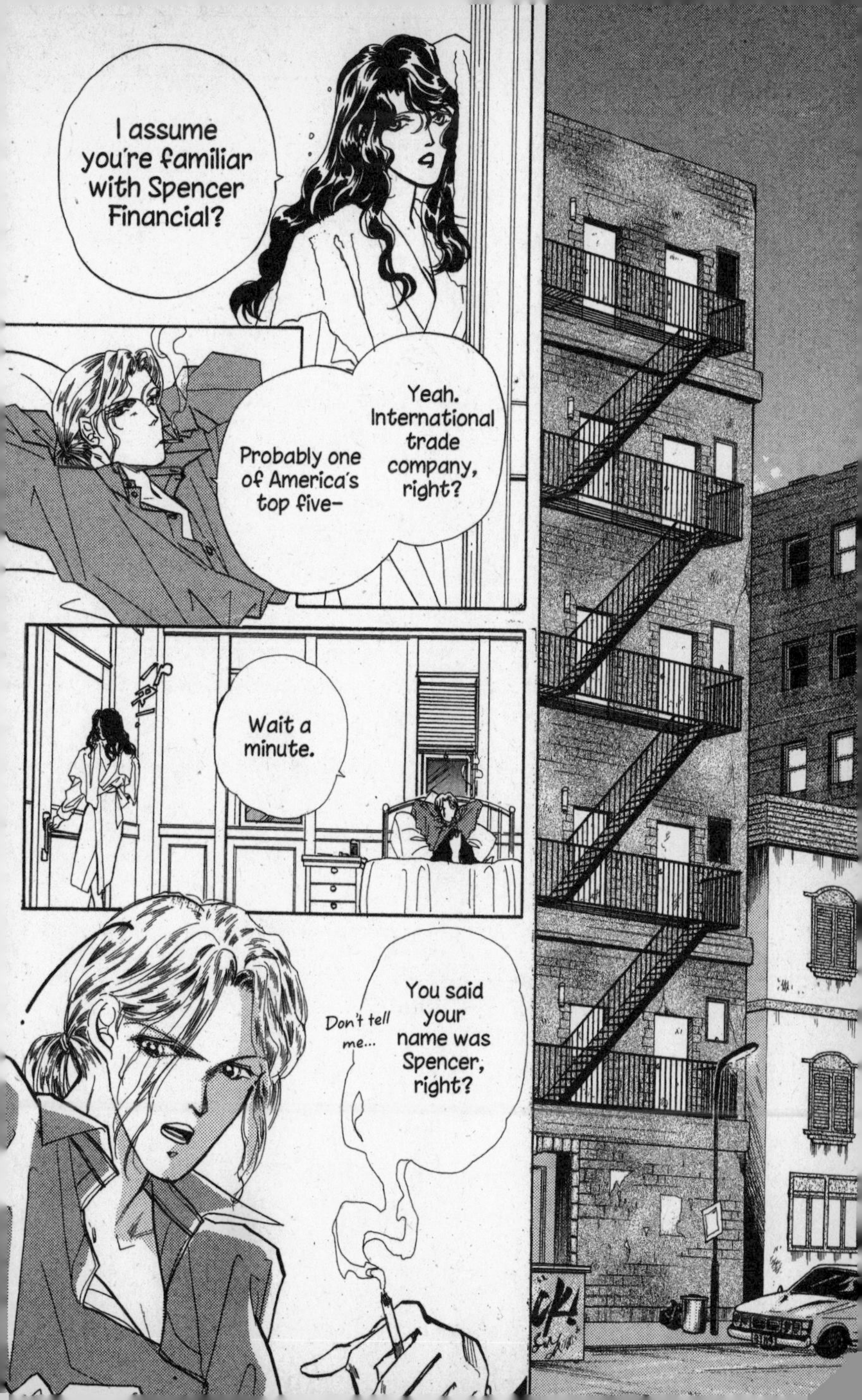
I assume you're familiar with Spencer Financial?
Yeah. International trade company, right?
Probably one of America's top five-
Wait a minute.
You said your name was Spencer, right?
Don't tell me...

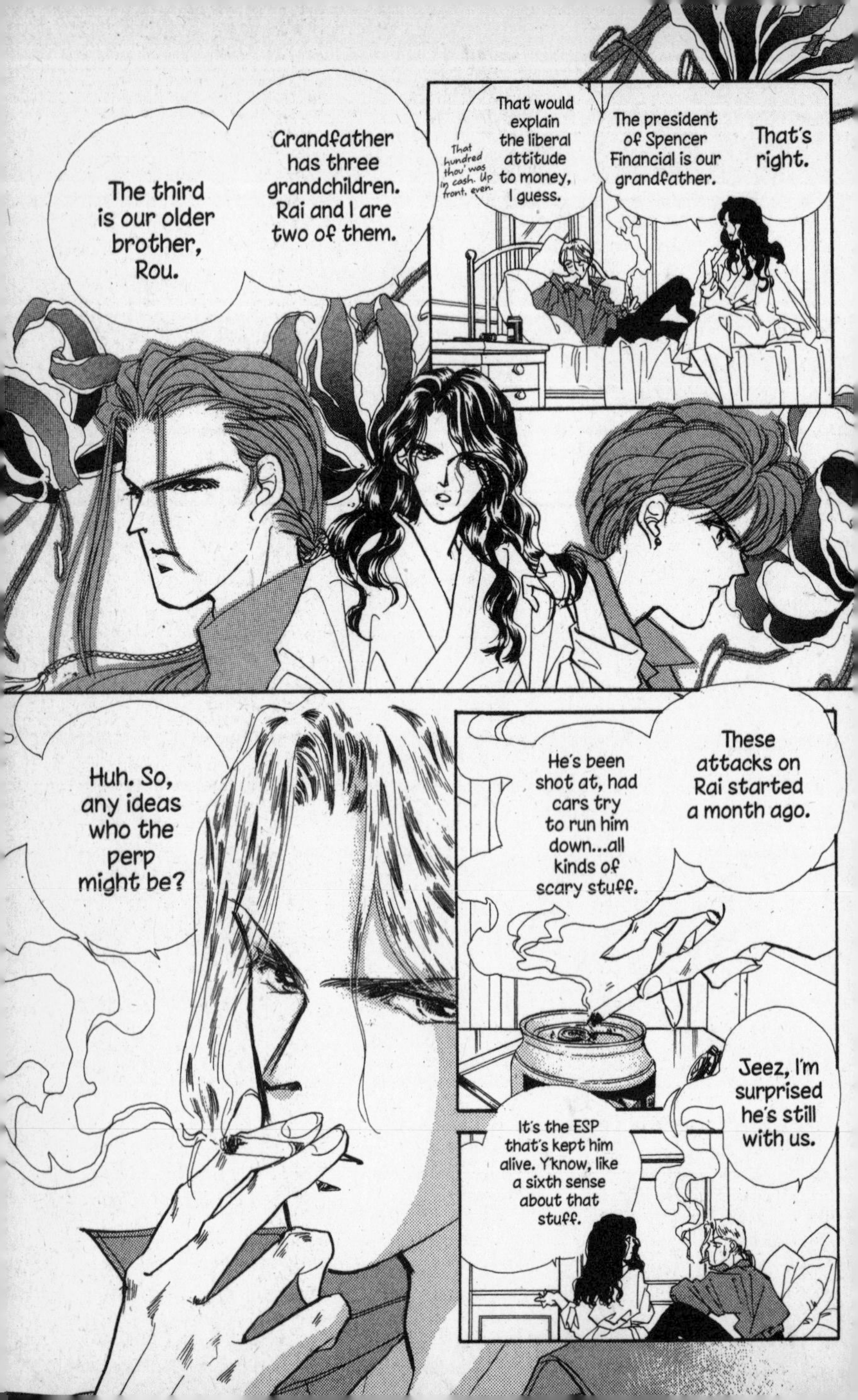
That's right.
The president of Spencer Financial is our grandfather.
That would explain the liberal attitude to money, I guess.
That hundred thou' was in cash. Up front, even.
Grandfather has three grandchildren. Rai and I are two of them.
The third is our older brother, Rou.
These attacks on Rai started a month ago.
He's been shot at, had cars try to run him down...all kinds of scary stuff.
Jeez, I'm surprised he's still with us.
It's the ESP that's kept him alive. Y'know, like a sixth sense about that stuff.
Huh. So, any ideas who the perp might be?

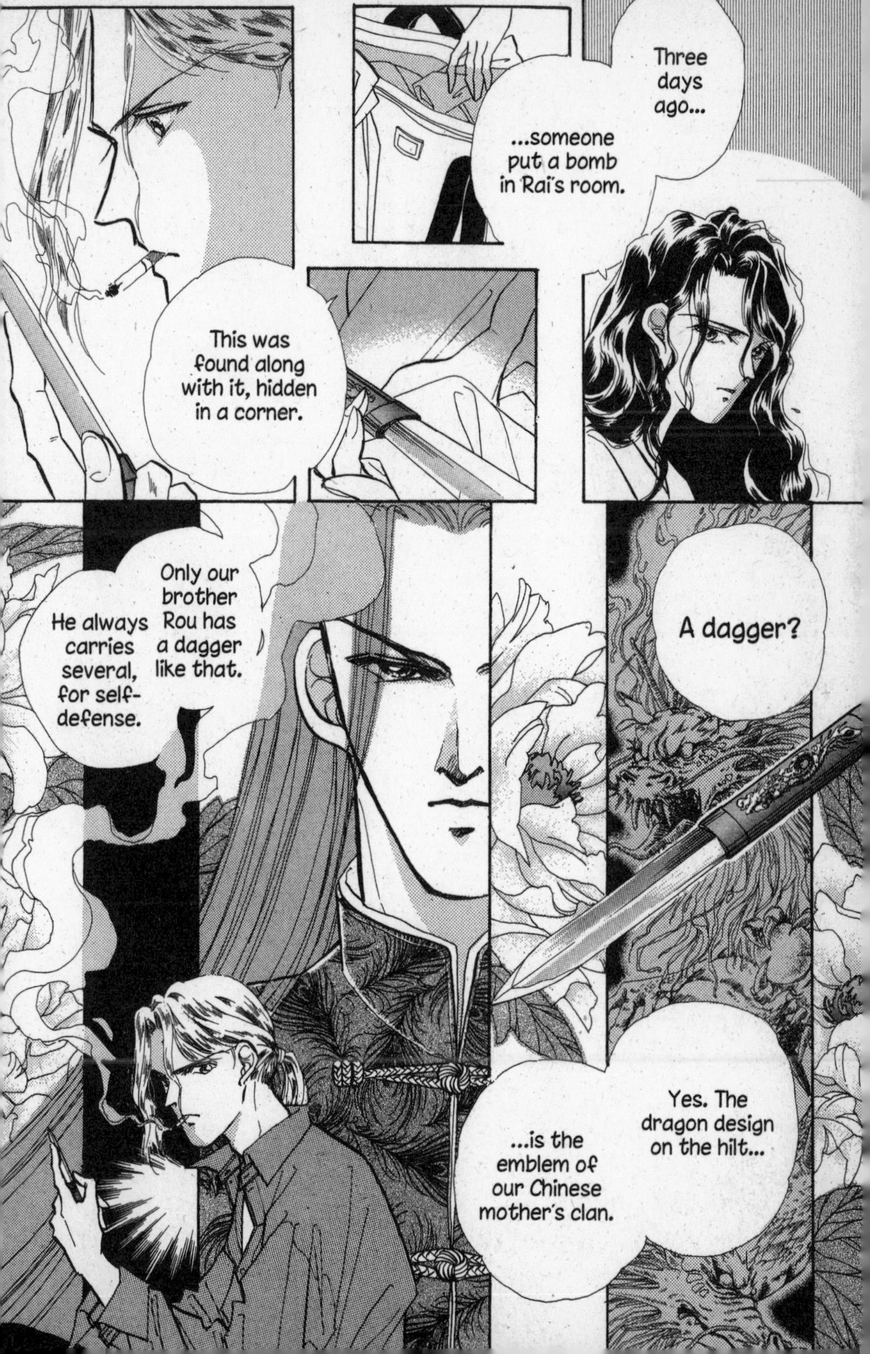
Three days ago...
...someone put a bomb in Rai's room.
This was found along with it, hidden in a corner.
A dagger?
Yes. The dragon design on the hilt...
...is the emblem of our Chinese mother's clan.
Only our brother Rou has a dagger like that.
He always carries several, for self-defense.

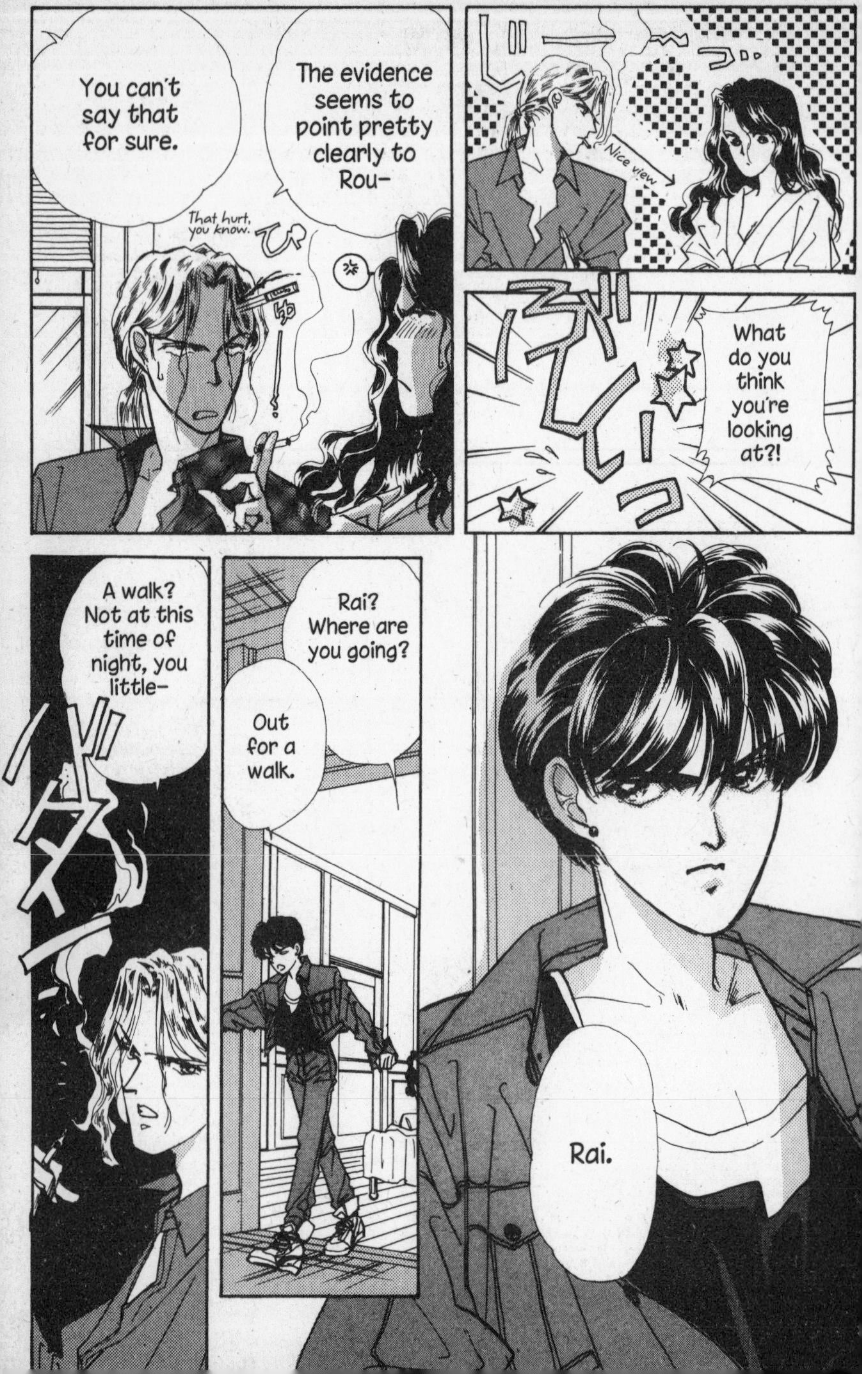
Nice view
What do you think you're looking at?!
The evidence seems to point pretty clearly to Rou-
You can't say that for sure.
That hurt, you know.
Rai.
Rai? Where are you going?
Out for a walk.
A walk? Not at this time of night, you little-

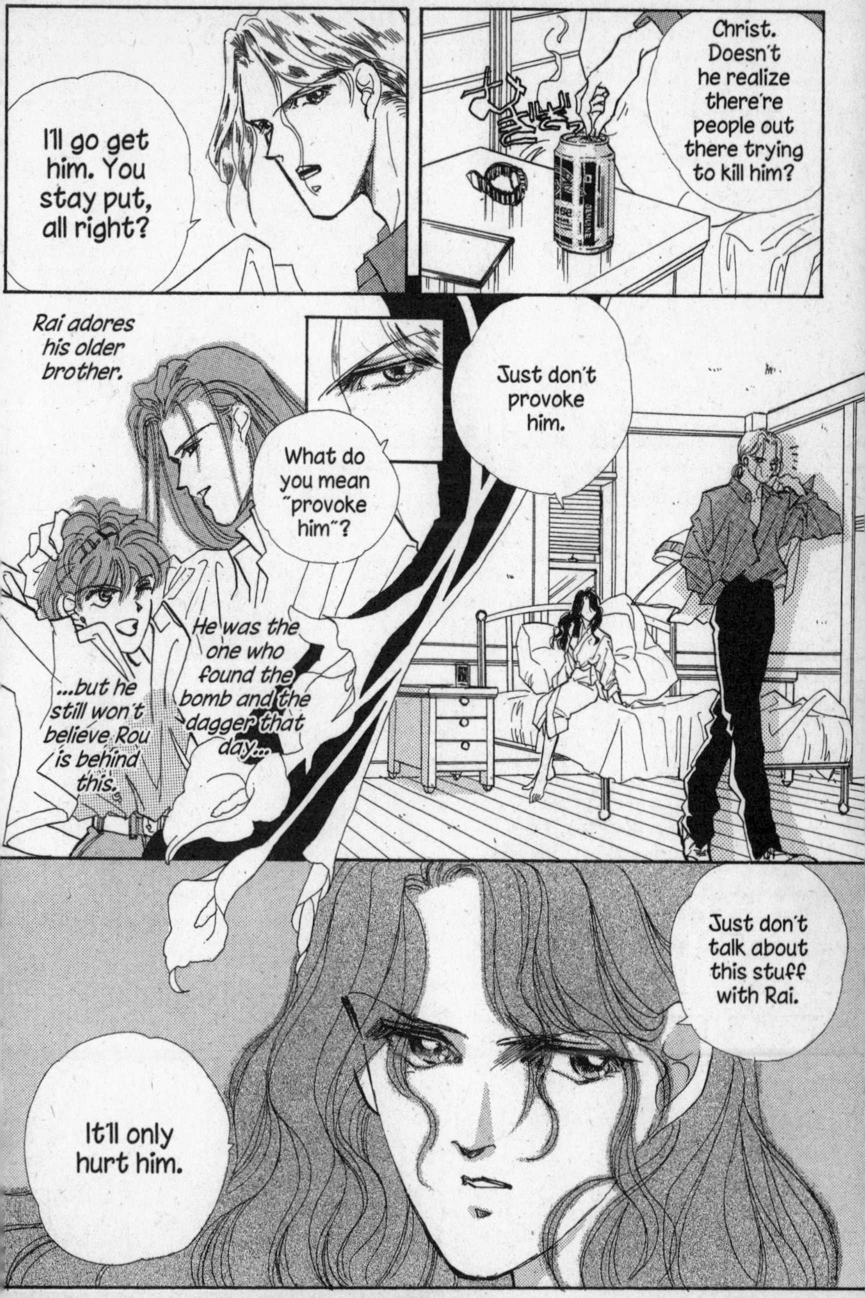
Christ. Doesn't he realize there're people out there trying to kill him?
I'll go get him. You stay put, all right?
Just don't provoke him.
What do you mean "provoke him"?
Rai adores his older brother.
He was the one who found the bomb and the dagger that day...
...but he still won't believe Rou is behind this.
Just don't talk about this stuff with Rai.
It'll only hurt him.

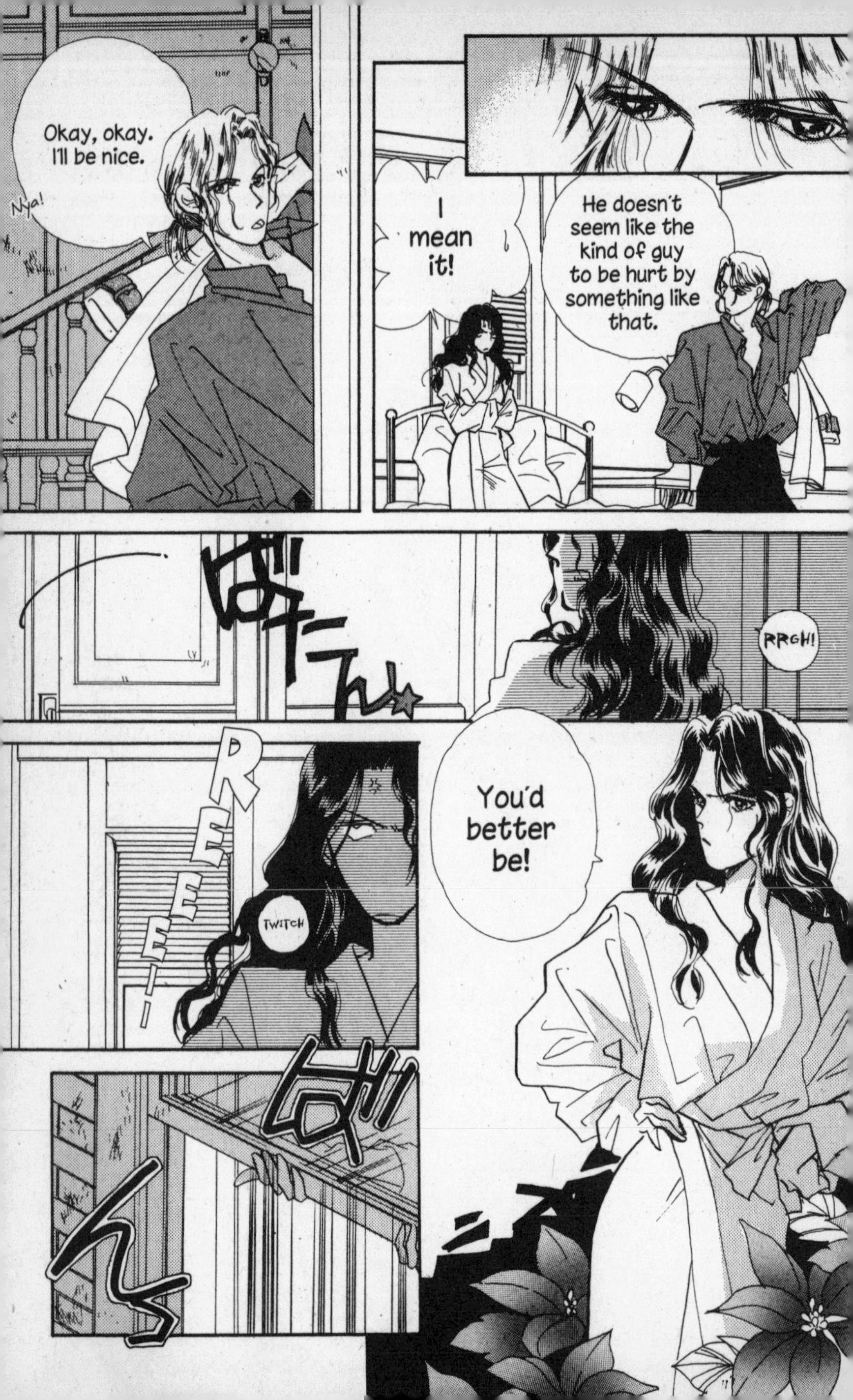
He doesn't seem like the kind of guy to be hurt by something like that.
I mean it!
Okay, okay. I'll be nice.
Nya!
RRGH!
ばたーん
You'd better be!
REEEE!!
TWITCH
ばん

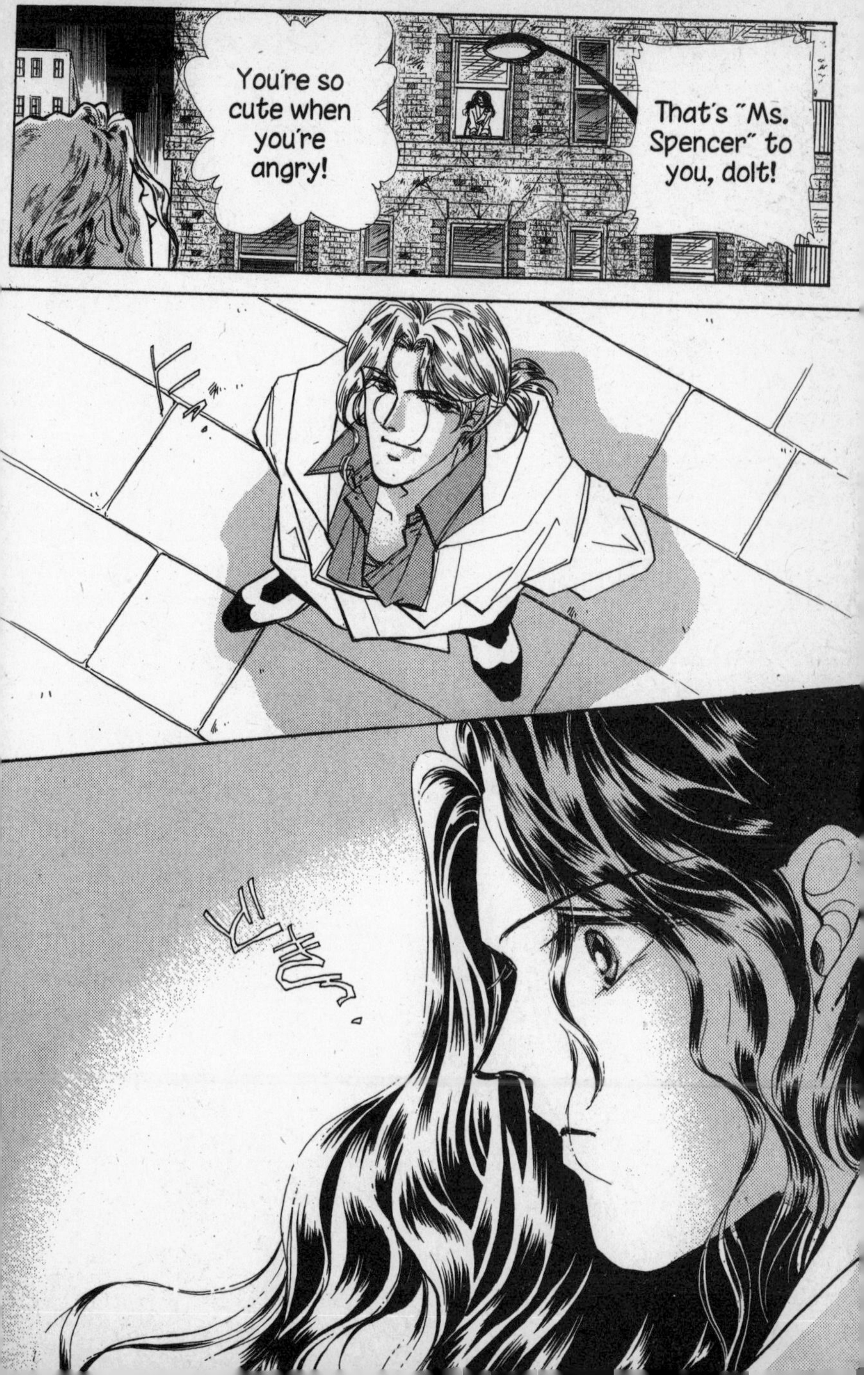
That's "Ms. Spencer" to you, dolt!
You're so cute when you're angry!

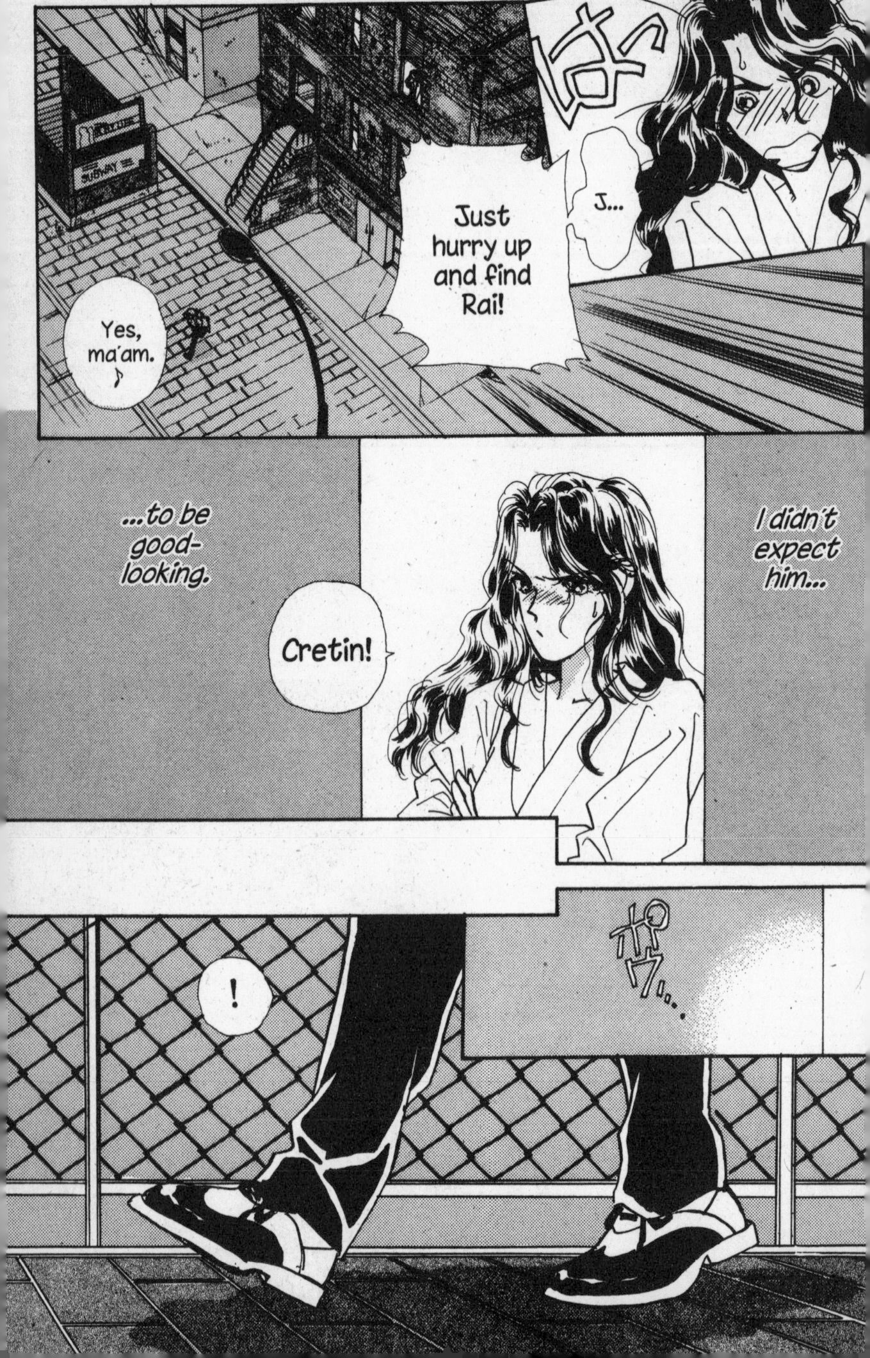
はっ
J...
Just hurry up and find Rai!
Yes, ma'am. ♪
I didn't expect him...
Cretin!
...to be good-looking.
!

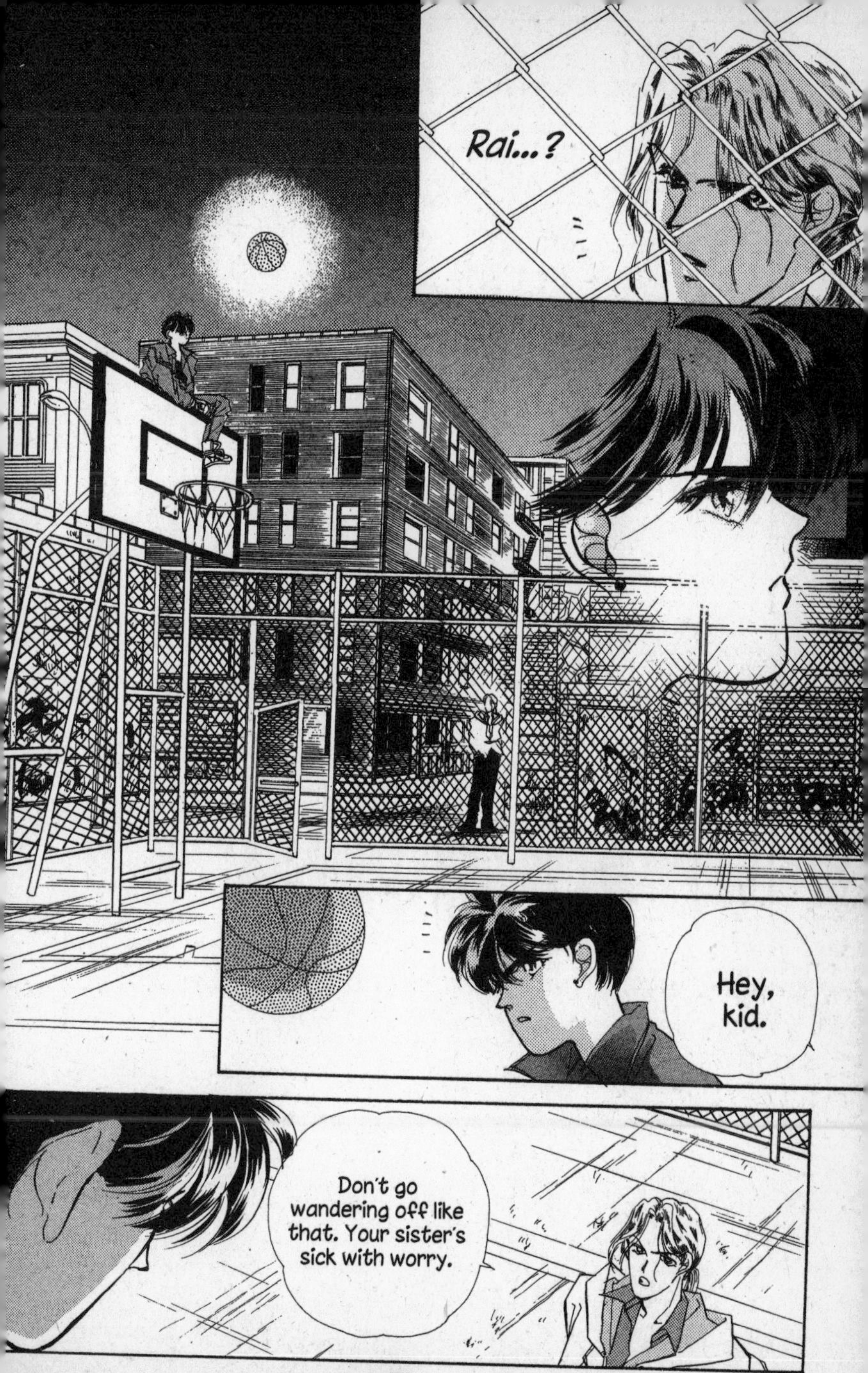
Rai...?
Hey, kid.
Don't go wandering off like that. Your sister's sick with worry.

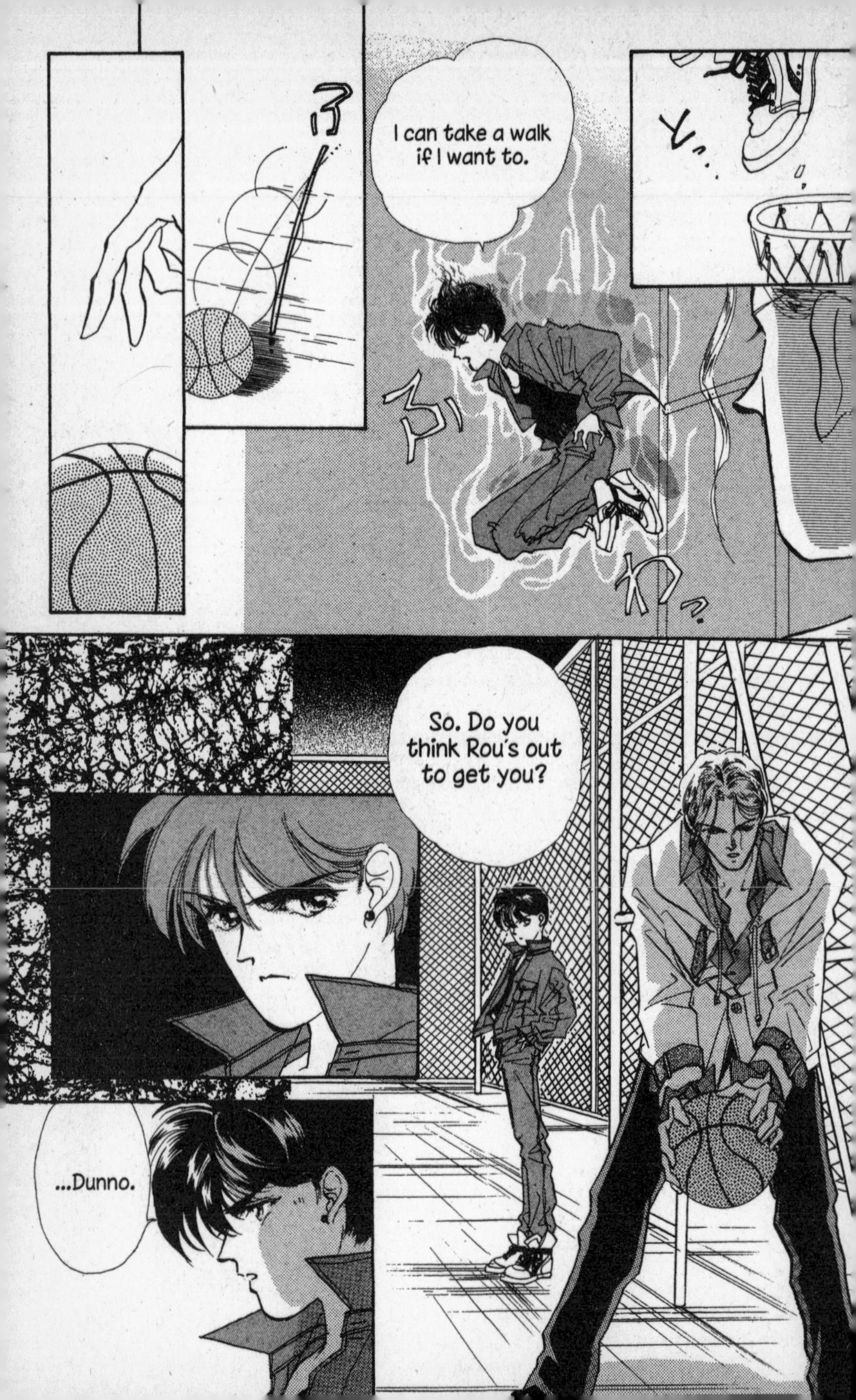
I can take a walk if I want to.
So. Do you think Rou's out to get you?
...Dunno.

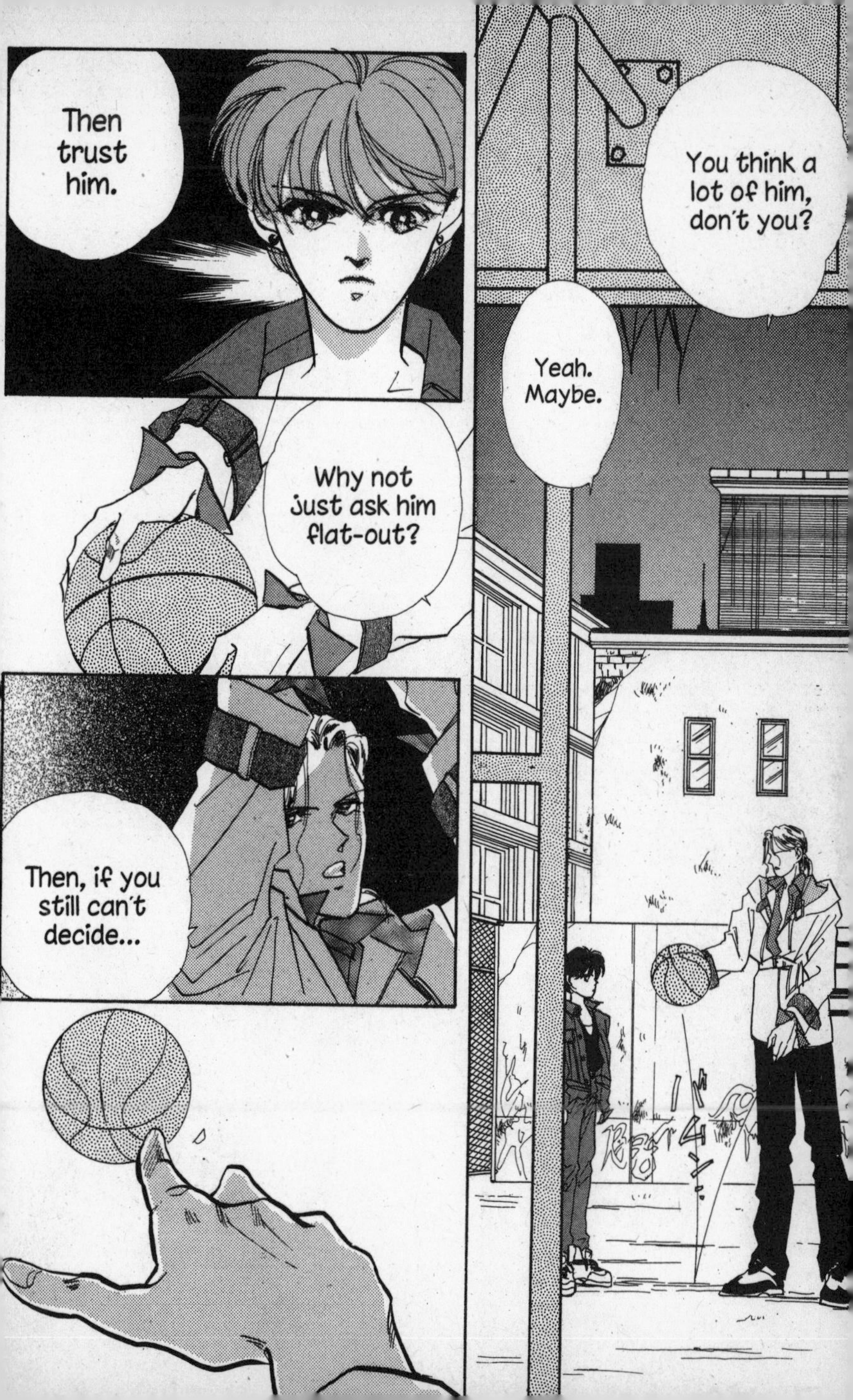
You think a lot of him, don't you?
Yeah. Maybe.
Then trust him.
Why not just ask him flat-out?
Then, if you still can't decide...

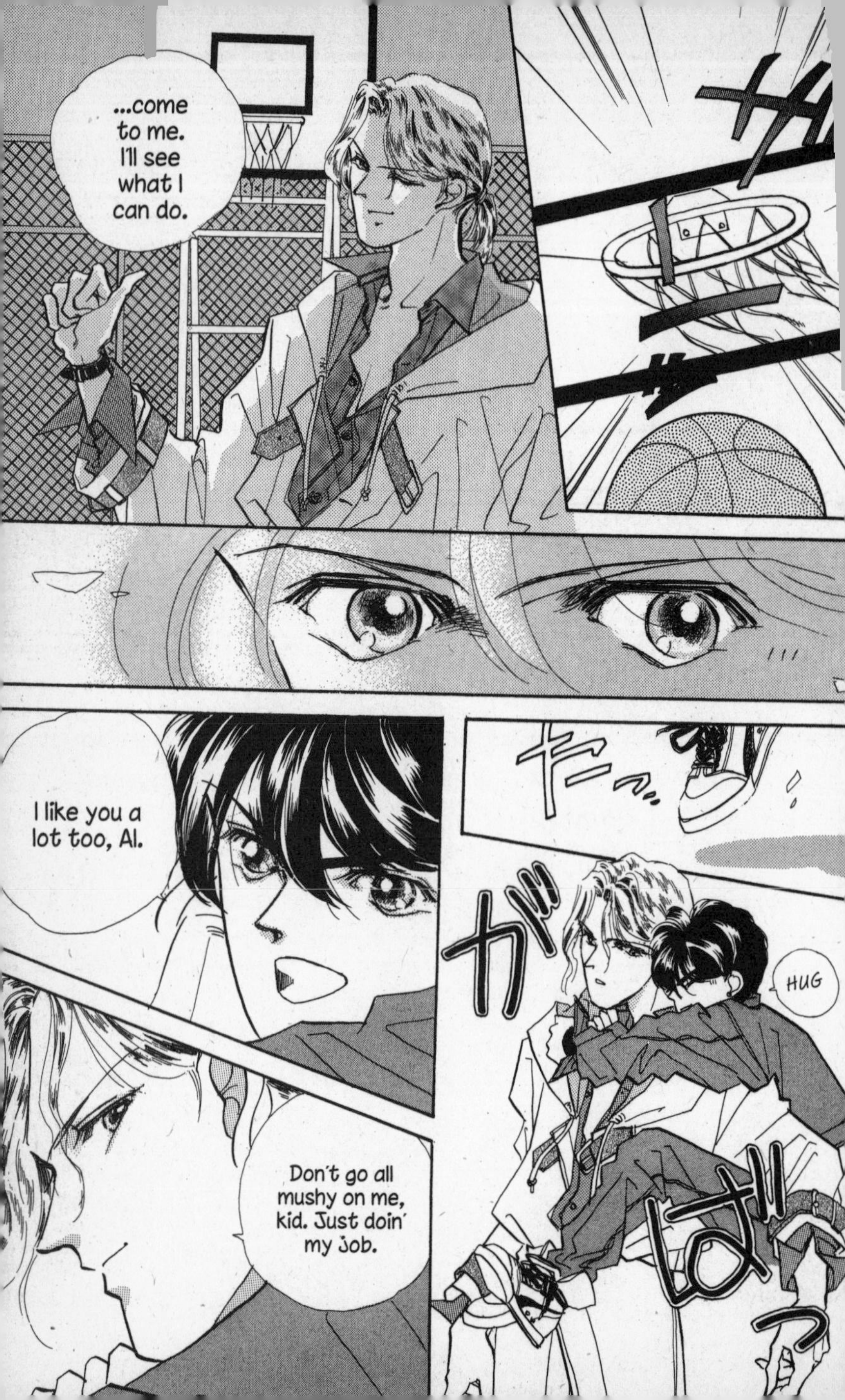
...come to me. I'll see what I can do.
HUG
I like you a lot too, Al.
Don't go all mushy on me, kid. Just doin' my job.

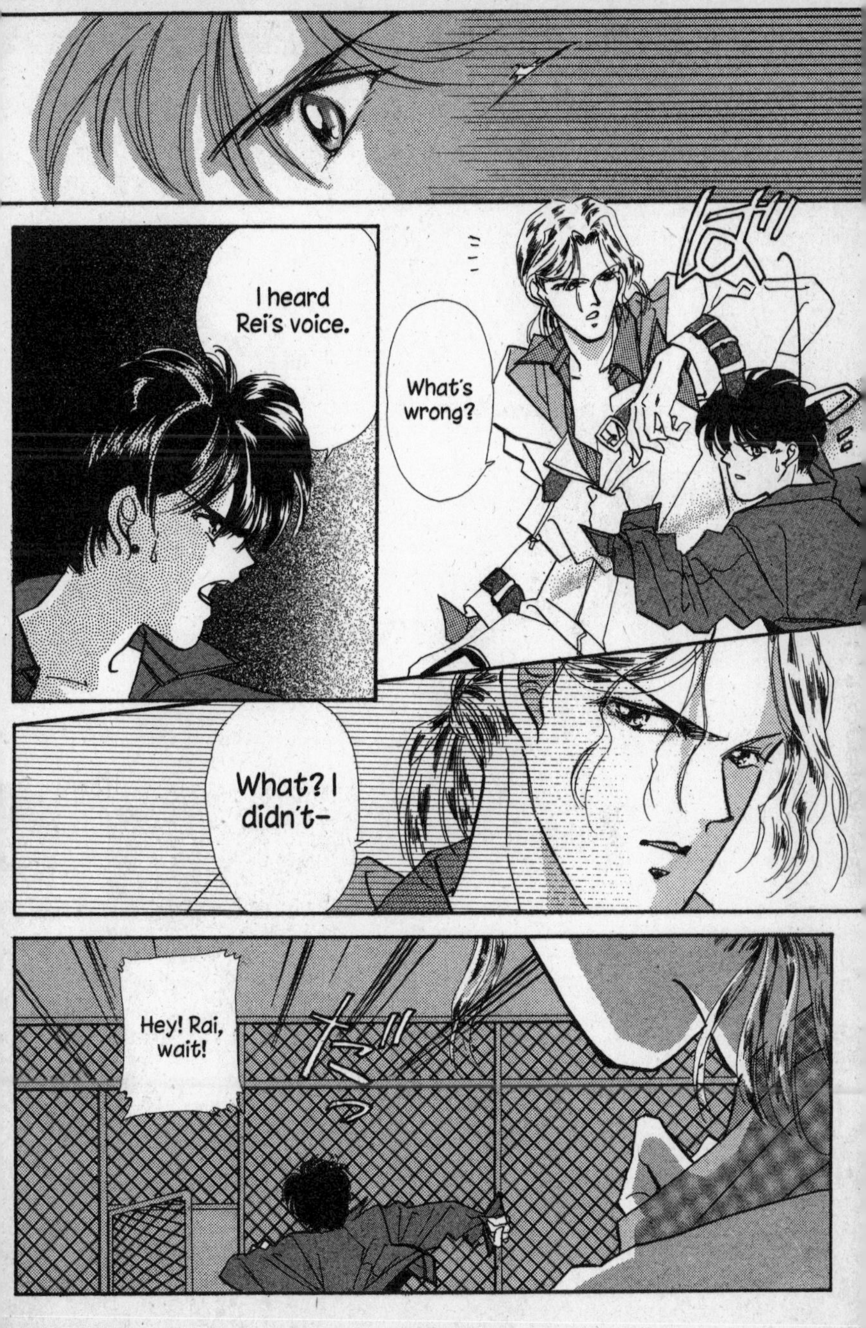
What's wrong?
I heard Rei's voice.
What? I didn't-
Hey! Rai, wait!

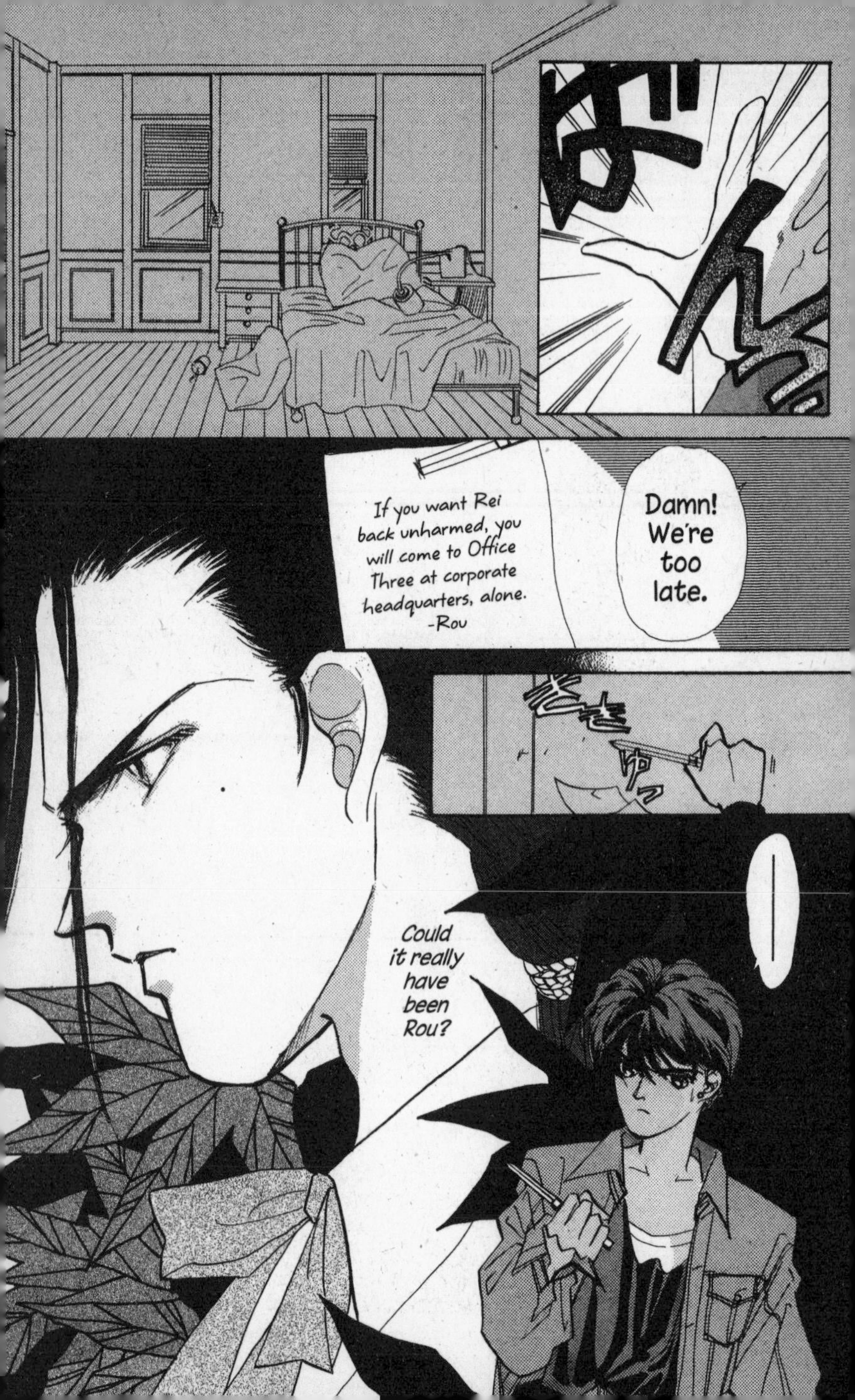
Damn! We're too late.
If you want Rei back unharmed, you will come to Office Three at corporate headquarters, alone. -Rou
Could it really have been Rou?

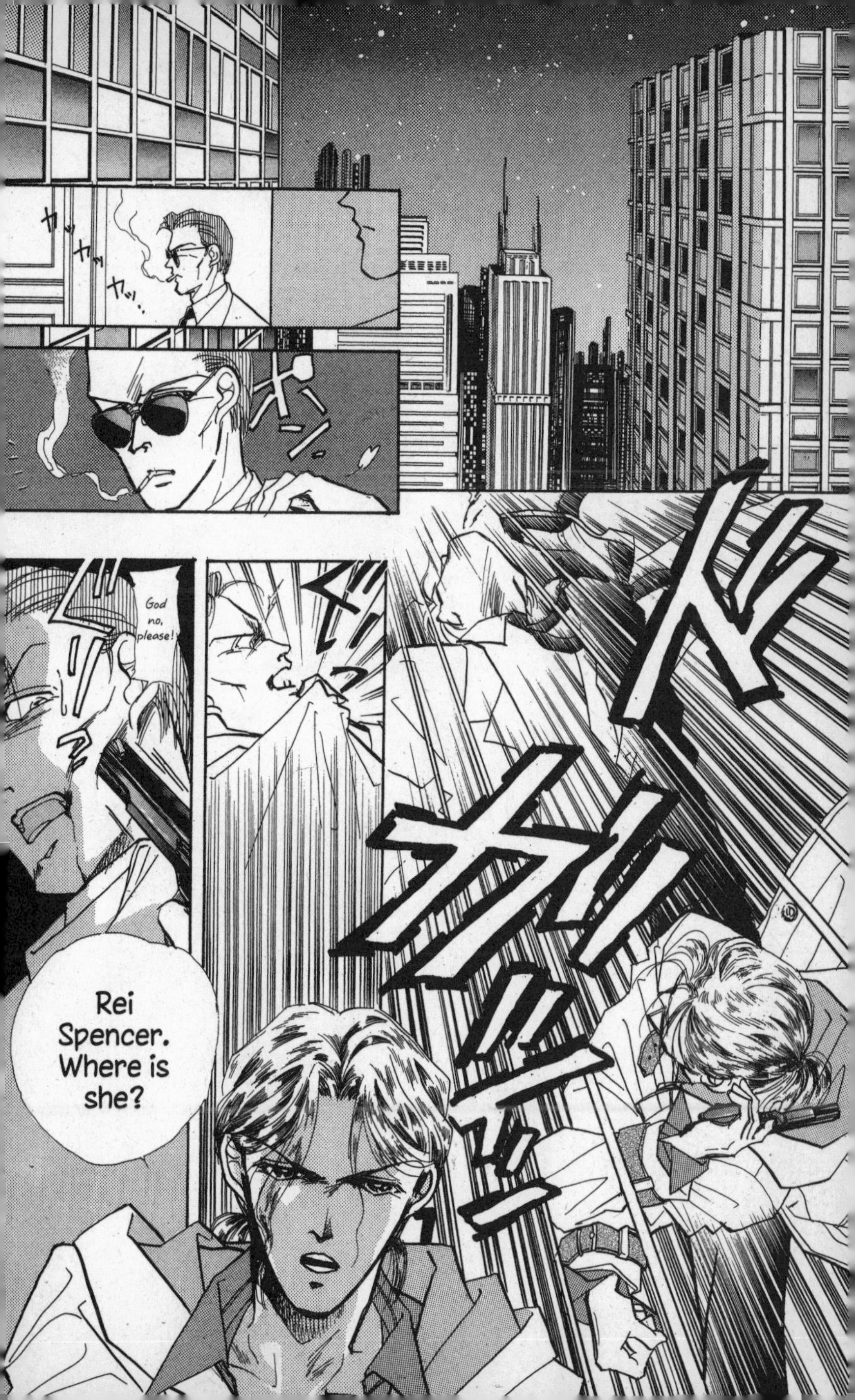
God no, please!
Rei Spencer. Where is she?

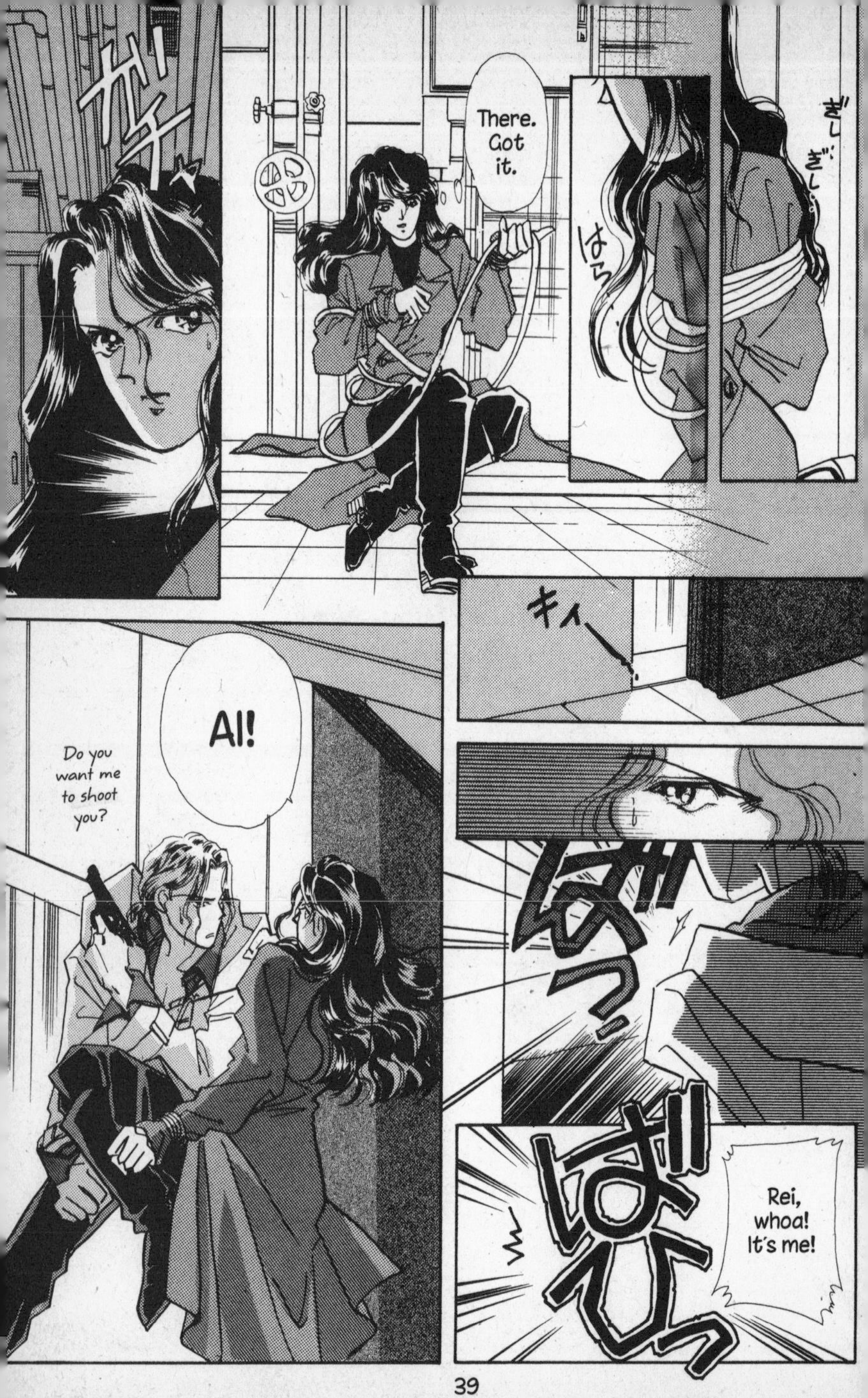
ぎし ぎし
はら
There. Got it.
カチ
キィー
Rei, whoa! It's me!
AI!
Do you want me to shoot you?

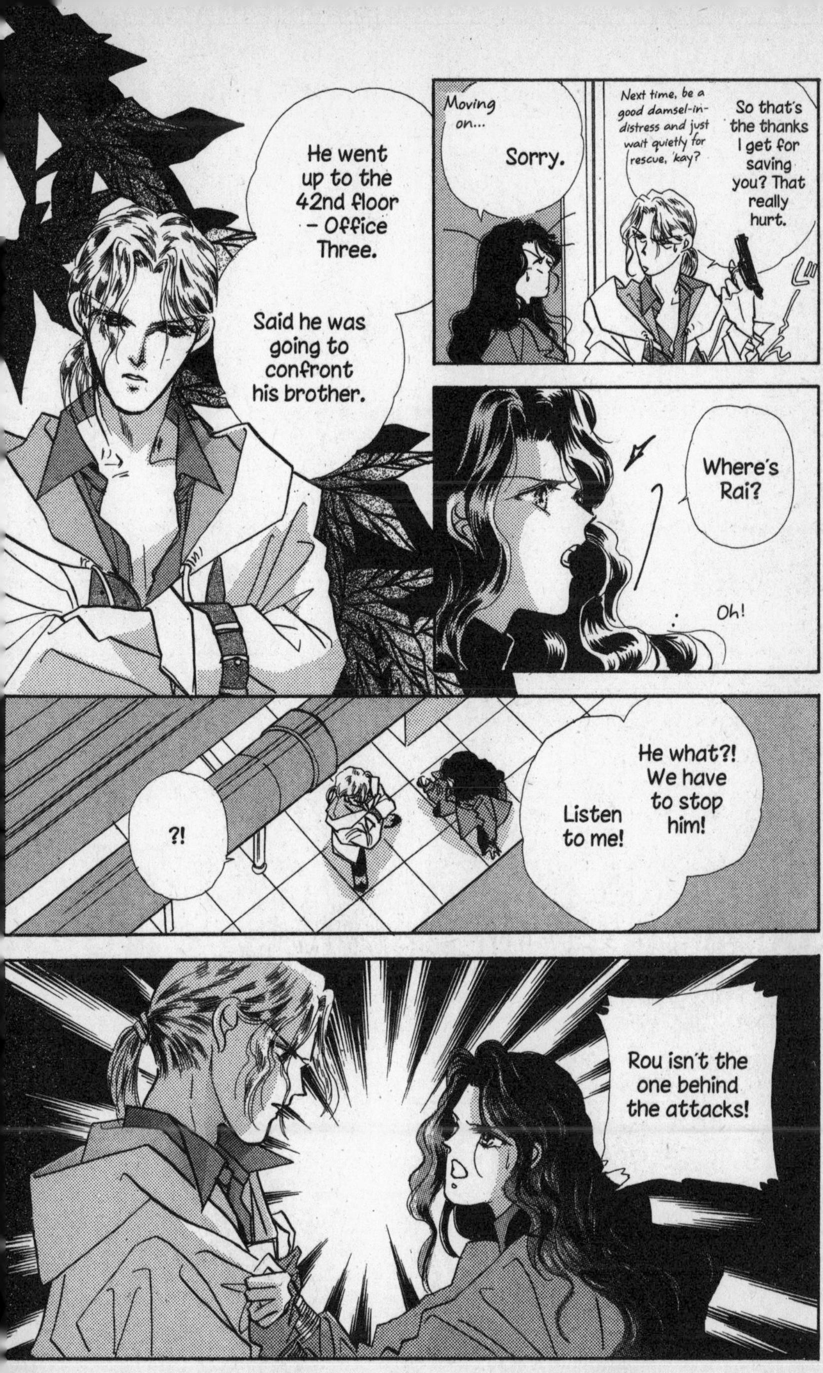
So that's the thanks I get for saving you? That really hurt.
Next time, be a good damsel-in-distress and just wait quietly for rescue, 'kay?
Moving on...
Sorry.
Where's Rai?
Oh!
He went up to the 42nd floor – Office Three.
Said he was going to confront his brother.
He what?! We have to stop him!
Listen to me!
?!
Rou isn't the one behind the attacks!

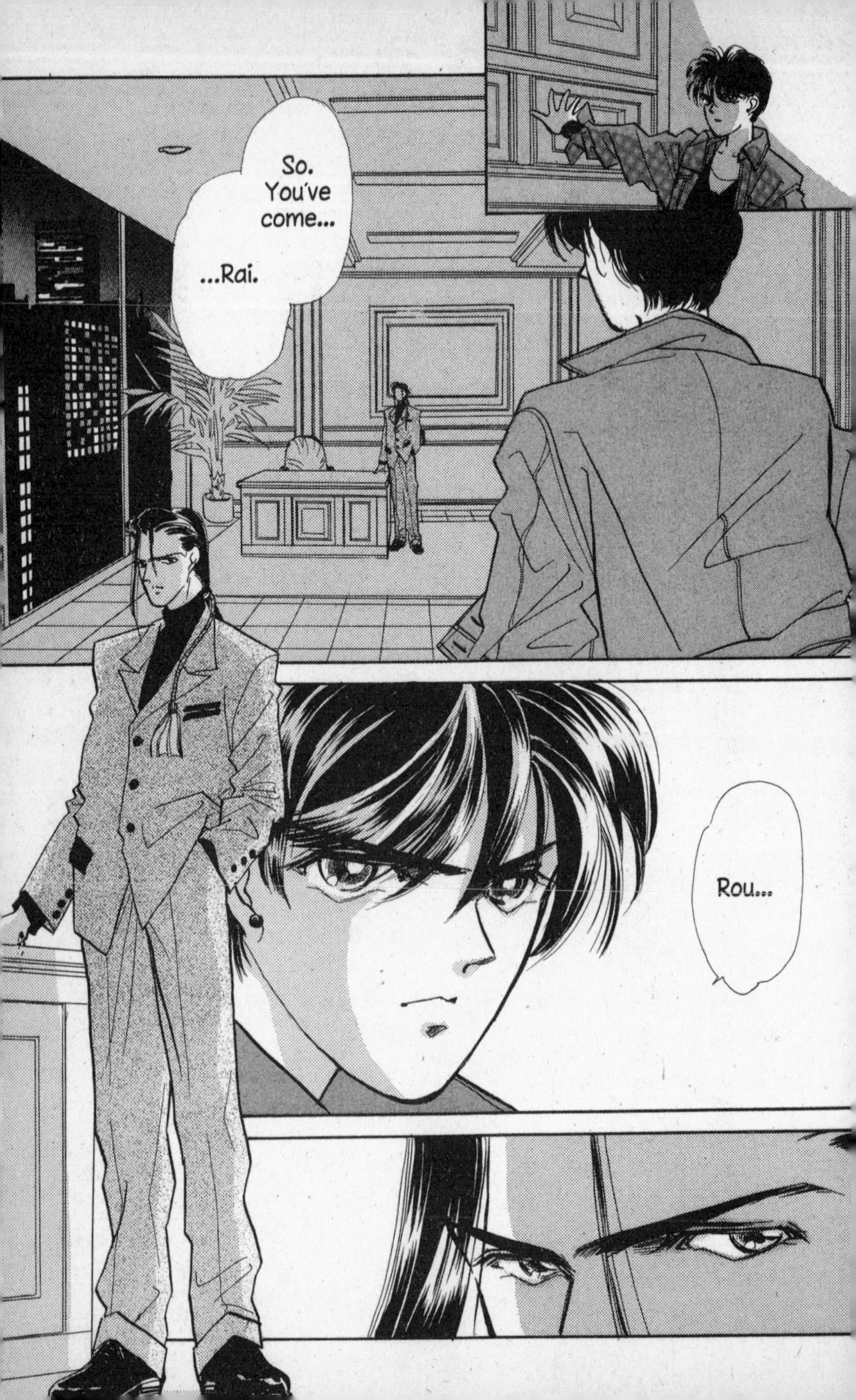
So. You've come...
...Rai.
Rou...

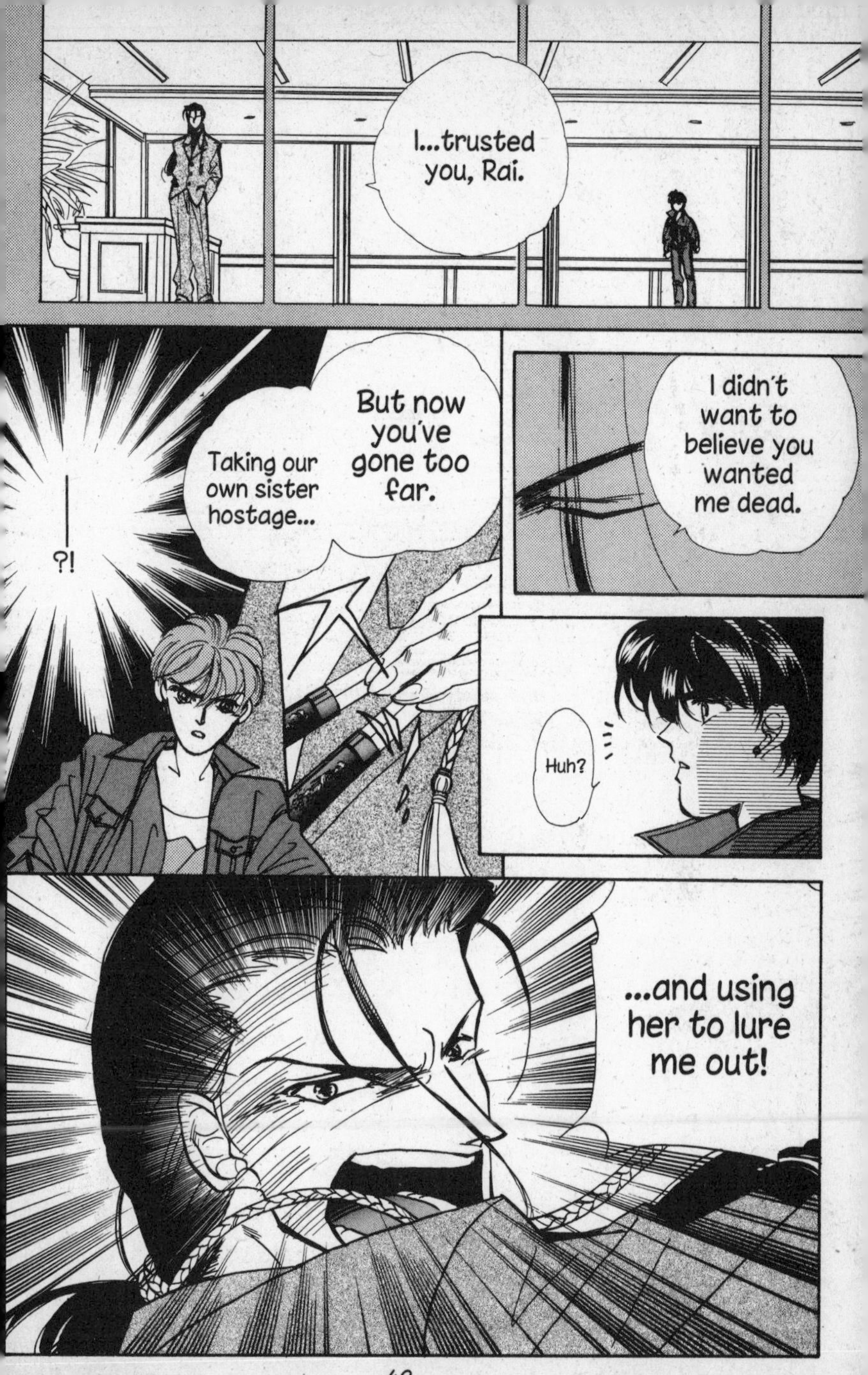
I...trusted you, Rai.
I didn't want to believe you wanted me dead.
Huh?
But now you've gone too far.
Taking our own sister hostage...
?!
...and using her to lure me out!

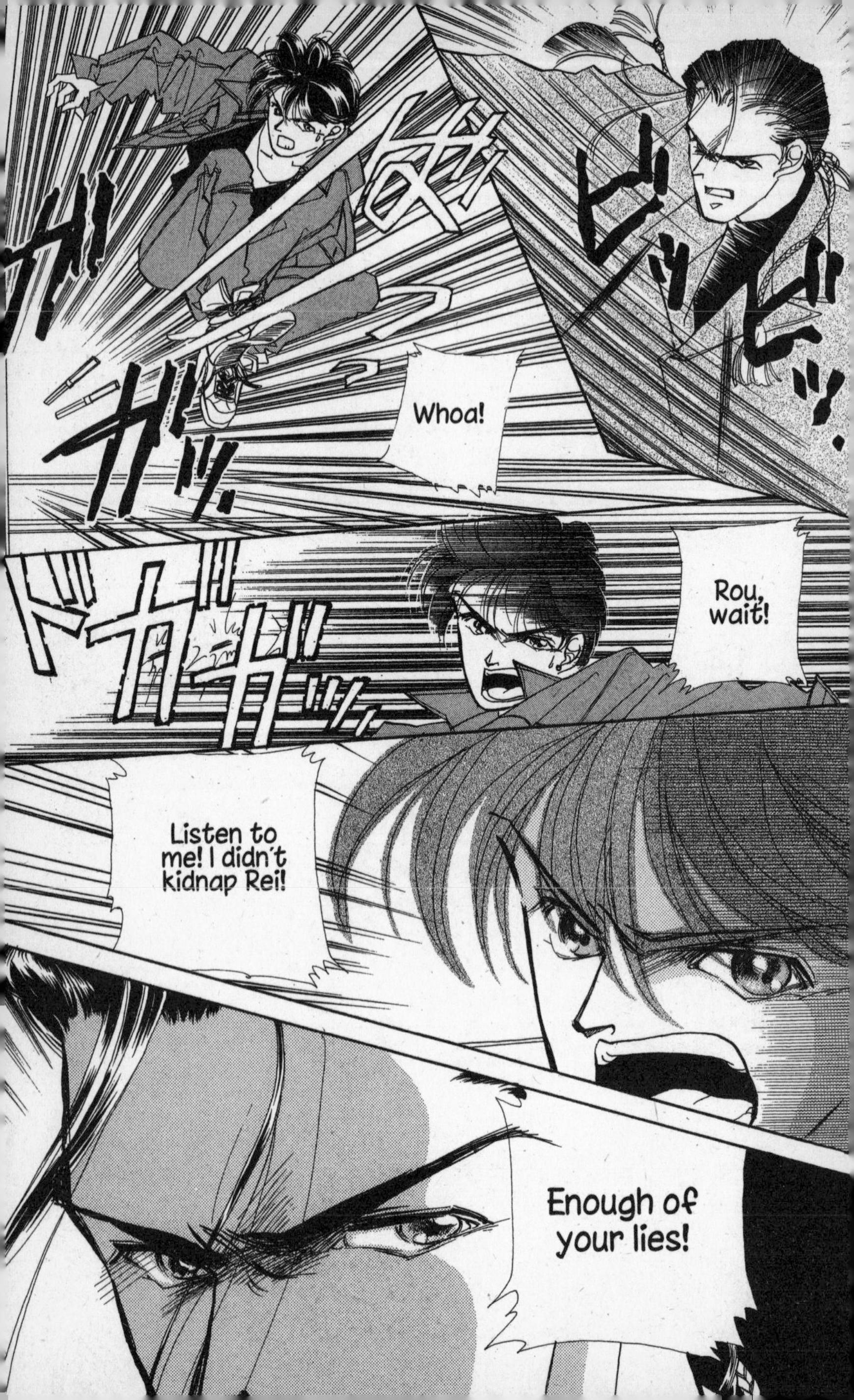
Whoa!
Rou, wait!
Listen to me! I didn't kidnap Rei!
Enough of your lies!

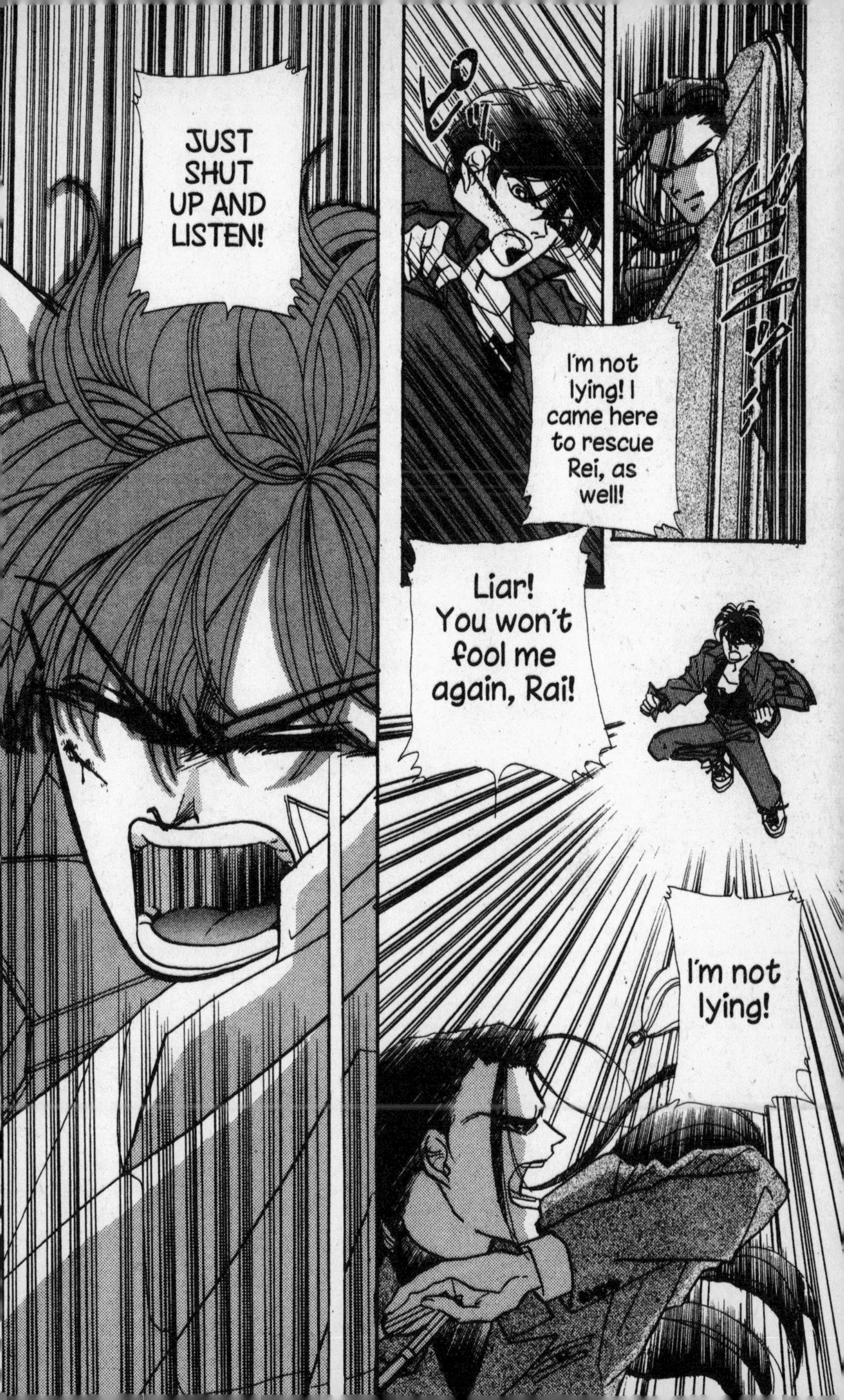
I'm not lying! I came here to rescue Rei, as well!
Liar! You won't fool me again, Rai!
I'm not lying!
JUST SHUT UP AND LISTEN!

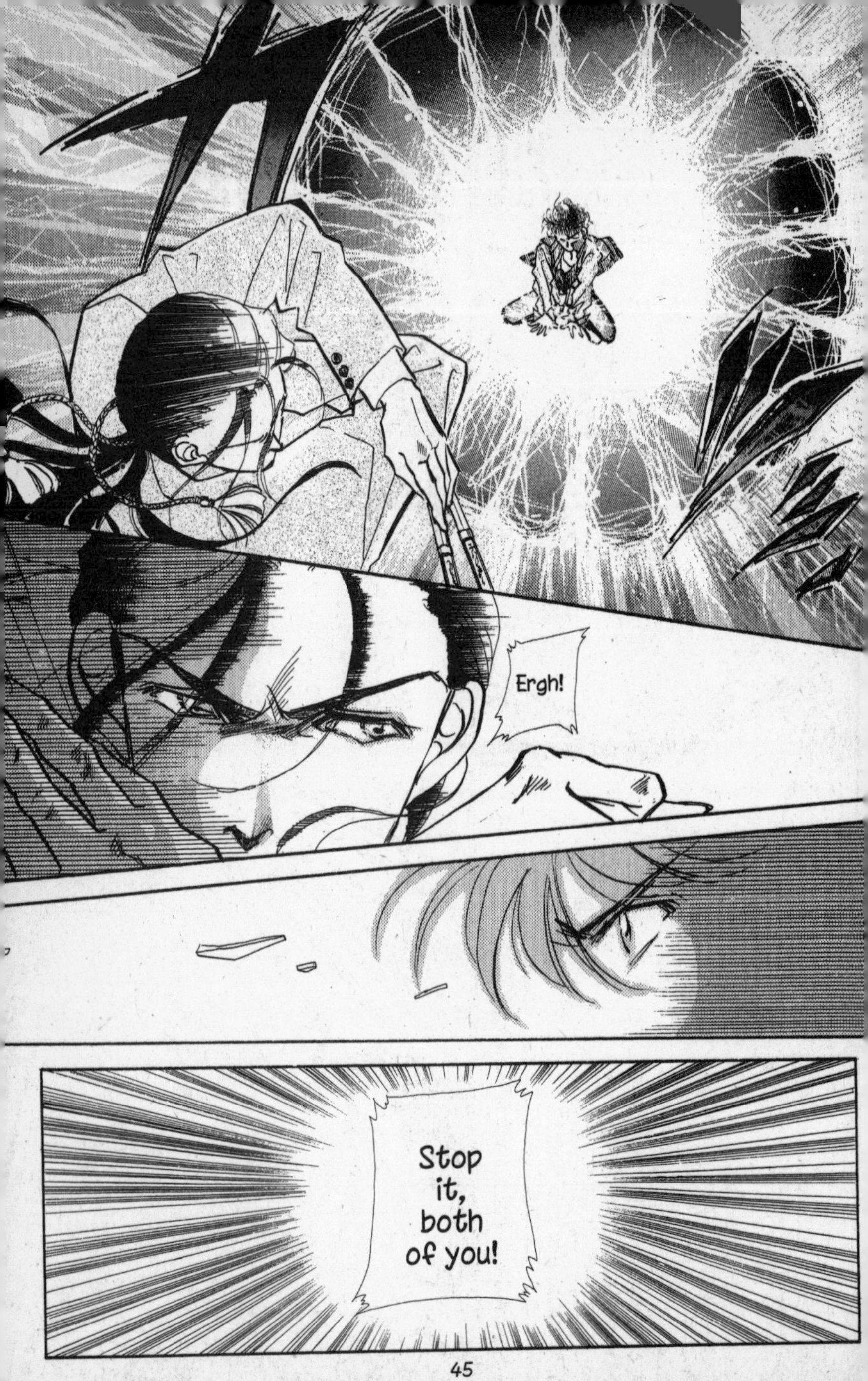
Ergh!
Stop it, both of you!

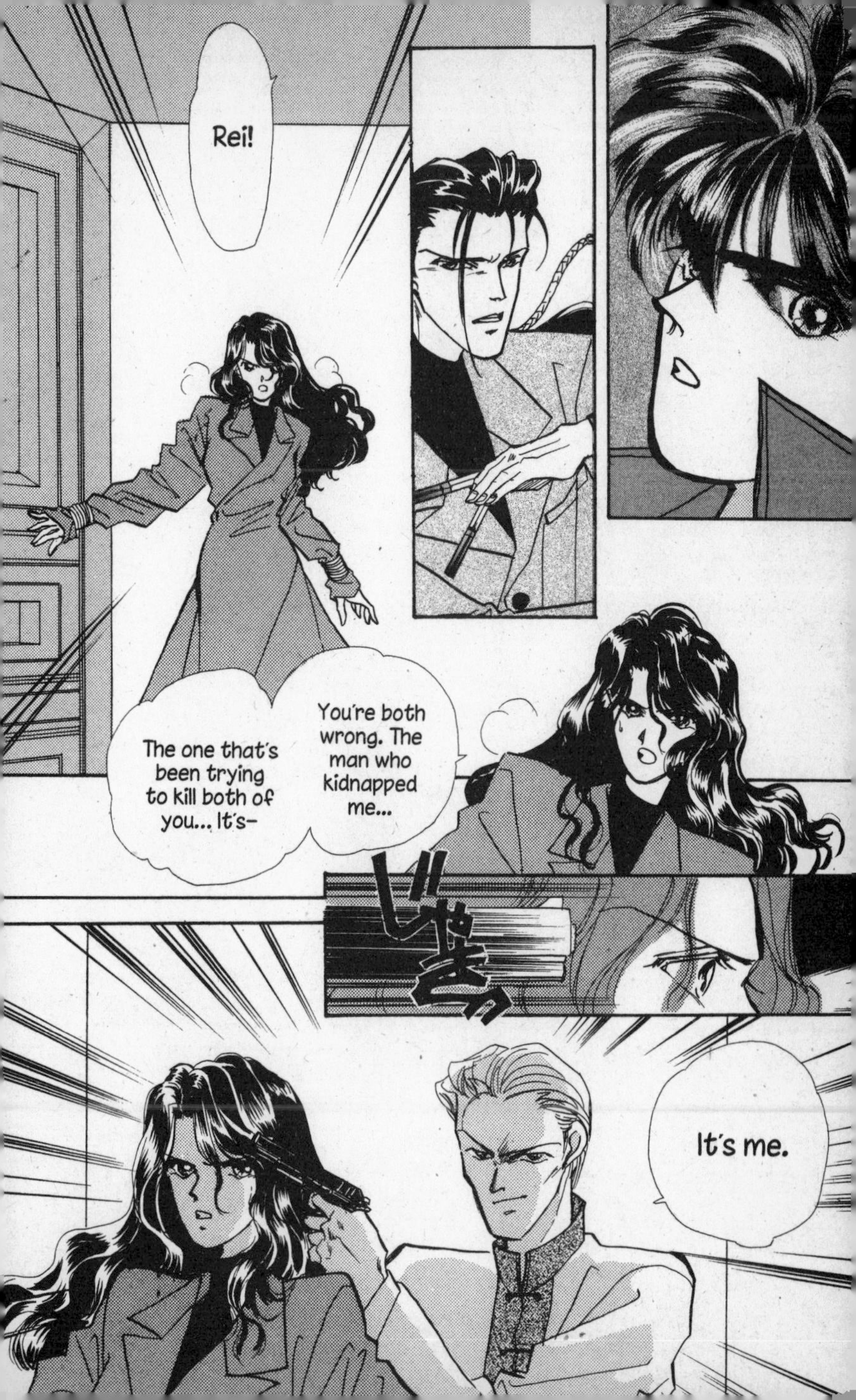
Rei!
You're both wrong. The man who kidnapped me...
The one that's been trying to kill both of you... It's-
じゃきっ
It's me.

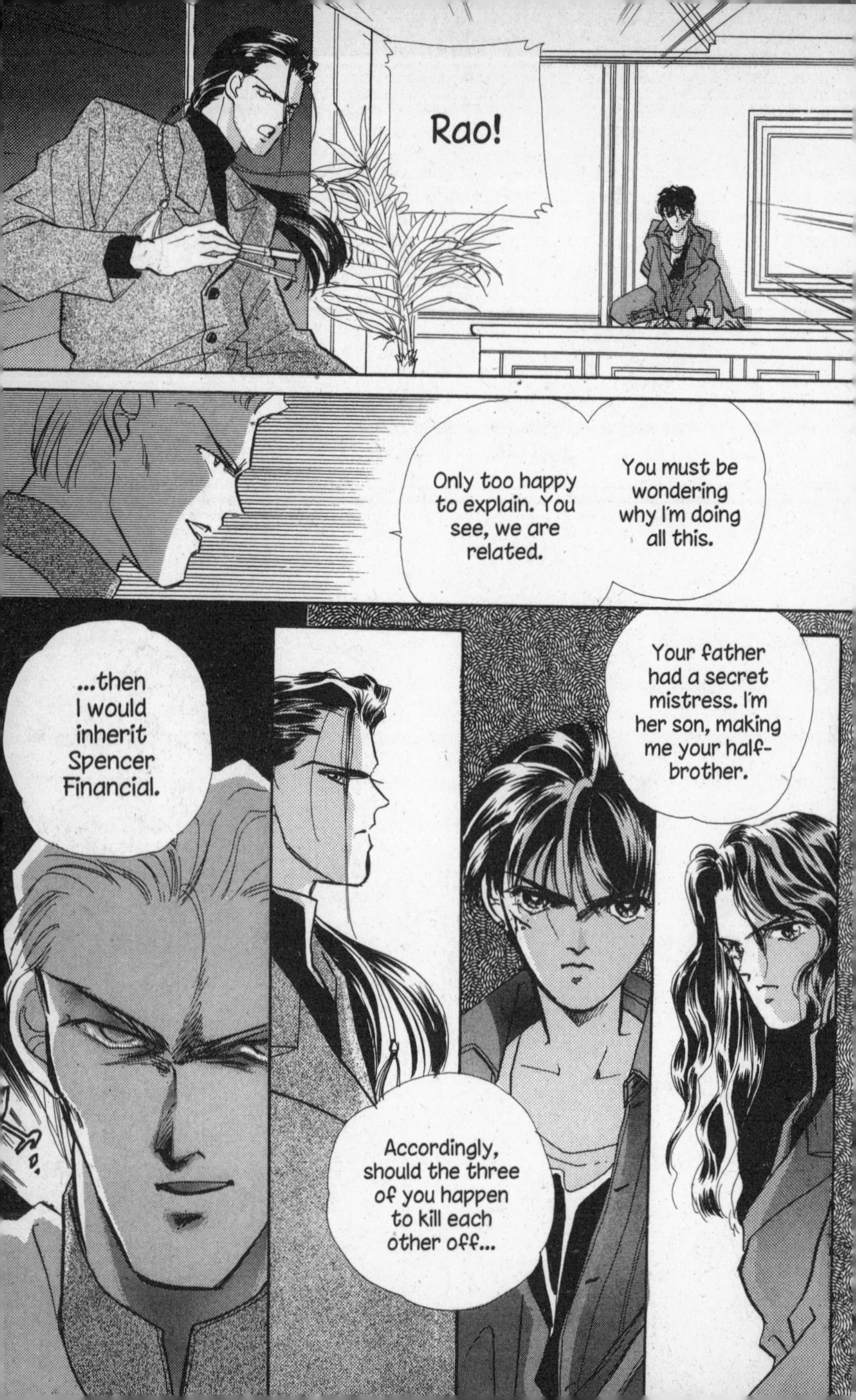
Rao!
You must be wondering why I'm doing all this.
Only too happy to explain. You see, we are related.
Your father had a secret mistress. I'm her son, making me your half-brother.
Accordingly, should the three of you happen to kill each other off...
...then I would inherit Spencer Financial.

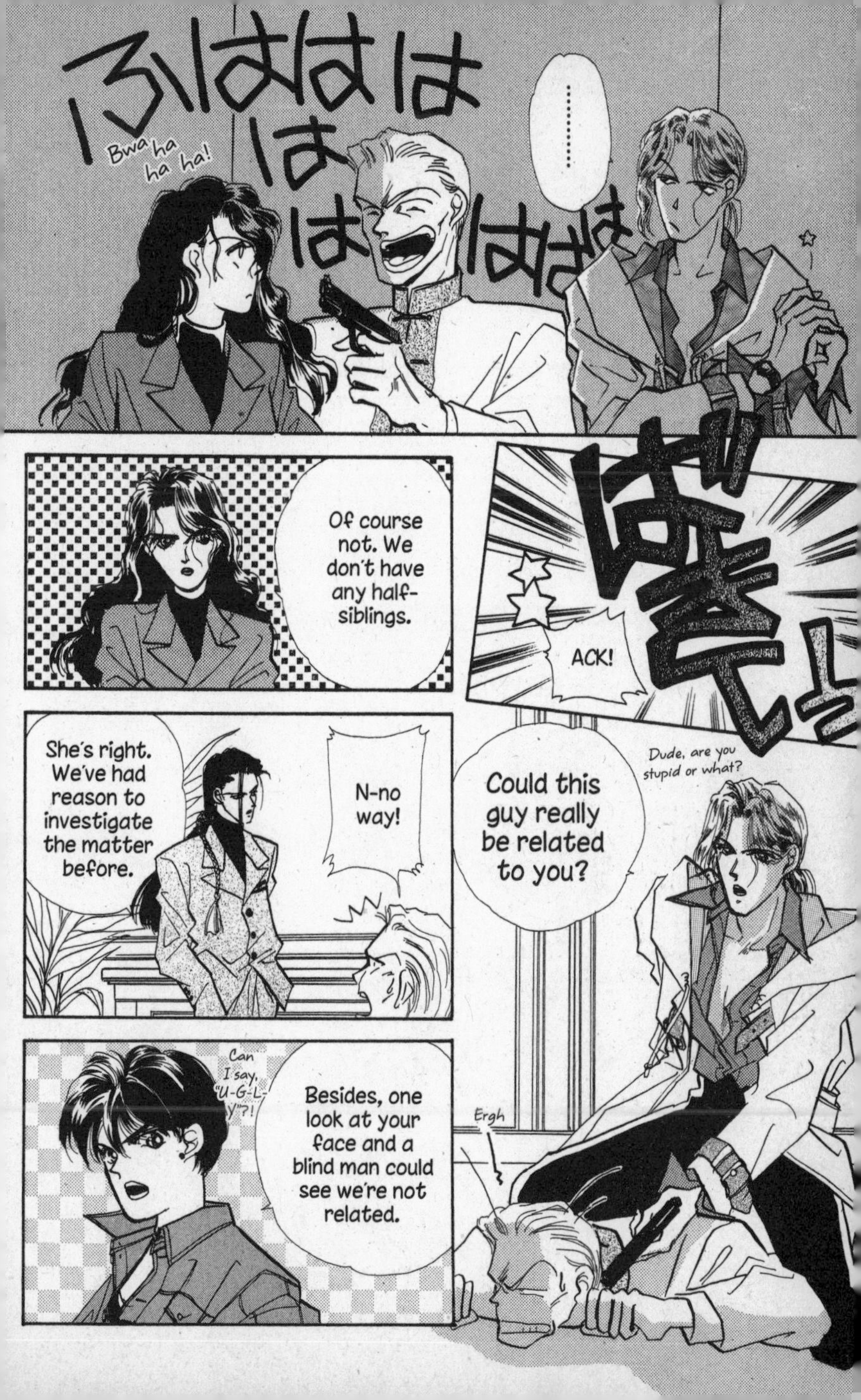
……
ふははははははは
Bwa ha ha ha!
ばきっ
ACK!
Of course not. We don't have any half-siblings.
Dude, are you stupid or what?
Could this guy really be related to you?
Ergh
N-no way!
She's right. We've had reason to investigate the matter before.
Besides, one look at your face and a blind man could see we're not related.
Can I say, "U-G-L-Y"?!

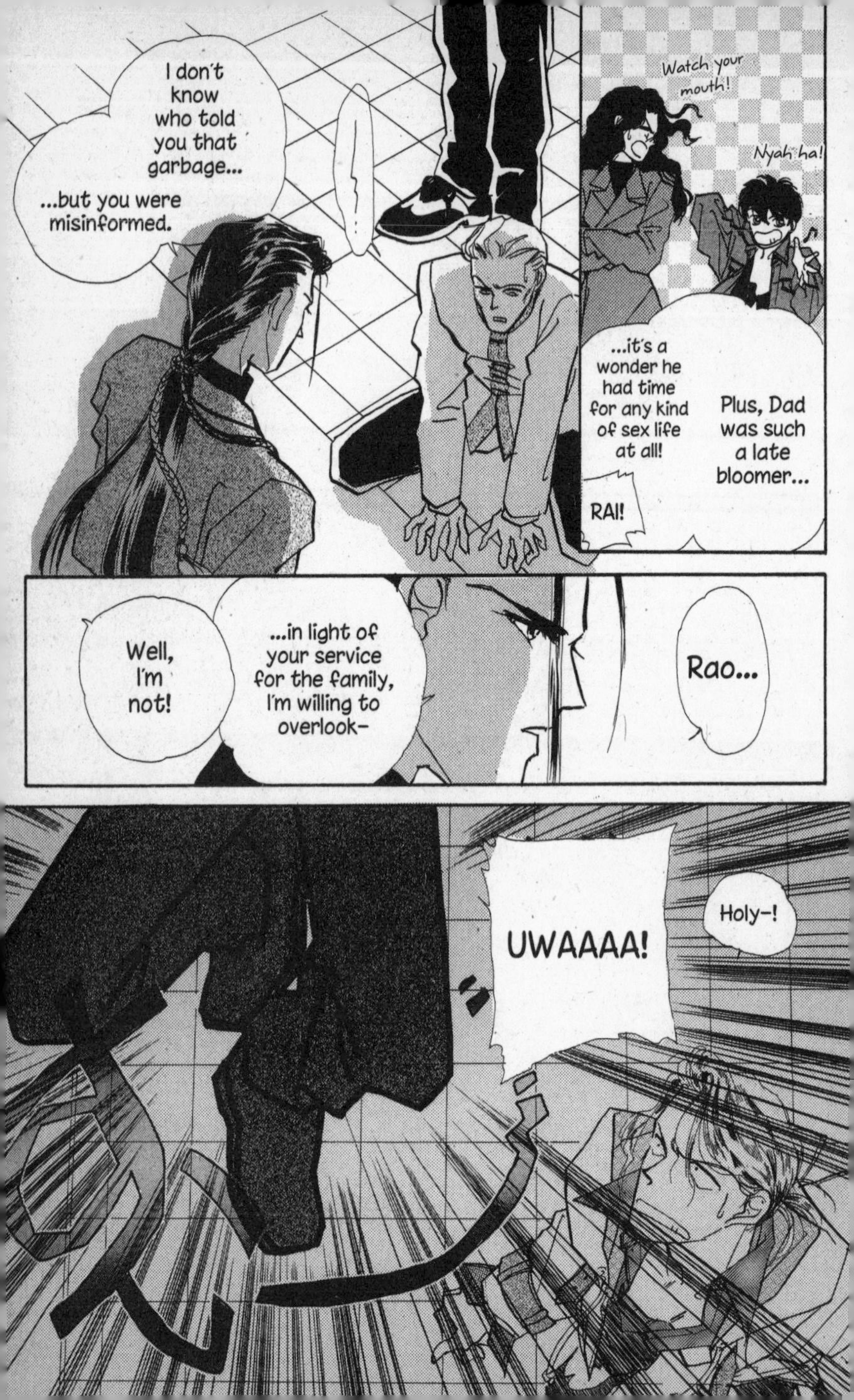
Plus, Dad was such a late bloomer...
...it's a wonder he had time for any kind of sex life at all!
RAI!
Watch your mouth!
Nyah ha!
I don't know who told you that garbage...
...but you were misinformed.
Rao...
...in light of your service for the family, I'm willing to overlook-
Well, I'm not!
Holy-!
UWAAAA!

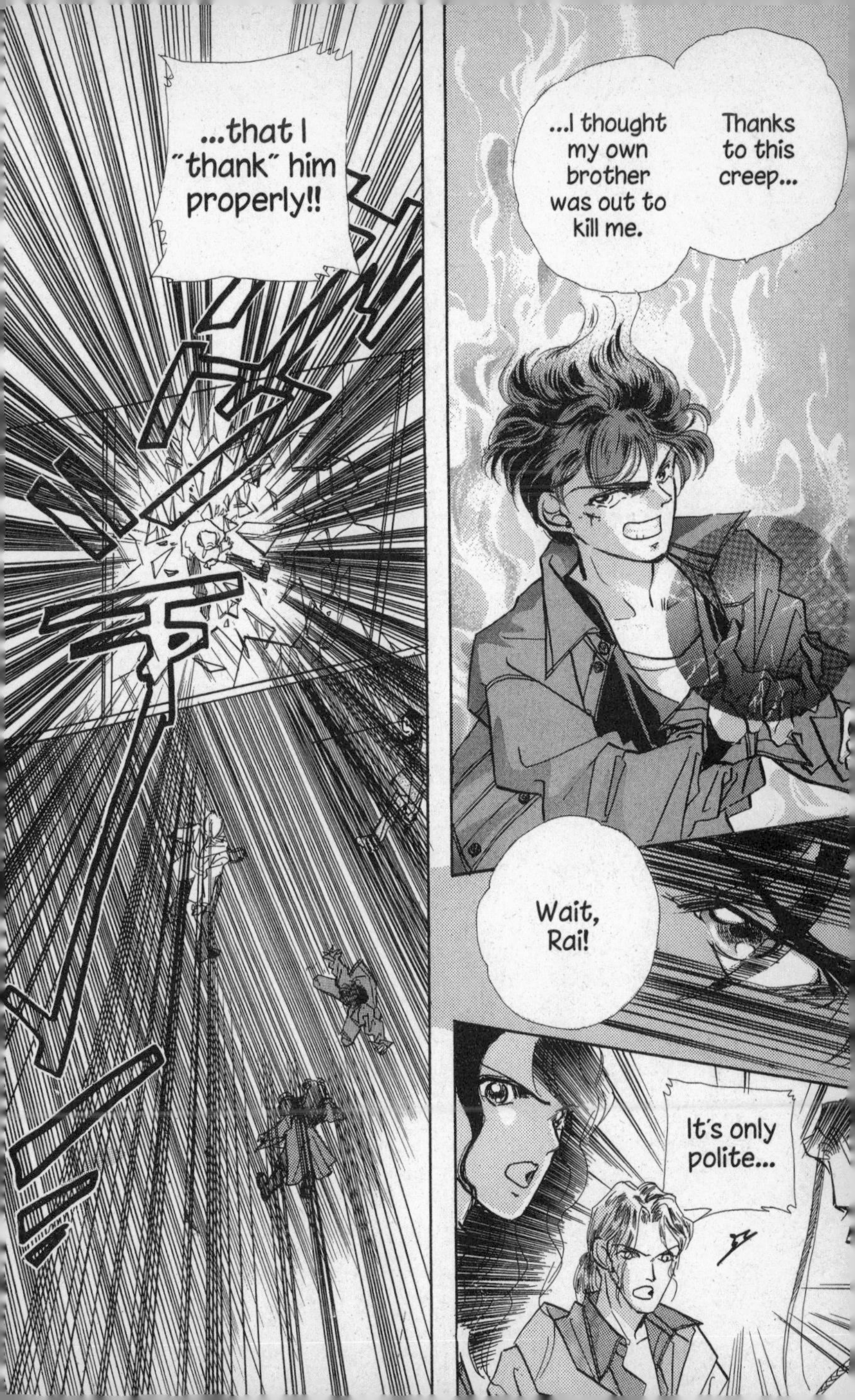
Thanks to this creep...
...I thought my own brother was out to kill me.
Wait, Rai!
It's only polite...
...that I "thank" him properly!!

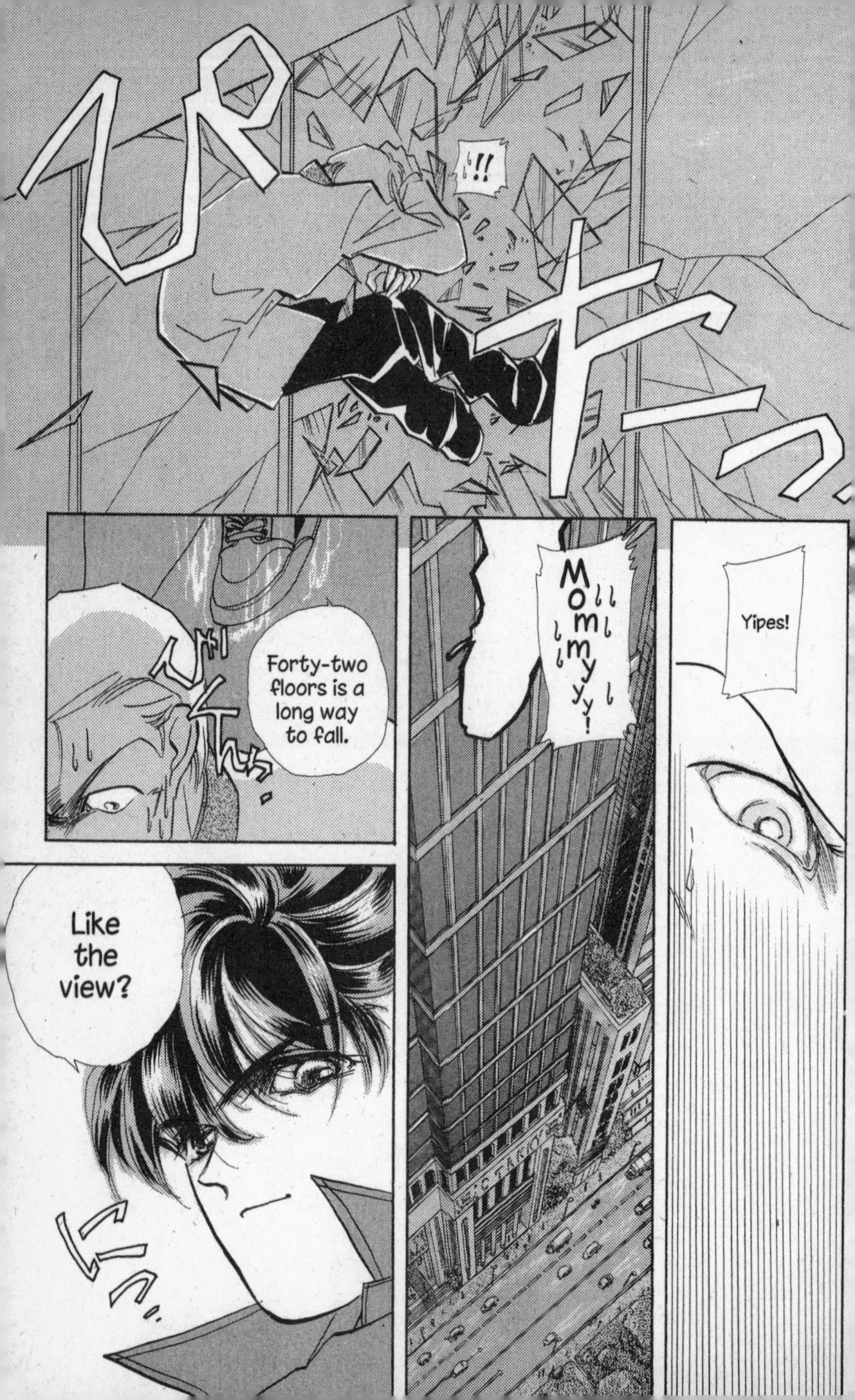
!!
Yipes!
Mommyyy!
Forty-two floors is a long way to fall.
Like the view?

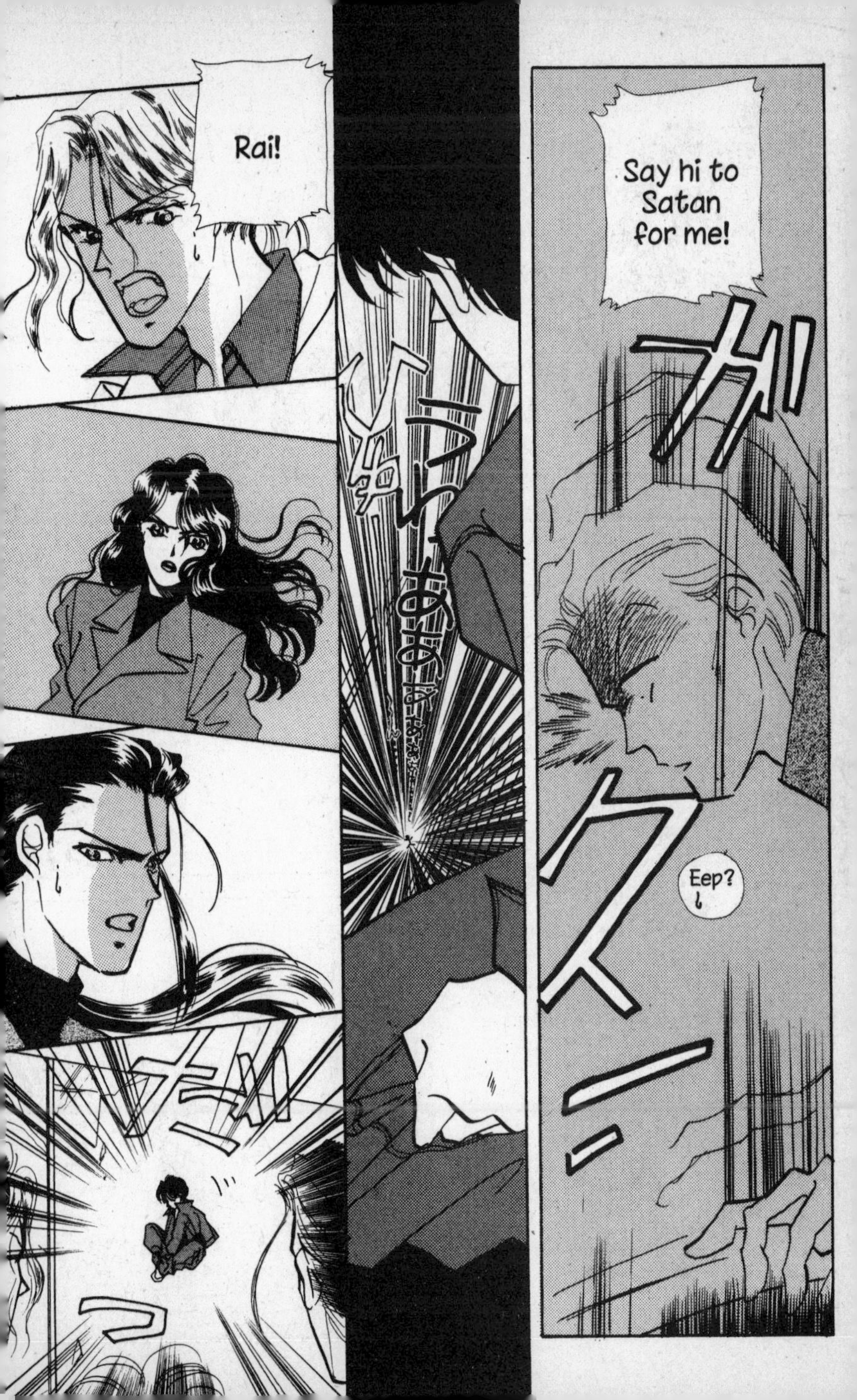
Say hi to Satan for me!
Eep?
Rai!

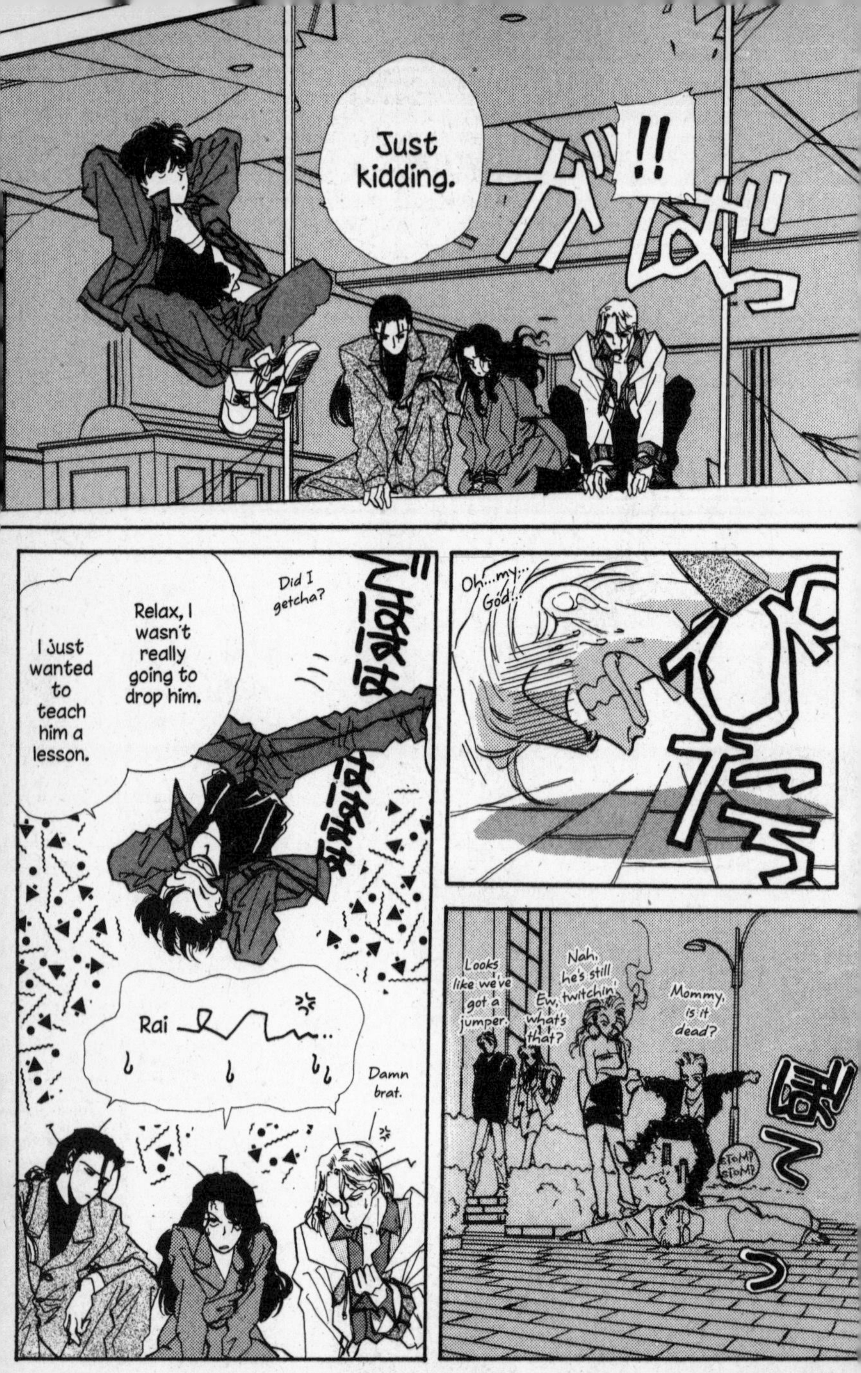

Just kidding.
!!
がばっ
Oh...my... God!...
Mommy, is it dead?
Nah, he's still twitchin'.
Ew, what's that?
Looks like we've got a jumper.
STOMP STOMP
ぽてっ
Did I getcha?
Relax, I wasn't really going to drop him.
I just wanted to teach him a lesson.
Rai ~~...
Damn brat.

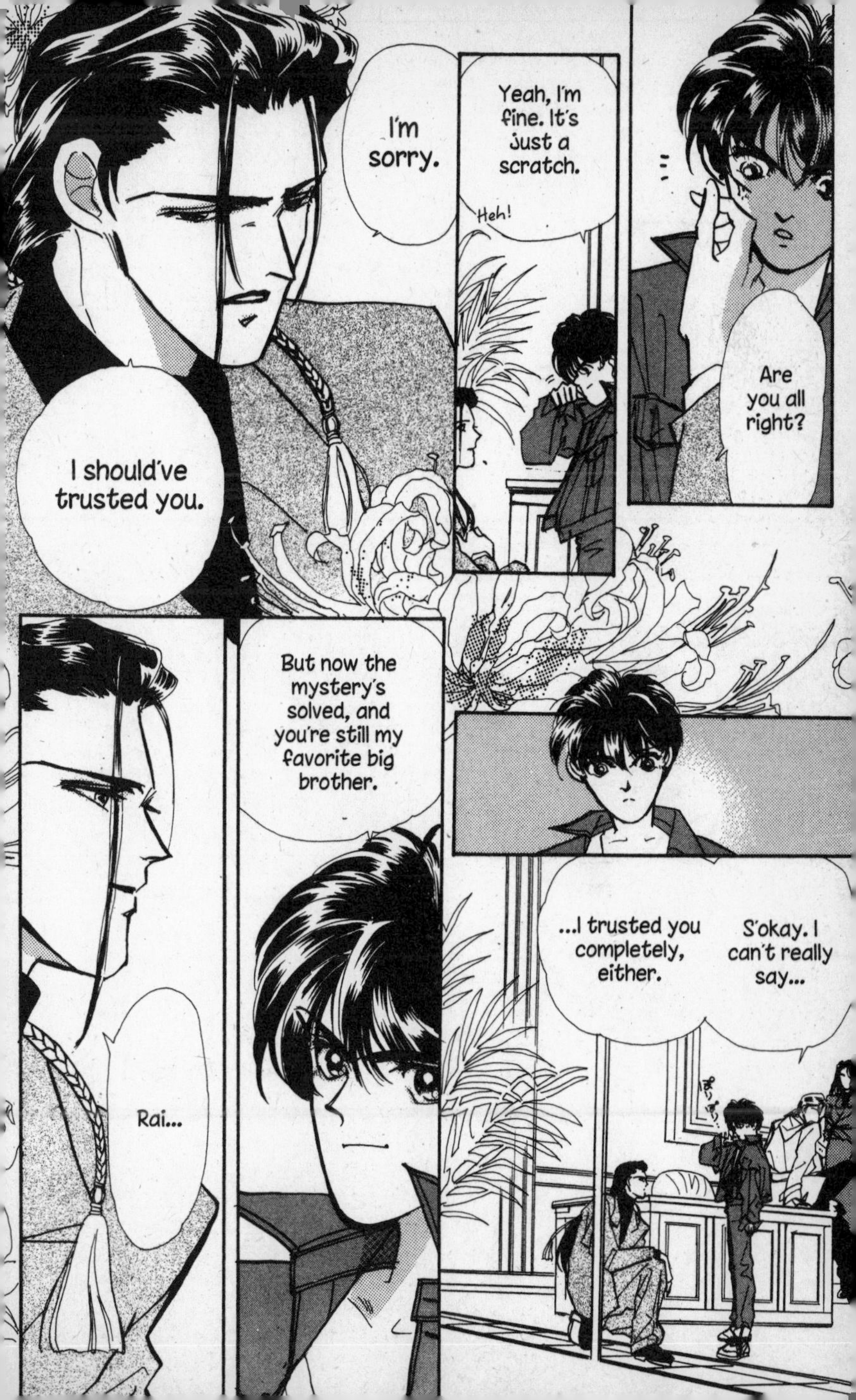
Are you all right?
Yeah, I'm fine. It's just a scratch.
Heh!
I'm sorry.
I should've trusted you.
S'okay. I can't really say...
...I trusted you completely, either.
But now the mystery's solved, and you're still my favorite big brother.
Rai...

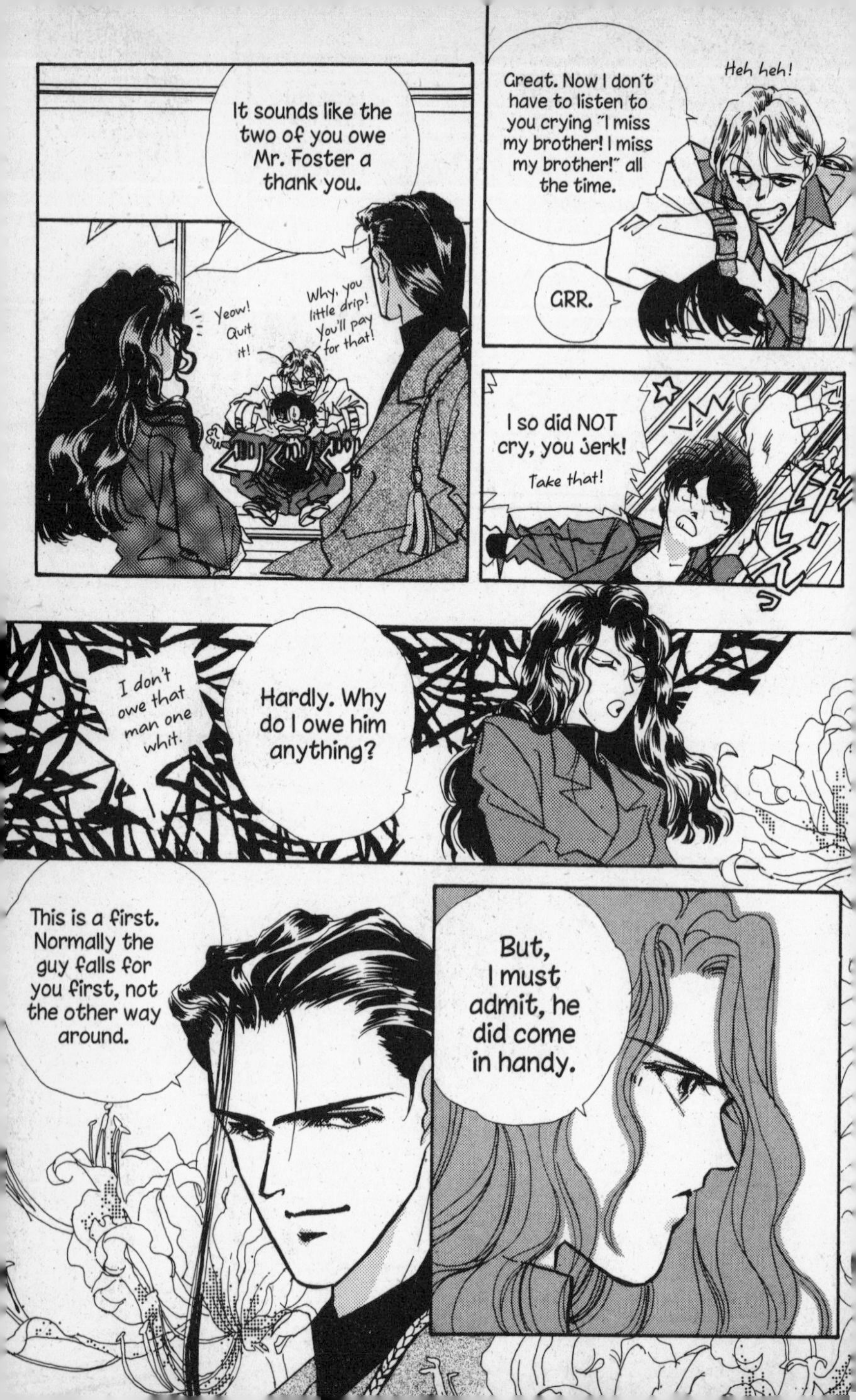
Heh heh!
Great. Now I don't have to listen to you crying "I miss my brother! I miss my brother!" all the time.
GRR.
I so did NOT cry, you jerk!
Take that!
It sounds like the two of you owe Mr. Foster a thank you.
Why, you little drip! You'll pay for that!
Yeow! Quit it!
Hardly. Why do I owe him anything?
I don't owe that man one whit.
But, I must admit, he did come in handy.
This is a first. Normally the guy falls for you first, not the other way around.

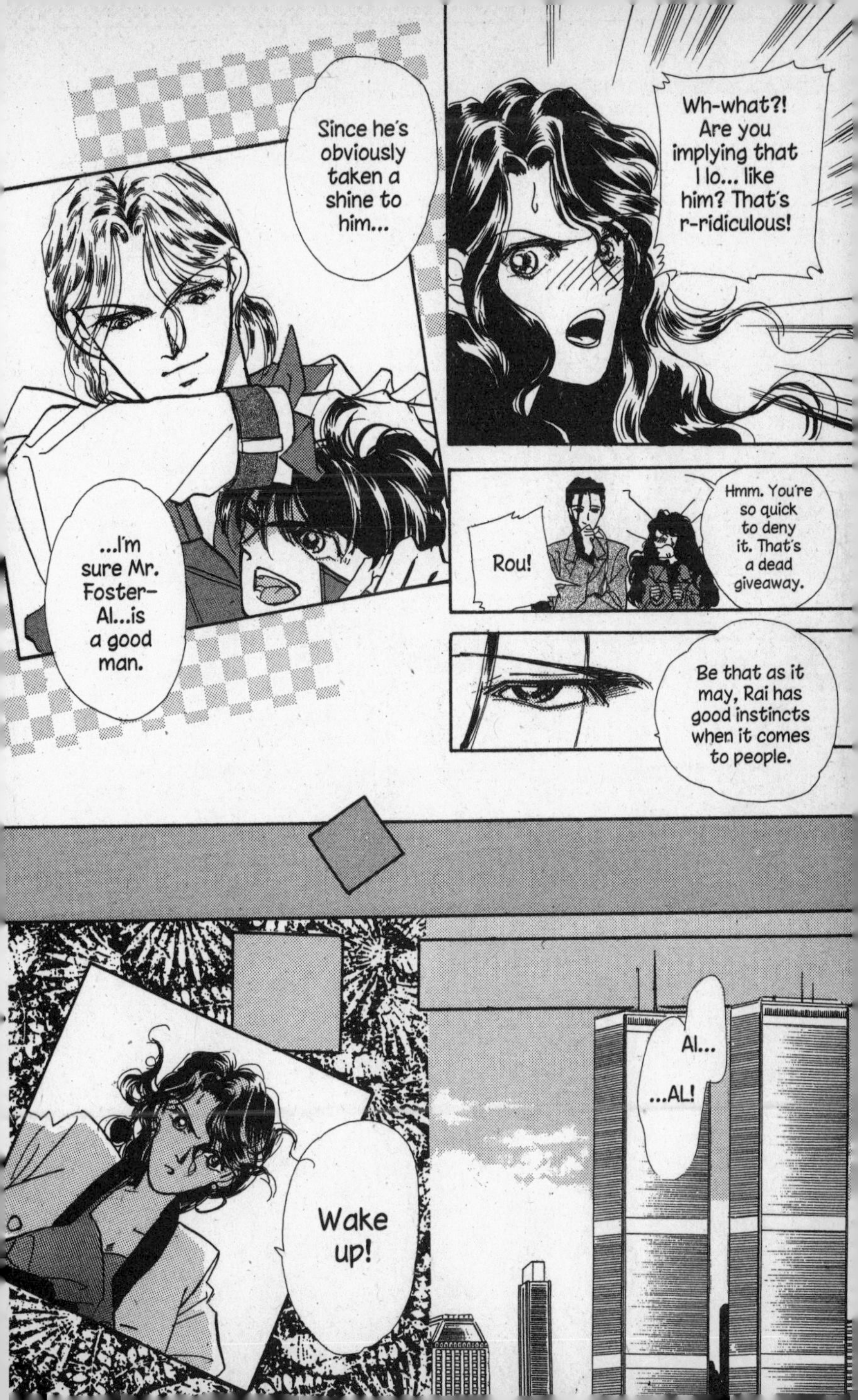

Wh-what?! Are you implying that I lo... like him? That's r-ridiculous!
Hmm. You're so quick to deny it. That's a dead giveaway.
Rou!
Be that as it may, Rai has good instincts when it comes to people.
Since he's obviously taken a shine to him...
...I'm sure Mr. Foster-Al...is a good man.
Al...
...AL!
Wake up!

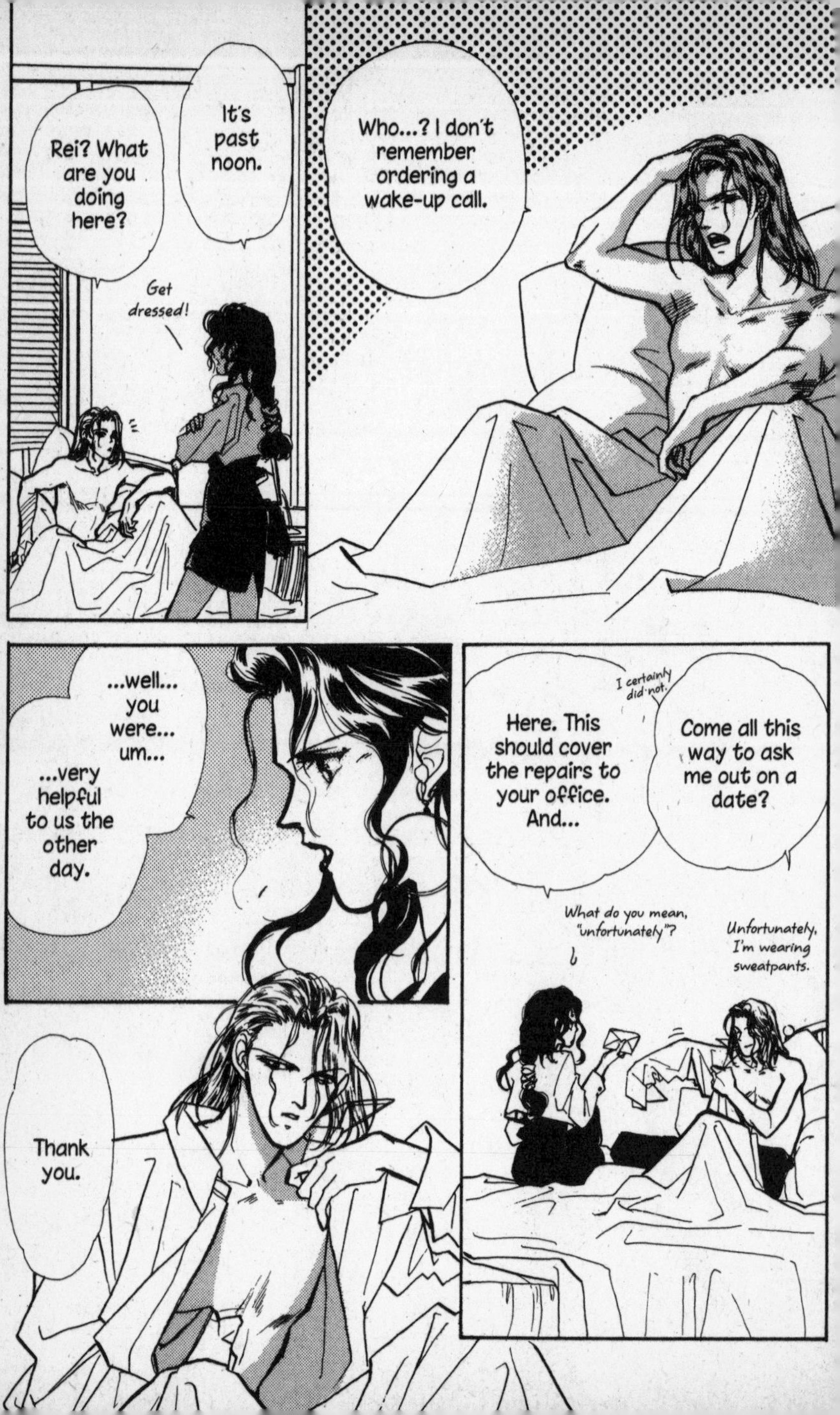
Who...? I don't remember ordering a wake-up call.
It's past noon.
Rei? What are you doing here?
Get dressed!
Come all this way to ask me out on a date?
I certainly did not.
Here. This should cover the repairs to your office. And...
Unfortunately, I'm wearing sweatpants.
What do you mean, "unfortunately"?
...well... you were... um...
...very helpful to us the other day.
Thank you.

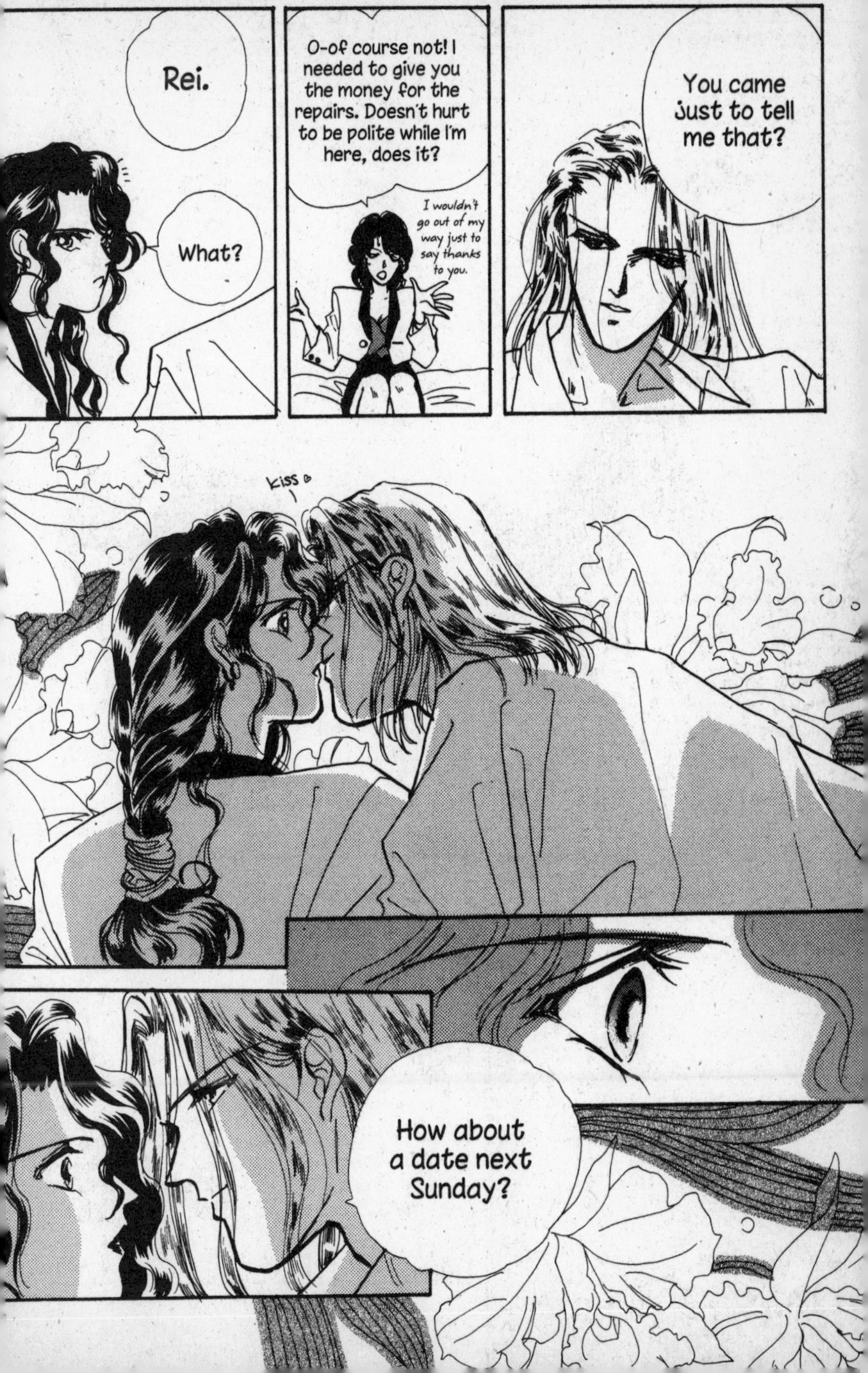
You came just to tell me that?
O-of course not! I needed to give you the money for the repairs. Doesn't hurt to be polite while I'm here, does it?
I wouldn't go out of my way just to say thanks to you.
Rei.
What?
kiss
How about a date next Sunday?

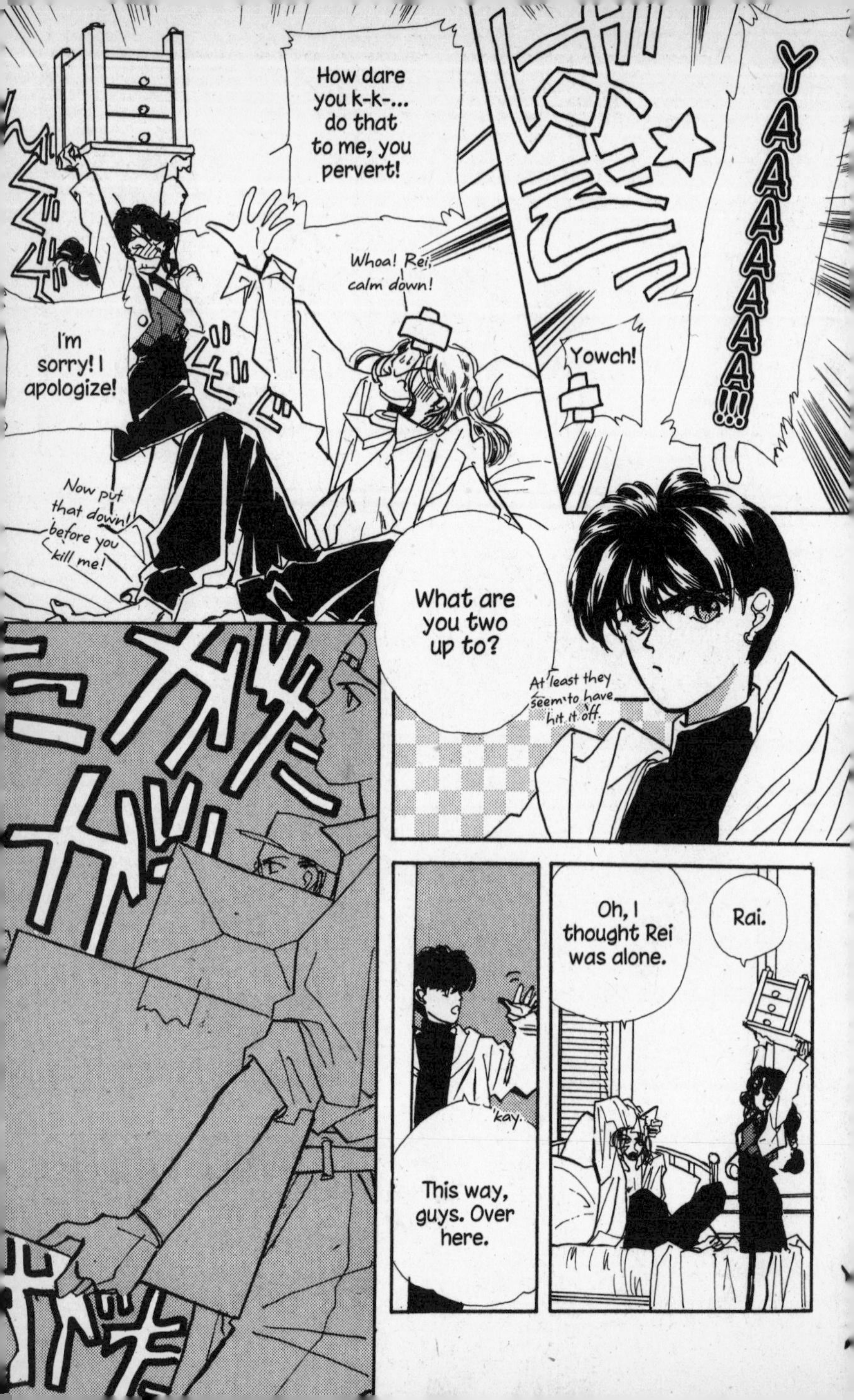
YAAAAAAAA!!!
Yowch!
How dare you k-k-... do that to me, you pervert!
Whoa! Rei, calm down!
I'm sorry! I apologize!
Now put that down before you kill me!
What are you two up to?
At least they seem to have hit it off.
Rai.
Oh, I thought Rei was alone.
'kay.
This way, guys. Over here.

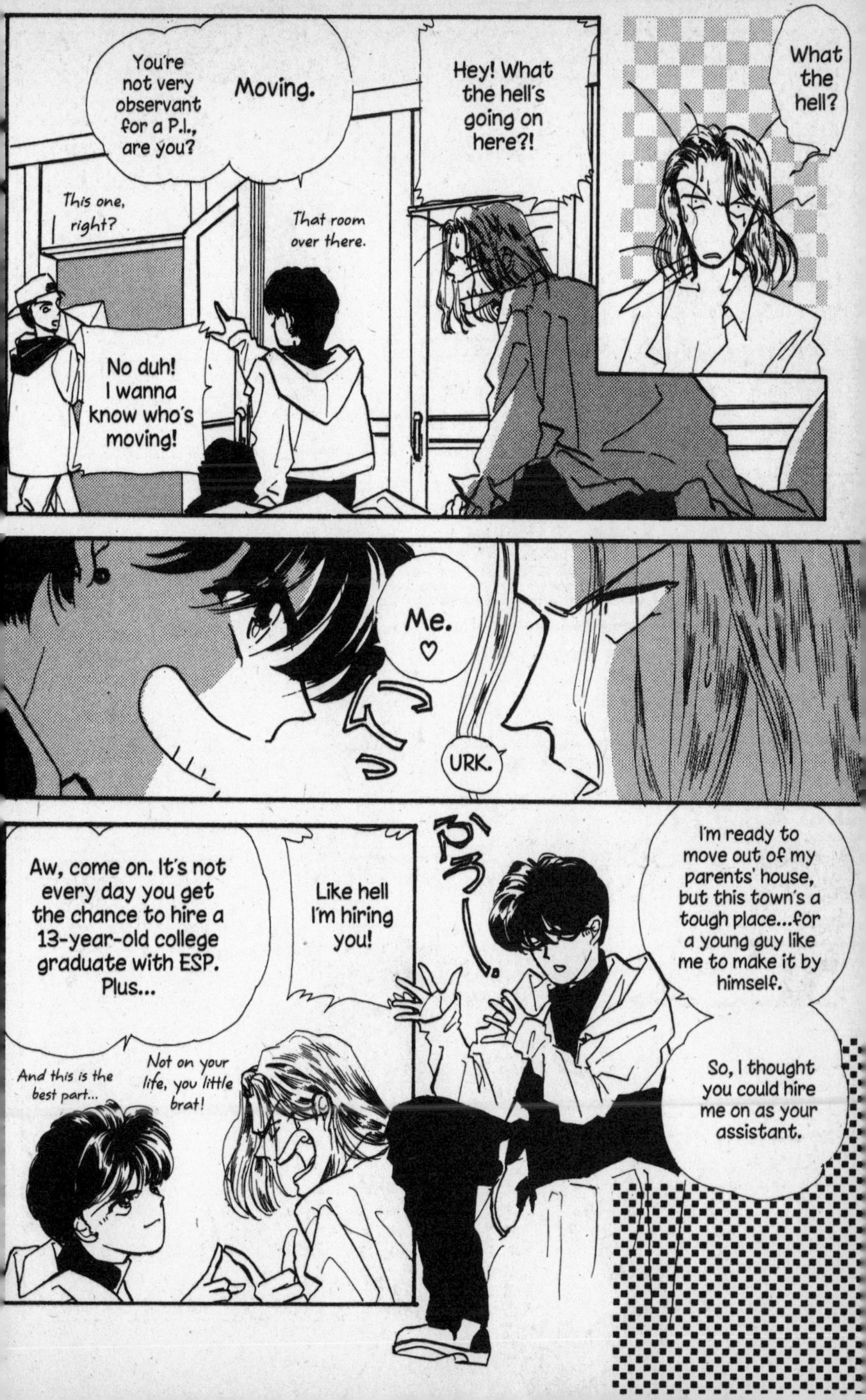
What the hell?
Hey! What the hell's going on here?!
Moving.
You're not very observant for a P.I., are you?
That room over there.
This one, right?
No duh! I wanna know who's moving!
Me. ♡
URK.
I'm ready to move out of my parents' house, but this town's a tough place...for a young guy like me to make it by himself.
So, I thought you could hire me on as your assistant.
Like hell I'm hiring you!
Aw, come on. It's not every day you get the chance to hire a 13-year-old college graduate with ESP. Plus...
Not on your life, you little brat!
And this is the best part...

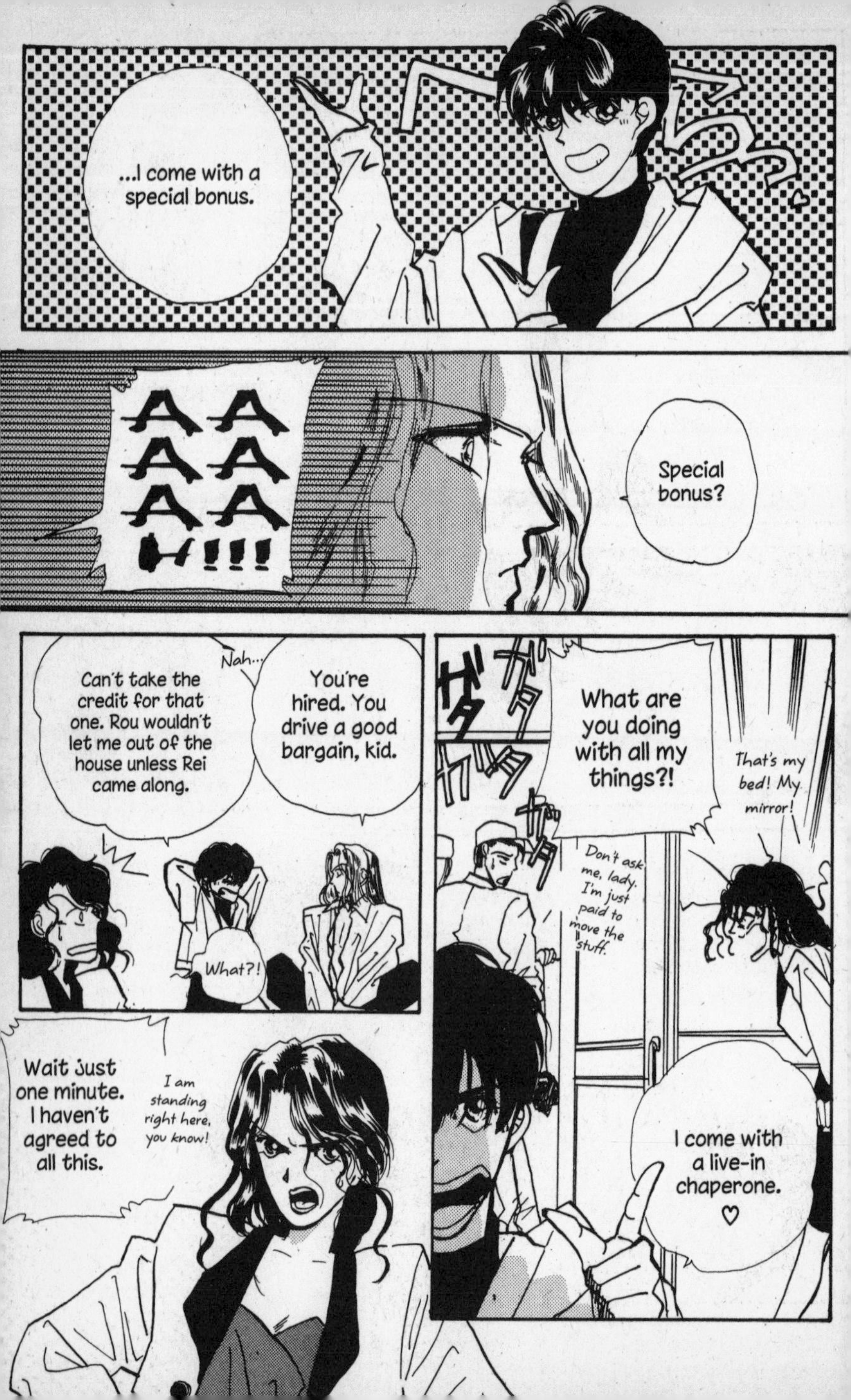
...I come with a special bonus.
Special bonus?
AAAAAAH!!!
ガタガタ
What are you doing with all my things?!
That's my bed! My mirror!
Don't ask me, lady. I'm just paid to move the stuff.
I come with a live-in chaperone. ♡
You're hired. You drive a good bargain, kid.
Nah...
Can't take the credit for that one. Rou wouldn't let me out of the house unless Rei came along.
What?!
I am standing right here, you know!
Wait just one minute. I haven't agreed to all this.

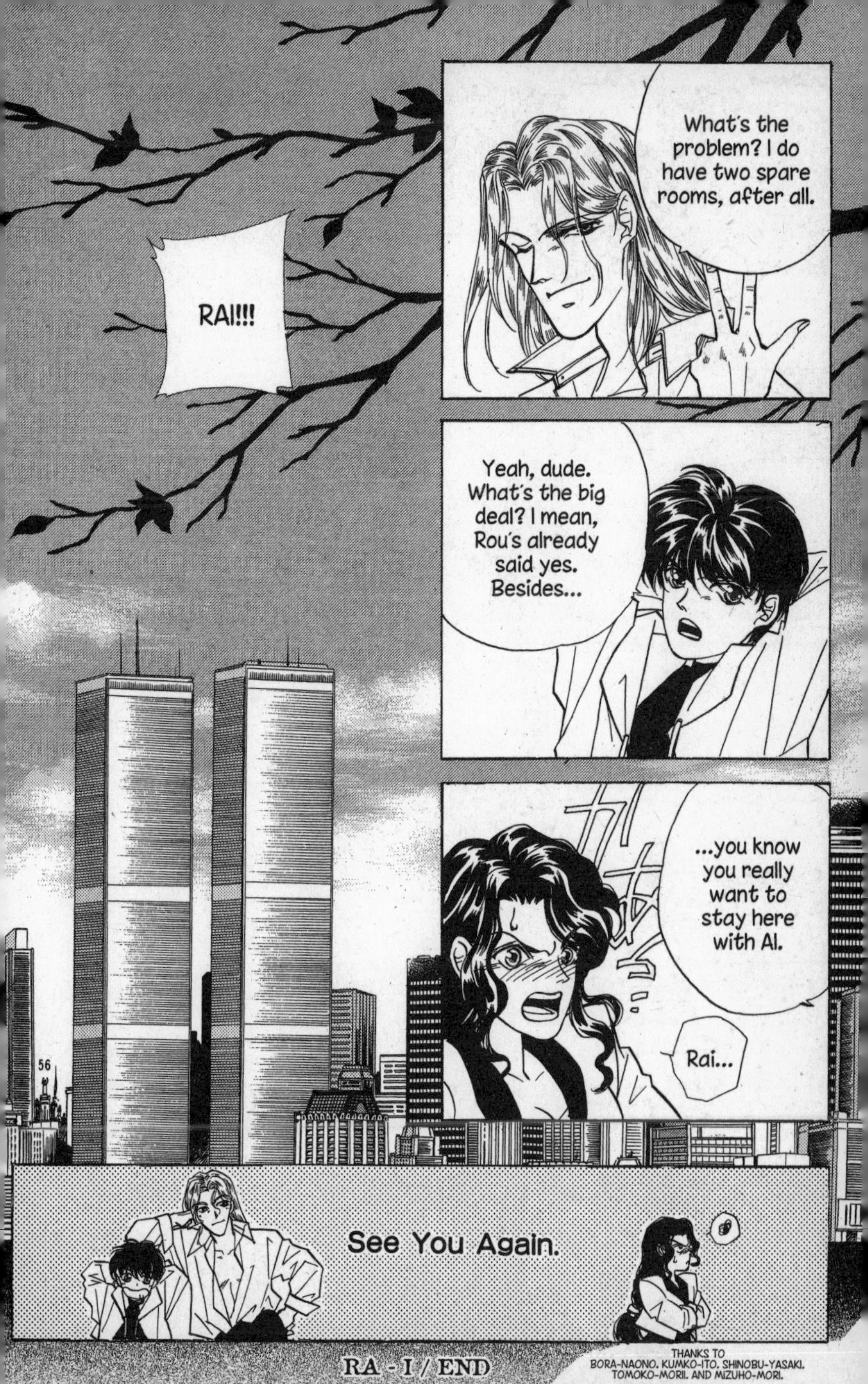

What's the problem? I do have two spare rooms, after all.
Yeah, dude. What's the big deal? I mean, Rou's already said yes. Besides...
...you know you really want to stay here with AI.
Rai...
RAI!!!
56
See You Again.
RA - I / END
THANKS TO
BORA-NAONO. KUMKO-ITO. SHINOBU-YASAKI.
TOMOKO-MORII. AND MIZUHO-MORI.

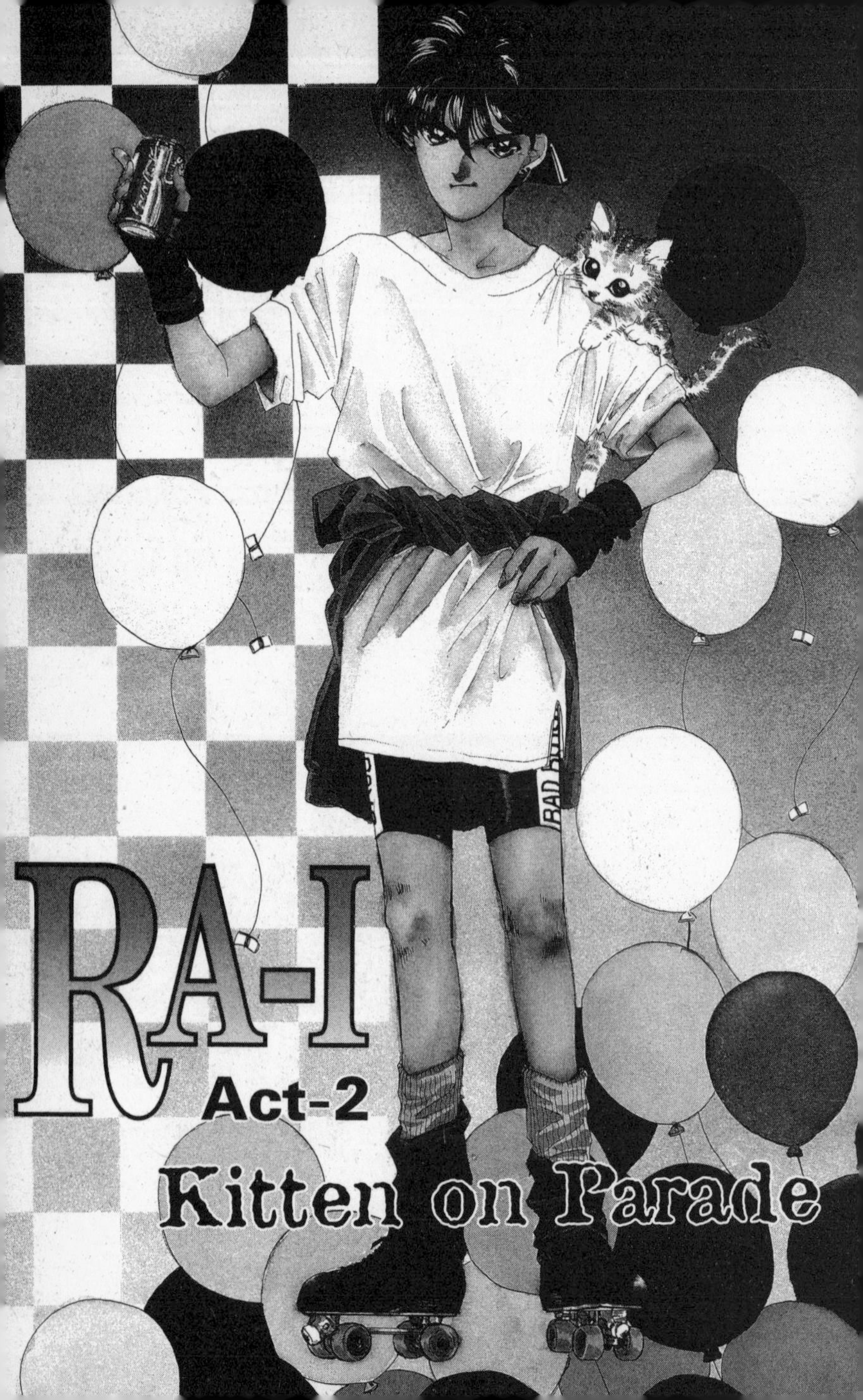
RA-I
Act-2
Kitten on Parade

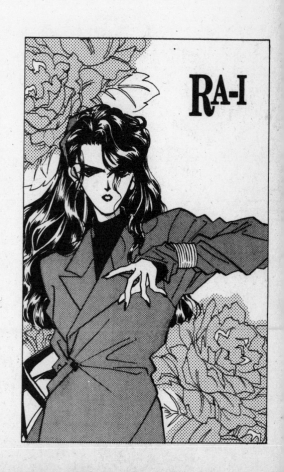

RA-I

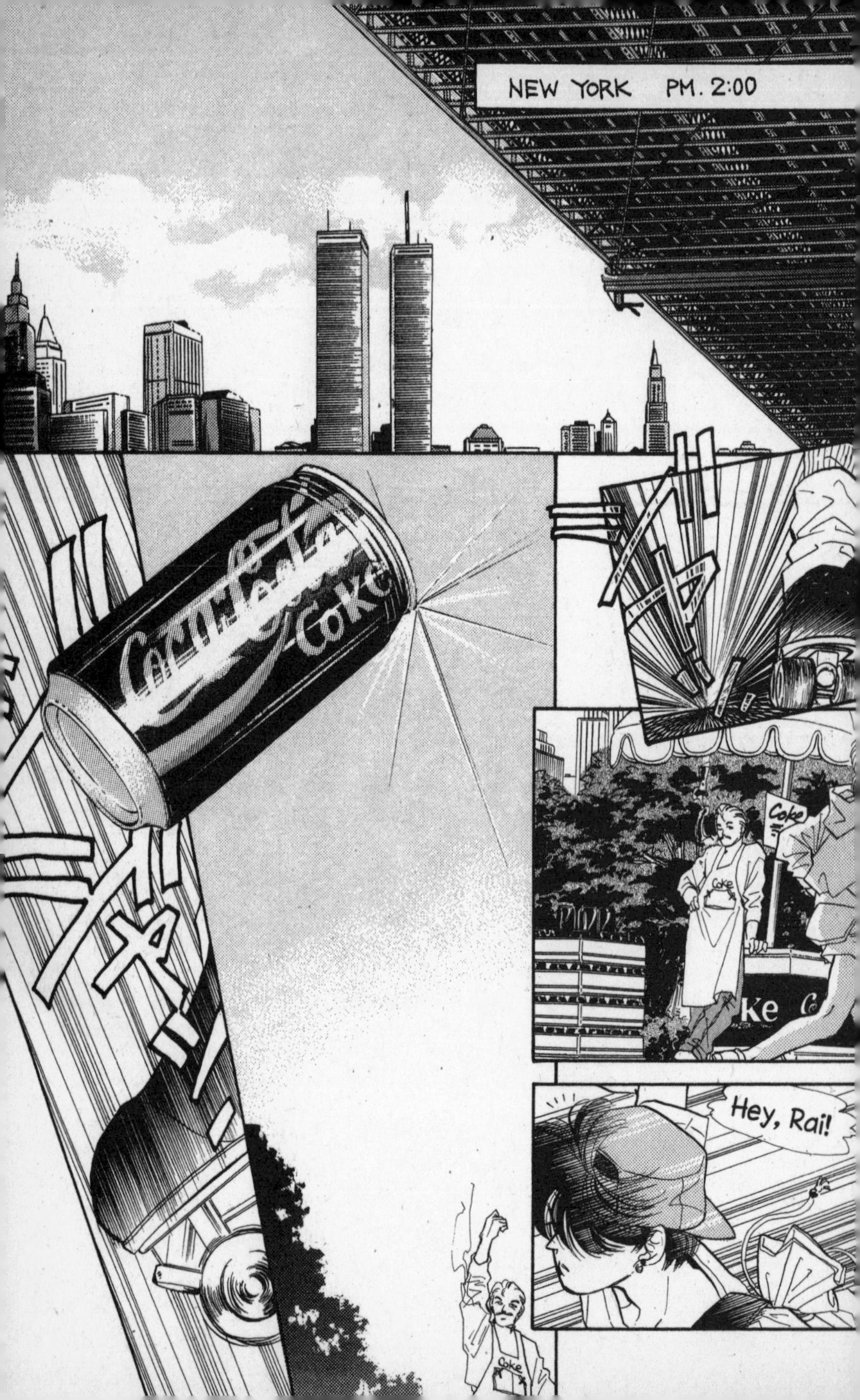
NEW YORK PM. 2:00
Coke
Coke
Hey, Rai!
Coke
Coke

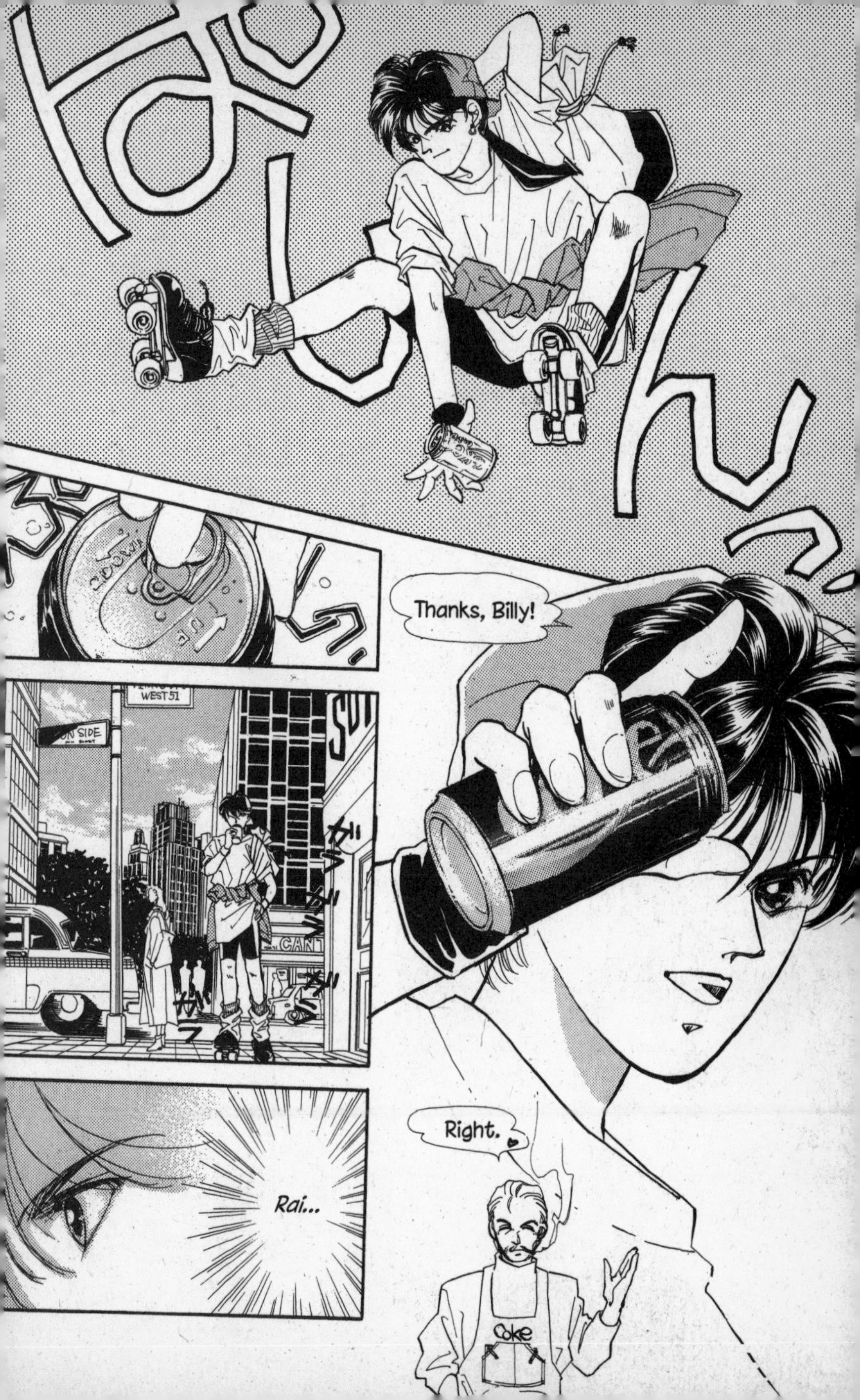
Thanks, Billy!
Right.
Coke
WEST 51
Rai...

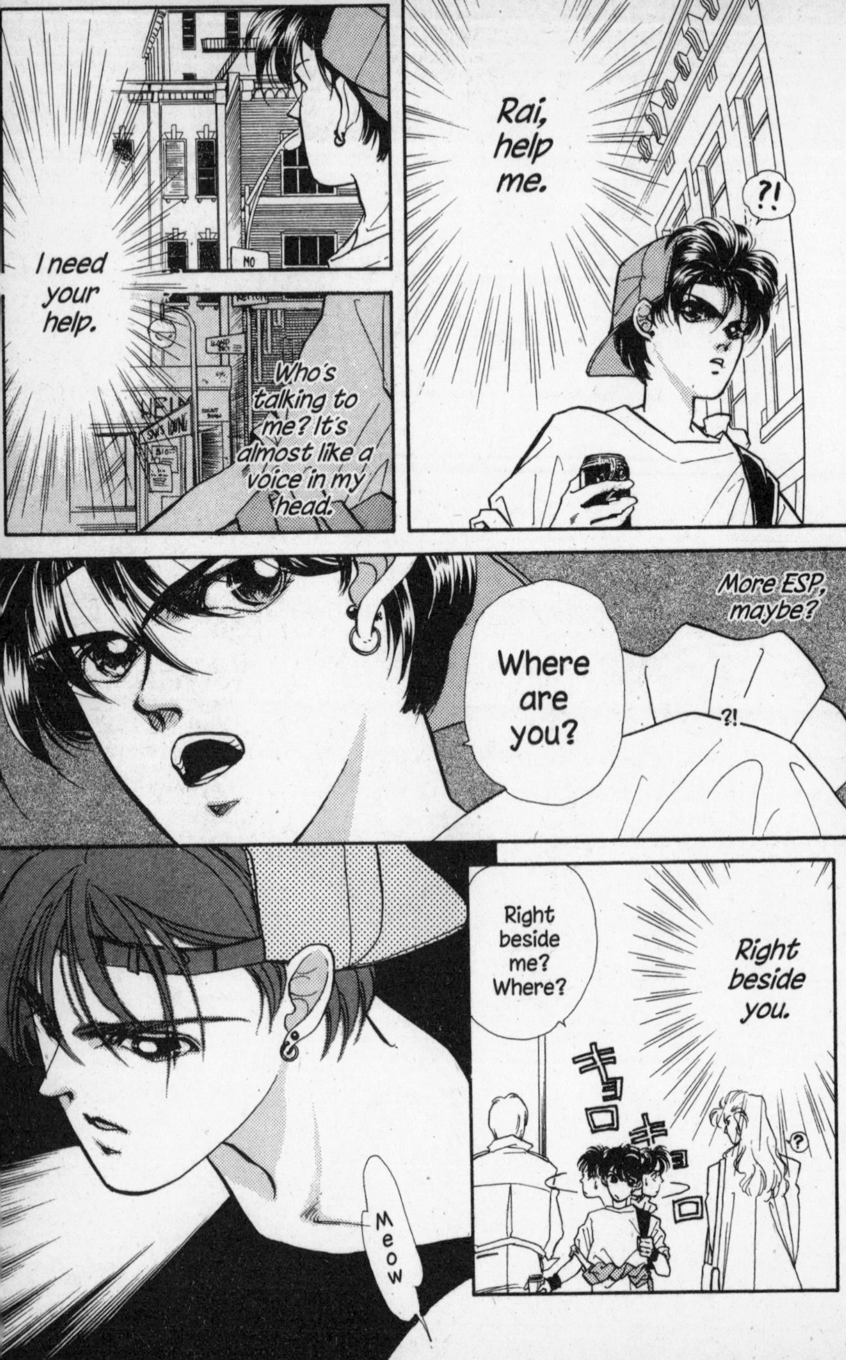
Rai, help me.
?!
I need your help.
Who's talking to me? It's almost like a voice in my head.
More ESP, maybe?
Where are you?
?!
Right beside you.
Right beside me? Where?
キョロキョロ
?
Meow

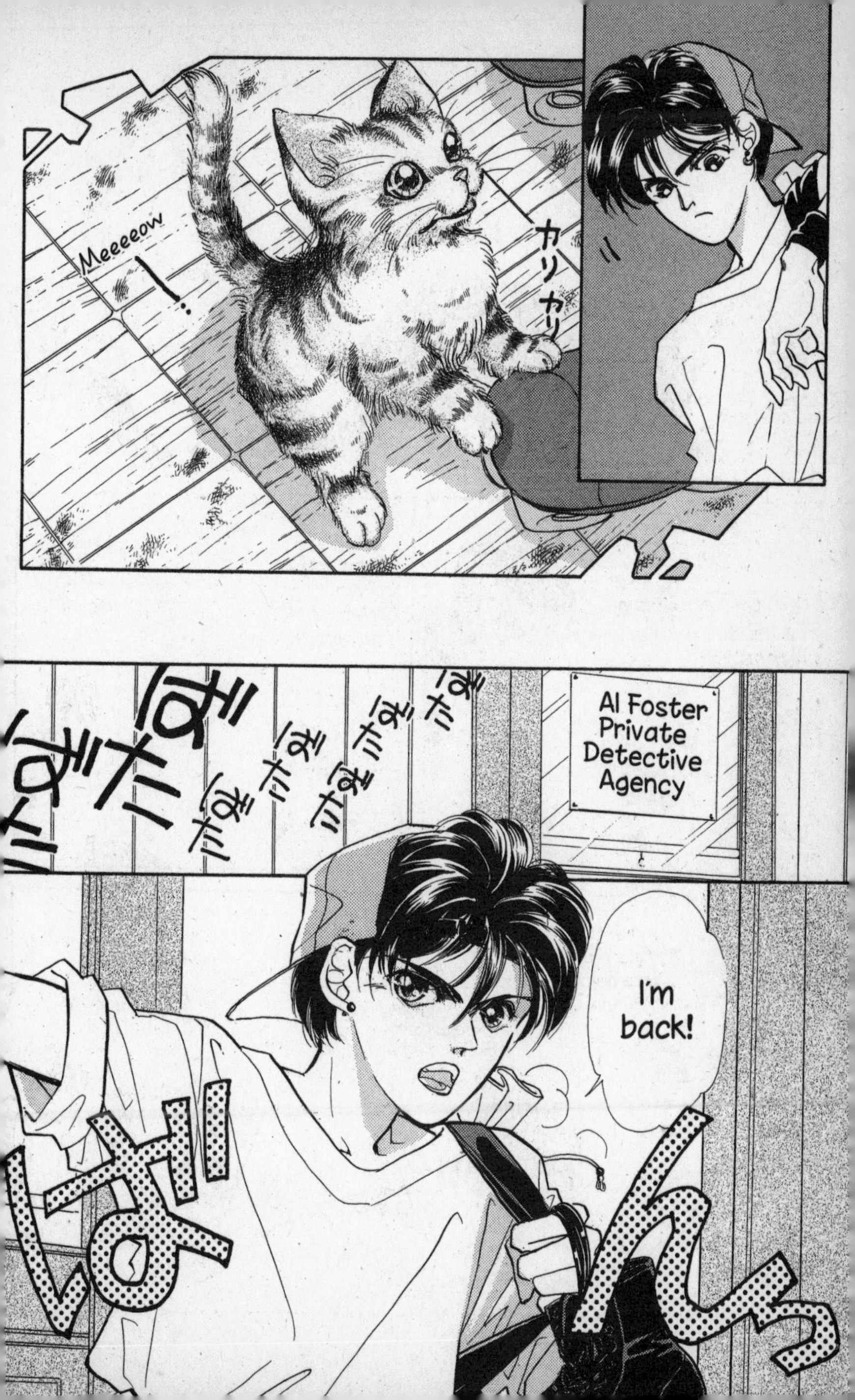
カリ カリ
Meeeeow
Al Foster Private Detective Agency
ぱた ぱたぱた ぱたぱた
ぱたぱたっ
I'm back!
ばんっ

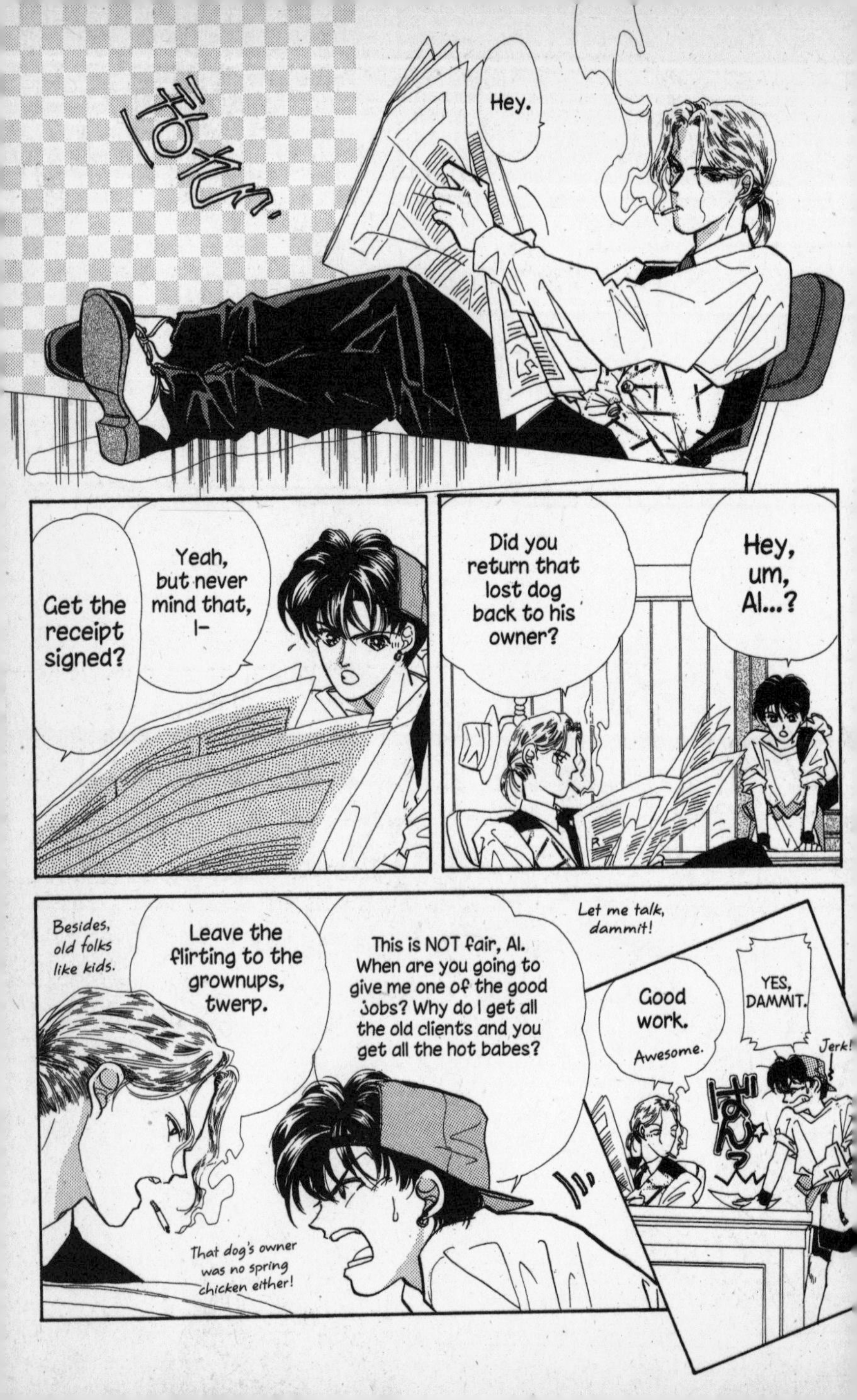
Hey.
Hey, um, Al...?
Did you return that lost dog back to his owner?
Yeah, but never mind that, I–
Get the receipt signed?
YES, DAMMIT.
Good work.
Awesome.
Jerk!
Let me talk, dammit!
This is NOT fair, Al. When are you going to give me one of the good jobs? Why do I get all the old clients and you get all the hot babes?
Leave the flirting to the grownups, twerp.
Besides, old folks like kids.
That dog's owner was no spring chicken either!

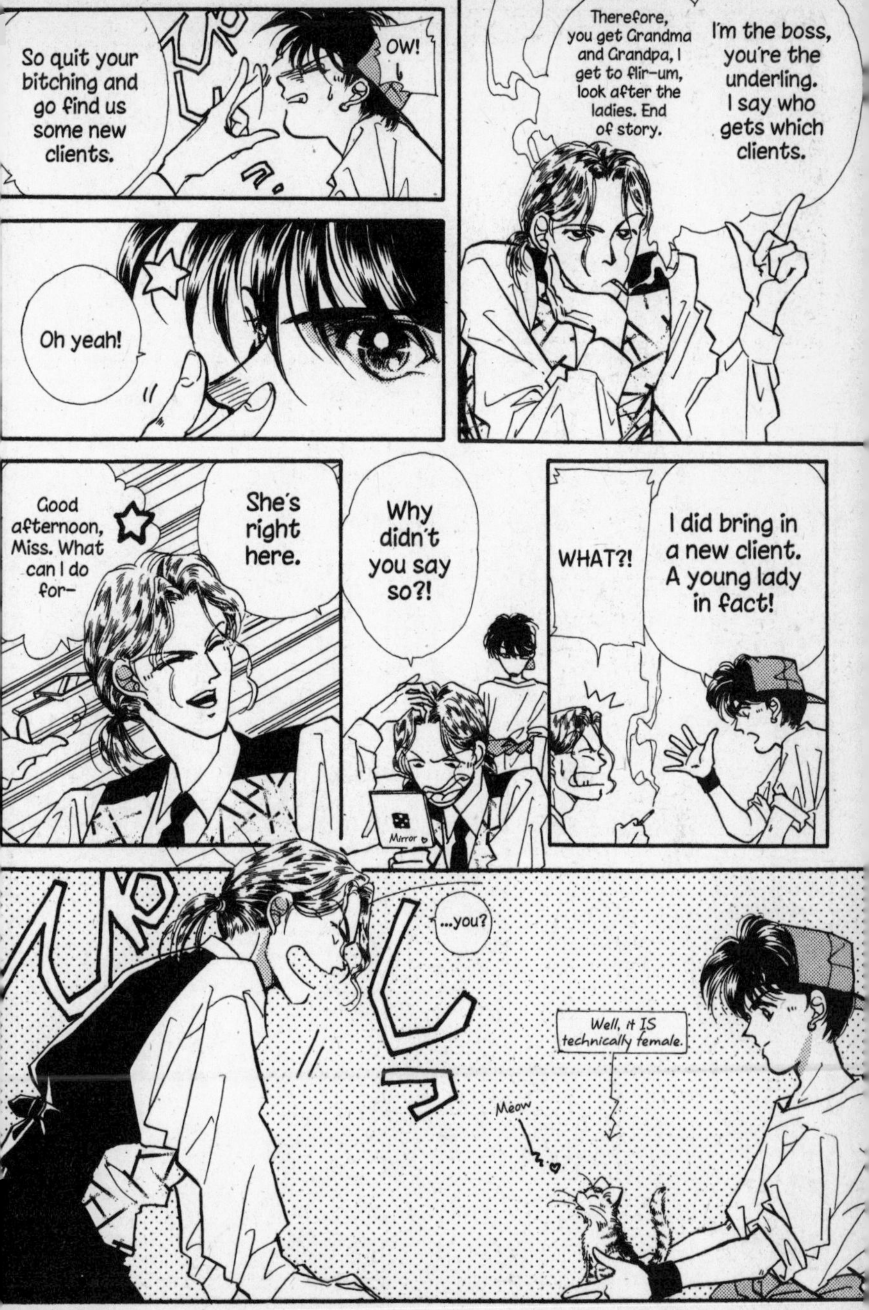
I'm the boss, you're the underling. I say who gets which clients.
Therefore, you get Grandma and Grandpa, I get to flir-um, look after the ladies. End of story.
OW!
So quit your bitching and go find us some new clients.
Oh yeah!
I did bring in a new client. A young lady in fact!
WHAT?!
Why didn't you say so?!
Mirror
She's right here.
Good afternoon, Miss. What can I do for-
...you?
Well, it IS technically female.
Meow

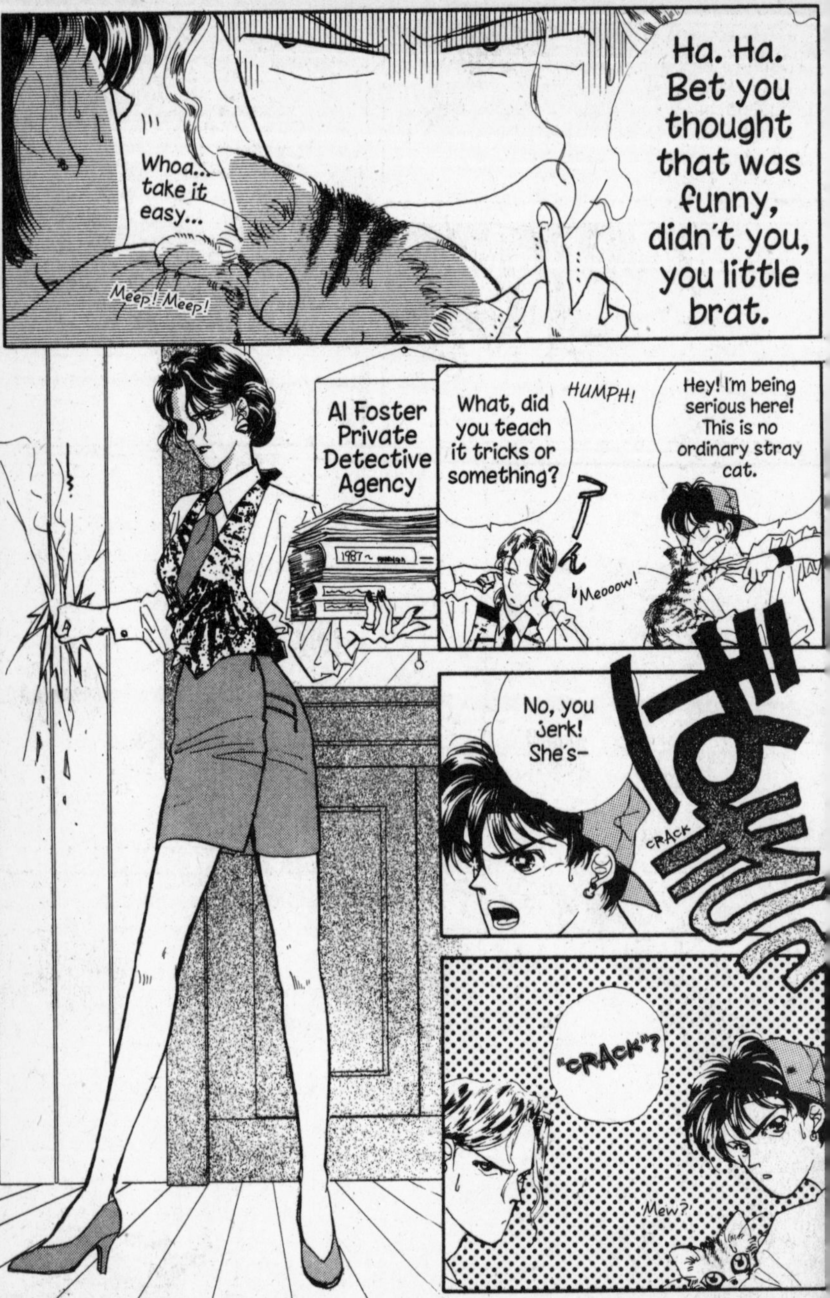
Ha. Ha. Bet you thought that was funny, didn't you, you little brat.
Whoa... take it easy...
Meep! Meep!
Hey! I'm being serious here! This is no ordinary stray cat.
HUMPH!
What, did you teach it tricks or something?
Meeoow!
No, you jerk! She's-
CRACK
"CRACK"?
Mew?
Al Foster Private Detective Agency
1987~

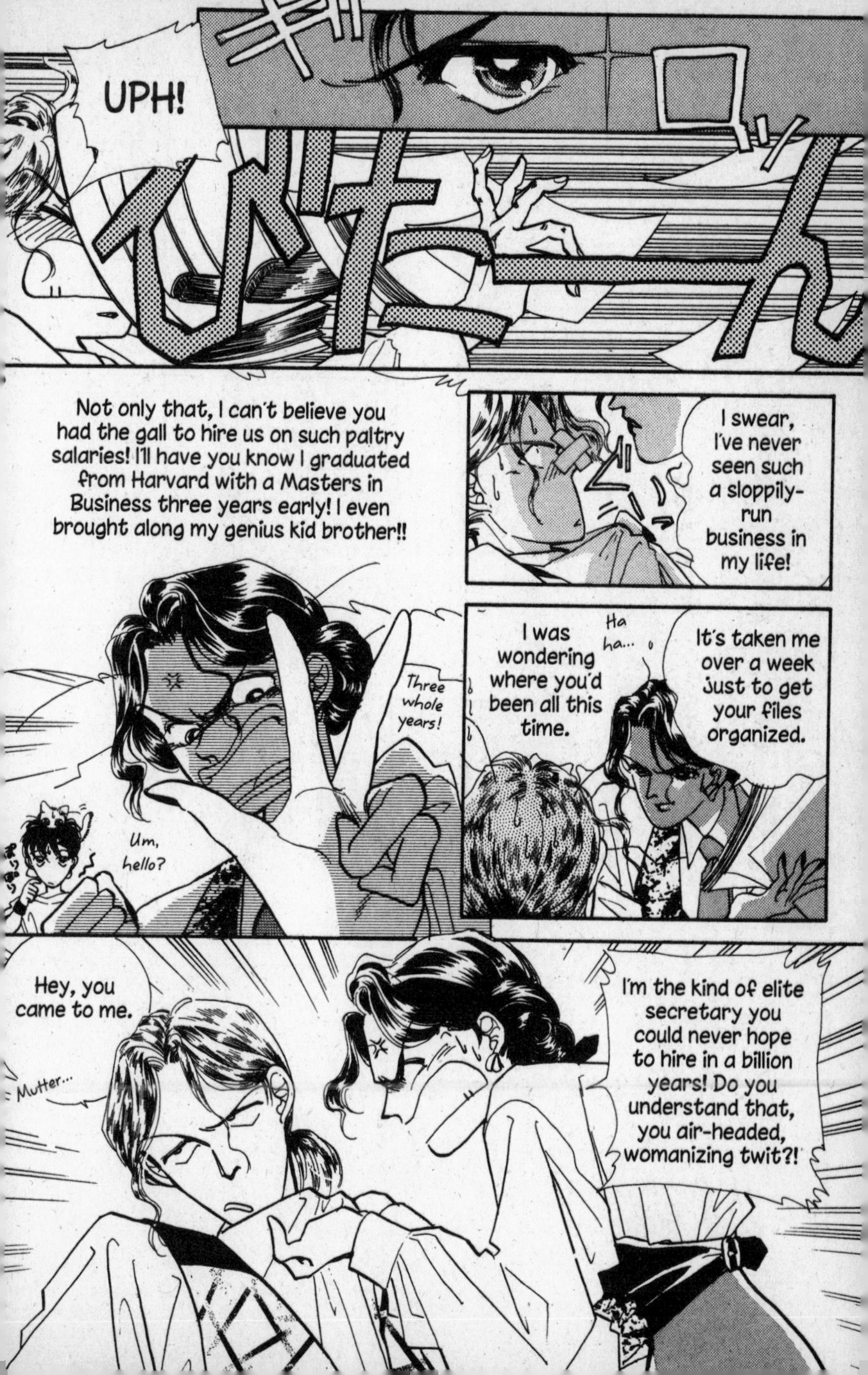

UPH!
I swear, I've never seen such a sloppily-run business in my life!
It's taken me over a week just to get your files organized.
Ha ha...
I was wondering where you'd been all this time.
Not only that, I can't believe you had the gall to hire us on such paltry salaries! I'll have you know I graduated from Harvard with a Masters in Business three years early! I even brought along my genius kid brother!!
Three whole years!
Um, hello?
I'm the kind of elite secretary you could never hope to hire in a billion years! Do you understand that, you air-headed, womanizing twit?!
Hey, you came to me.
Mutter...

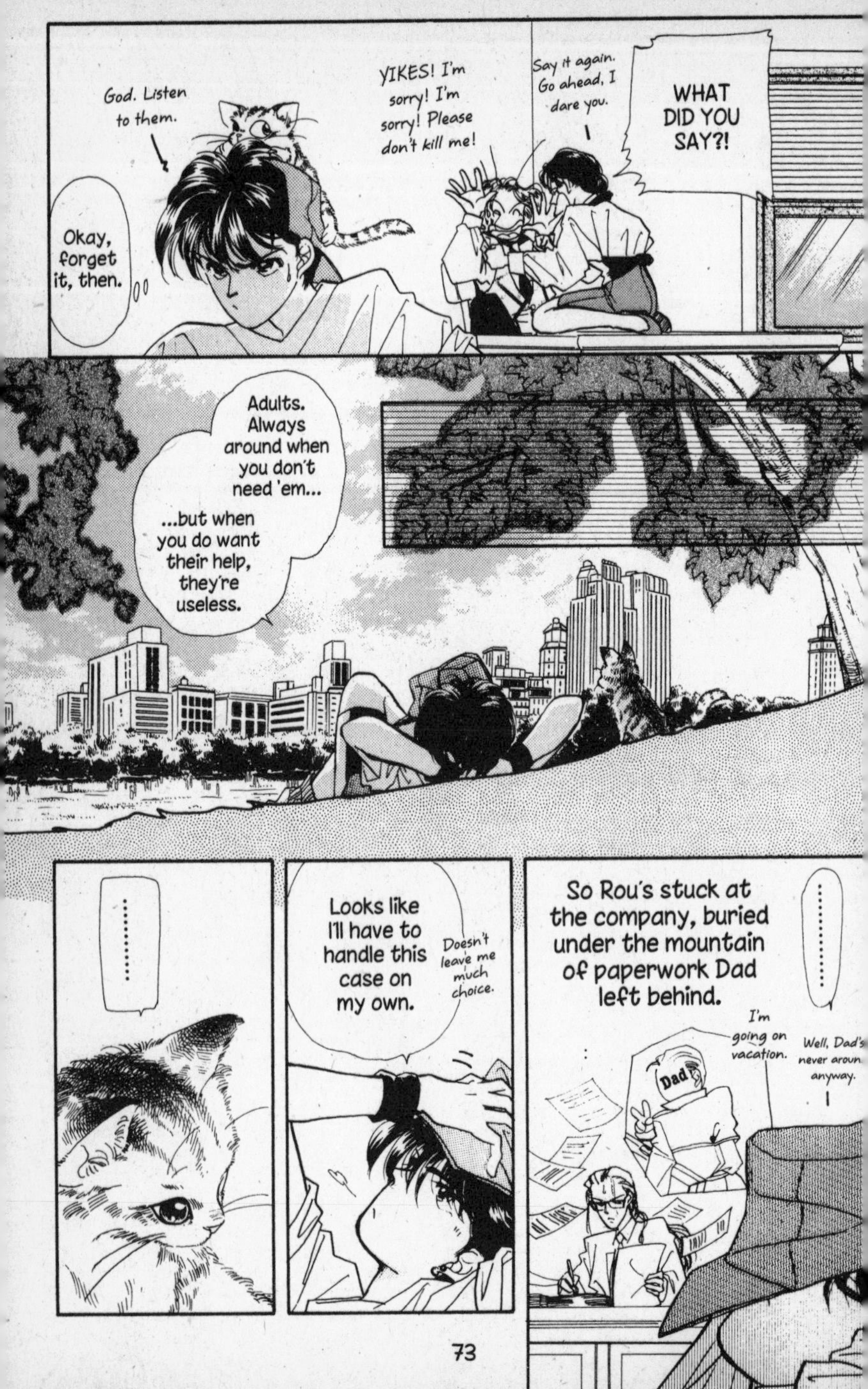
WHAT DID YOU SAY?!
Say it again. Go ahead, I dare you.
YIKES! I'm sorry! I'm sorry! Please don't kill me!
God. Listen to them.
Okay, forget it, then.
Adults. Always around when you don't need 'em...
...but when you do want their help, they're useless.
......
So Rou's stuck at the company, buried under the mountain of paperwork Dad left behind.
Well, Dad's never aroun anyway.
I'm going on vacation.
Dad
Looks like I'll have to handle this case on my own.
Doesn't leave me much choice.
....

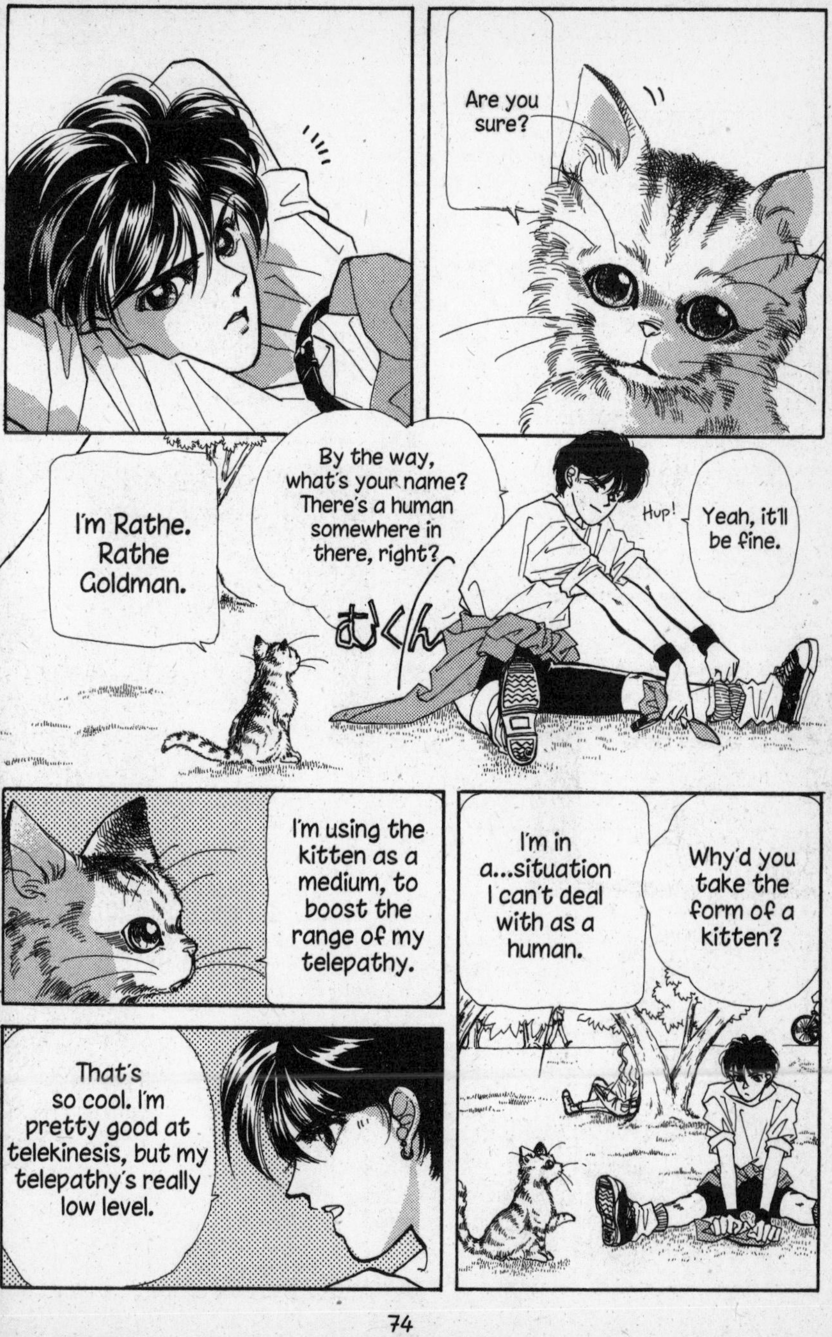

Are you sure?
Hup!
Yeah, it'll be fine.
By the way, what's your name? There's a human somewhere in there, right?
I'm Rathe. Rathe Goldman.
Why'd you take the form of a kitten?
I'm in a...situation I can't deal with as a human.
I'm using the kitten as a medium, to boost the range of my telepathy.
That's so cool. I'm pretty good at telekinesis, but my telepathy's really low level.

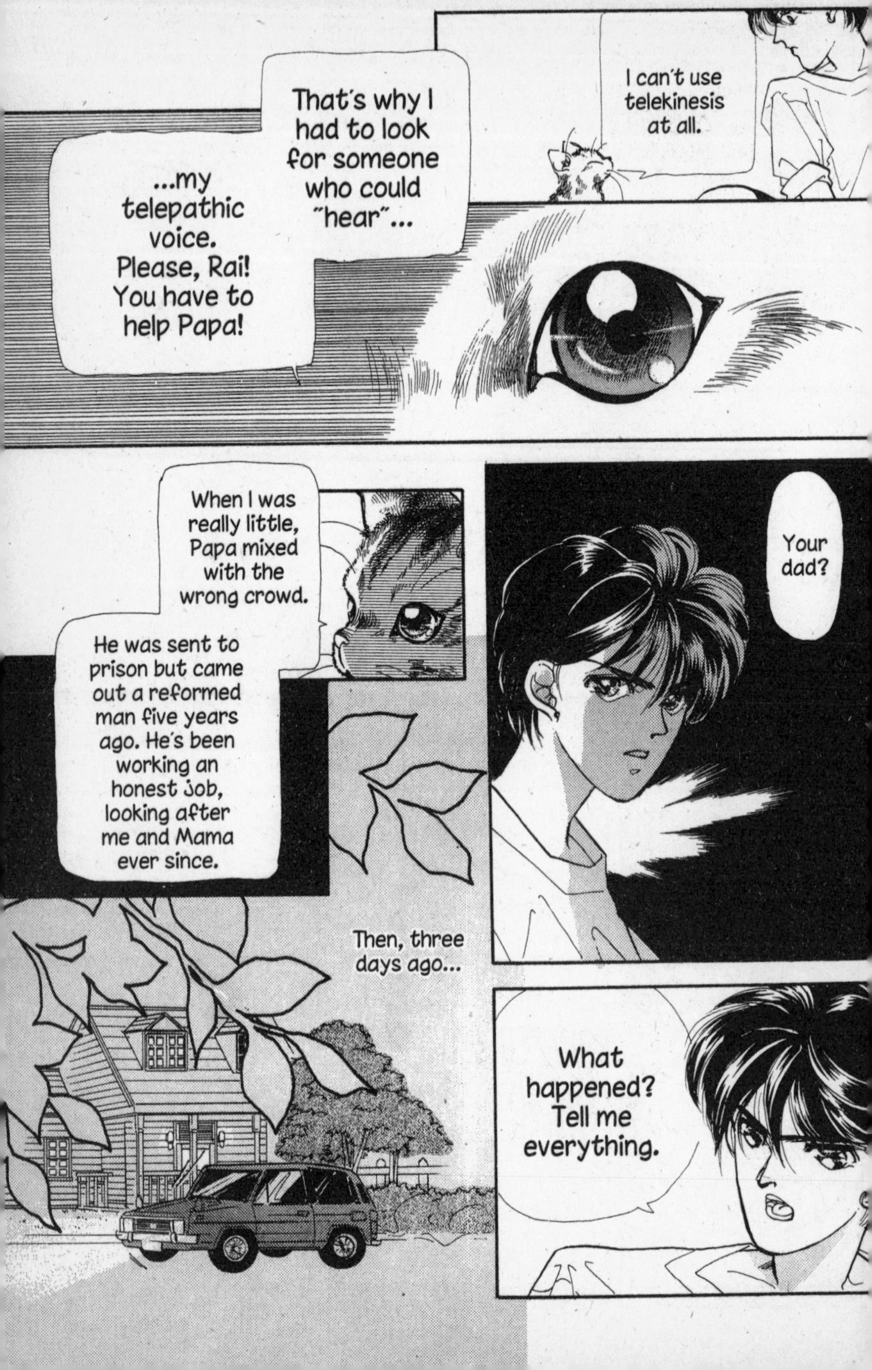
I can't use telekinesis at all.
That's why I had to look for someone who could "hear"...
...my telepathic voice. Please, Rai! You have to help Papa!
Your dad?
When I was really little, Papa mixed with the wrong crowd.
He was sent to prison but came out a reformed man five years ago. He's been working an honest job, looking after me and Mama ever since.
What happened? Tell me everything.
Then, three days ago...

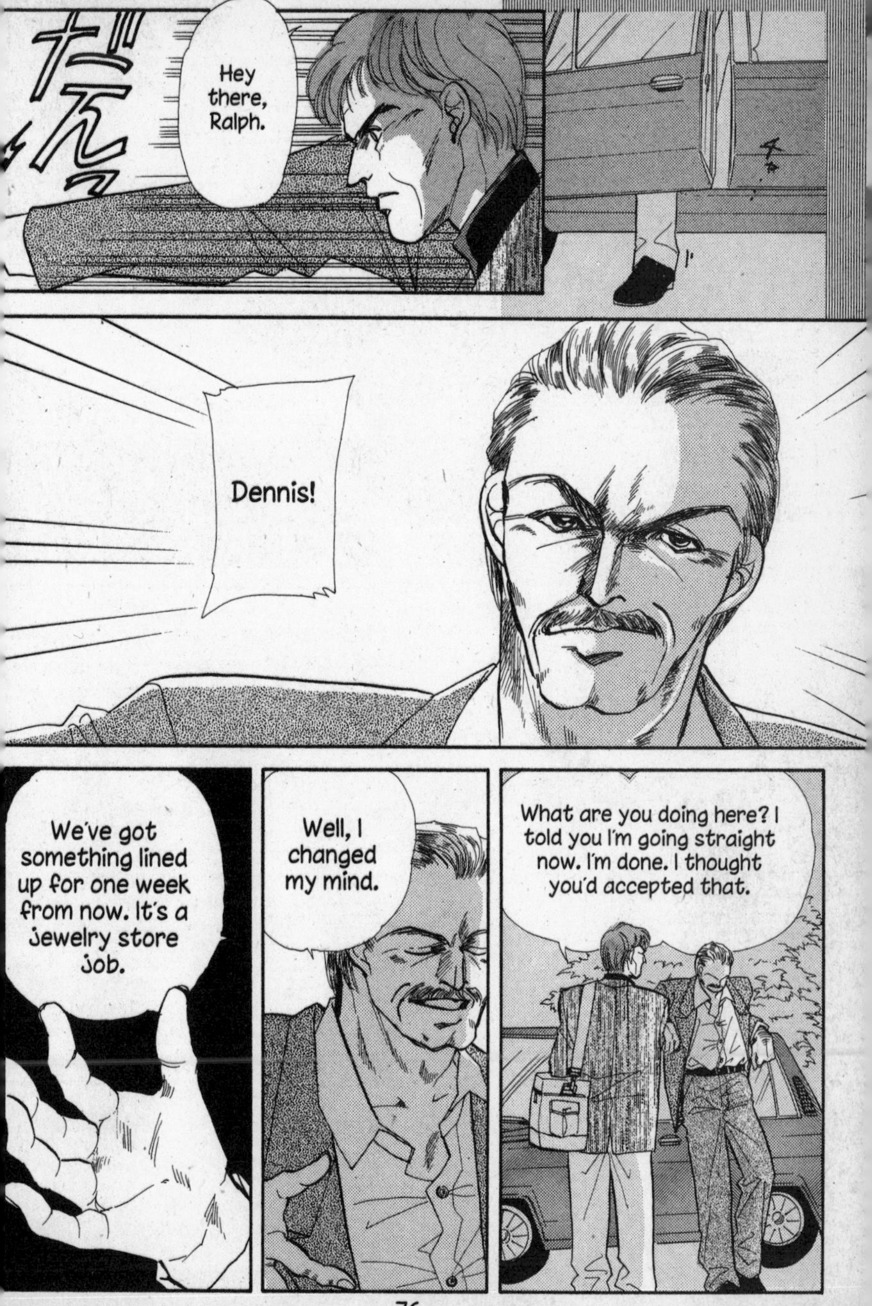
Hey there, Ralph.
Dennis!
What are you doing here? I told you I'm going straight now. I'm done. I thought you'd accepted that.
Well, I changed my mind.
We've got something lined up for one week from now. It's a jewelry store job.

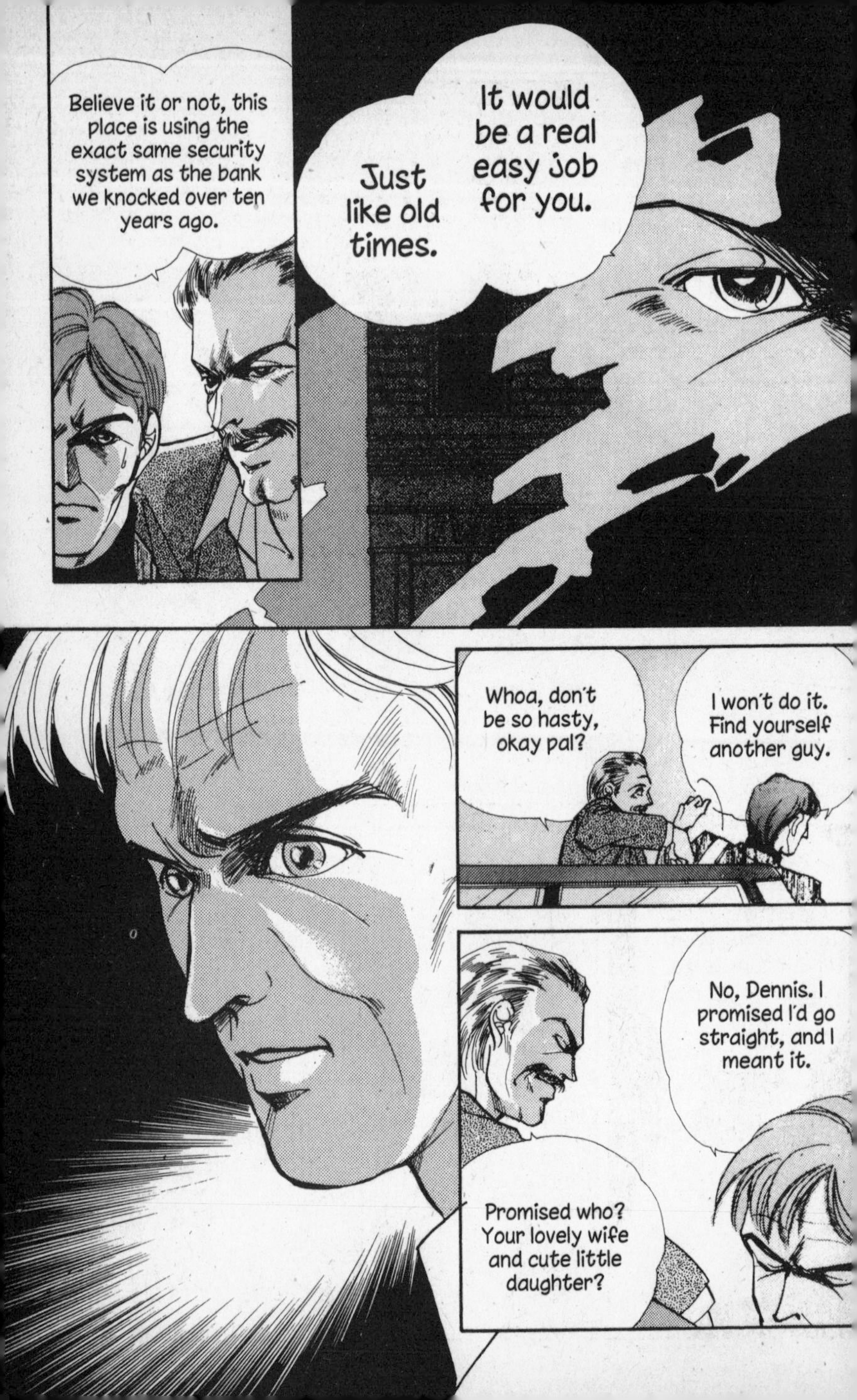
It would be a real easy job for you.
Just like old times.
Believe it or not, this place is using the exact same security system as the bank we knocked over ten years ago.
I won't do it. Find yourself another guy.
Whoa, don't be so hasty, okay pal?
No, Dennis. I promised I'd go straight, and I meant it.
Promised who? Your lovely wife and cute little daughter?

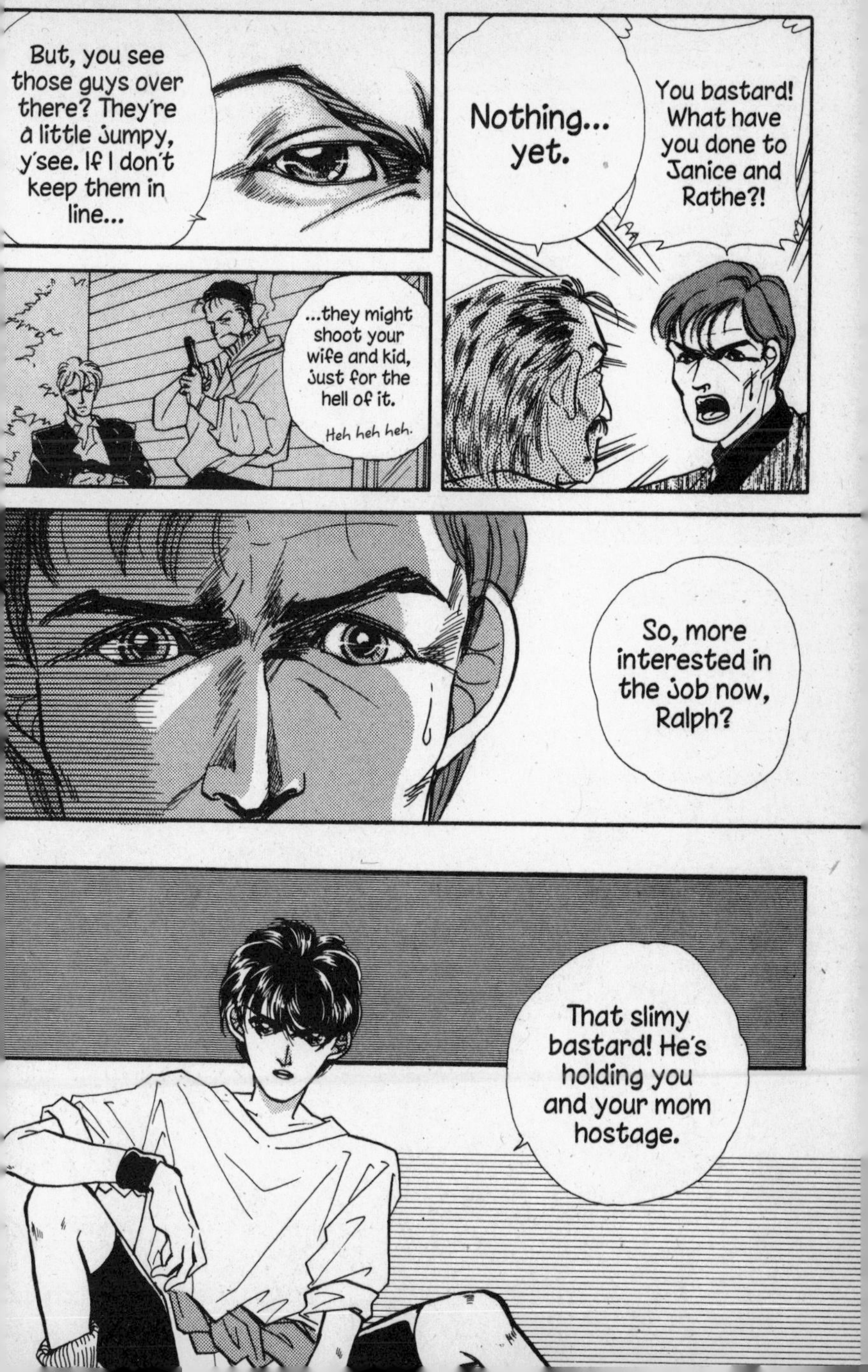
You bastard! What have you done to Janice and Rathe?!
Nothing... yet.
But, you see those guys over there? They're a little jumpy, y'see. If I don't keep them in line...
...they might shoot your wife and kid, just for the hell of it.
Heh heh heh.
So, more interested in the job now, Ralph?
That slimy bastard! He's holding you and your mom hostage.

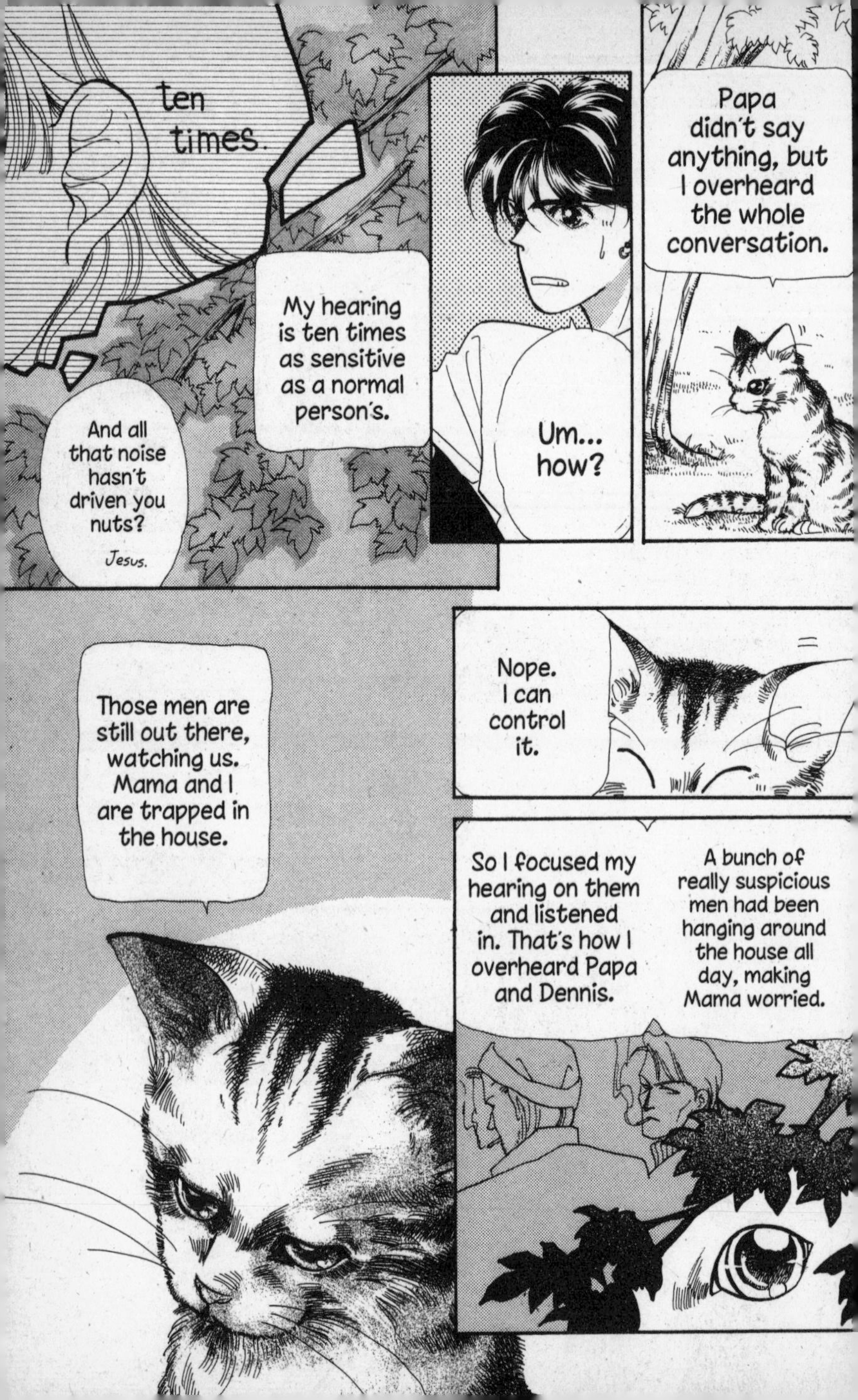
Papa didn't say anything, but I overheard the whole conversation.
Um... how?
My hearing is ten times as sensitive as a normal person's.
ten times.
And all that noise hasn't driven you nuts?
Jesus.
Nope. I can control it.
A bunch of really suspicious men had been hanging around the house all day, making Mama worried.
So I focused my hearing on them and listened in. That's how I overheard Papa and Dennis.
Those men are still out there, watching us. Mama and I are trapped in the house.

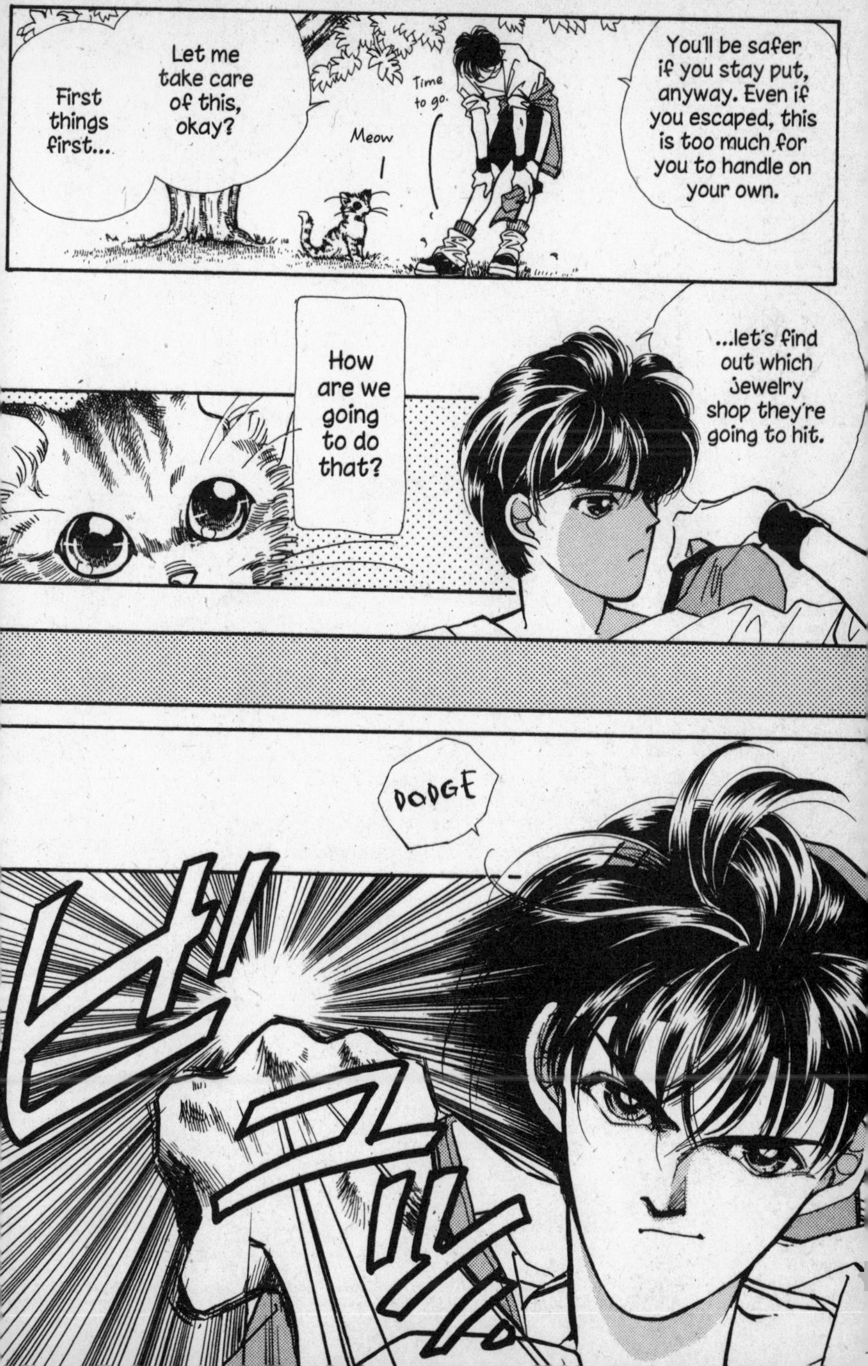
You'll be safer if you stay put, anyway. Even if you escaped, this is too much for you to handle on your own.
Time to go.
Meow
Let me take care of this, okay?
First things first...
...let's find out which jewelry shop they're going to hit.
How are we going to do that?
DODGE
ビュッ

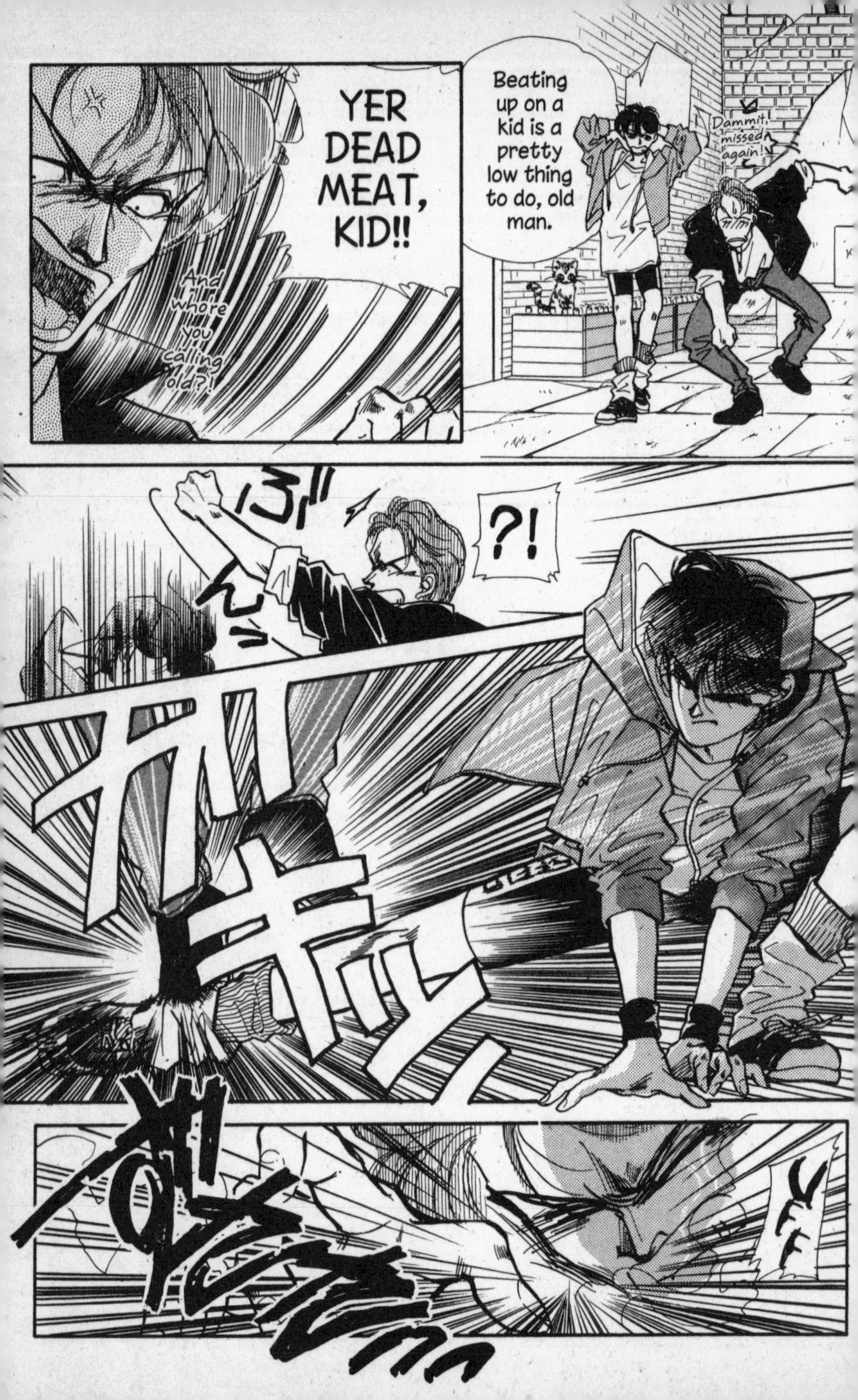
Beating up on a kid is a pretty low thing to do, old man.
Dammit, missed again!
YER DEAD MEAT, KID!!
And whore you calling old?!
?!
ガキッ

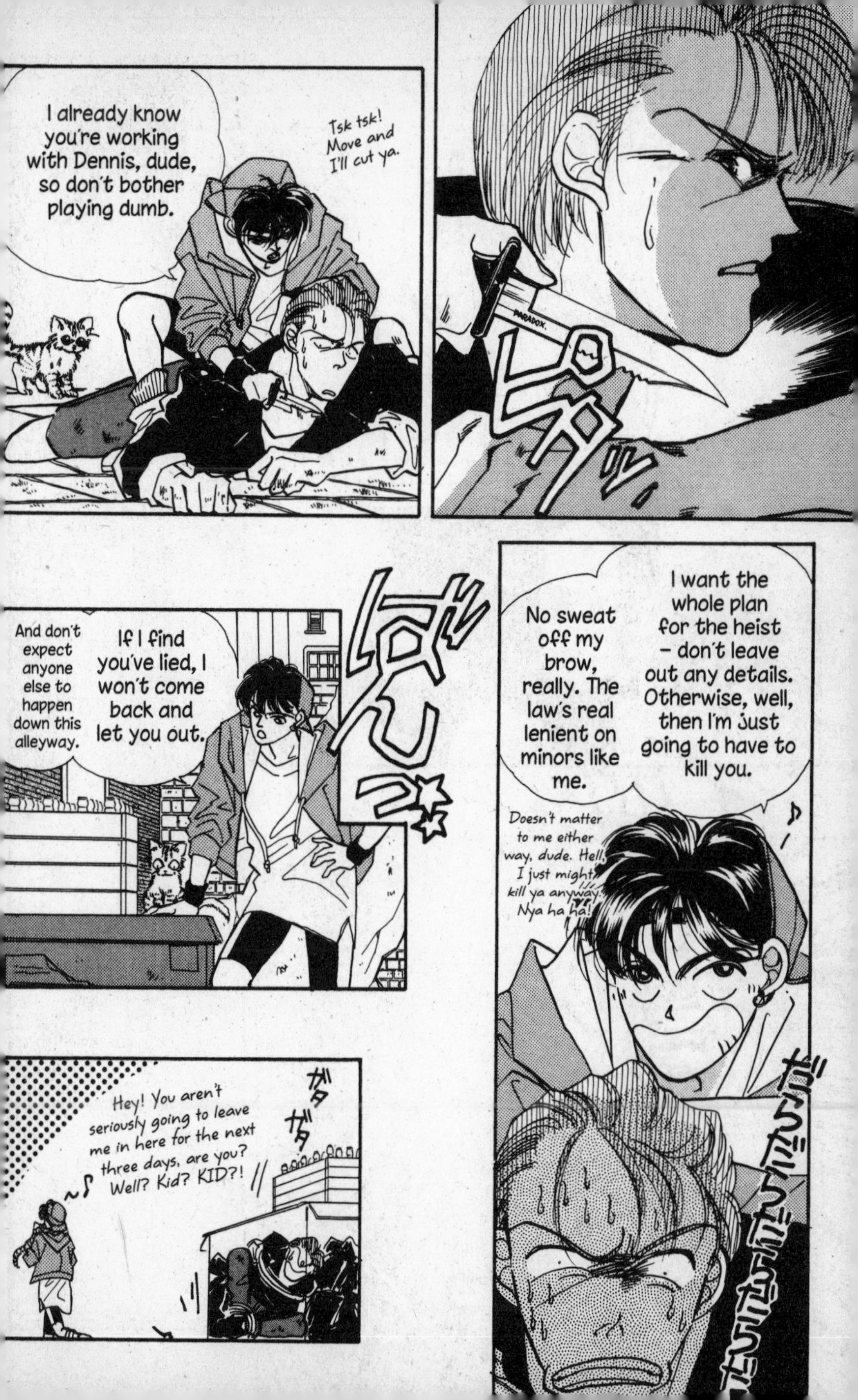
PARADOX.
ピタッ
Tsk tsk! Move and I'll cut ya.
I already know you're working with Dennis, dude, so don't bother playing dumb.
I want the whole plan for the heist – don't leave out any details. Otherwise, well, then I'm just going to have to kill you.
No sweat off my brow, really. The law's real lenient on minors like me.
Doesn't matter to me either way, dude. Hell, I just might kill ya anyway. Nya ha ha!
だらだらだらだら
ばんっ
If I find you've lied, I won't come back and let you out.
And don't expect anyone else to happen down this alleyway.
ガタ ガタ
Hey! You aren't seriously going to leave me in here for the next three days, are you? Well? Kid? KID?!

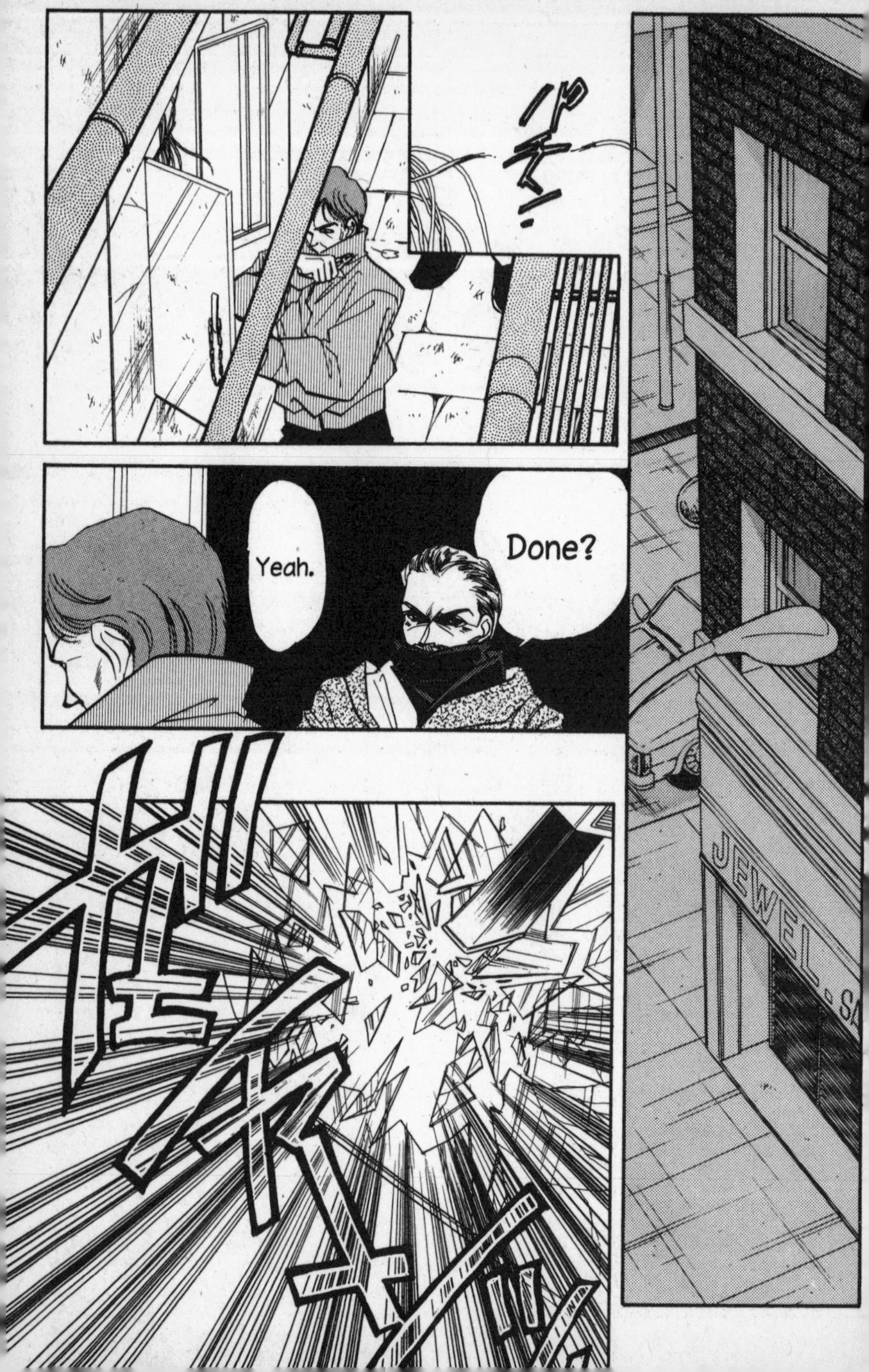
JEWEL
Done?
Yeah.

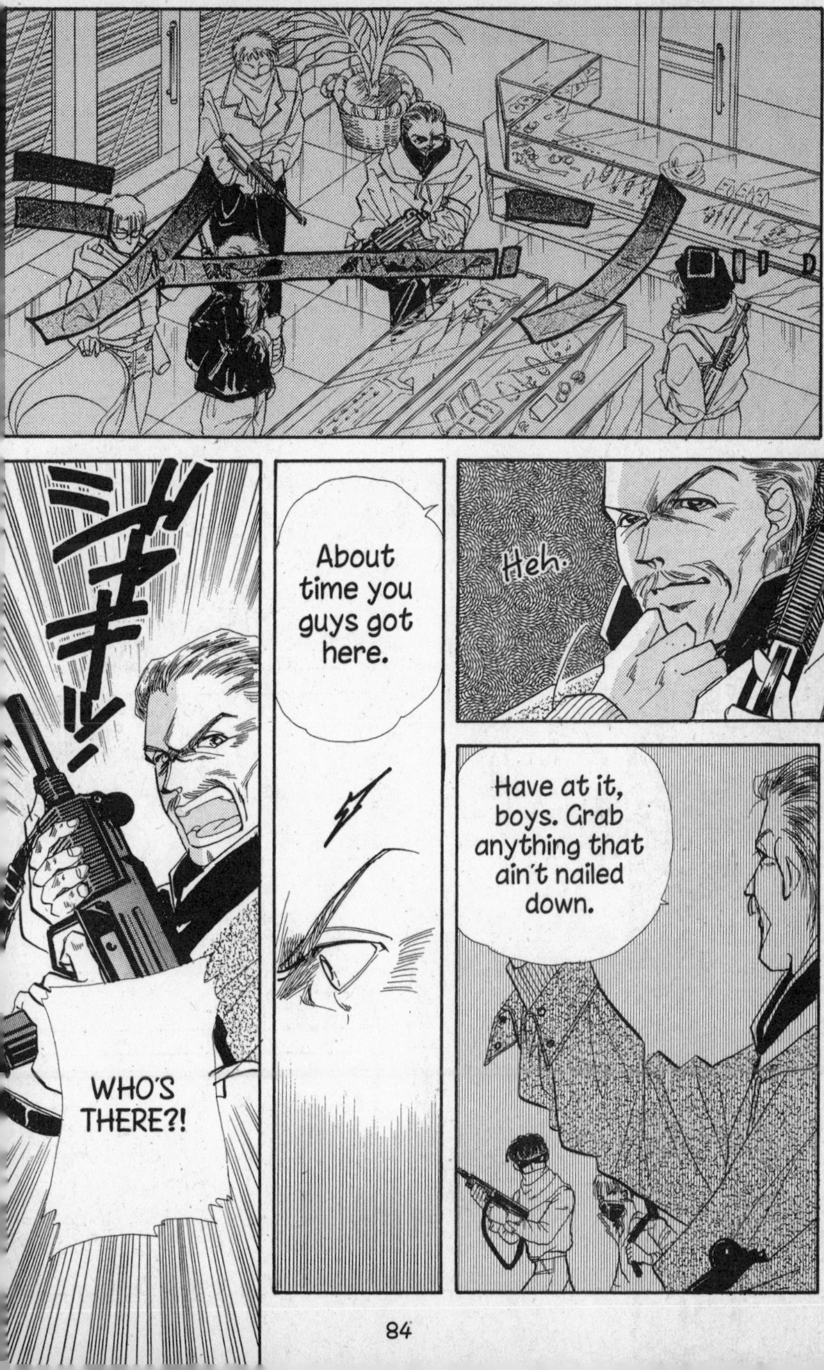
Heh.
Have at it, boys. Grab anything that ain't nailed down.
About time you guys got here.
WHO'S THERE?!

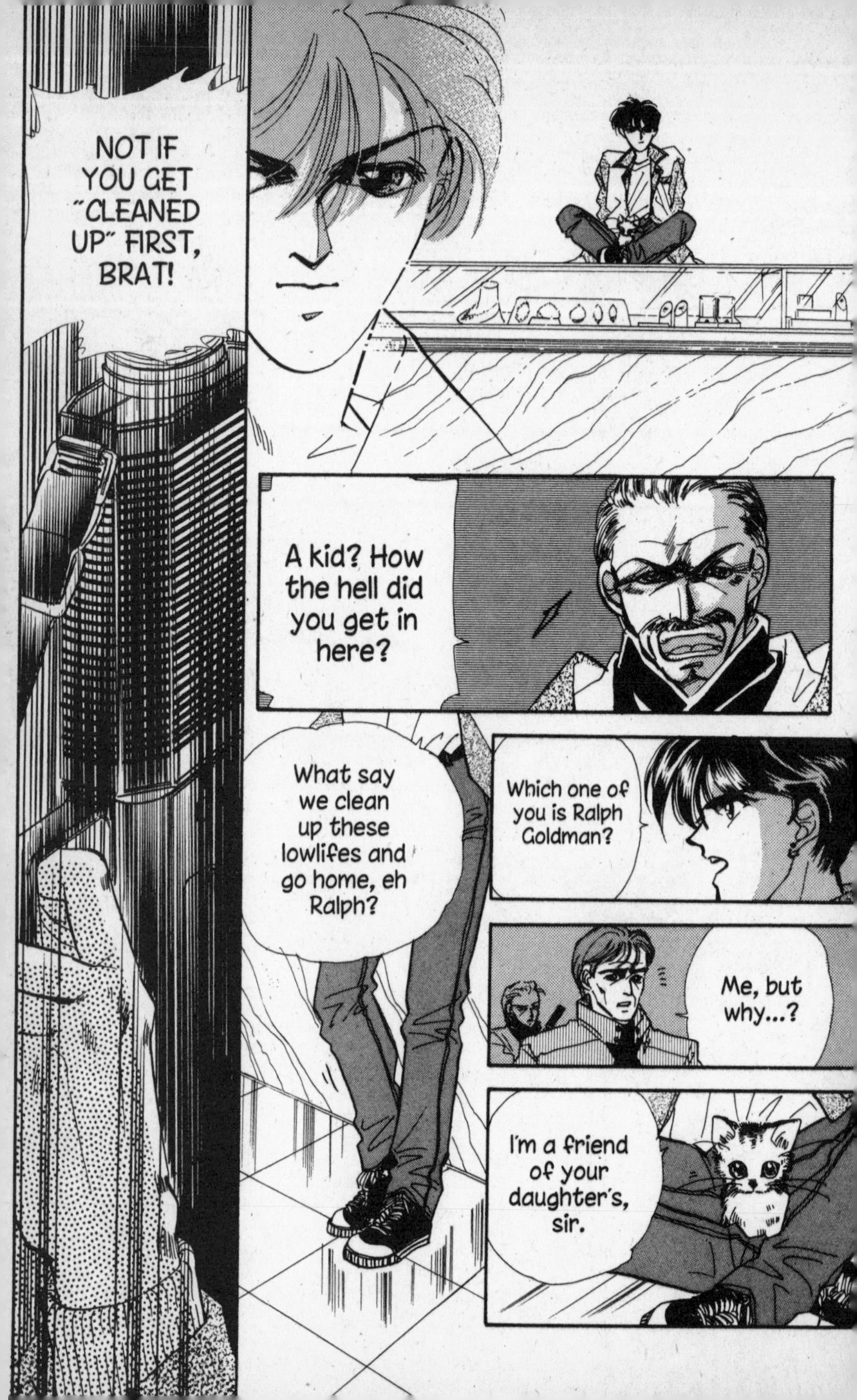
A kid? How the hell did you get in here?
Which one of you is Ralph Goldman?
Me, but why...?
I'm a friend of your daughter's, sir.
What say we clean up these lowlifes and go home, eh Ralph?
NOT IF YOU GET "CLEANED UP" FIRST, BRAT!

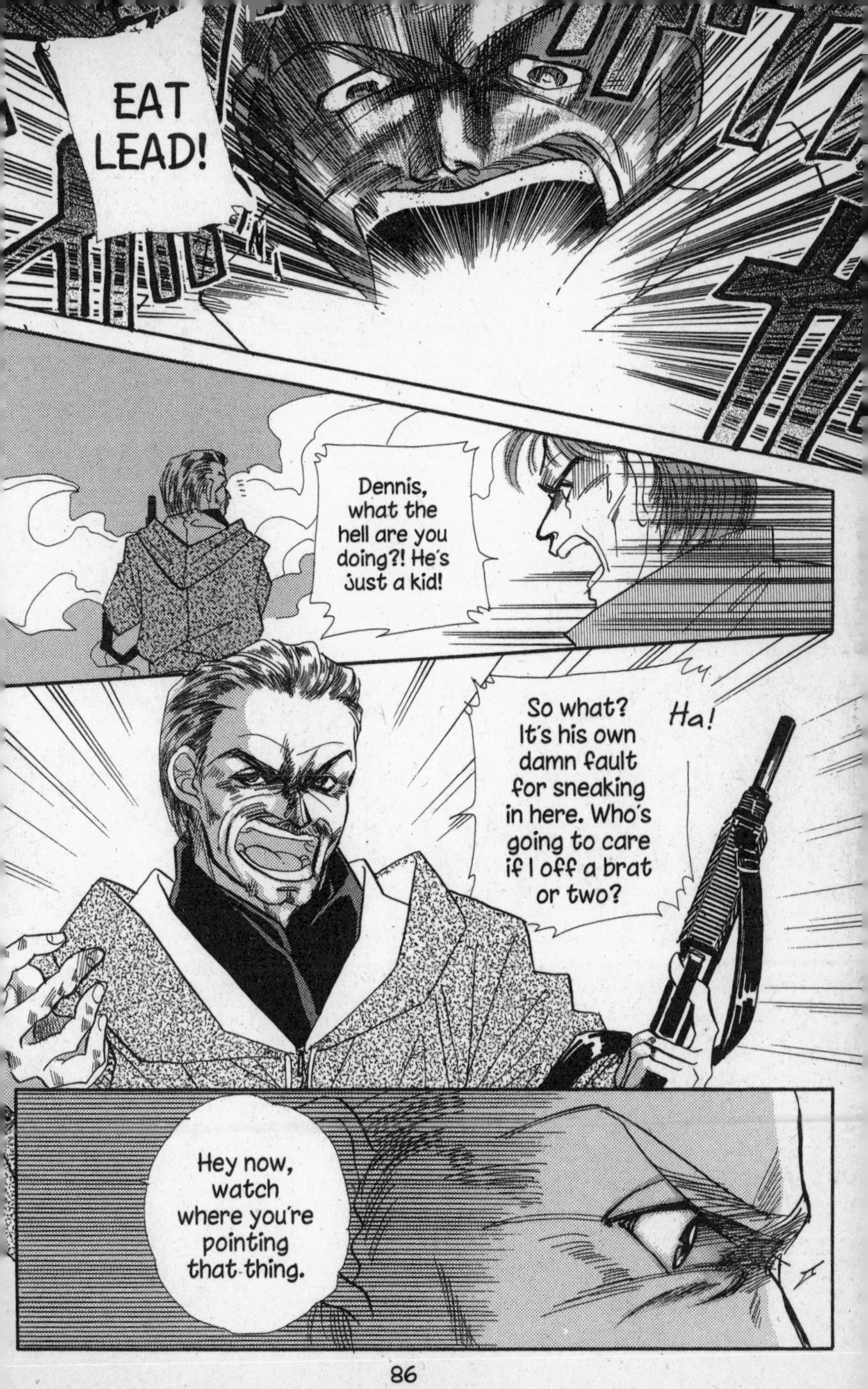
EAT LEAD!
Dennis, what the hell are you doing?! He's just a kid!
Ha!
So what? It's his own damn fault for sneaking in here. Who's going to care if I off a brat or two?
Hey now, watch where you're pointing that thing.

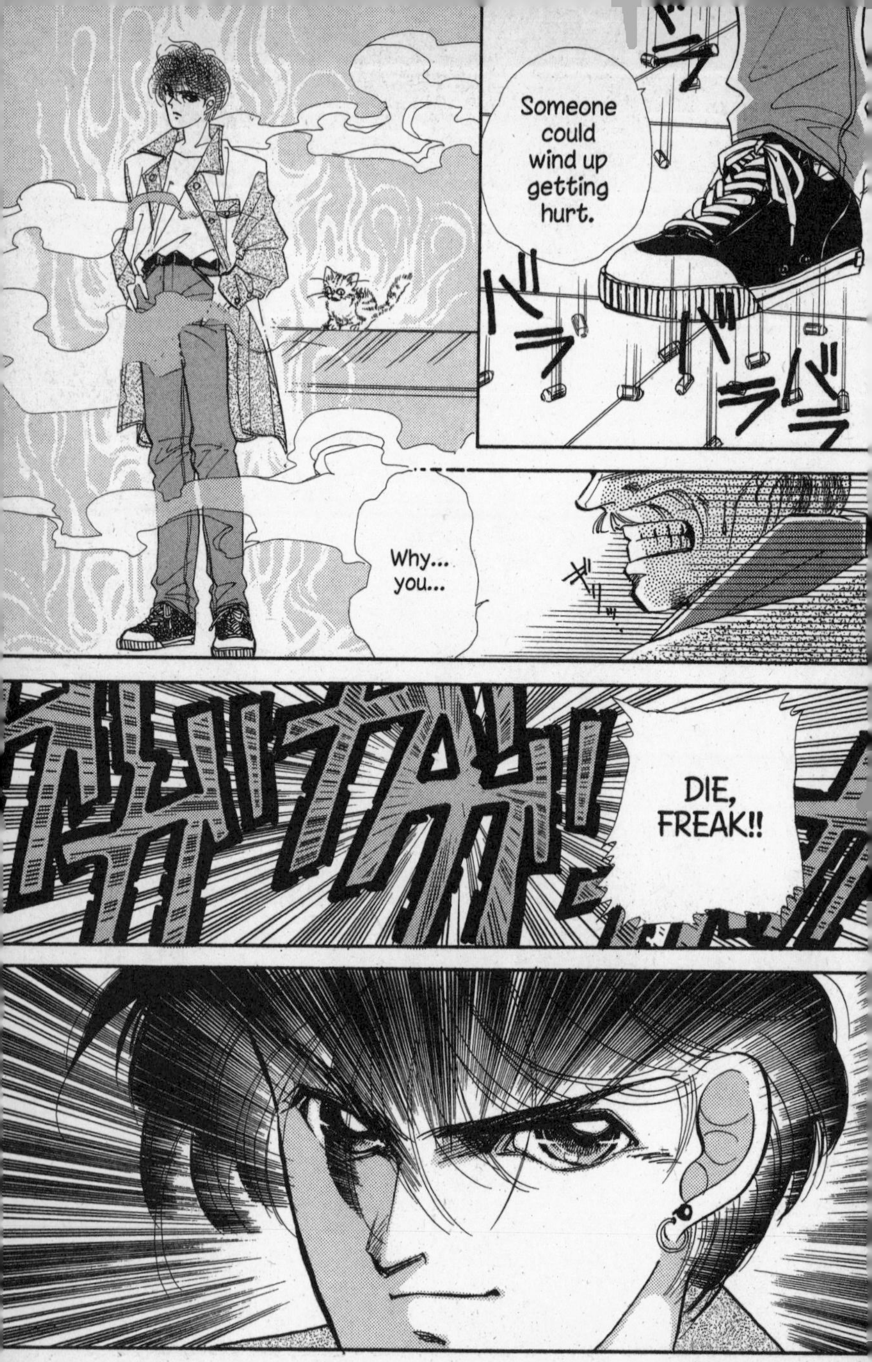
Someone could wind up getting hurt.
Why... you...
DIE, FREAK!!

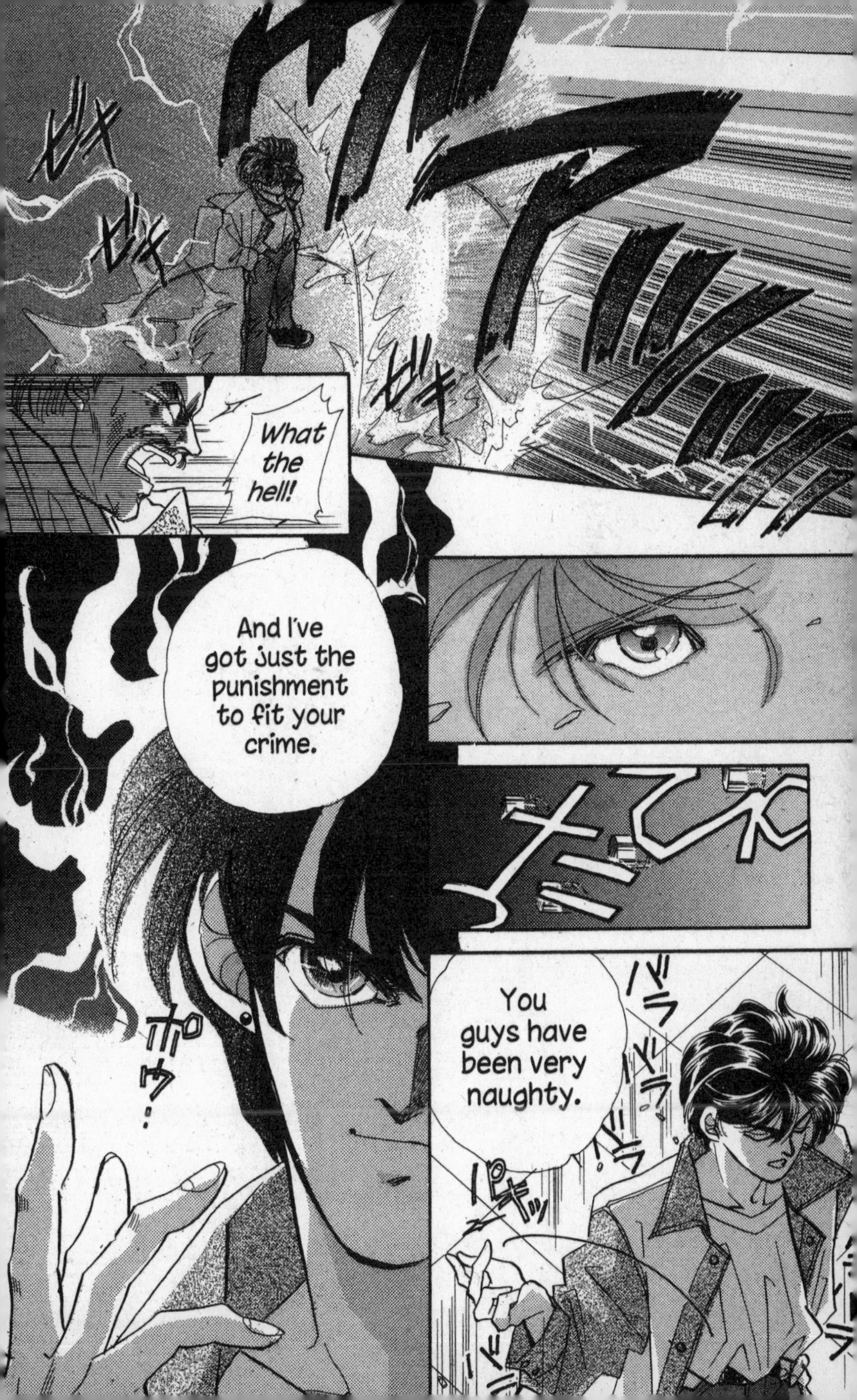
What the hell!
You guys have been very naughty.
And I've got just the punishment to fit your crime.

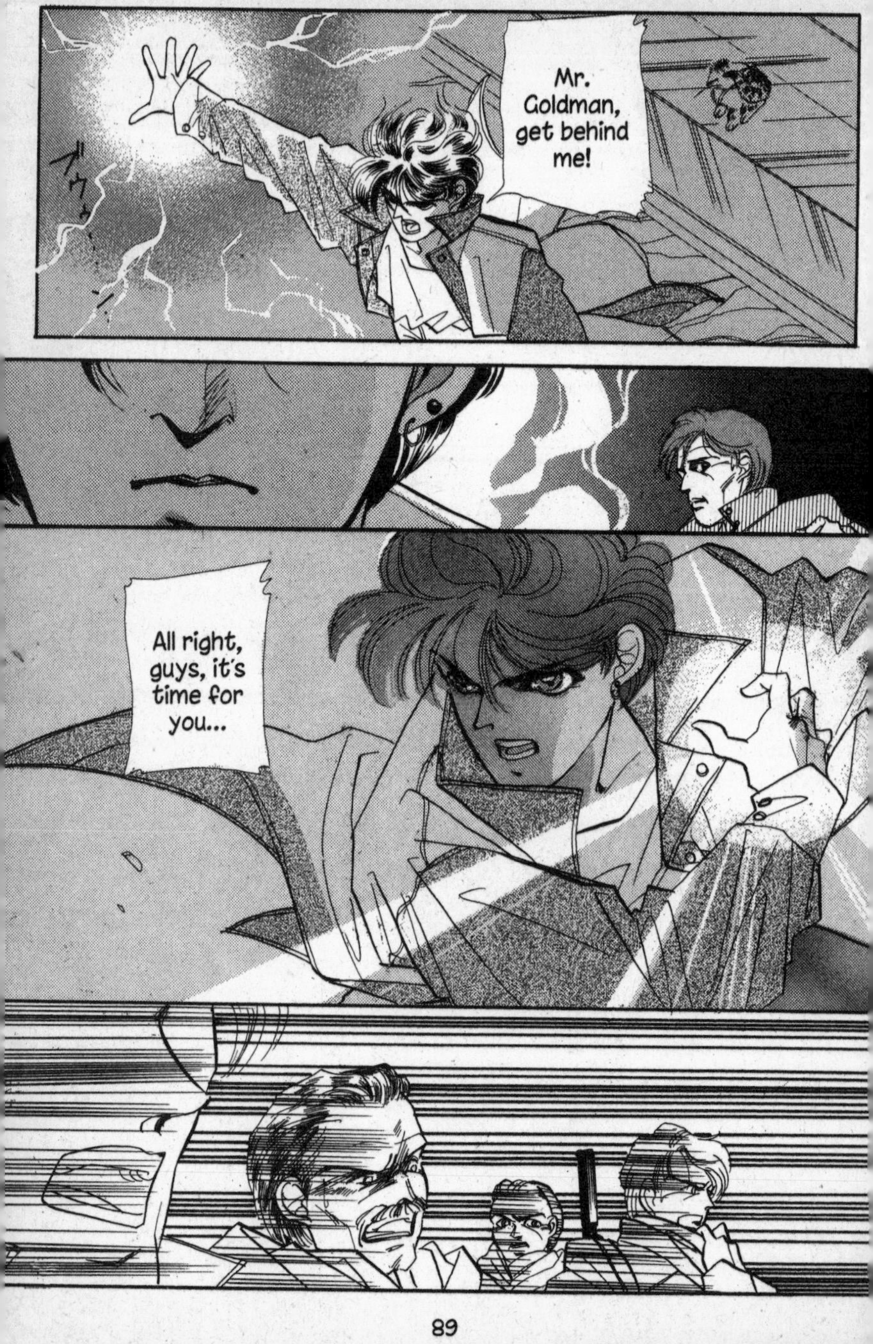
Mr. Goldman, get behind me!
All right, guys, it's time for you...

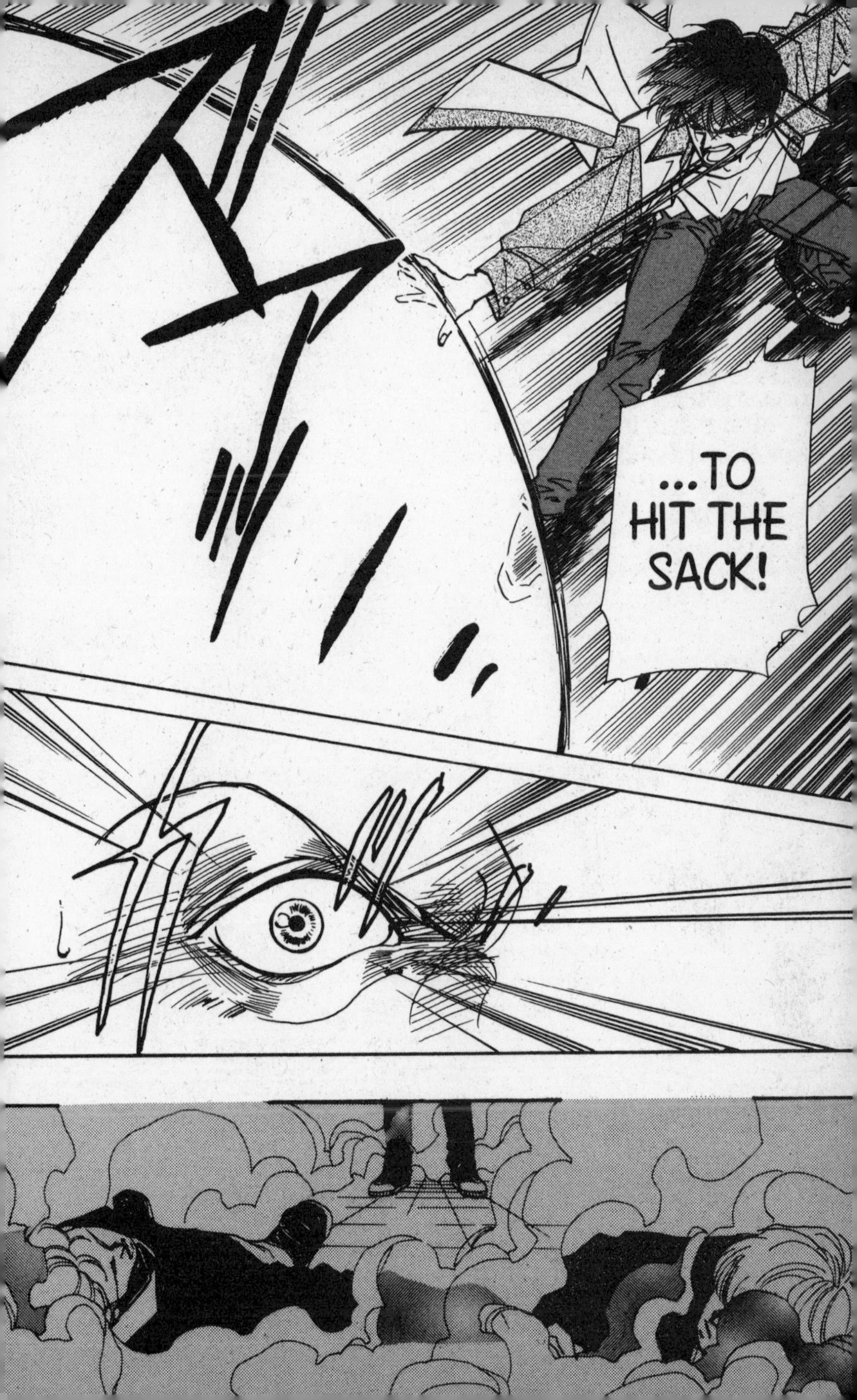
...TO HIT THE SACK!

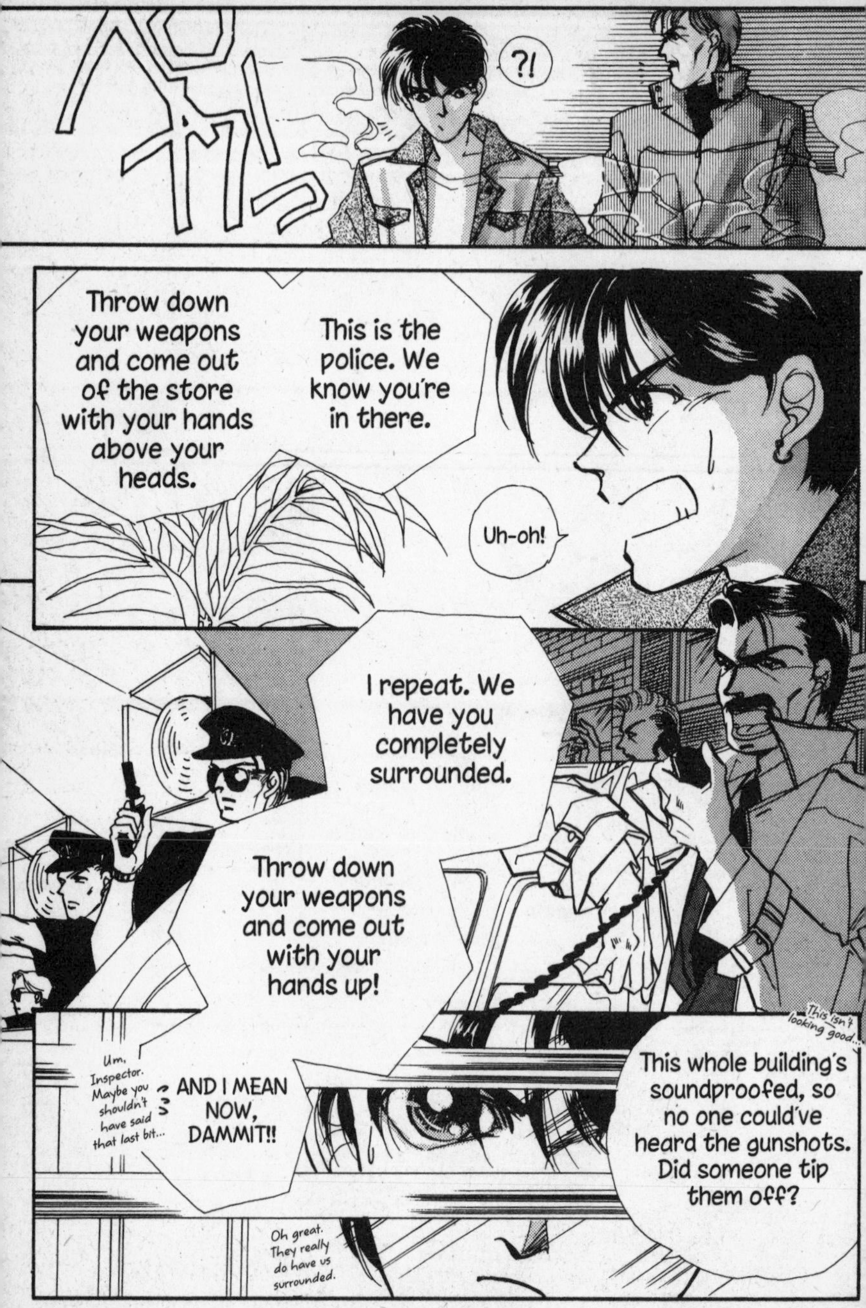
?!
This is the police. We know you're in there.
Throw down your weapons and come out of the store with your hands above your heads.
Uh-oh!
I repeat. We have you completely surrounded.
Throw down your weapons and come out with your hands up!
This isn't looking good...
This whole building's soundproofed, so no one could've heard the gunshots. Did someone tip them off?
AND I MEAN NOW, DAMMIT!!
Um, Inspector. Maybe you shouldn't have said that last bit...
Oh great. They really do have us surrounded.

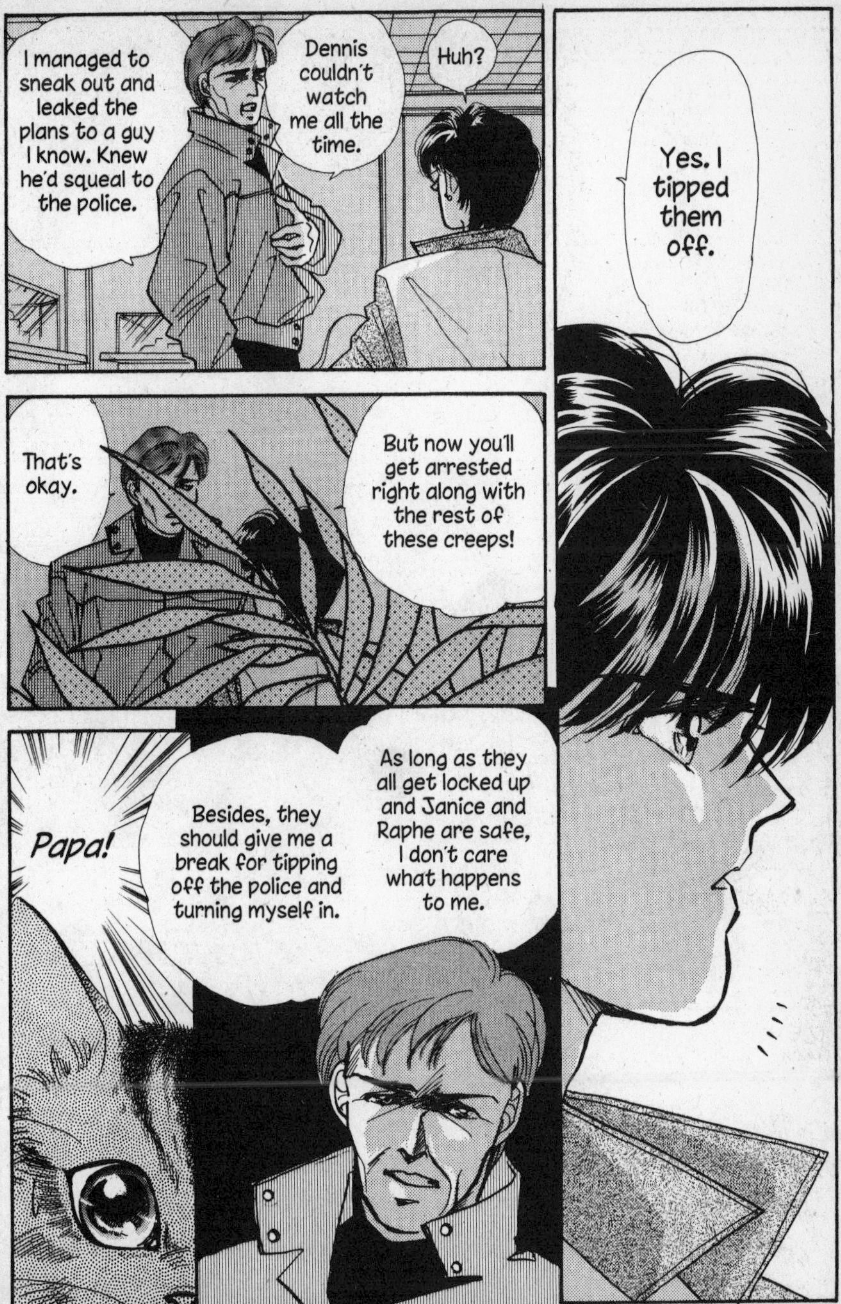
Yes. I tipped them off.
Huh?
Dennis couldn't watch me all the time.
I managed to sneak out and leaked the plans to a guy I know. Knew he'd squeal to the police.
But now you'll get arrested right along with the rest of these creeps!
That's okay.
As long as they all get locked up and Janice and Raphe are safe, I don't care what happens to me.
Besides, they should give me a break for tipping off the police and turning myself in.
Papa!

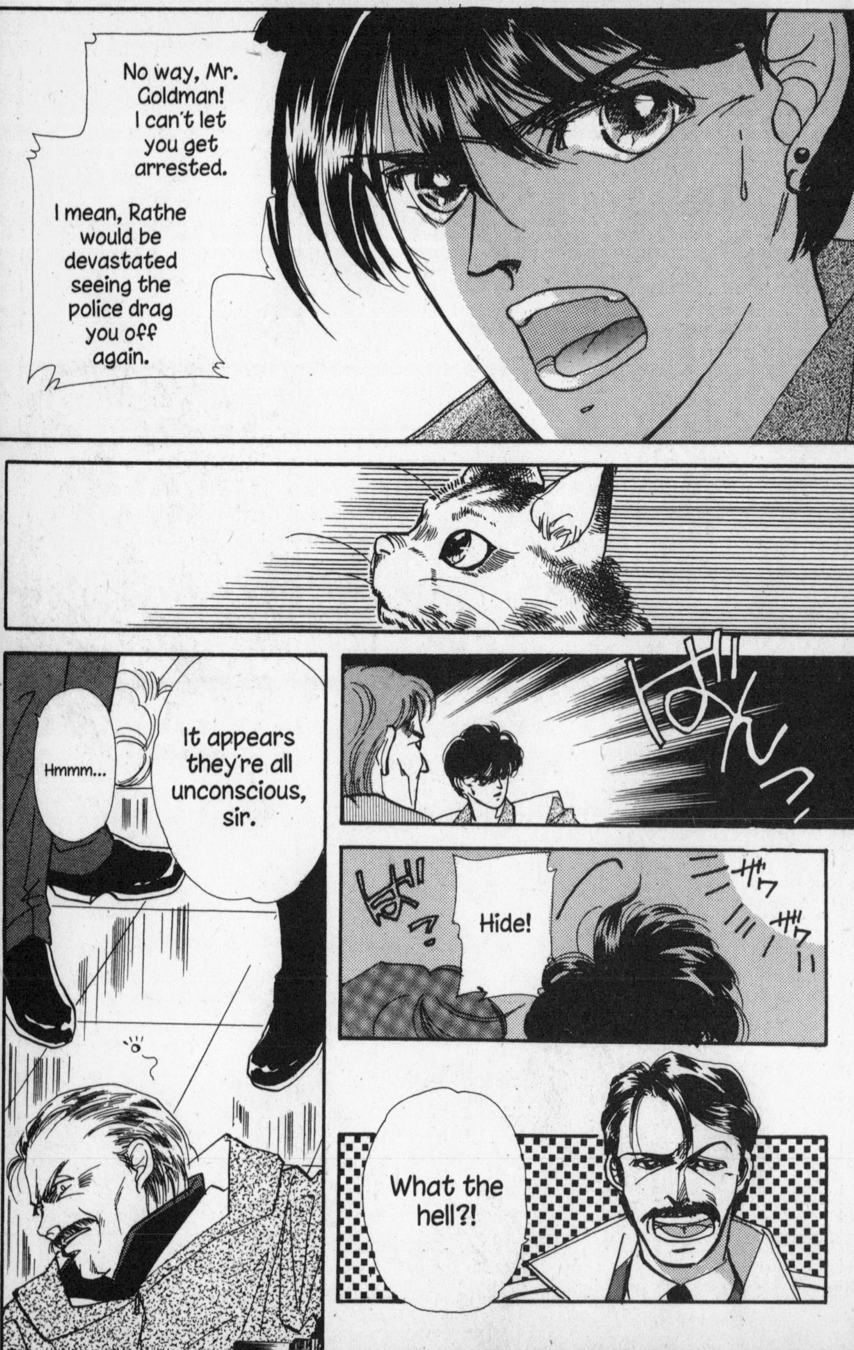
No way, Mr. Goldman! I can't let you get arrested.
I mean, Rathe would be devastated seeing the police drag you off again.
ばんっ
ばっ
Hide!
ザワ
ザワ
What the hell?!
It appears they're all unconscious, sir.
Hmmm...

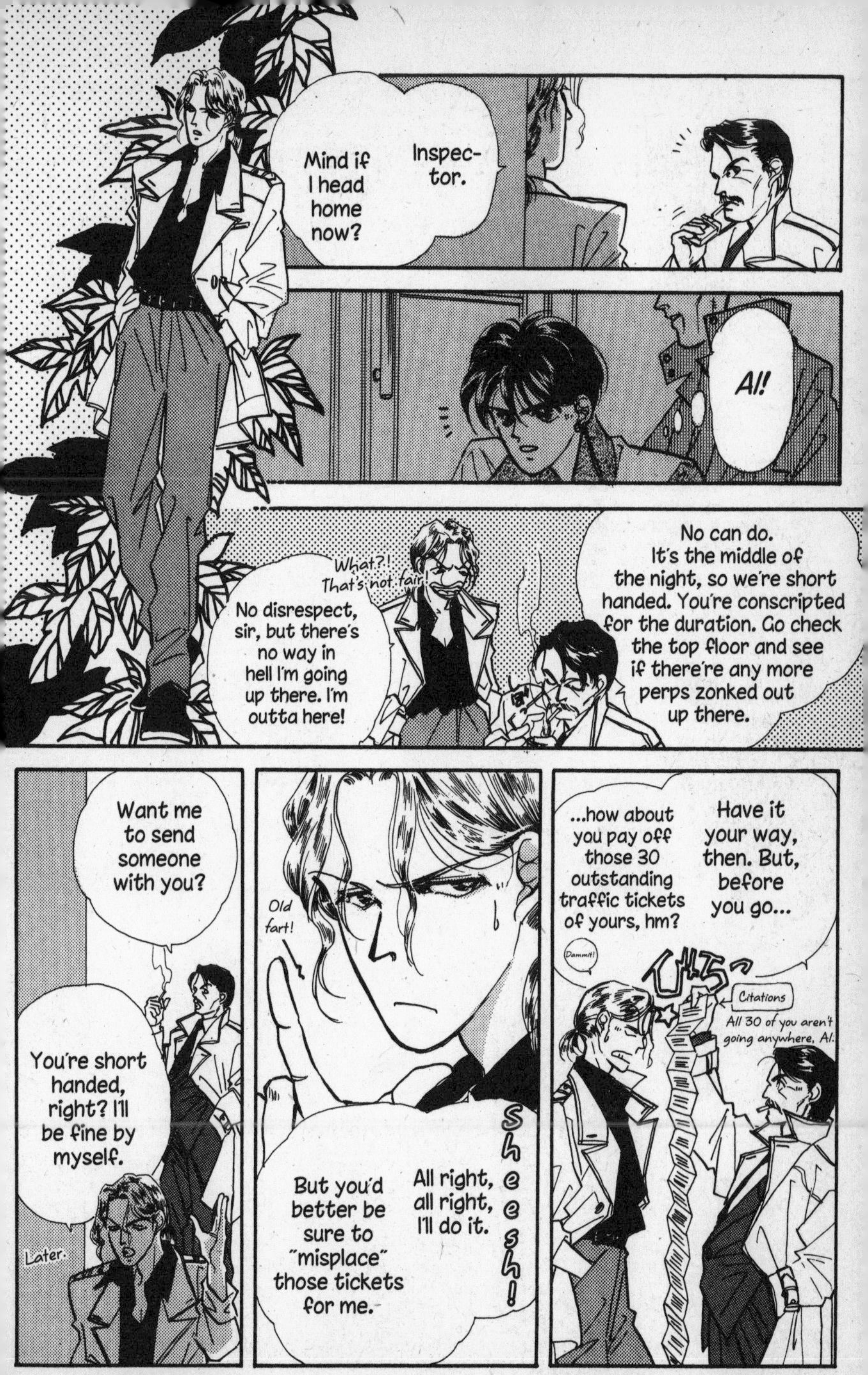
Al!
Inspector.
Mind if I head home now?
No can do. It's the middle of the night, so we're short handed. You're conscripted for the duration. Go check the top floor and see if there're any more perps zonked out up there.
What?! That's not fair
No disrespect, sir, but there's no way in hell I'm going up there. I'm outta here!
Have it your way, then. But, before you go...
...how about you pay off those 30 outstanding traffic tickets of yours, hm?
Dammit!
Citations
All 30 of you aren't going anywhere, Al.
Sheesh!
Old fart!
All right, all right, I'll do it.
But you'd better be sure to "misplace" those tickets for me.
Want me to send someone with you?
You're short handed, right? I'll be fine by myself.
Later.

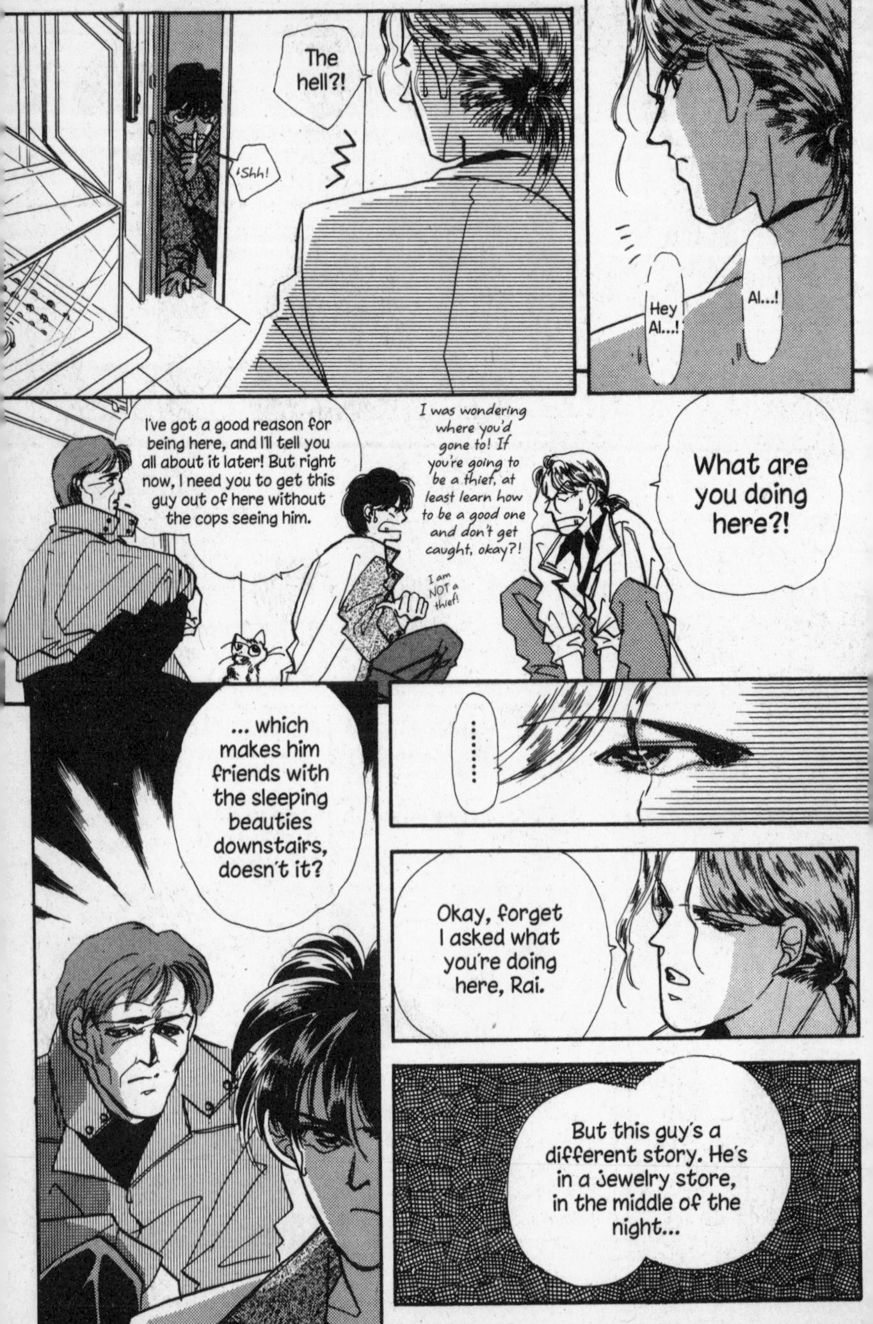

Al...!
Hey Al...!
The hell?!
'Shh!
What are you doing here?!
I was wondering where you'd gone to! If you're going to be a thief, at least learn how to be a good one and don't get caught, okay?!
I am NOT a thief!
I've got a good reason for being here, and I'll tell you all about it later! But right now, I need you to get this guy out of here without the cops seeing him.
......
Okay, forget I asked what you're doing here, Rai.
But this guy's a different story. He's in a jewelry store, in the middle of the night...
... which makes him friends with the sleeping beauties downstairs, doesn't it?

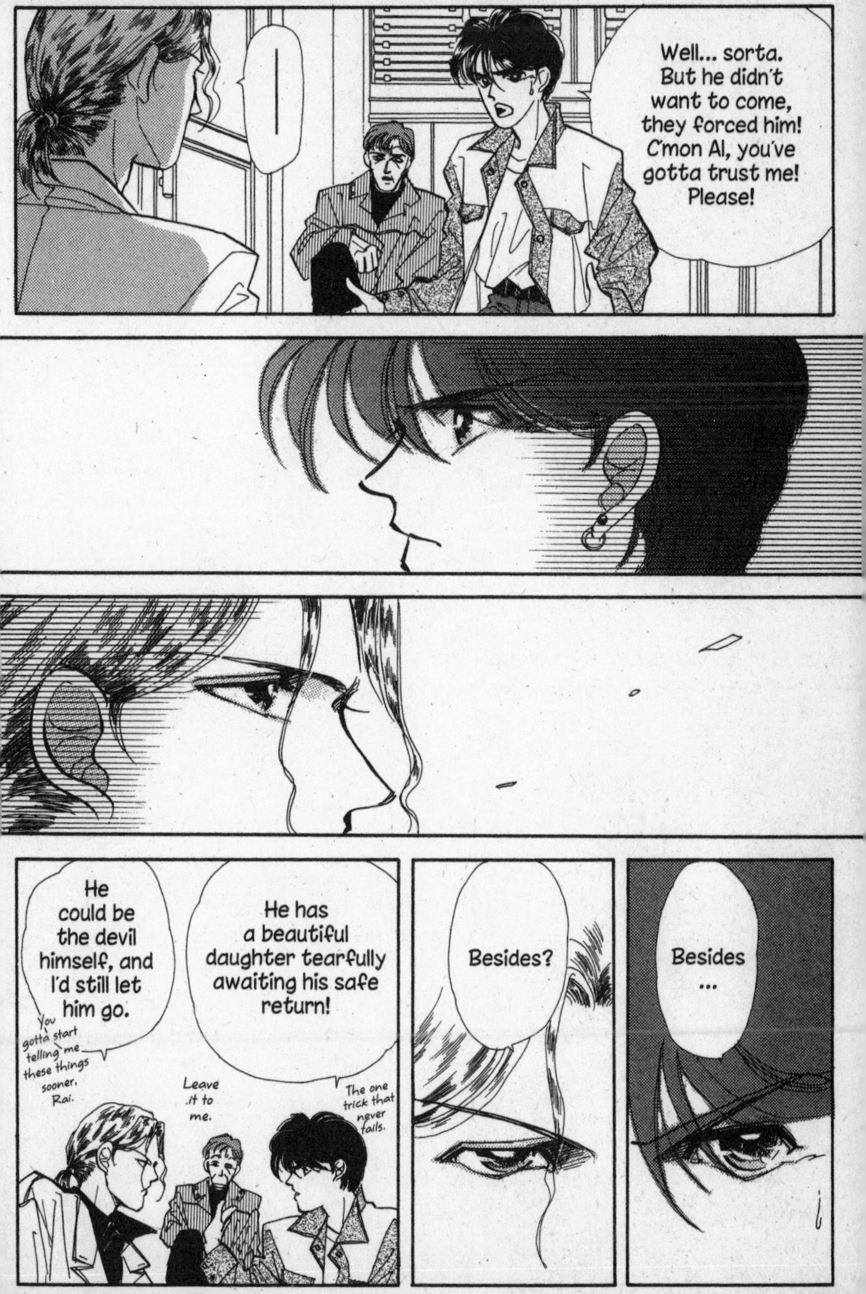
Well... sorta. But he didn't want to come, they forced him! C'mon Al, you've gotta trust me! Please!
Besides ...
Besides?
He has a beautiful daughter tearfully awaiting his safe return!
He could be the devil himself, and I'd still let him go.
The one trick that never fails.
Leave it to me.
You gotta start telling me these things sooner, Rai.

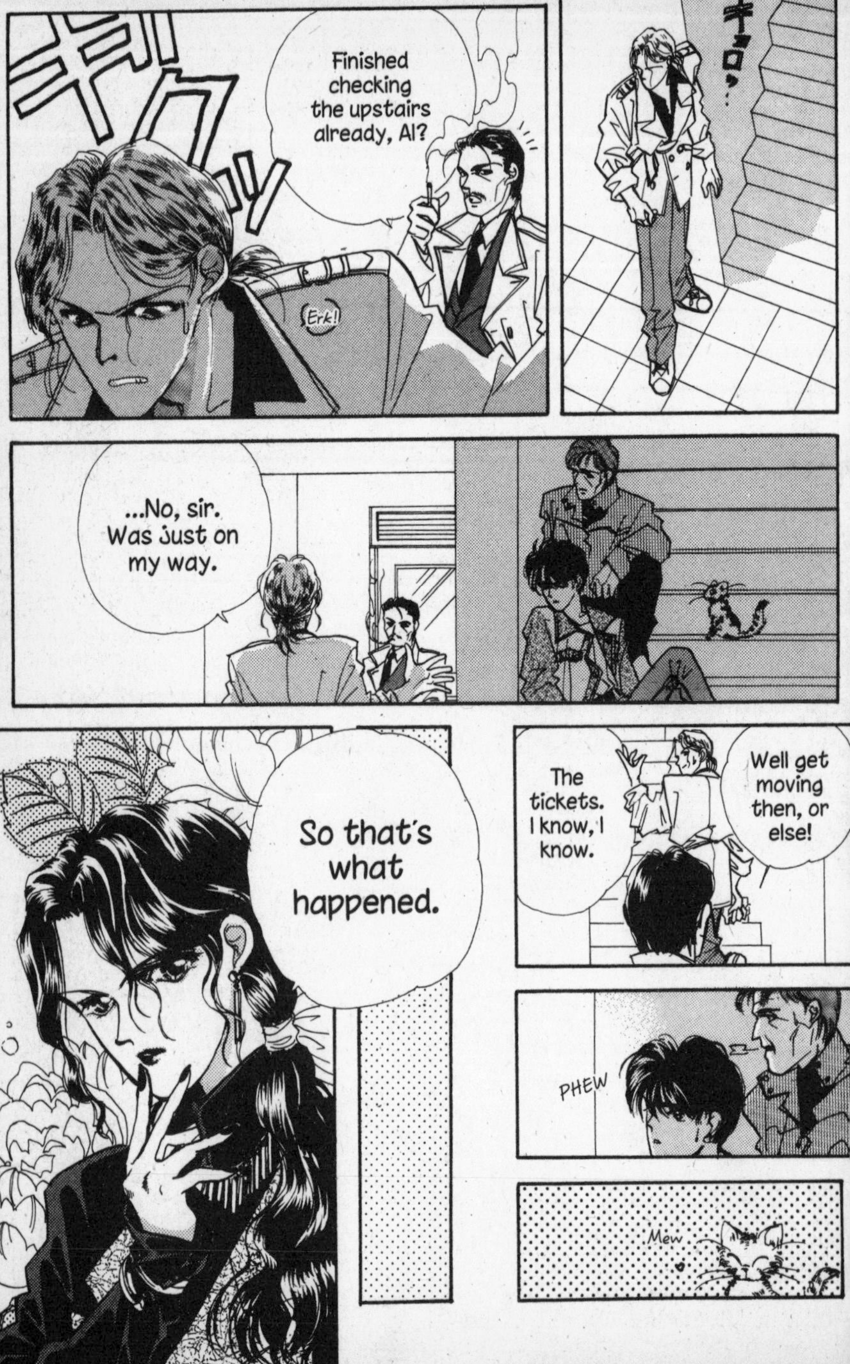

キョロッ...
ギクッ
Finished checking the upstairs already, Al?
Erk!
...No, sir. Was just on my way.
Well get moving then, or else!
The tickets. I know, I know.
PHEW
Mew
So that's what happened.

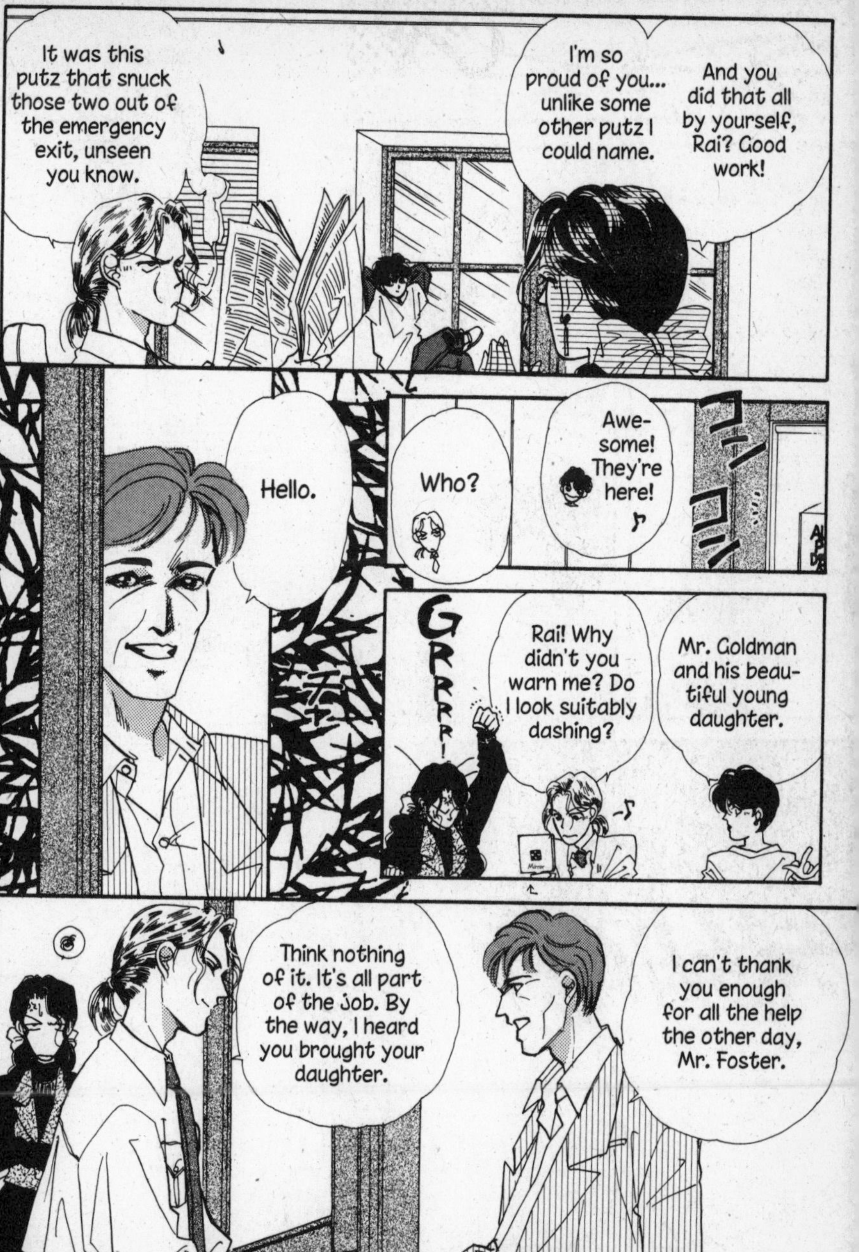
And you did that all by yourself, Rai? Good work!
I'm so proud of you... unlike some other putz I could name.
It was this putz that snuck those two out of the emergency exit, unseen you know.
Awe-some! They're here!
Who?
Mr. Goldman and his beau-tiful young daughter.
Rai! Why didn't you warn me? Do I look suitably dashing?
GRRRR!
Hello.
I can't thank you enough for all the help the other day, Mr. Foster.
Think nothing of it. It's all part of the job. By the way, I heard you brought your daughter.

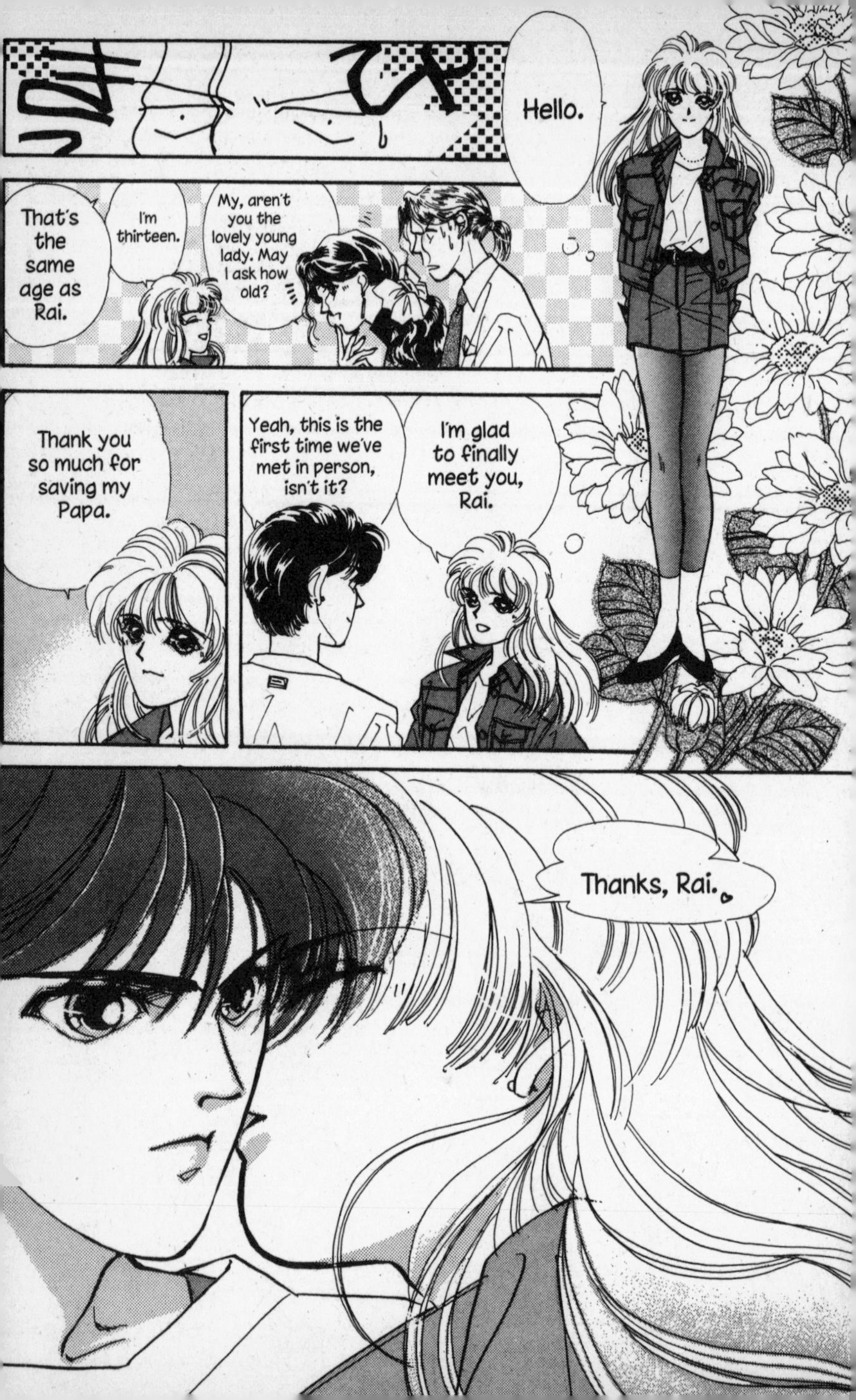
Hello.
My, aren't you the lovely young lady. May I ask how old?
I'm thirteen.
That's the same age as Rai.
I'm glad to finally meet you, Rai.
Yeah, this is the first time we've met in person, isn't it?
Thank you so much for saving my Papa.
Thanks, Rai. ♥

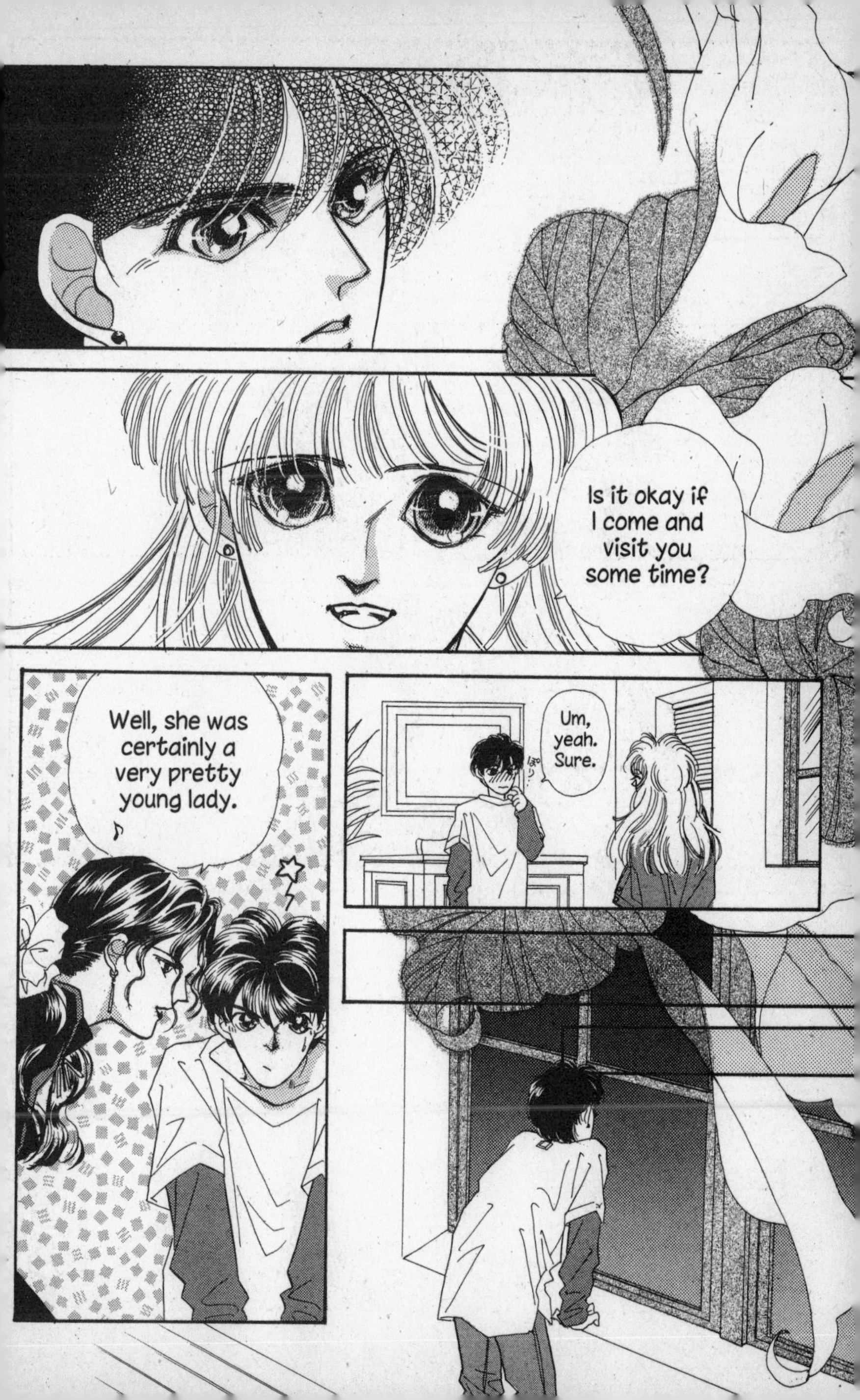
Is it okay if I come and visit you some time?
Um, yeah. Sure.
Well, she was certainly a very pretty young lady.

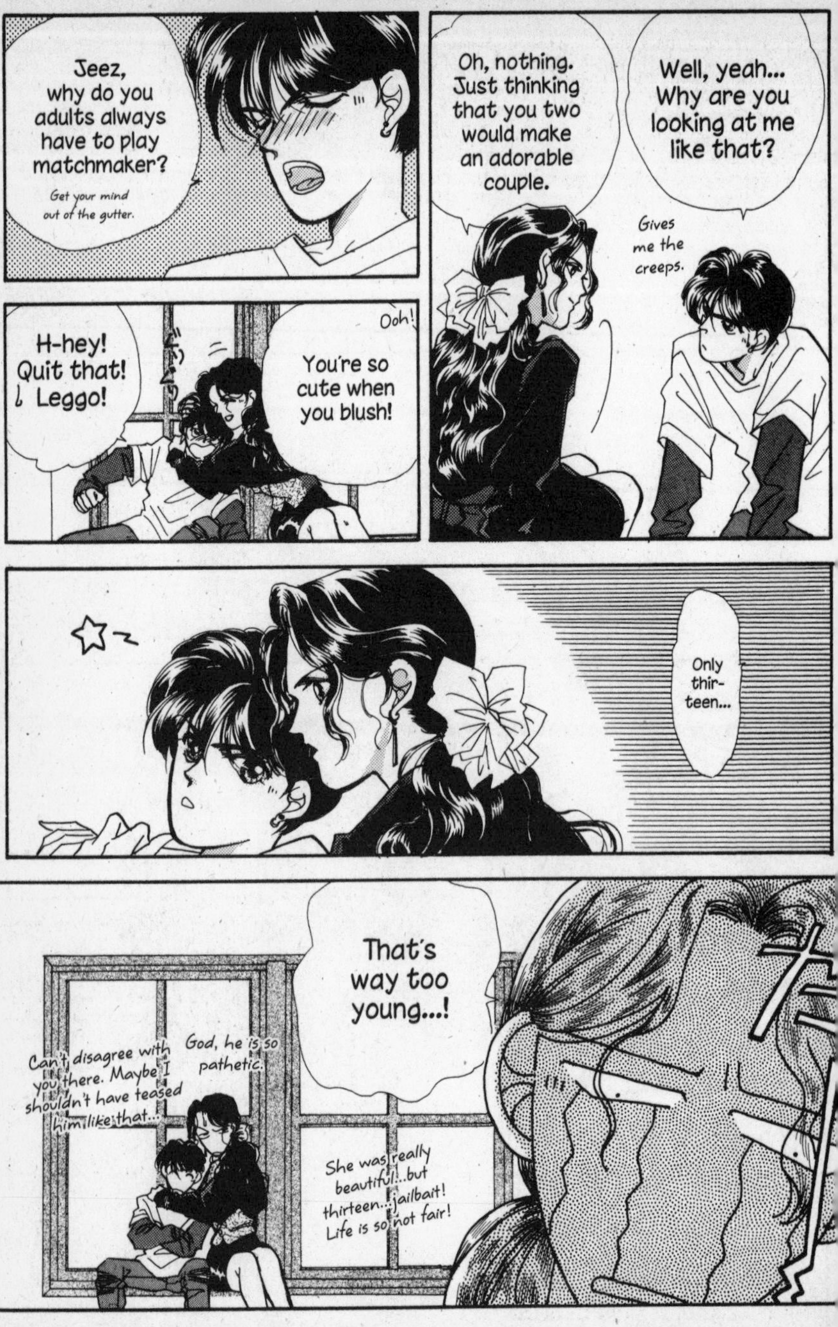
Well, yeah... Why are you looking at me like that?
Oh, nothing. Just thinking that you two would make an adorable couple.
Gives me the creeps.
Jeez, why do you adults always have to play matchmaker?
Get your mind out of the gutter.
Ooh!
You're so cute when you blush!
H-hey! Quit that! Leggo!
Only thir-teen...
That's way too young...!
She was really beautiful...but thirteen...jailbait! Life is so not fair!
God, he is so pathetic.
Can't disagree with you, there. Maybe I shouldn't have teased him like that...

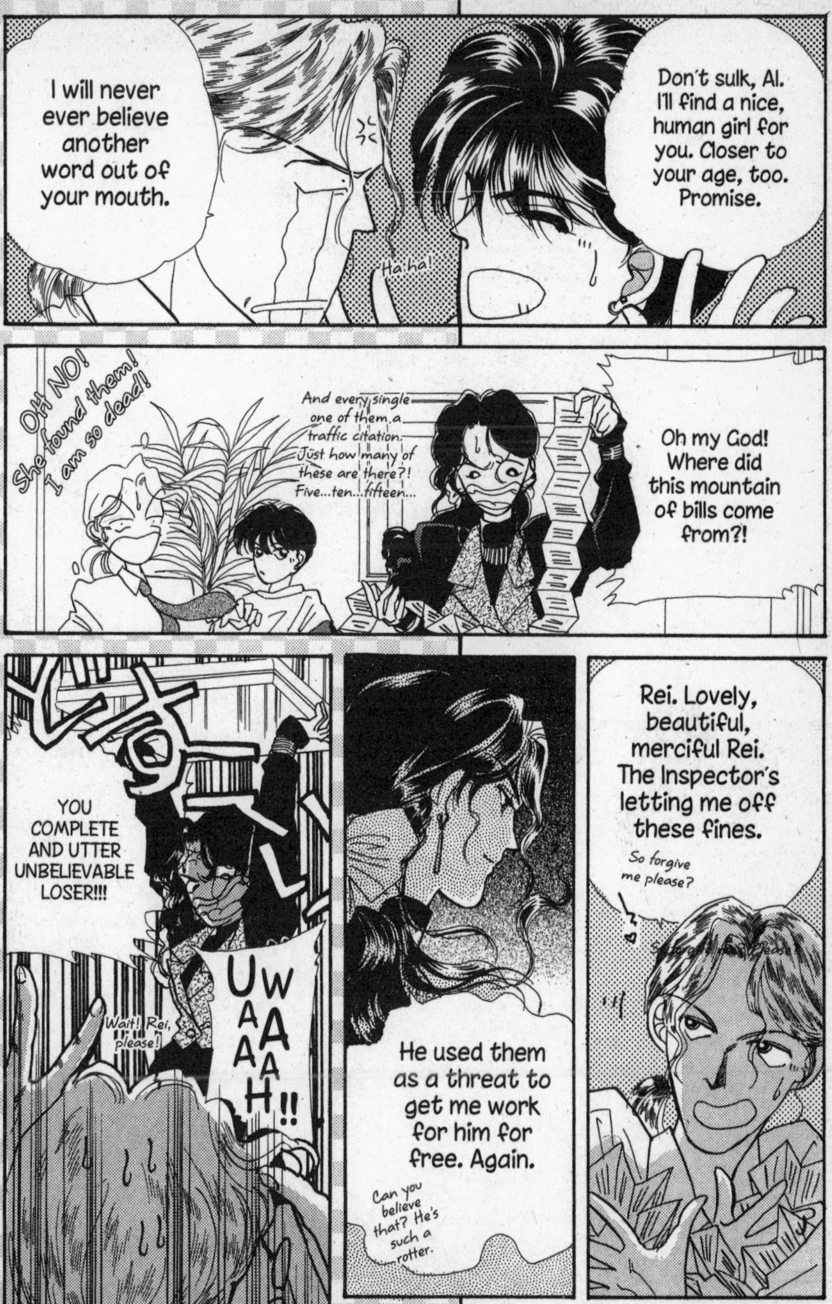
Don't sulk, Al. I'll find a nice, human girl for you. Closer to your age, too. Promise.
Ha ha!
I will never ever believe another word out of your mouth.
Oh my God! Where did this mountain of bills come from?!
And every single one of them a traffic citation. Just how many of these are there?! Five...ten...fifteen...
OH NO! She found them! I am so dead!
Rei. Lovely, beautiful, merciful Rei. The Inspector's letting me off these fines.
So forgive me please?
He used them as a threat to get me work for him for free. Again.
Can you believe that? He's such a rotter.
YOU COMPLETE AND UTTER UNBELIEVABLE LOSER!!!
UWAAAAH!!
Wait! Rei, please!

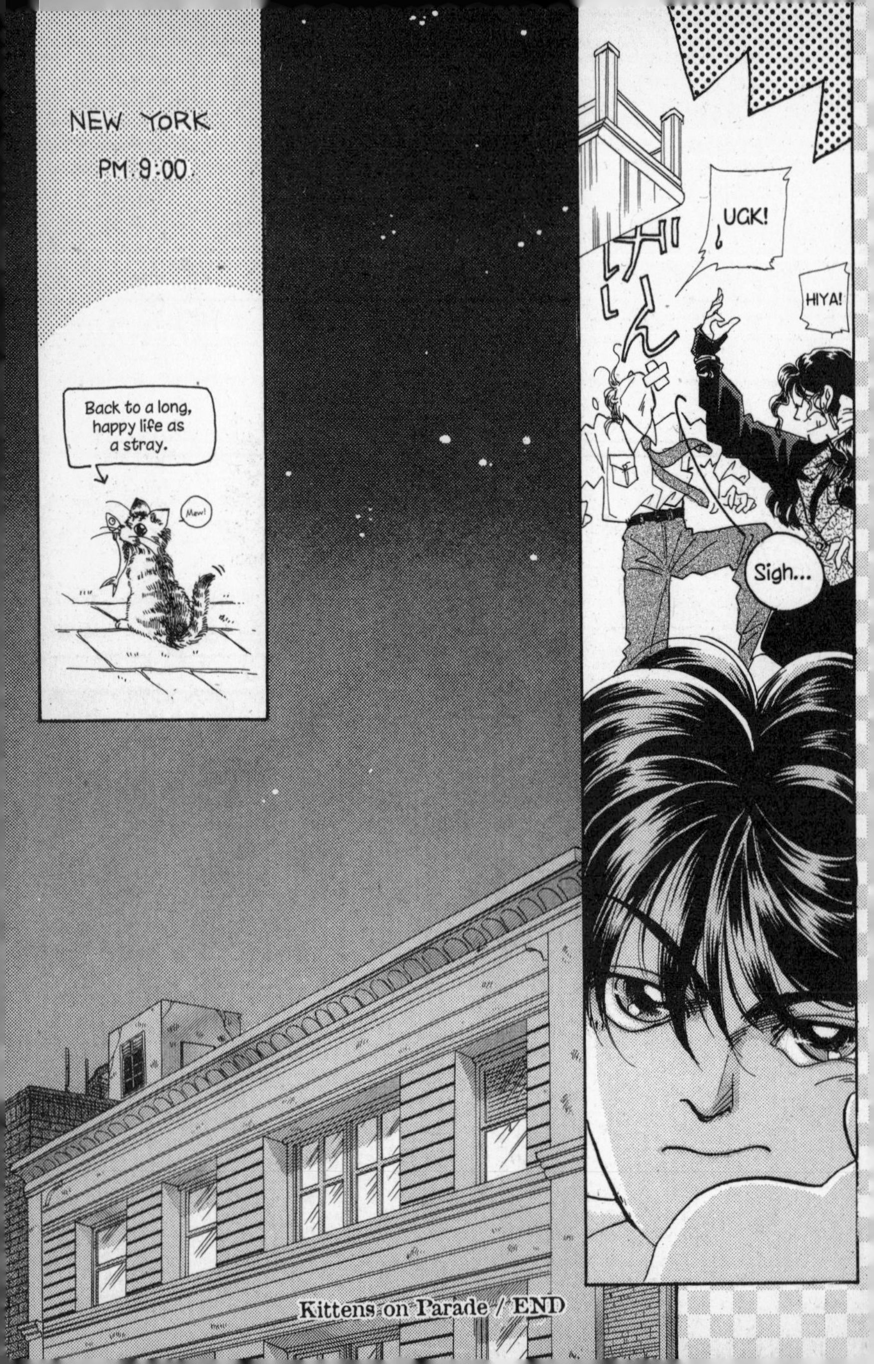
UGK!
HIYA!
Sigh...
NEW YORK
PM 9:00
Back to a long, happy life as a stray.
Mew!
Kittens on Parade / END

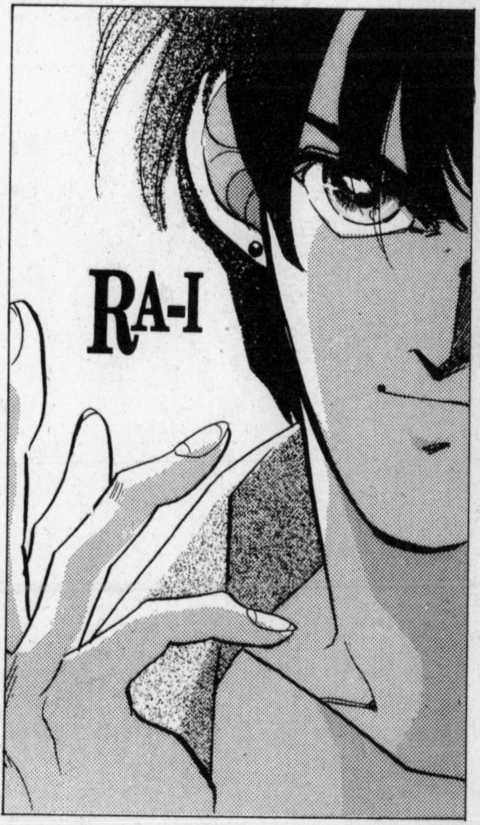
RA-I

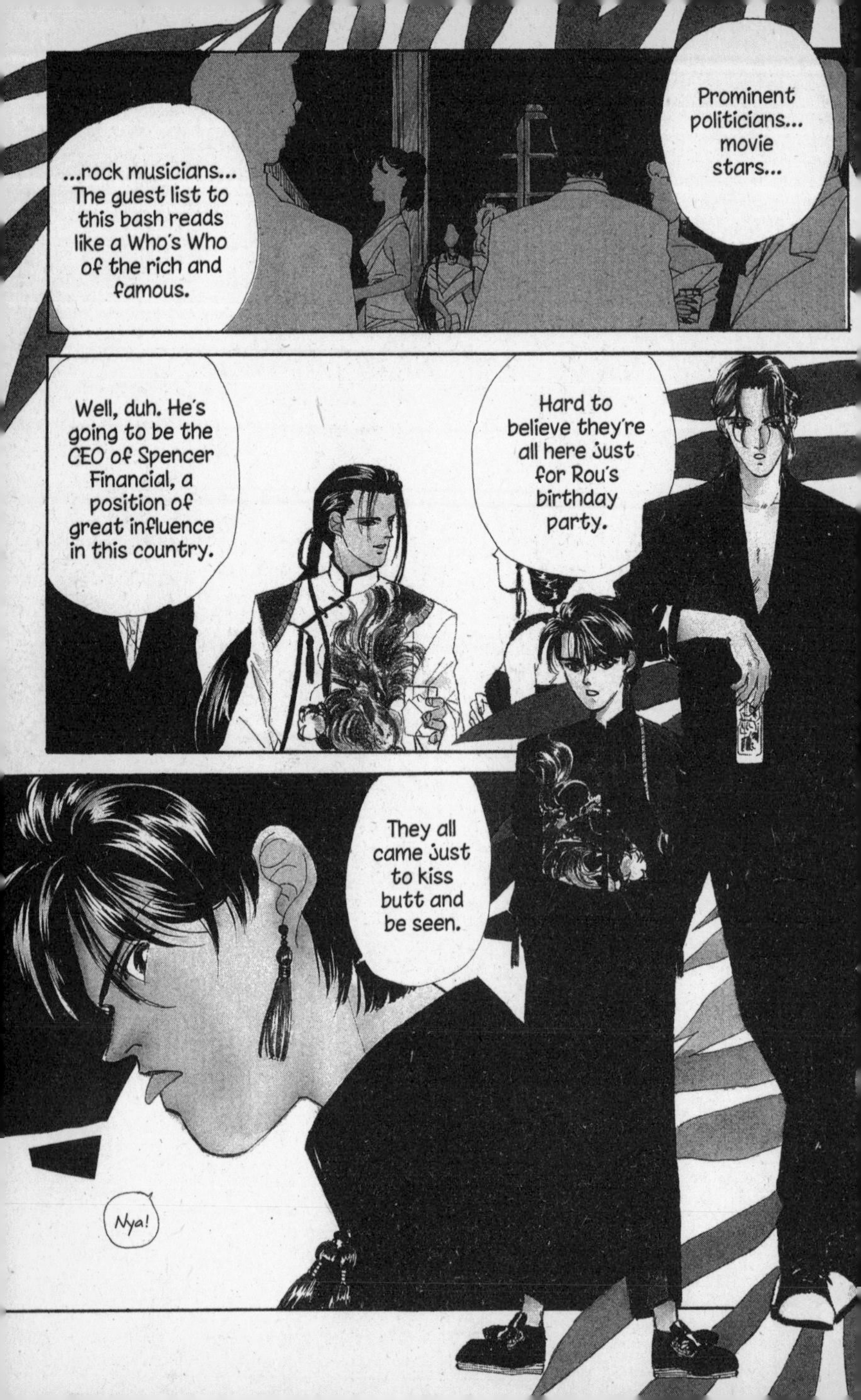

Prominent politicians... movie stars...
...rock musicians... The guest list to this bash reads like a Who's Who of the rich and famous.
Hard to believe they're all here just for Rou's birthday party.
Well, duh. He's going to be the CEO of Spencer Financial, a position of great influence in this country.
They all came just to kiss butt and be seen.
Nya!

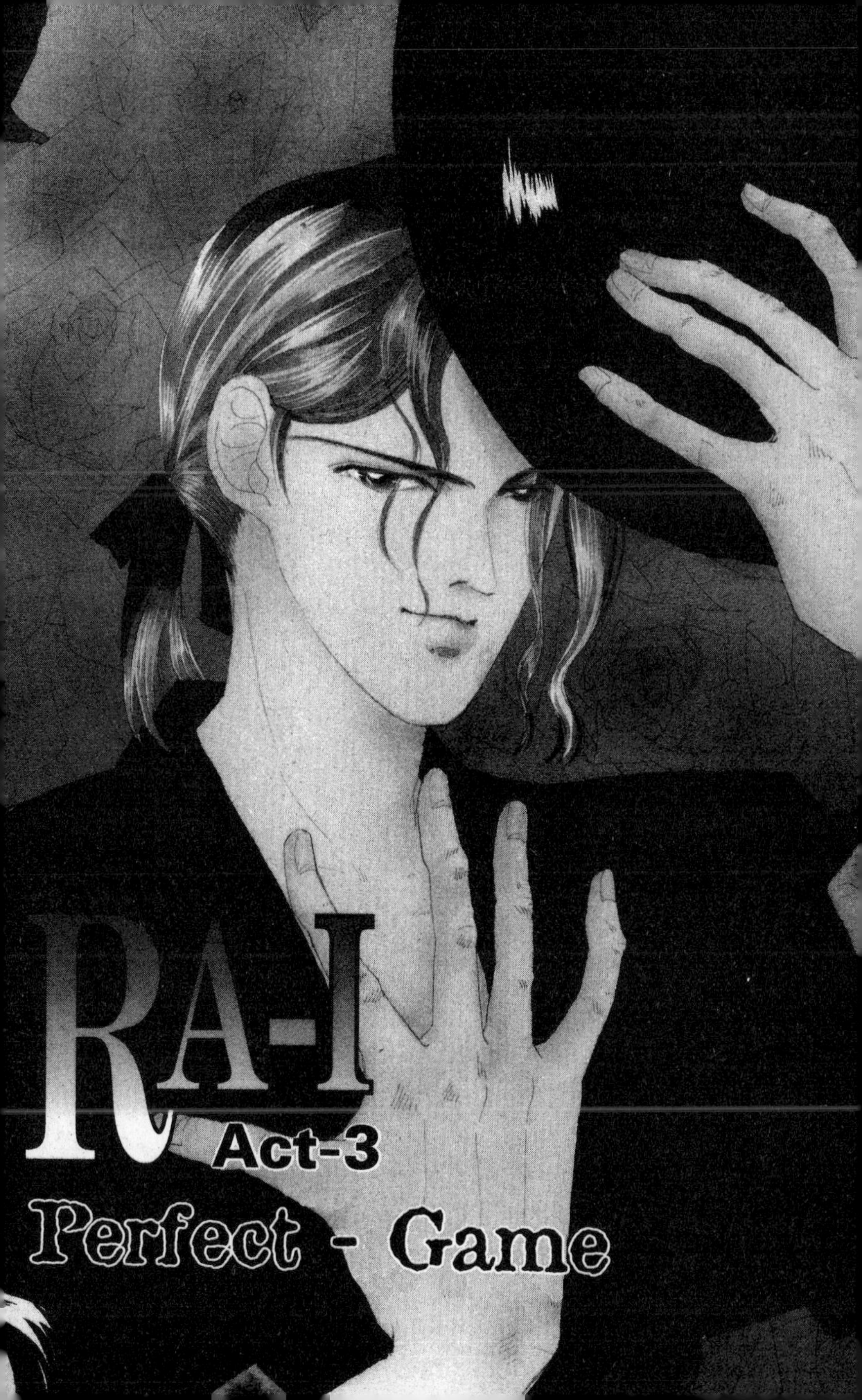
RA-I
Act-3
Perfect - Game

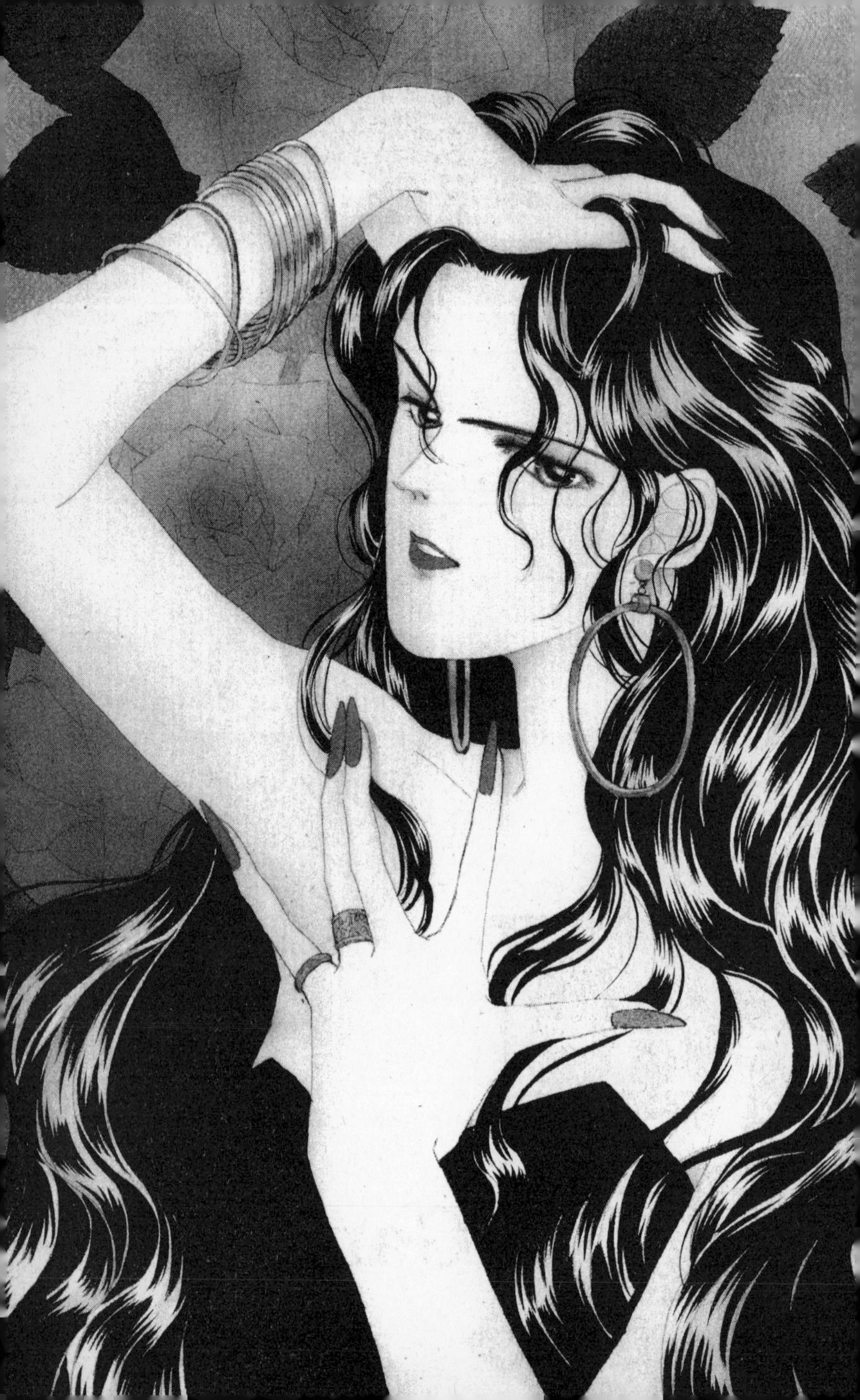

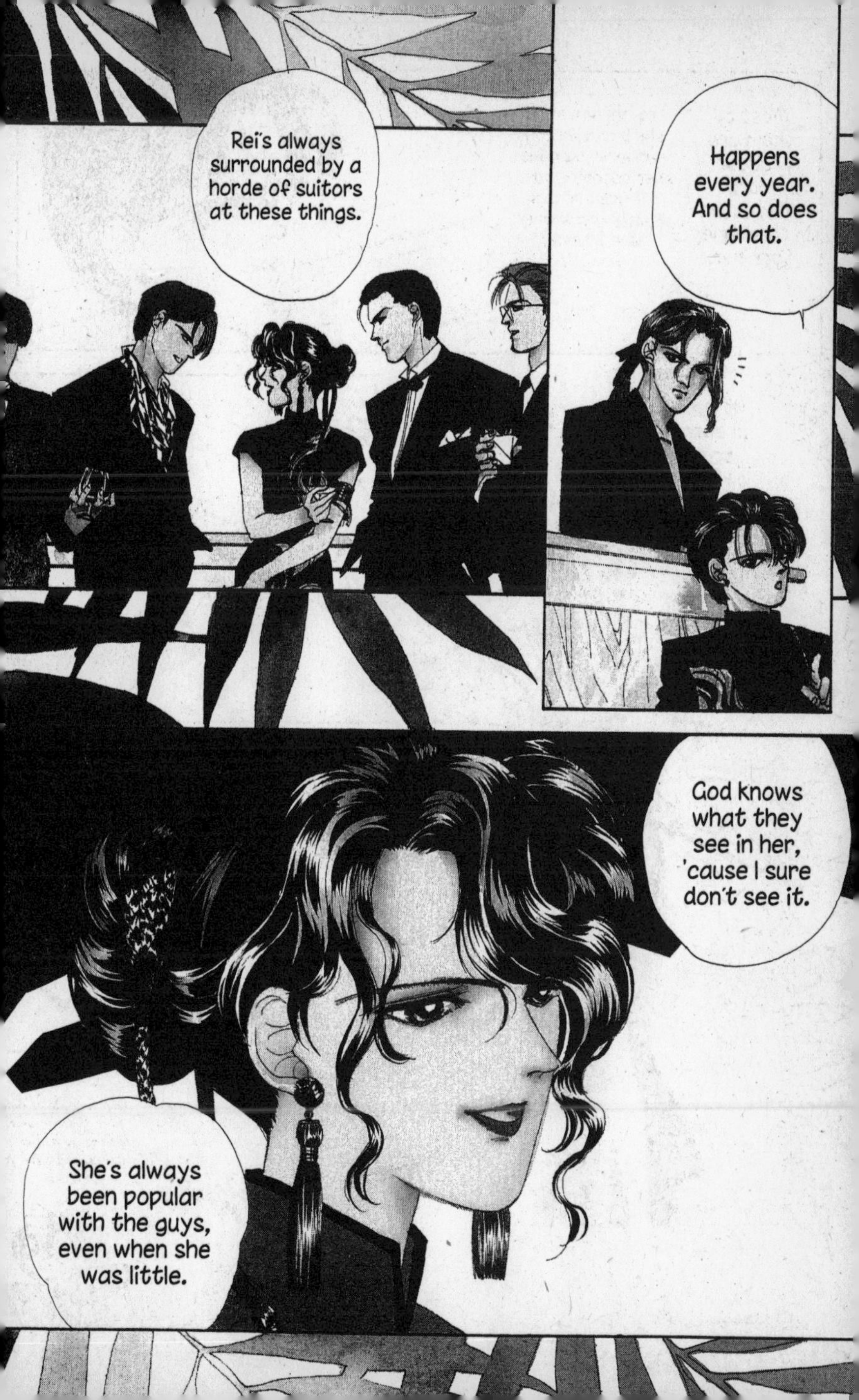
Happens every year. And so does that.
Rei's always surrounded by a horde of suitors at these things.
God knows what they see in her, 'cause I sure don't see it.
She's always been popular with the guys, even when she was little.

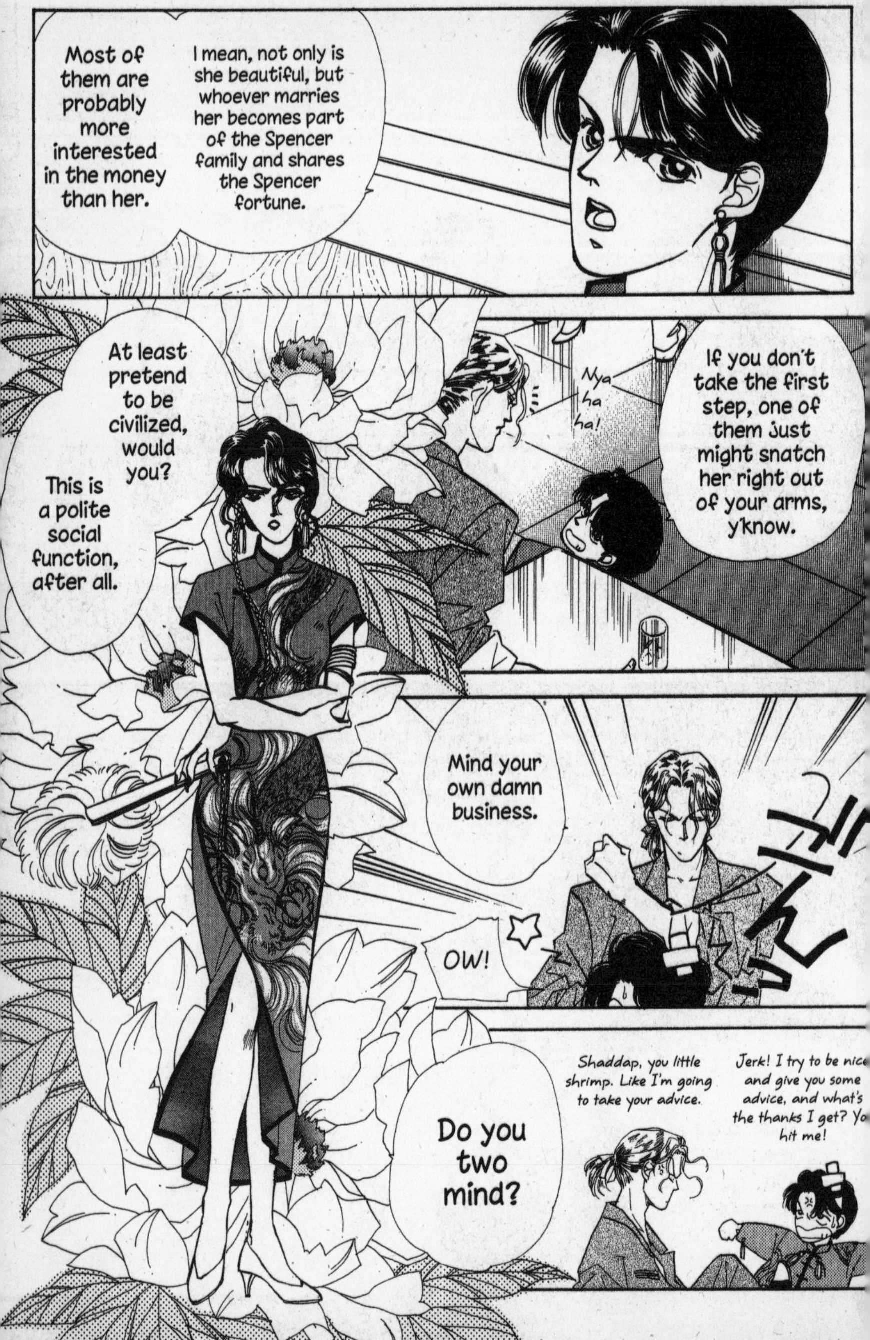
I mean, not only is she beautiful, but whoever marries her becomes part of the Spencer family and shares the Spencer fortune.
Most of them are probably more interested in the money than her.
If you don't take the first step, one of them just might snatch her right out of your arms, y'know.
Nya ha ha!
Mind your own damn business.
OW!
Jerk! I try to be nice and give you some advice, and what's the thanks I get? Yo hit me!
Shaddap, you little shrimp. Like I'm going to take your advice.
Do you two mind?
At least pretend to be civilized, would you?
This is a polite social function, after all.

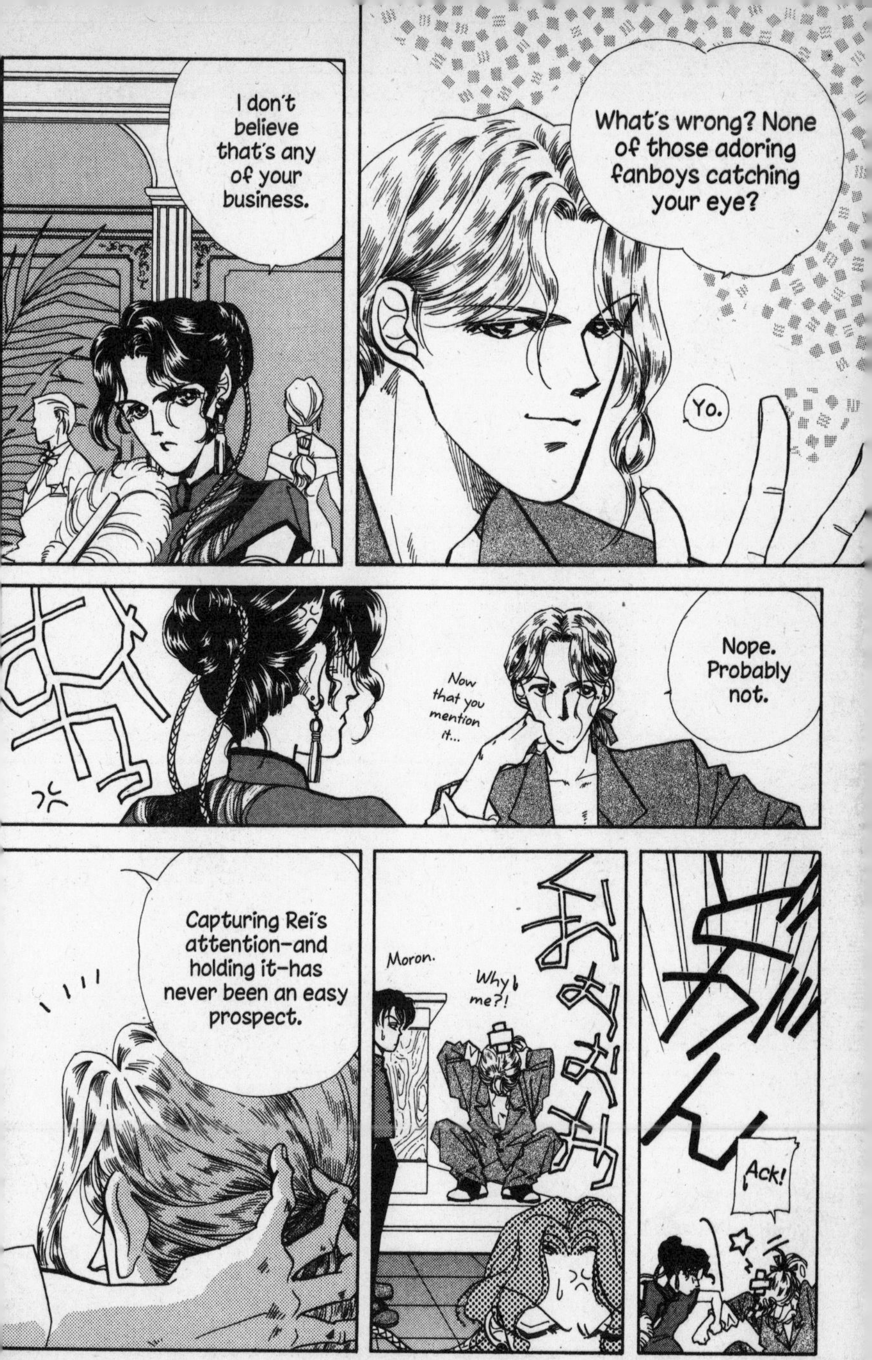

What's wrong? None of those adoring fanboys catching your eye?
Yo.
I don't believe that's any of your business.
Nope. Probably not.
Now that you mention it...
Ack!
Why me?!
Moron.
Capturing Rei's attention–and holding it–has never been an easy prospect.

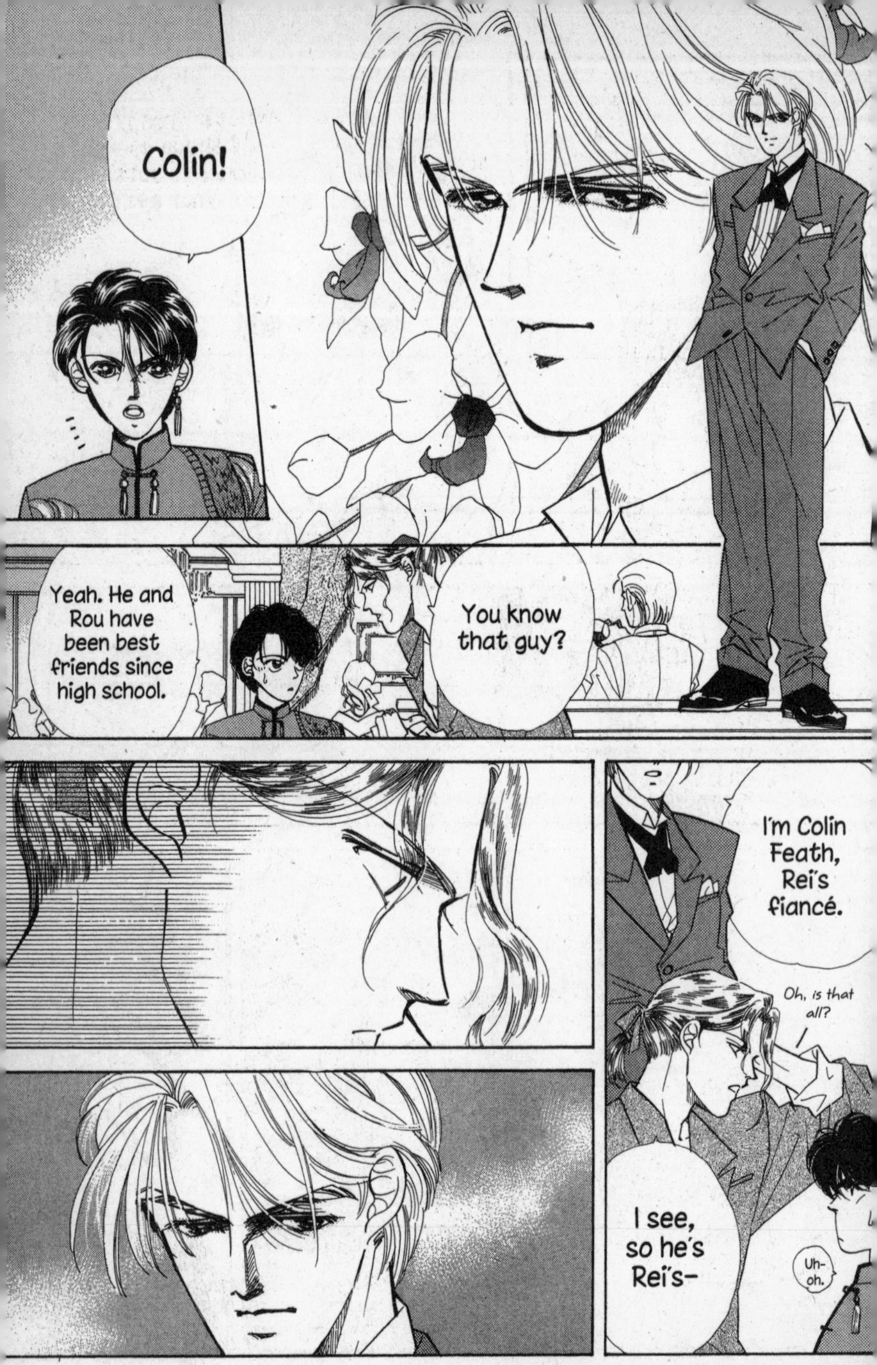
Colin!
You know that guy?
Yeah. He and Rou have been best friends since high school.
I'm Colin Feath, Rei's fiancé.
Oh, is that all?
I see, so he's Rei's-
Uh-oh.

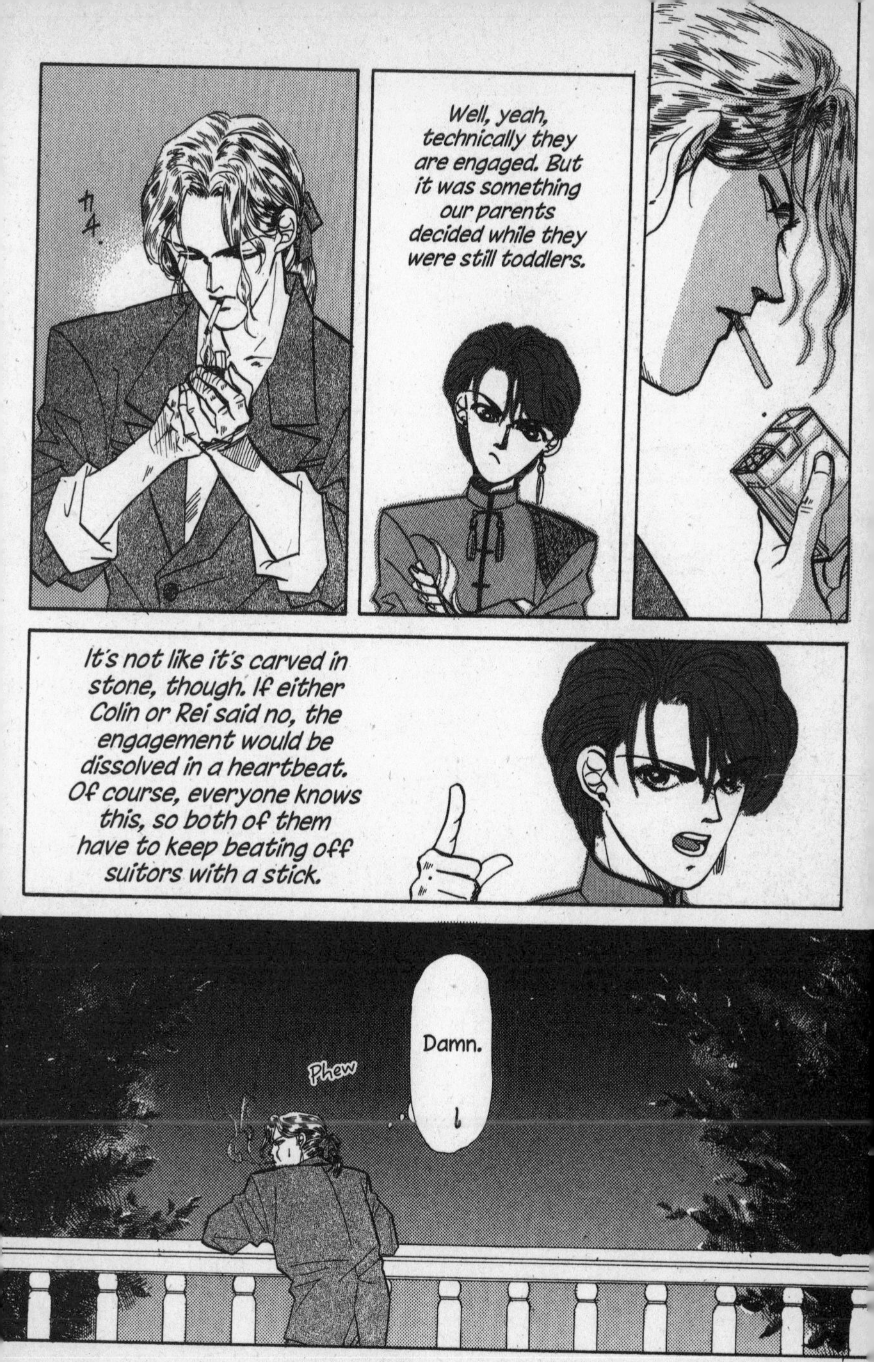

Well, yeah, technically they are engaged. But it was something our parents decided while they were still toddlers.
カチ
It's not like it's carved in stone, though. If either Colin or Rei said no, the engagement would be dissolved in a heartbeat. Of course, everyone knows this, so both of them have to keep beating off suitors with a stick.
Damn.
Phew

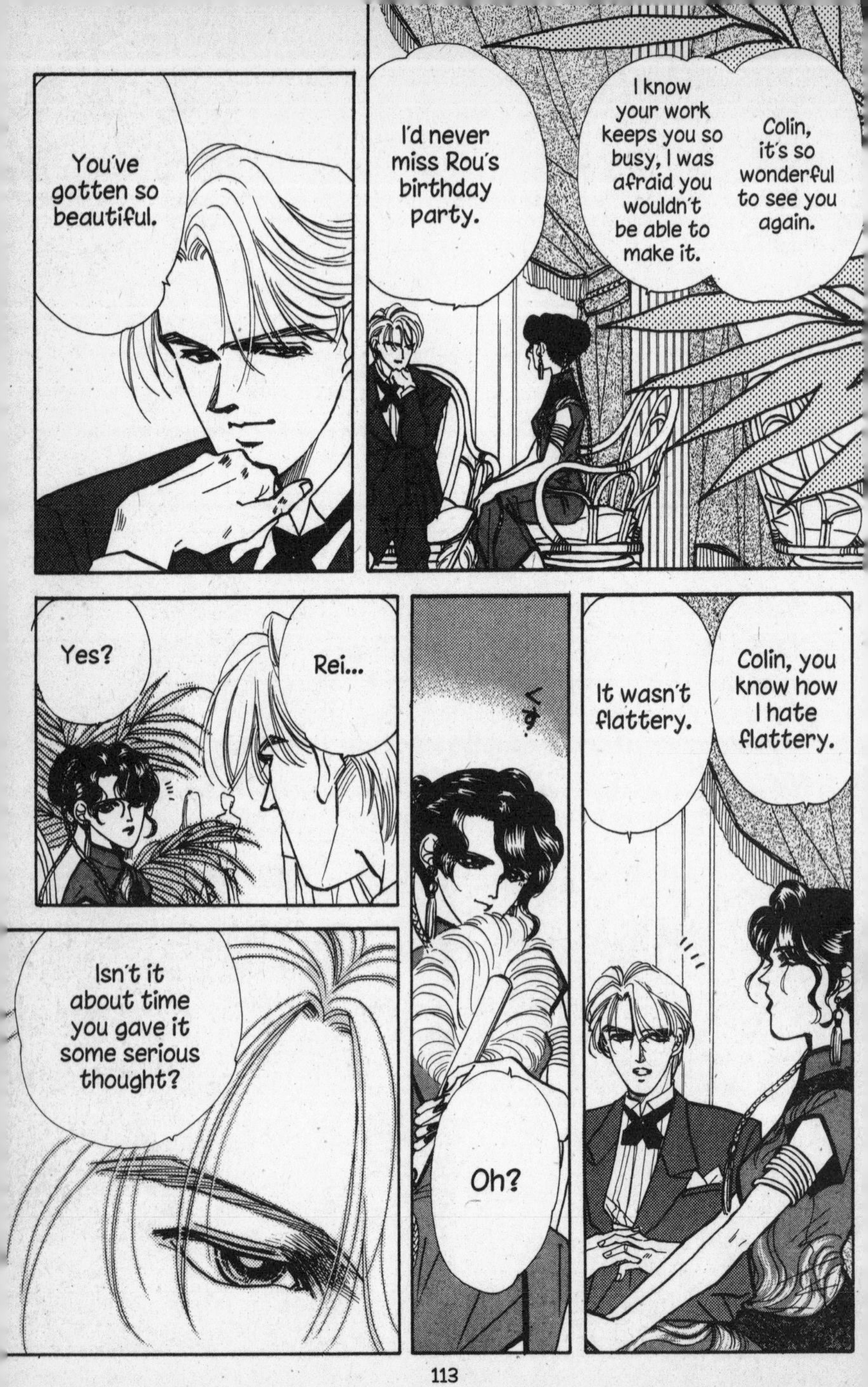
Colin, it's so wonderful to see you again.
I know your work keeps you so busy, I was afraid you wouldn't be able to make it.
I'd never miss Rou's birthday party.
You've gotten so beautiful.
Colin, you know how I hate flattery.
It wasn't flattery.
くす
Oh?
Rei...
Yes?
Isn't it about time you gave it some serious thought?

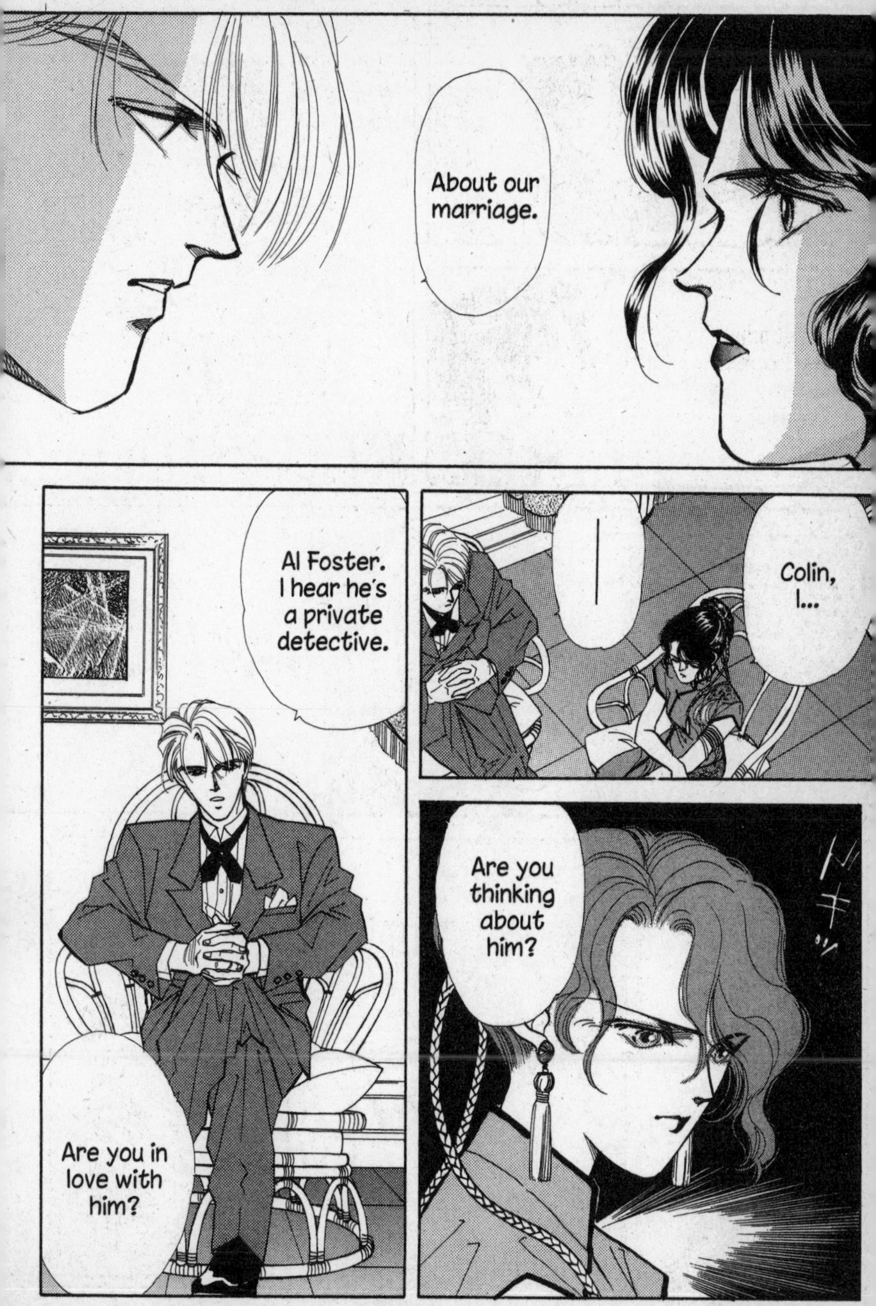
About our marriage.
Colin, I...
—
Are you thinking about him?
ドキッ
Al Foster. I hear he's a private detective.
Are you in love with him?

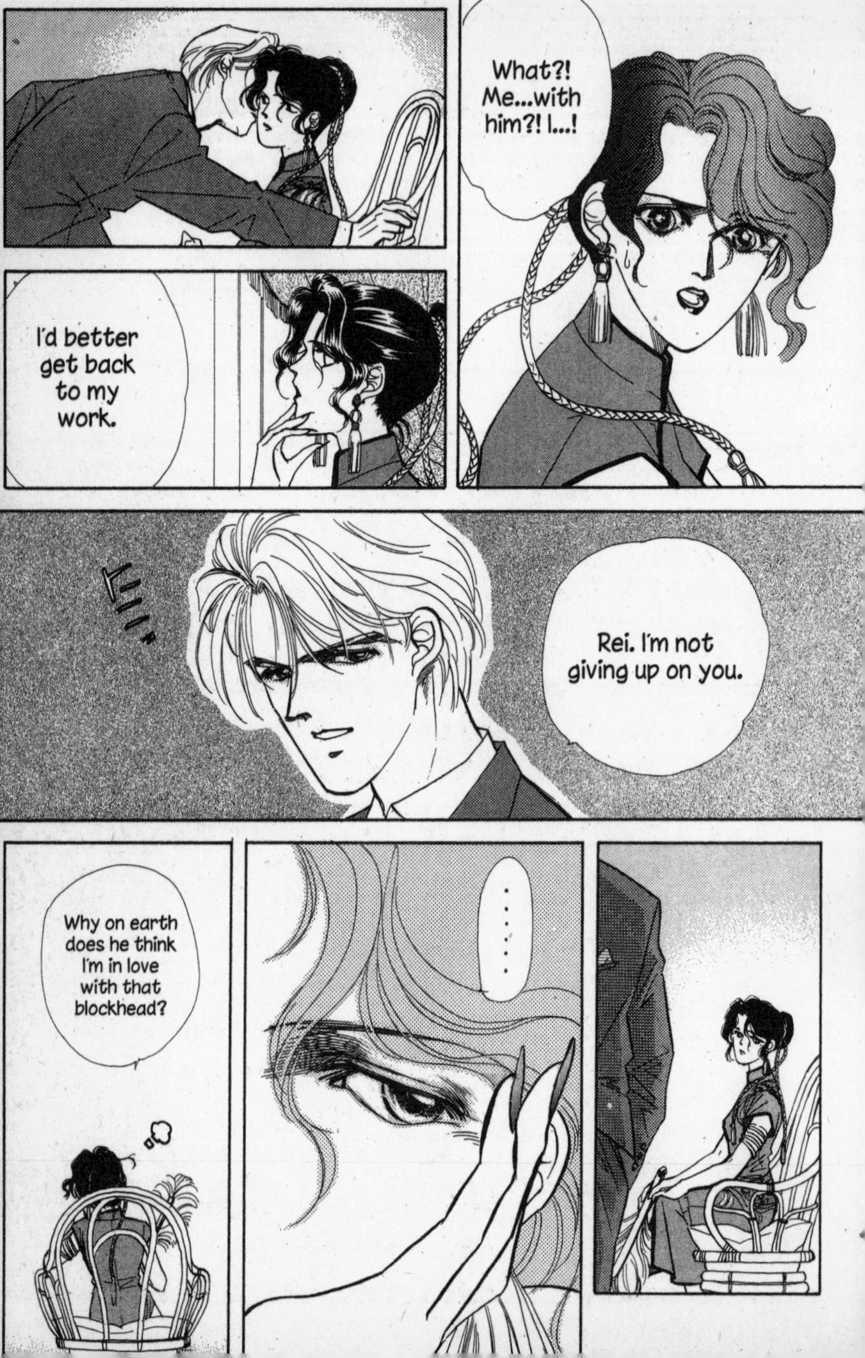
What?! Me...with him?! I...!
I'd better get back to my work.
Rei. I'm not giving up on you.
......
Why on earth does he think I'm in love with that blockhead?

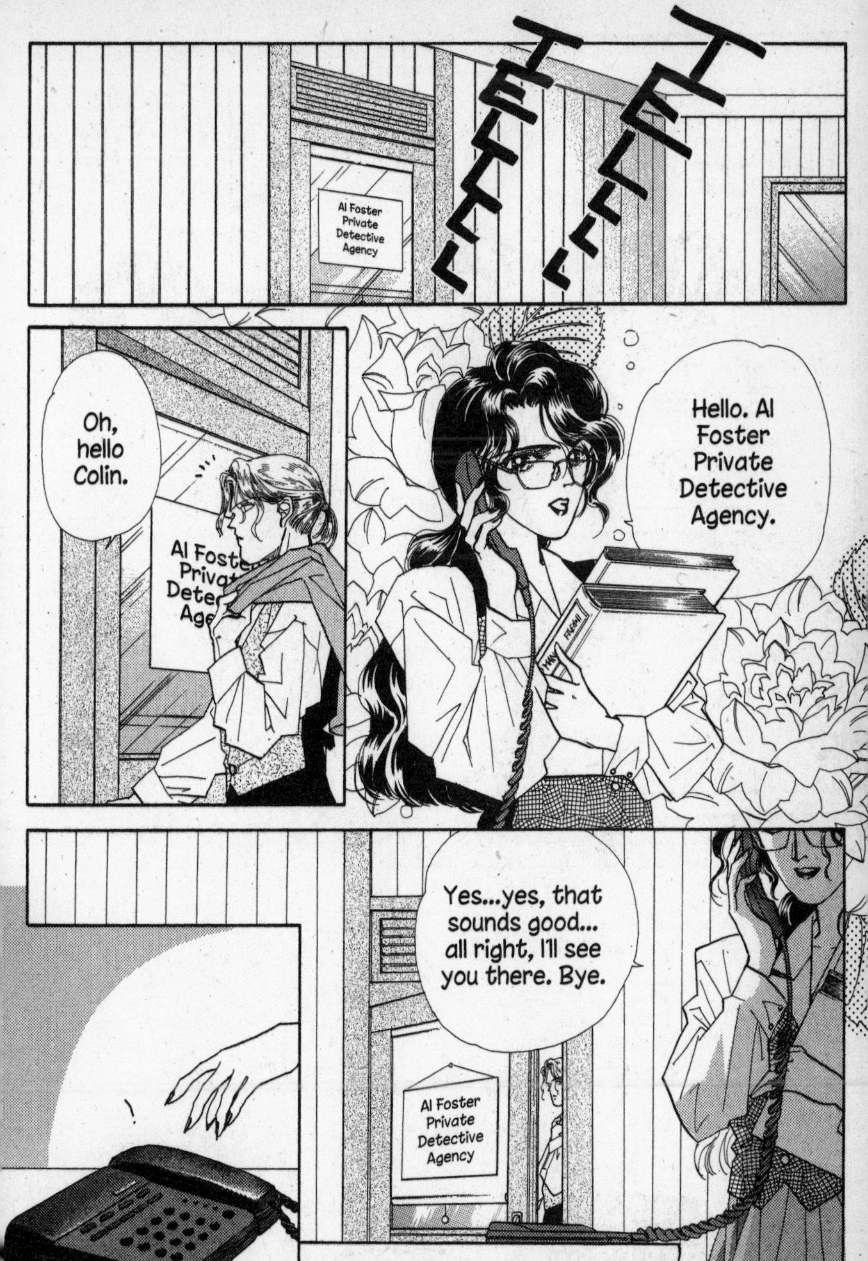
TELLLL
TELLLL
Al Foster Private Detective Agency
Hello. Al Foster Private Detective Agency.
Oh, hello Colin.
Yes...yes, that sounds good... all right, I'll see you there. Bye.
Al Foster Private Detective Agency

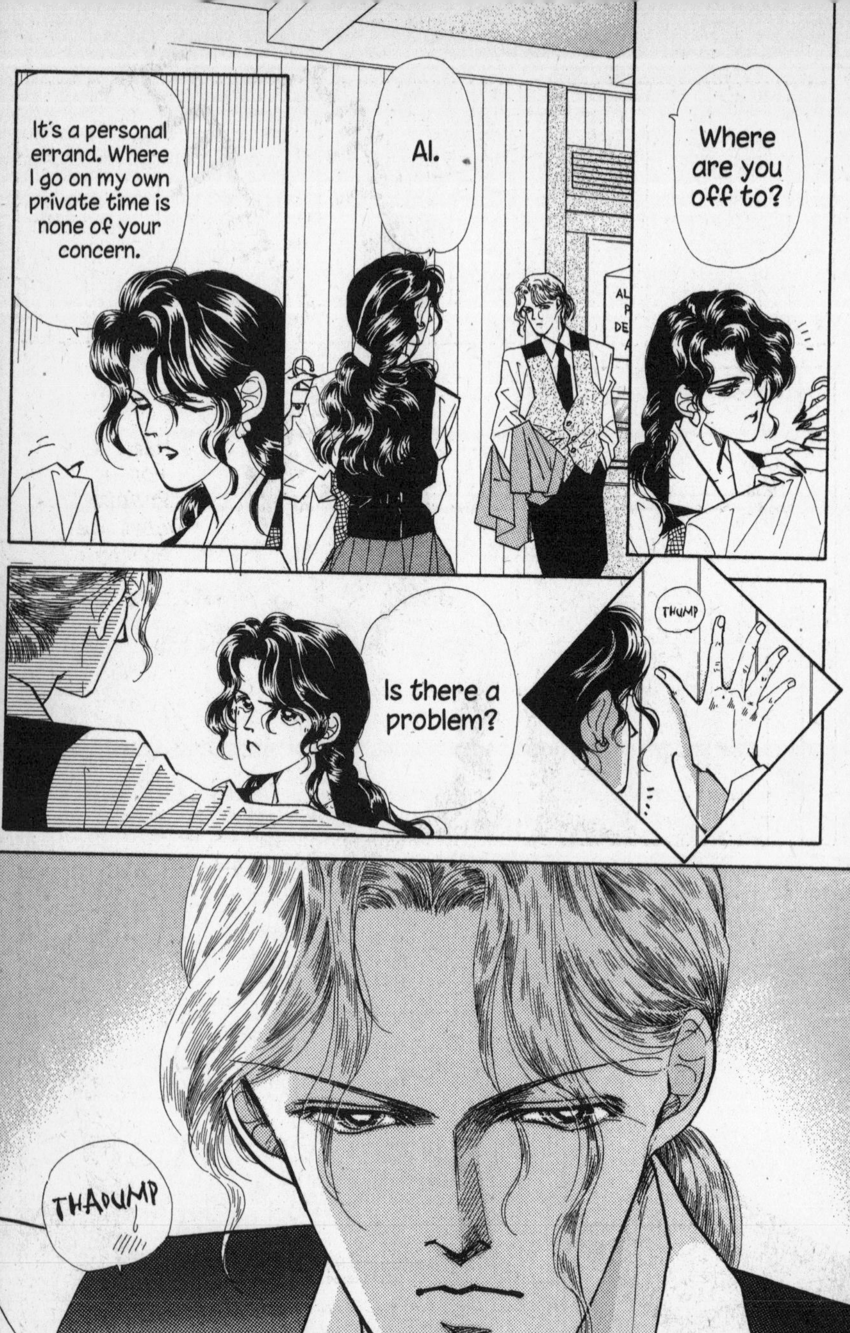
Where are you off to?
Al.
It's a personal errand. Where I go on my own private time is none of your concern.
THUMP
Is there a problem?
THADUMP

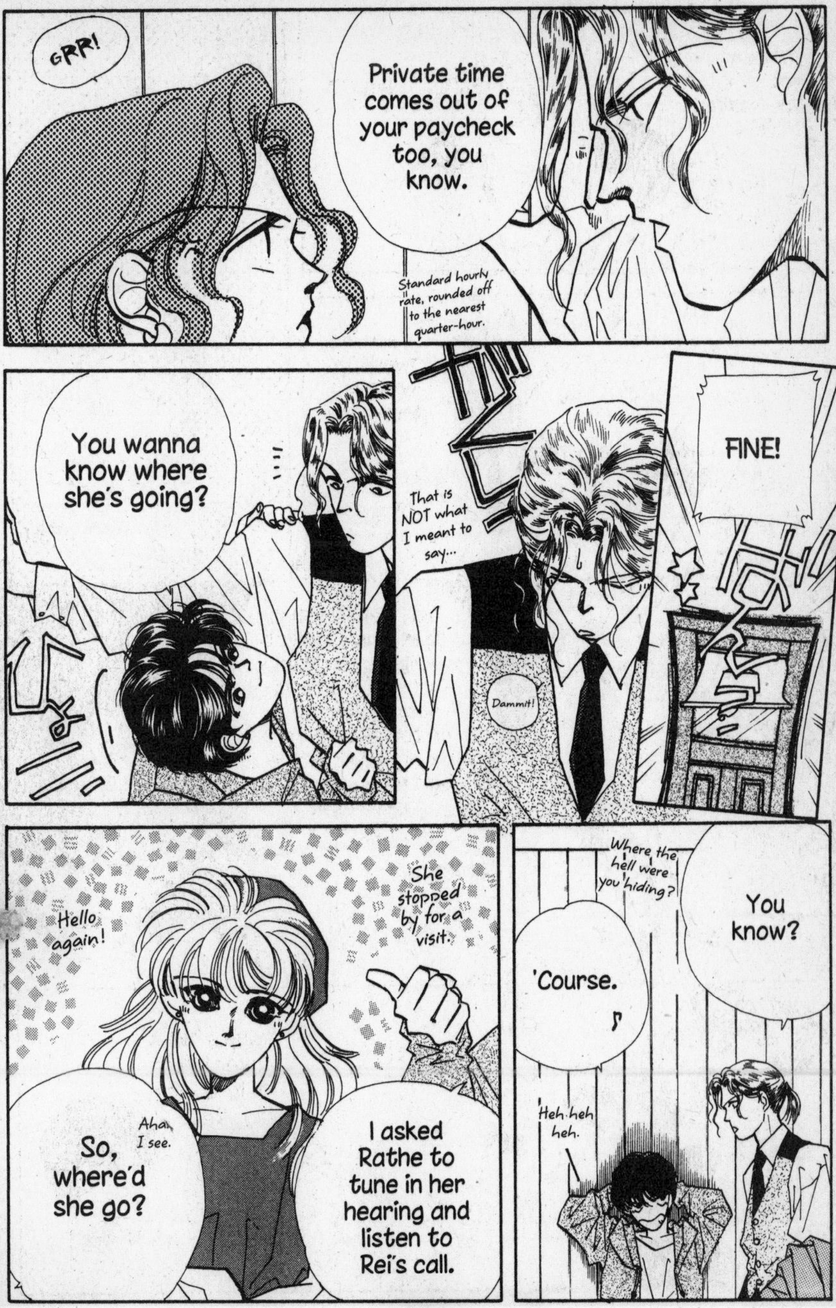
Private time comes out of your paycheck too, you know.
Standard hourly rate, rounded off to the nearest quarter-hour.
GRR!
FINE!
That is NOT what I meant to say...
Dammit!
You wanna know where she's going?
You know?
Where the hell were you hiding?
'Course.
Heh heh heh.
She stopped by for a visit.
Hello again!
I asked Rathe to tune in her hearing and listen to Rei's call.
Aha. I see.
So, where'd she go?

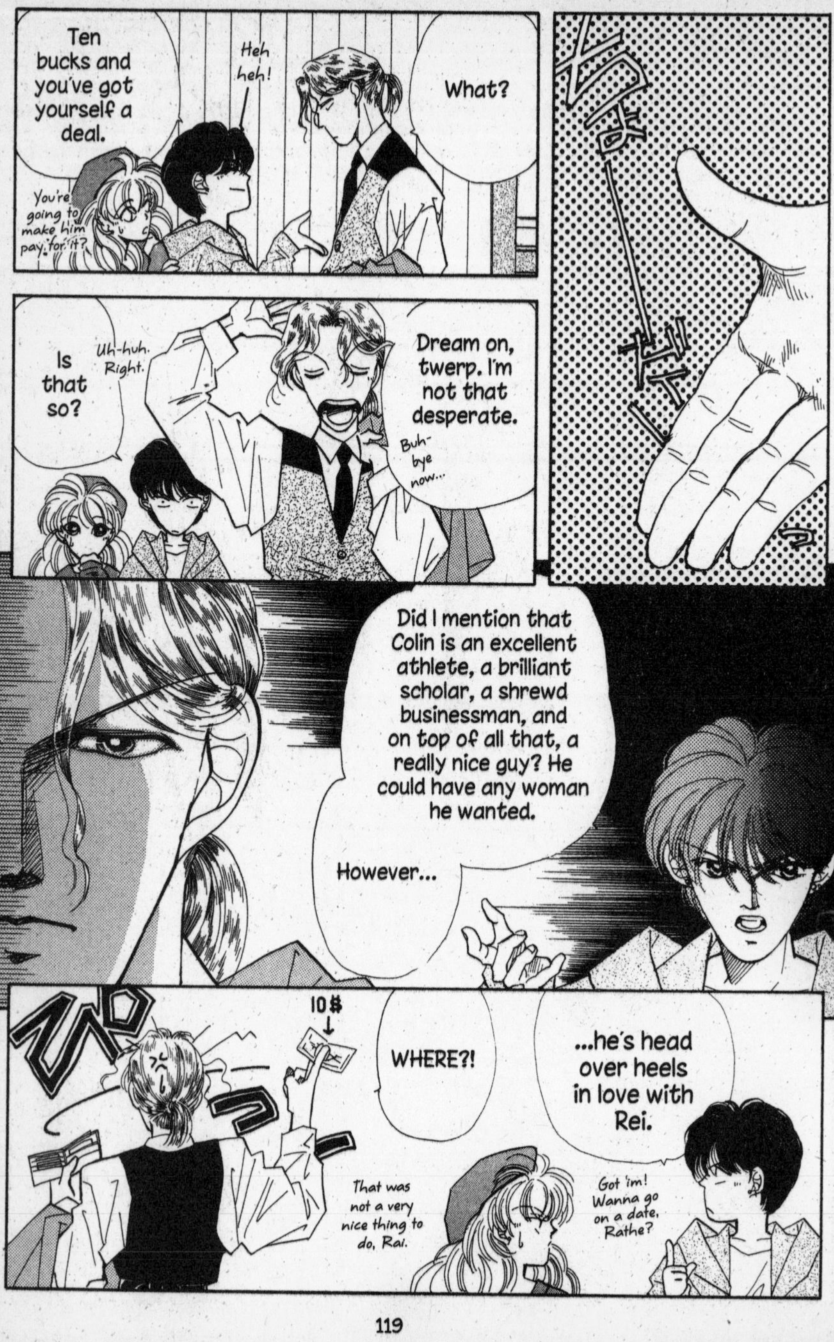
What?
Heh heh!
Ten bucks and you've got yourself a deal.
You're going to make him pay for it?
Dream on, twerp. I'm not that desperate.
Buh-bye now...
Uh-huh. Right.
Is that so?
Did I mention that Colin is an excellent athlete, a brilliant scholar, a shrewd businessman, and on top of all that, a really nice guy? He could have any woman he wanted.
However...
...he's head over heels in love with Rei.
Got 'im! Wanna go on a date, Rathe?
WHERE?!
10$
That was not a very nice thing to do, Rai.

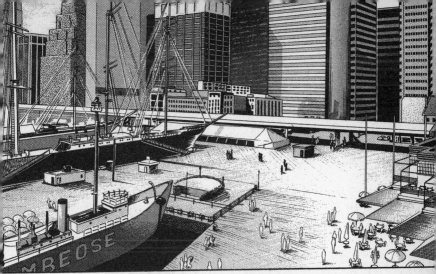

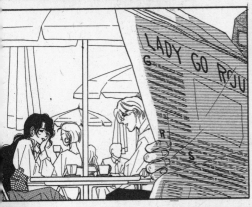

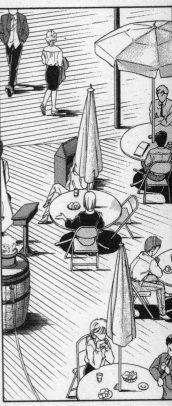

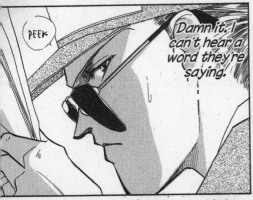

PEEK

Damn it. I can't hear a word they're saying.

Not at all suspicious, eh...?

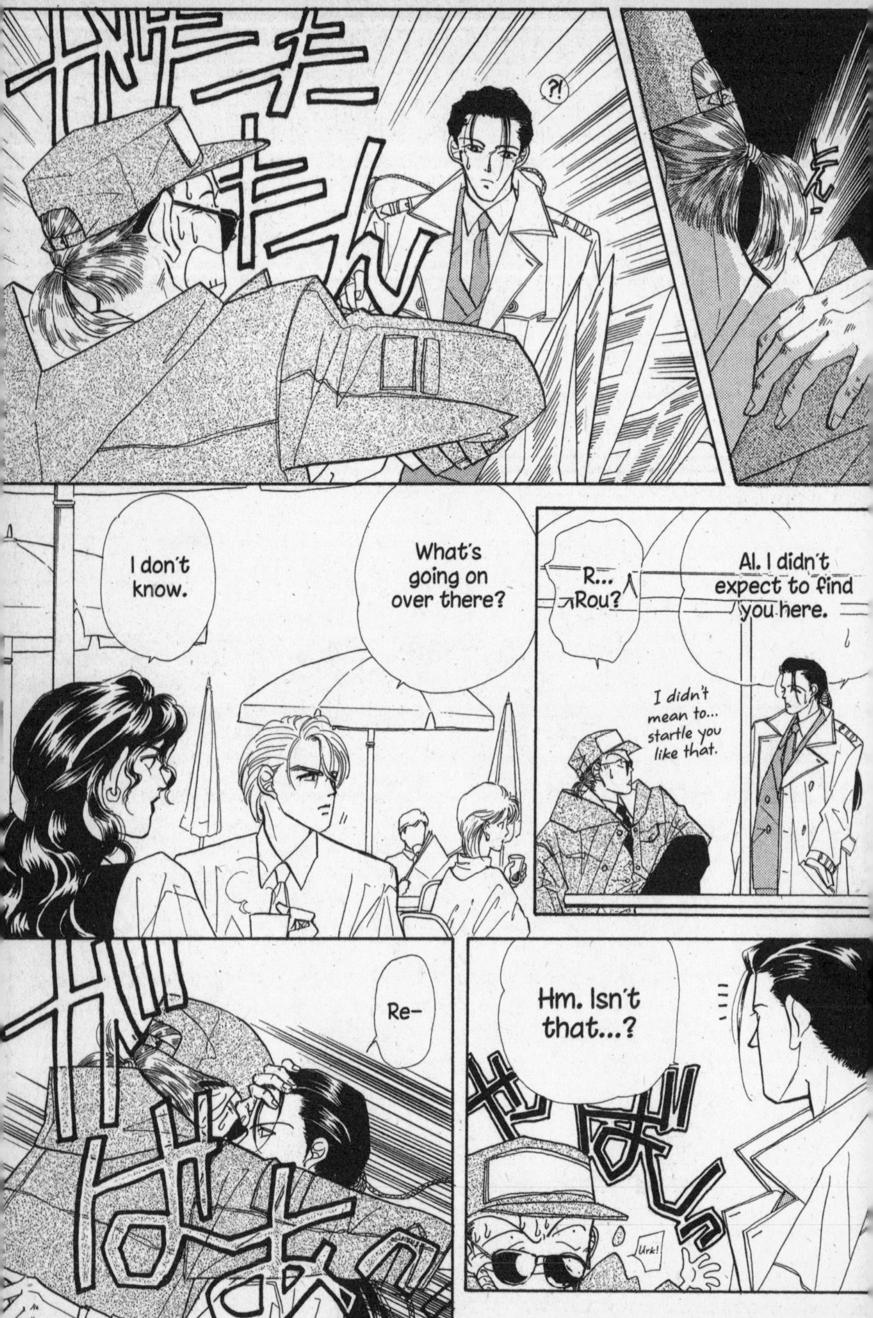

?!
Al. I didn't expect to find you here.
R... Rou?
I didn't mean to... startle you like that.
What's going on over there?
I don't know.
Hm. Isn't that...?
Urk!
Re-

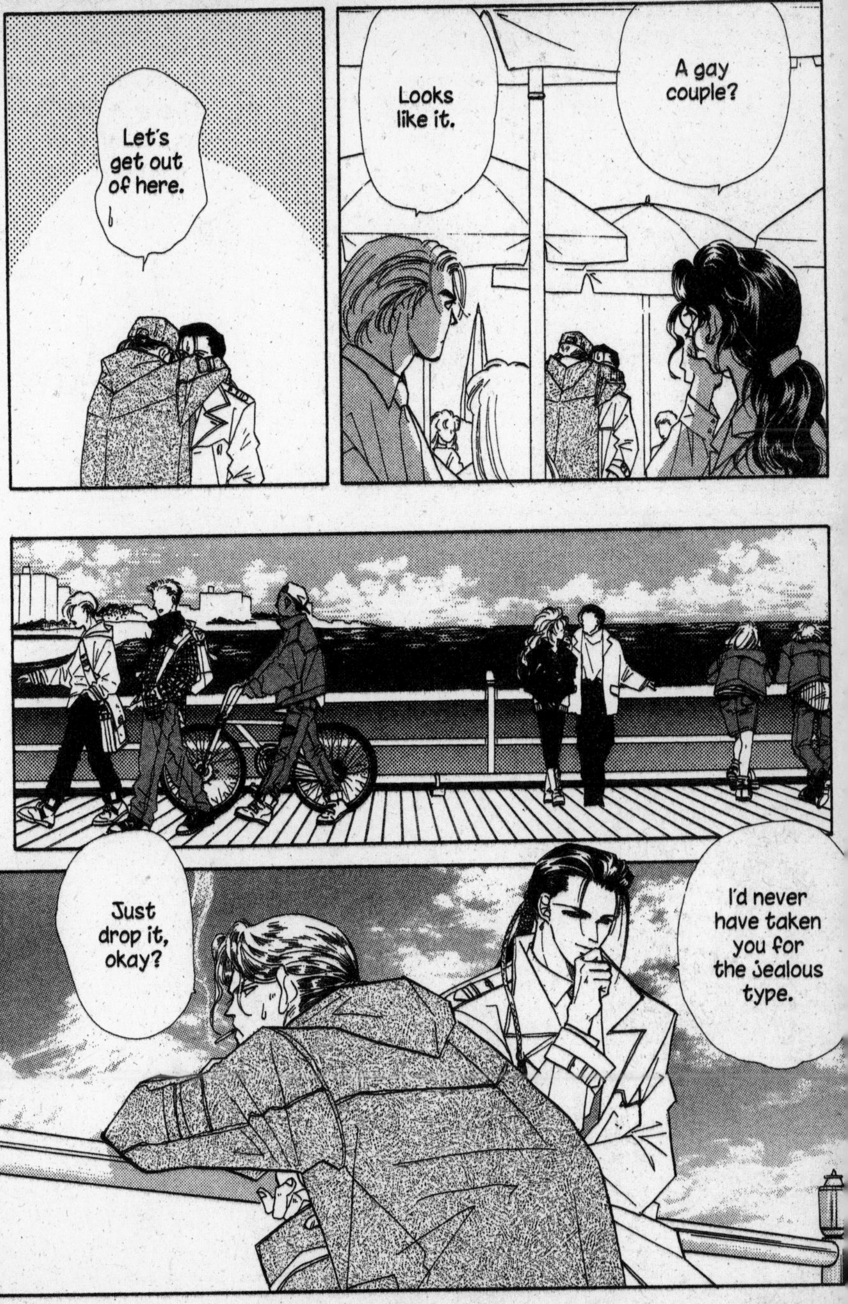
A gay couple?
Looks like it.
Let's get out of here.
I'd never have taken you for the jealous type.
Just drop it, okay?

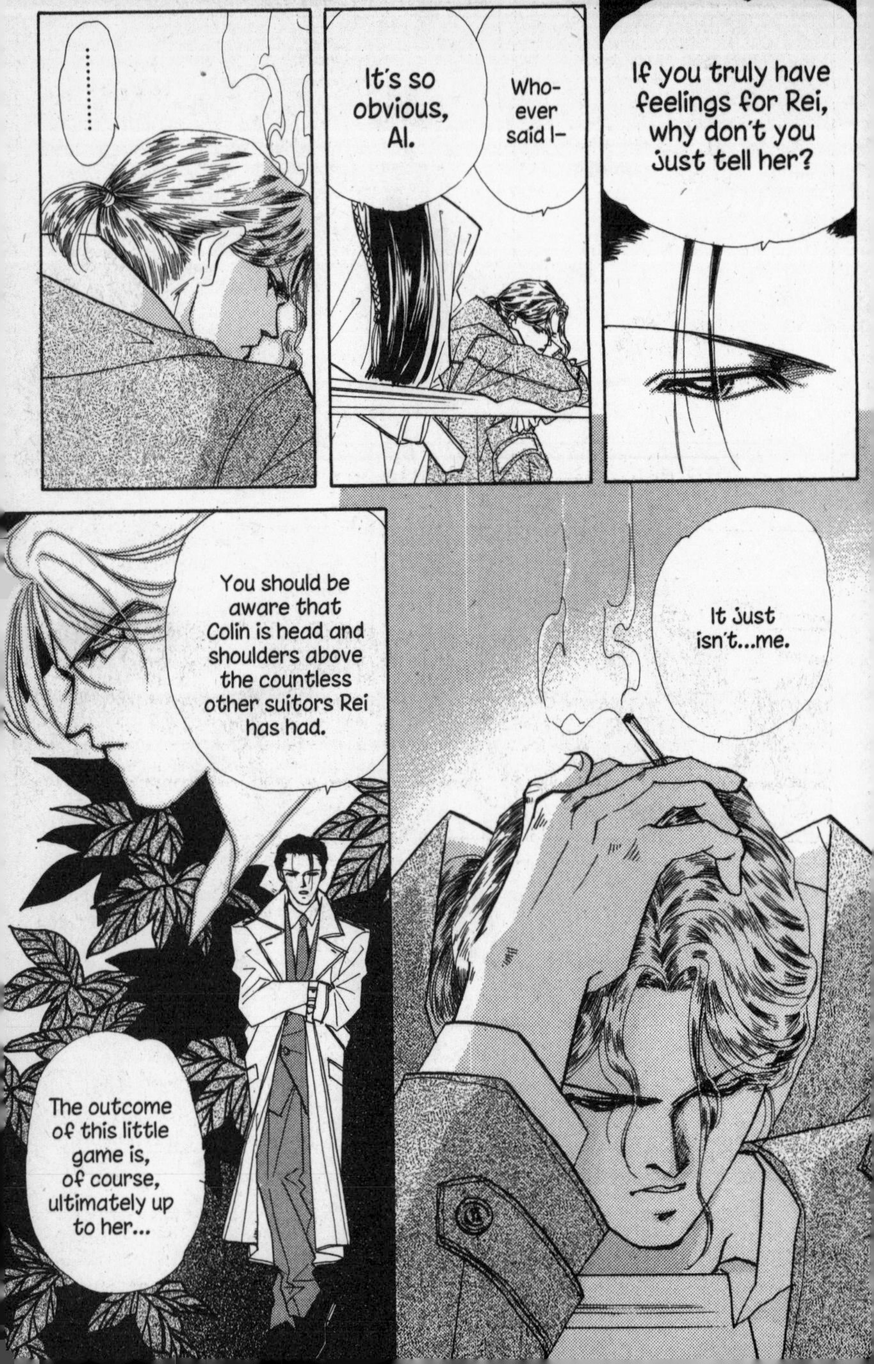
If you truly have feelings for Rei, why don't you just tell her?
Who-ever said I-
It's so obvious, Al.
....
It just isn't...me.
You should be aware that Colin is head and shoulders above the countless other suitors Rei has had.
The outcome of this little game is, of course, ultimately up to her...

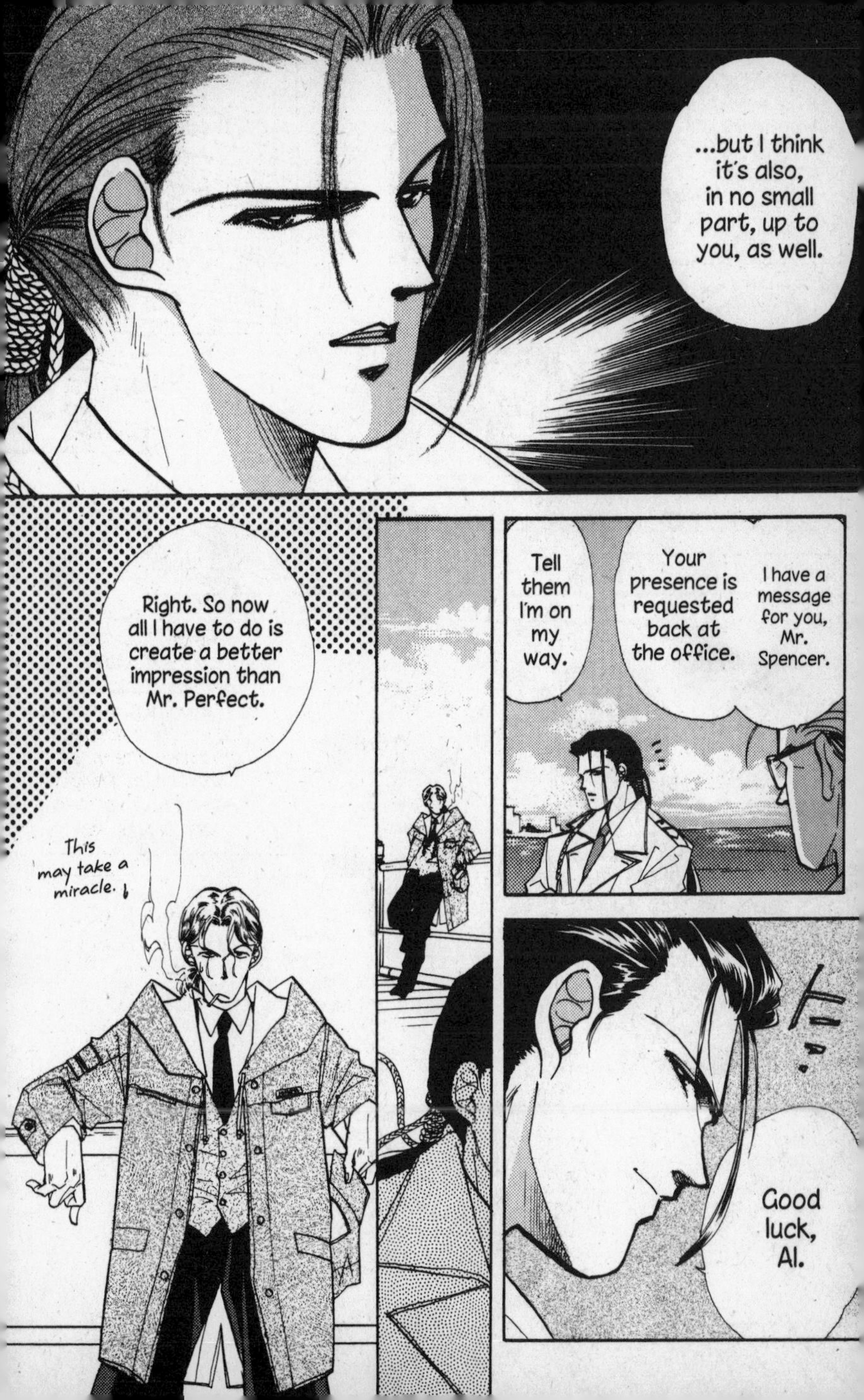
...but I think it's also, in no small part, up to you, as well.
I have a message for you, Mr. Spencer.
Your presence is requested back at the office.
Tell them I'm on my way.
Good luck, Al.
Right. So now all I have to do is create a better impression than Mr. Perfect.
This may take a miracle.

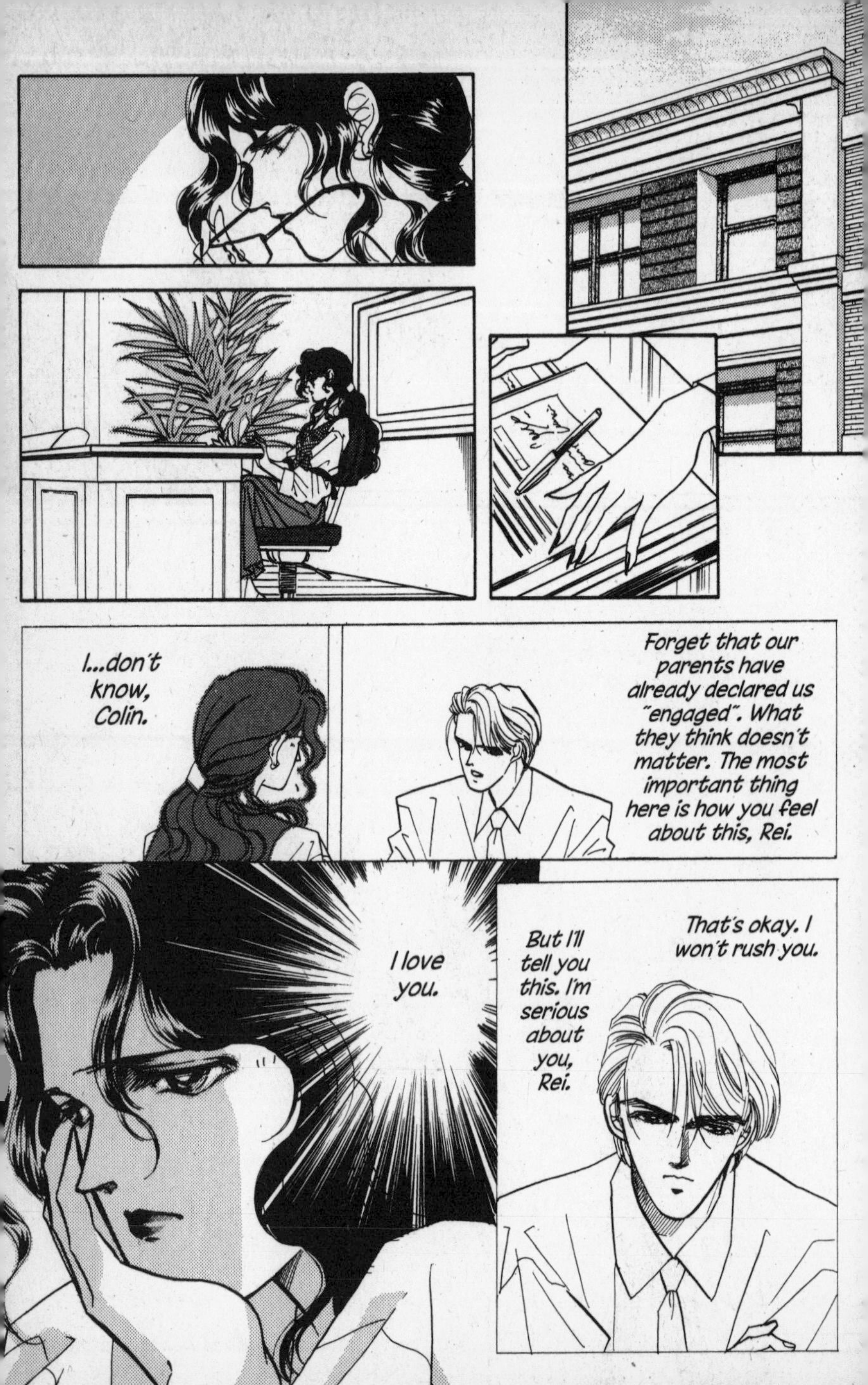
Forget that our parents have already declared us "engaged". What they think doesn't matter. The most important thing here is how you feel about this, Rei.
I...don't know, Colin.
That's okay. I won't rush you.
But I'll tell you this. I'm serious about you, Rei.
I love you.

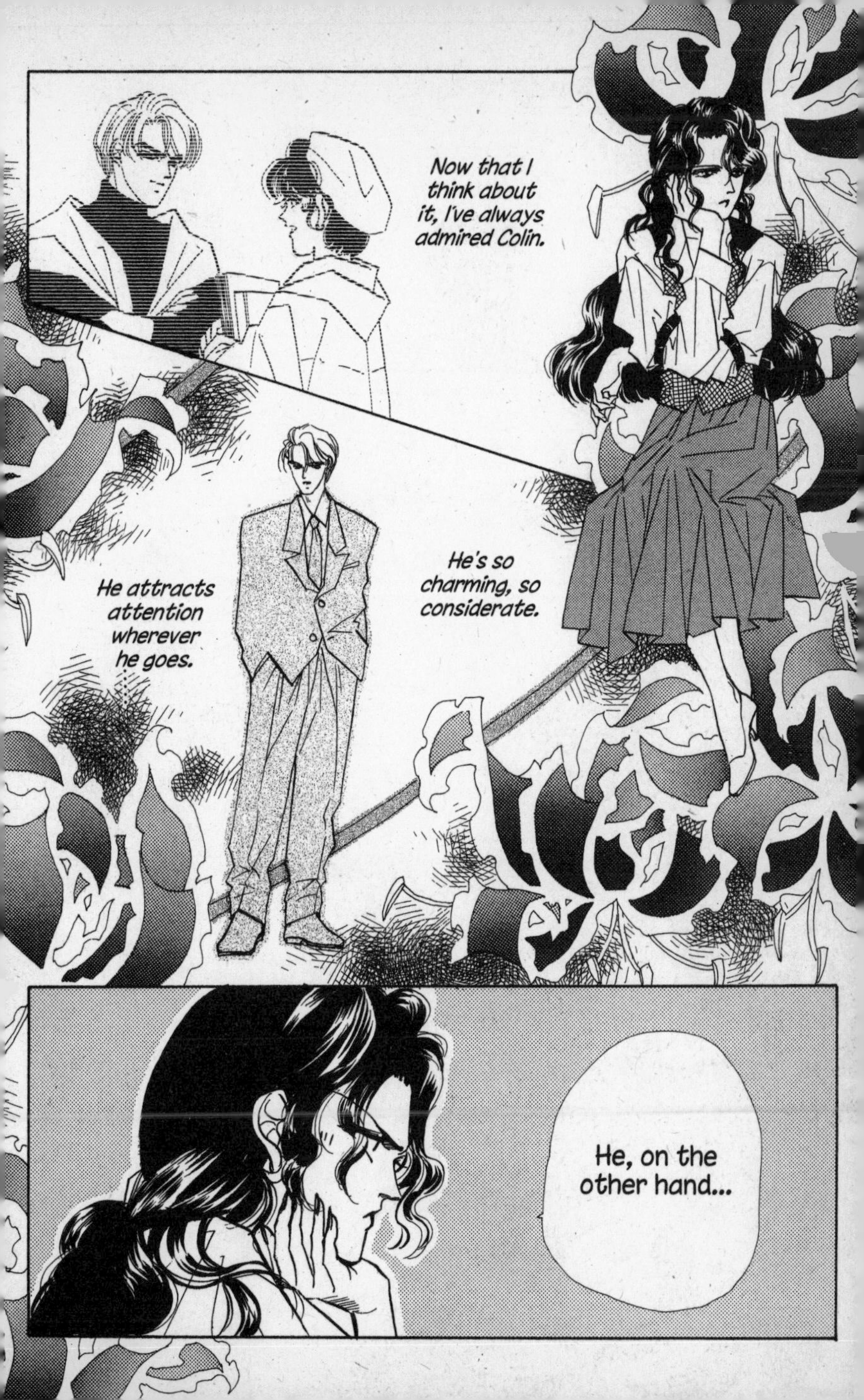
Now that I think about it, I've always admired Colin.
He's so charming, so considerate.
He attracts attention wherever he goes.
He, on the other hand...

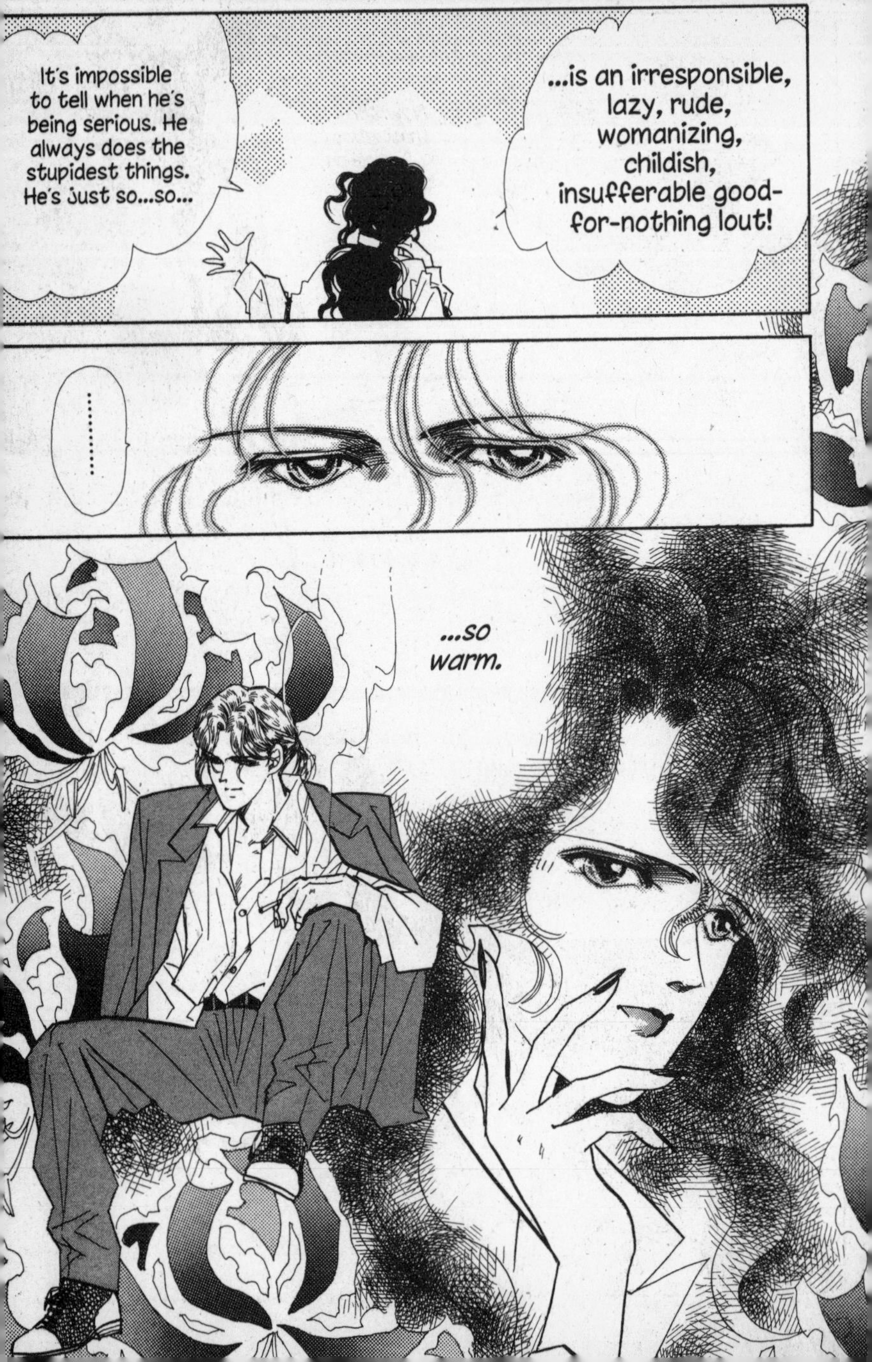
...is an irresponsible, lazy, rude, womanizing, childish, insufferable good-for-nothing lout!
It's impossible to tell when he's being serious. He always does the stupidest things. He's just so...so...
....
...so warm.

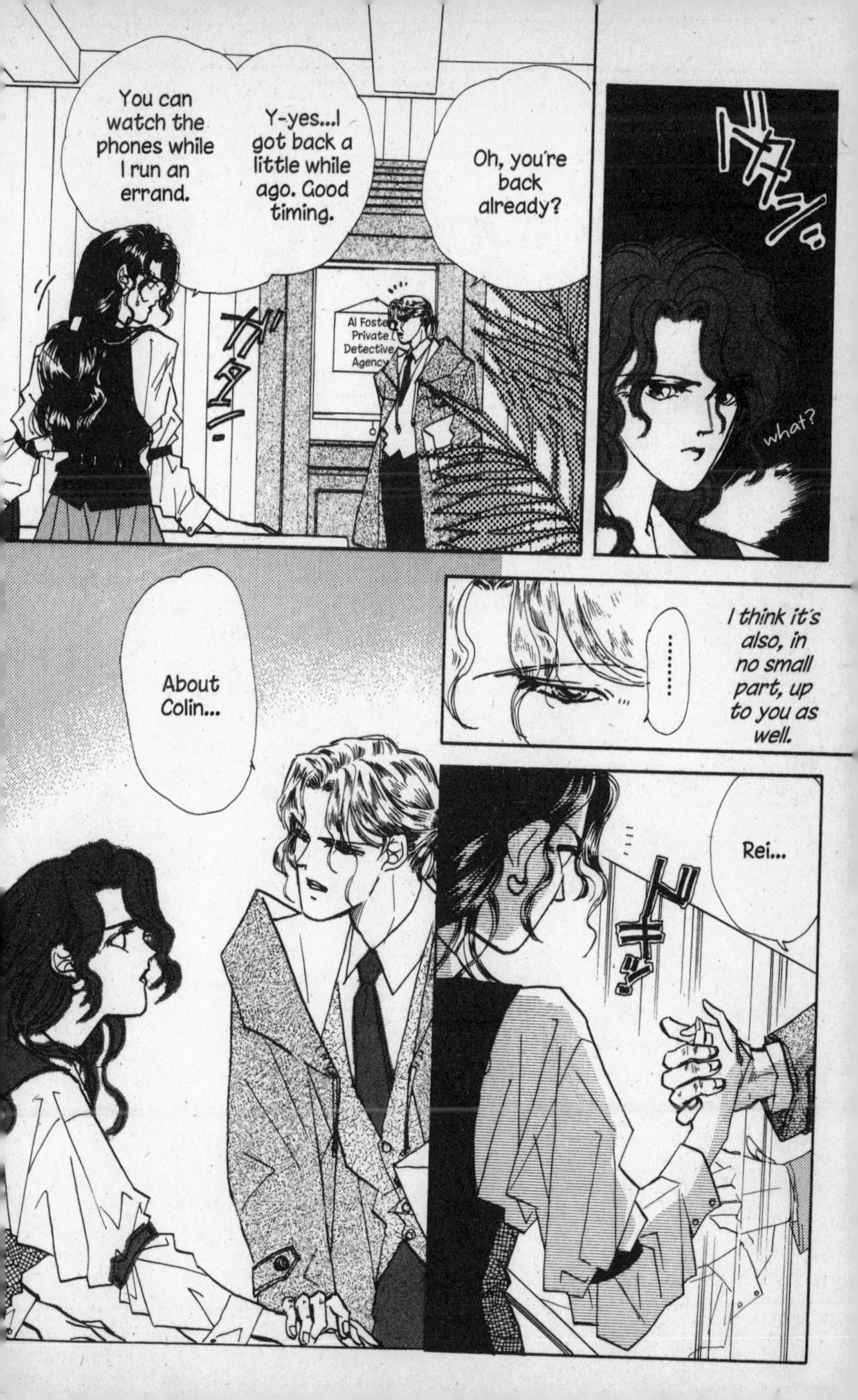
what?
Oh, you're back already?
Y-yes...I got back a little while ago. Good timing.
You can watch the phones while I run an errand.
Al Foste
Private
Detective
Agency
....
I think it's also, in no small part, up to you as well.
Rei...
About Colin...

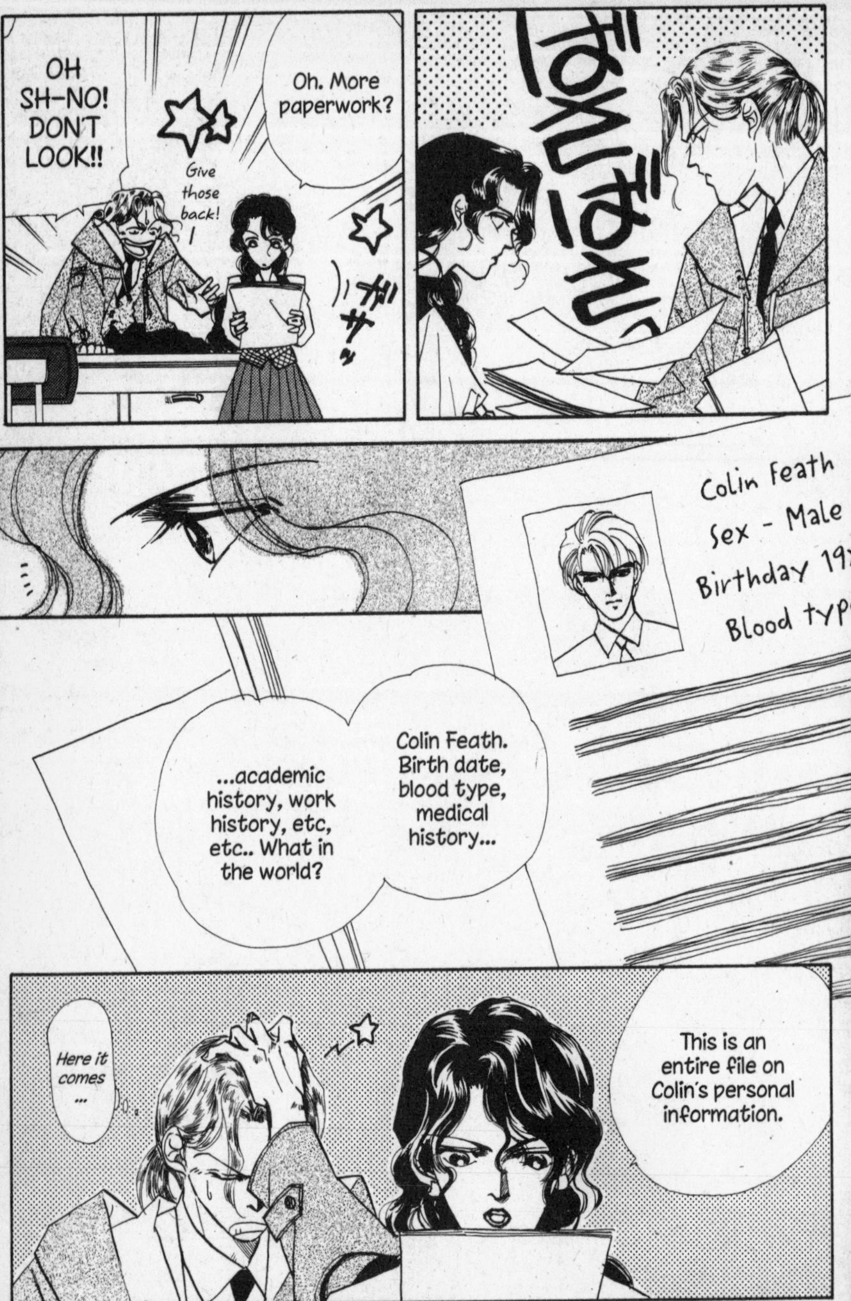
ばさばさっ
Oh. More paperwork?
OH SH-NO! DON'T LOOK!!
Give those back!
ガサッ
Colin Feath
Sex - Male
Birthday 19
Blood typ
Colin Feath. Birth date, blood type, medical history...
...academic history, work history, etc, etc.. What in the world?
This is an entire file on Colin's personal information.
Here it comes ...

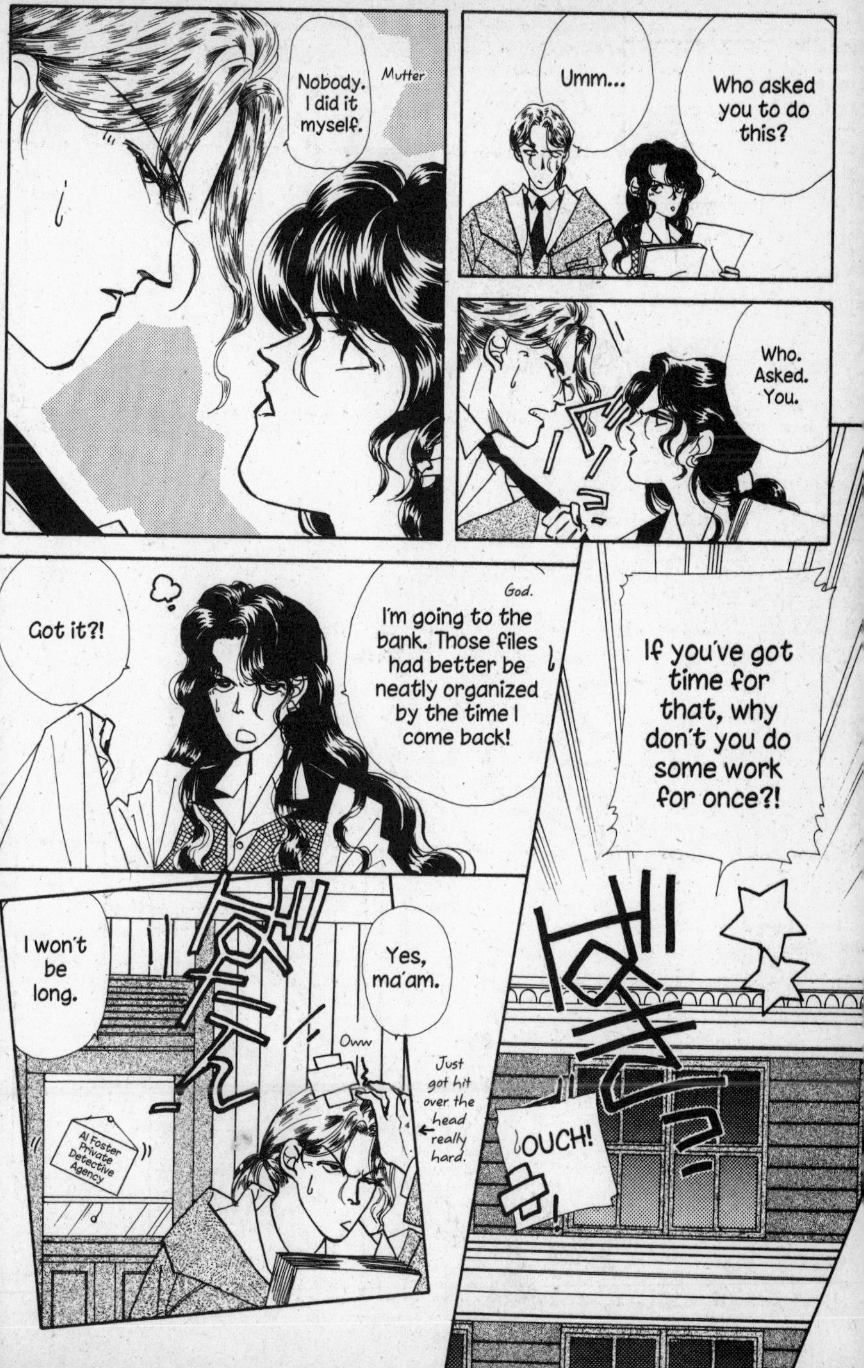
Who asked you to do this?
Umm...
Who. Asked. You.
Mutter
Nobody. I did it myself.
If you've got time for that, why don't you do some work for once?!
OUCH!
God.
I'm going to the bank. Those files had better be neatly organized by the time I come back!
Got it?!
Yes, ma'am.
I won't be long.
Oww
Just got hit over the head really hard.
Al Foster Private Detective Agency

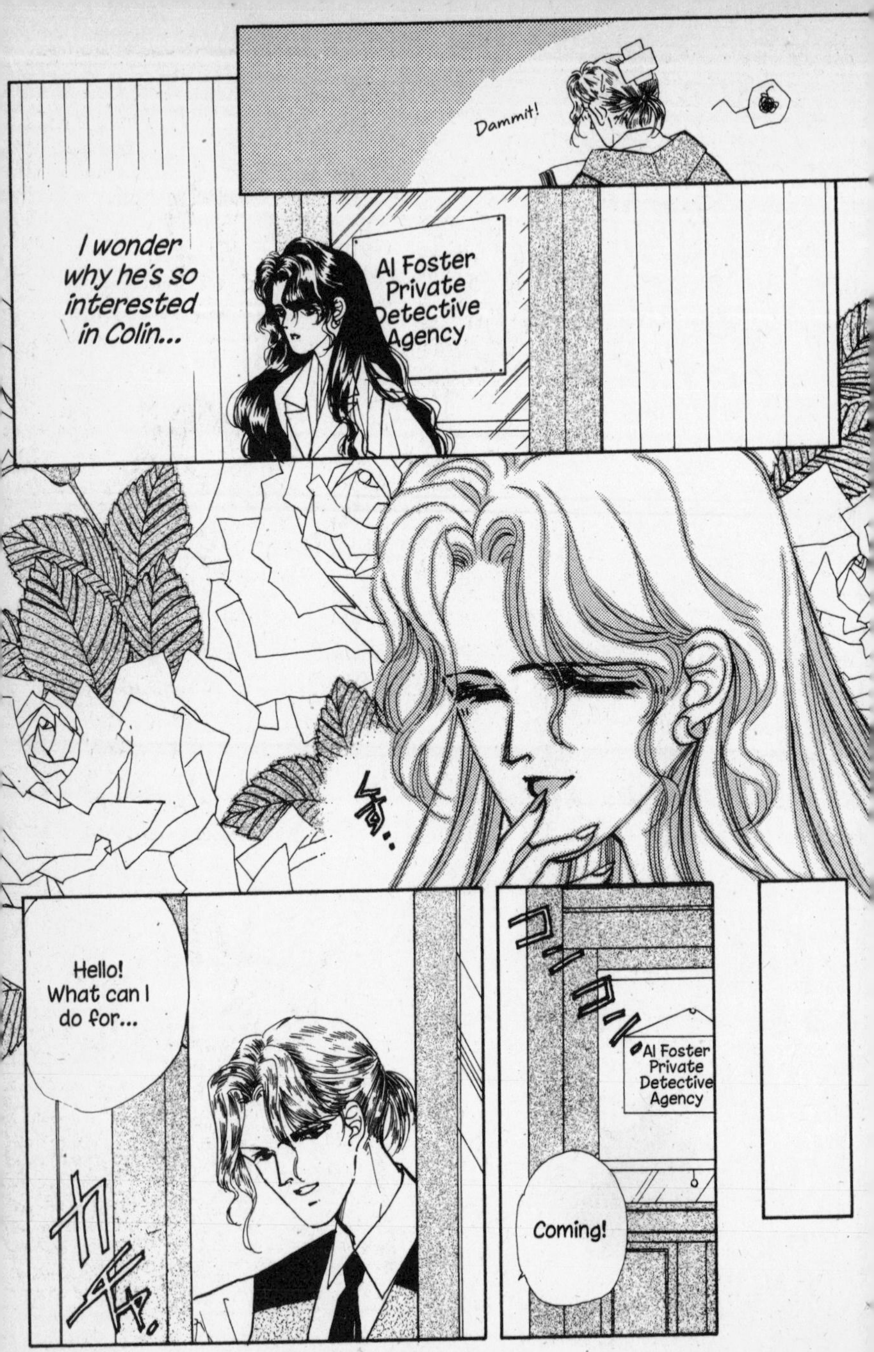
Dammit!
I wonder why he's so interested in Colin...
Al Foster Private Detective Agency
Al Foster Private Detective Agency
Coming!
Hello! What can I do for...

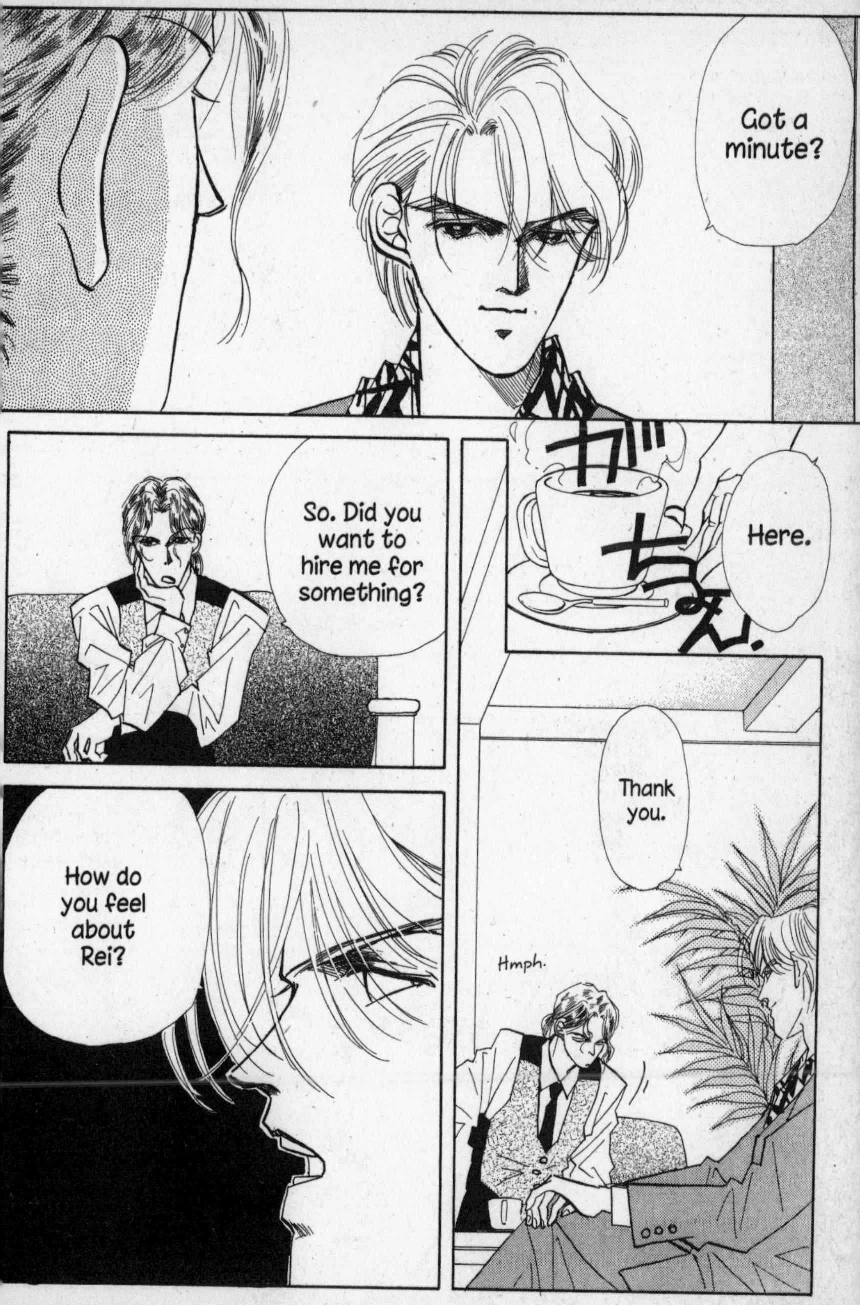

Got a minute?
がちゃん
Here.
Thank you.
Hmph.
So. Did you want to hire me for something?
How do you feel about Rei?

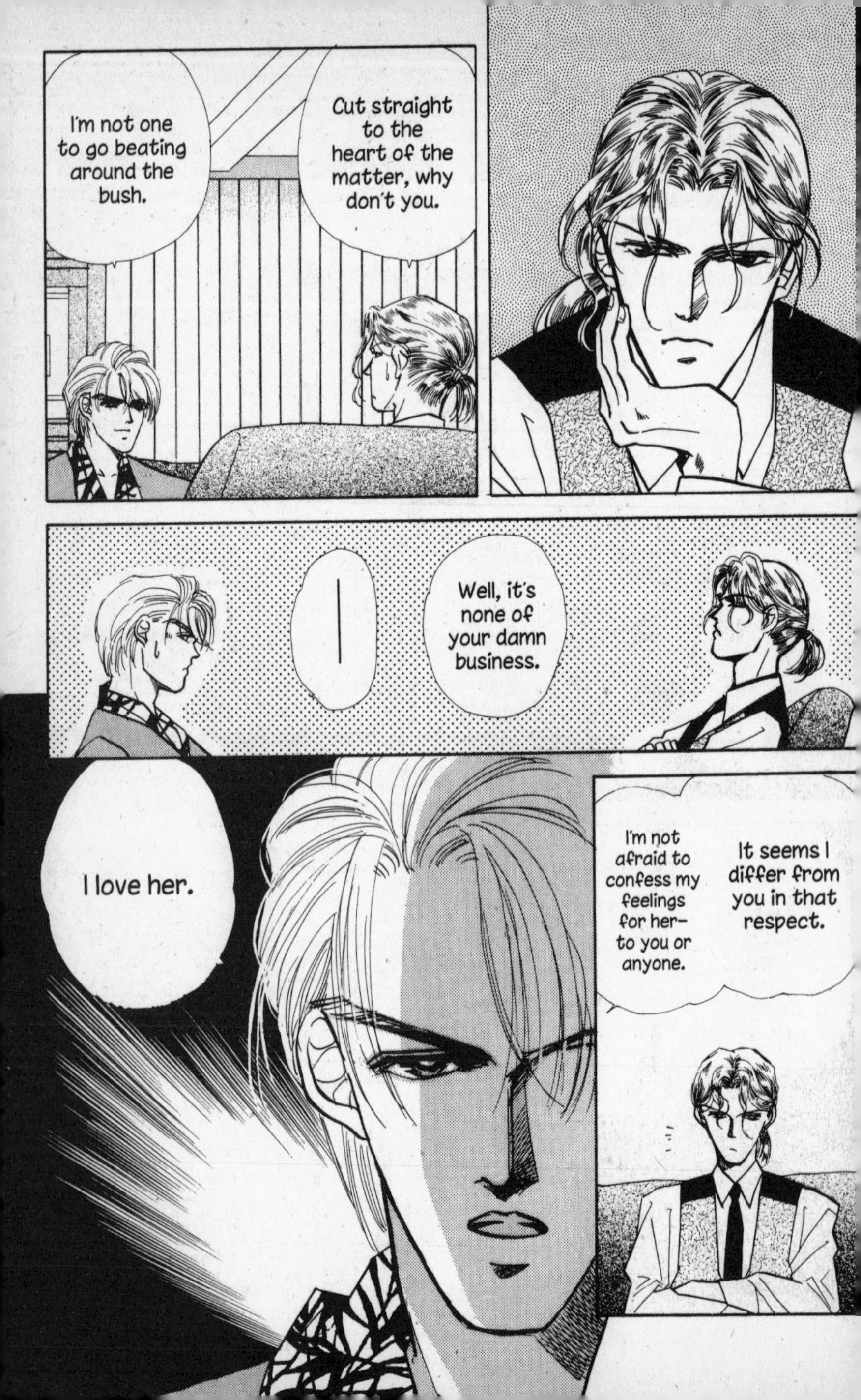
Cut straight to the heart of the matter, why don't you.
I'm not one to go beating around the bush.
Well, it's none of your damn business.
It seems I differ from you in that respect.
I'm not afraid to confess my feelings for her— to you or anyone.
I love her.

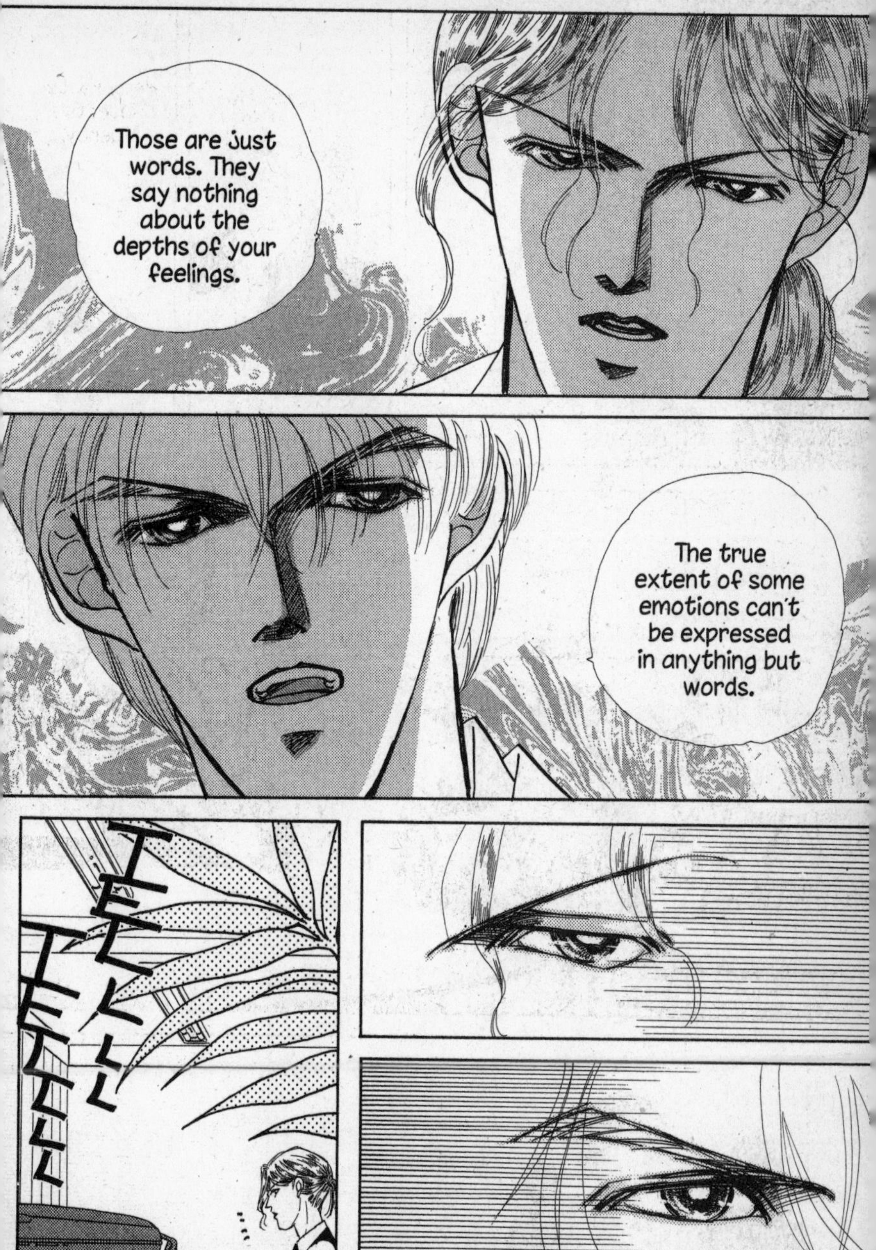

Those are just words. They say nothing about the depths of your feelings.
The true extent of some emotions can't be expressed in anything but words.

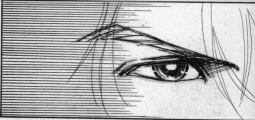

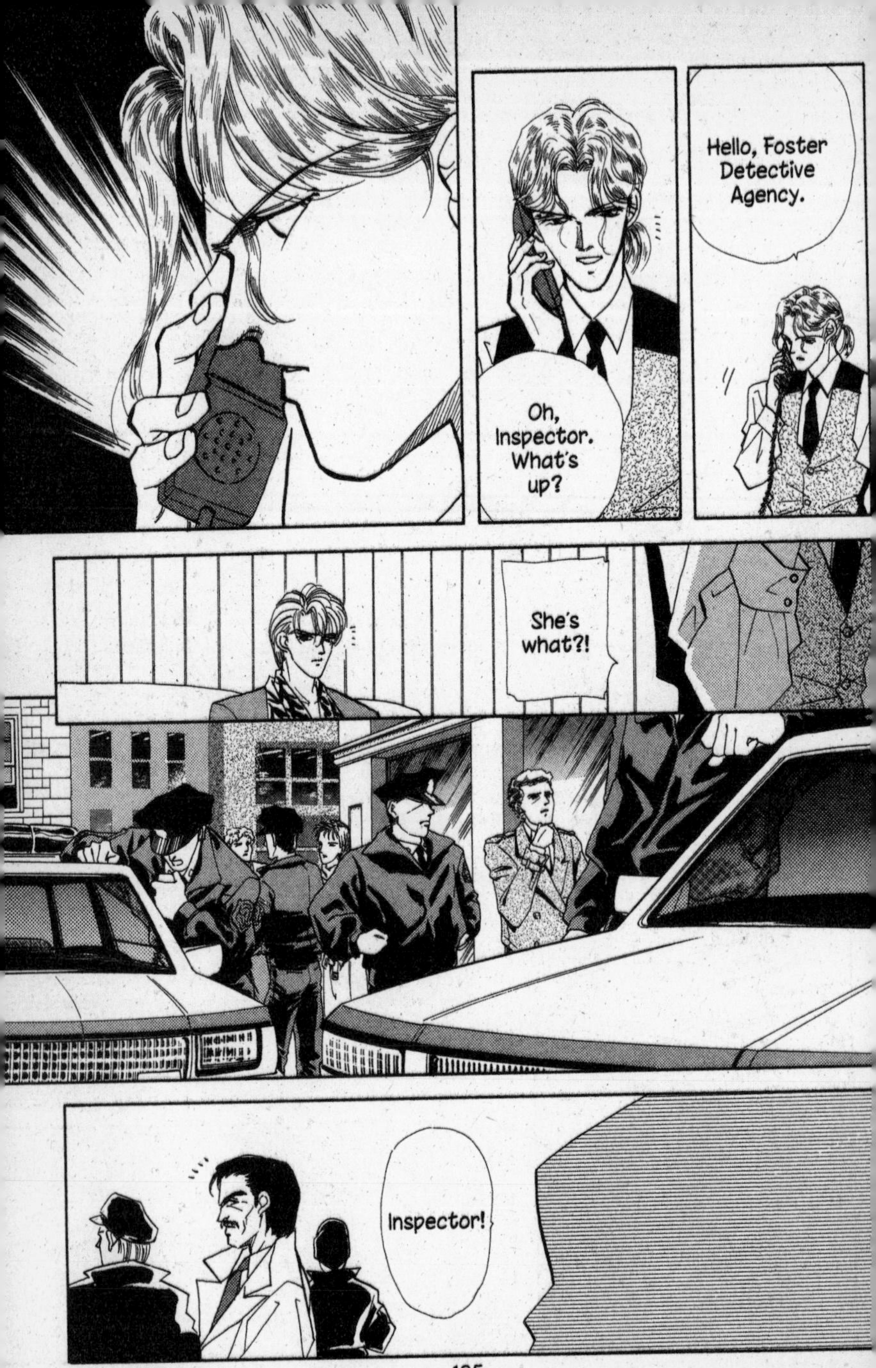
Hello, Foster Detective Agency.
Oh, Inspector. What's up?
She's what?!
Inspector!

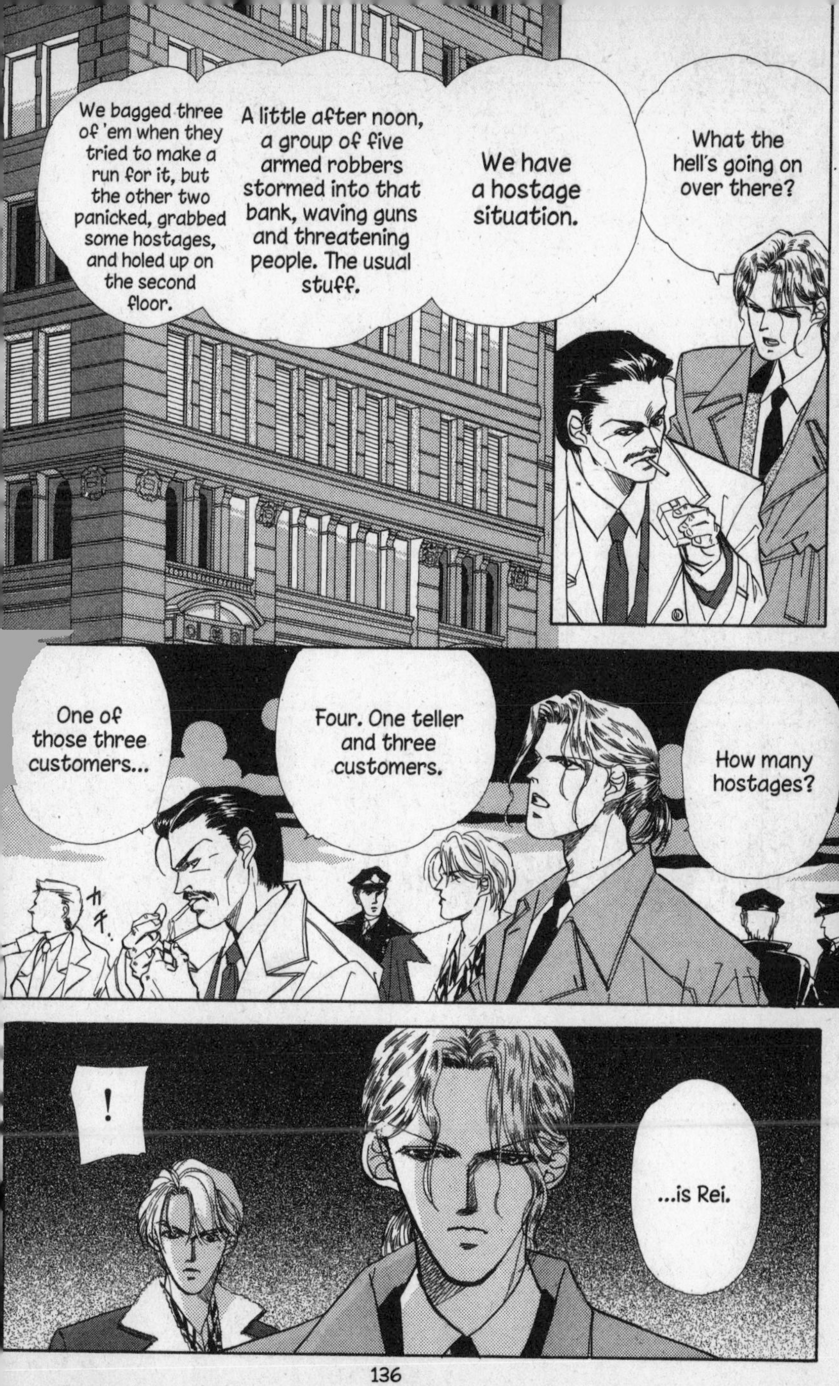
What the hell's going on over there?
We have a hostage situation.
A little after noon, a group of five armed robbers stormed into that bank, waving guns and threatening people. The usual stuff.
We bagged three of 'em when they tried to make a run for it, but the other two panicked, grabbed some hostages, and holed up on the second floor.
How many hostages?
Four. One teller and three customers.
One of those three customers...
カチ..
...is Rei.
!

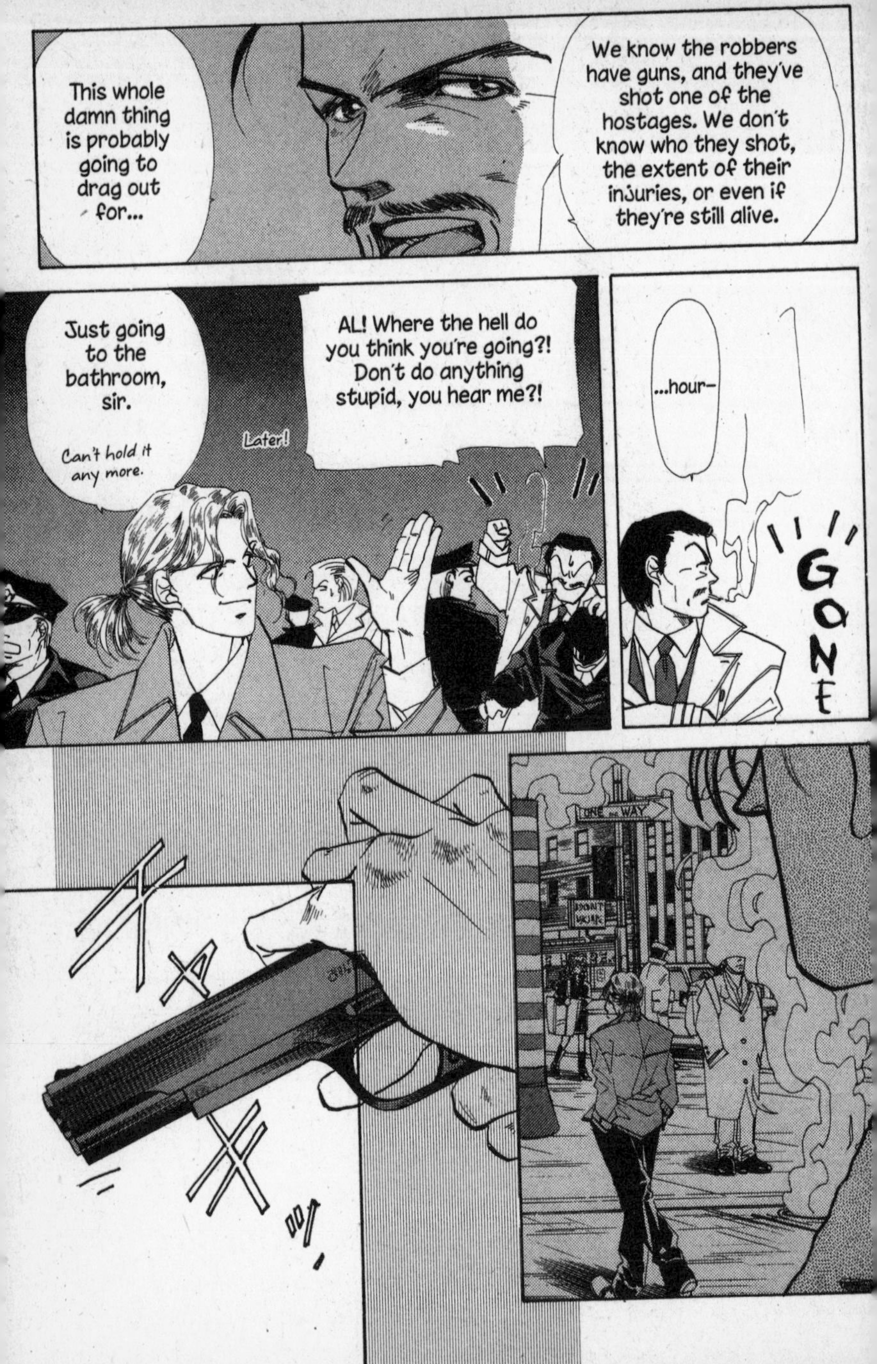

We know the robbers have guns, and they've shot one of the hostages. We don't know who they shot, the extent of their injuries, or even if they're still alive.
This whole damn thing is probably going to drag out for...
...hour-
GONE
AL! Where the hell do you think you're going?! Don't do anything stupid, you hear me?!
Later!
Just going to the bathroom, sir.
Can't hold it any more.
ONE WAY

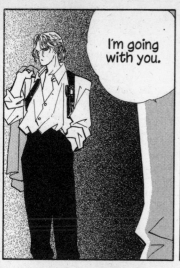

I'm going with you.

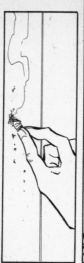

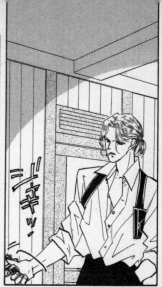

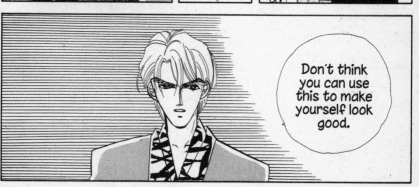

Don't think you can use this to make yourself look good.

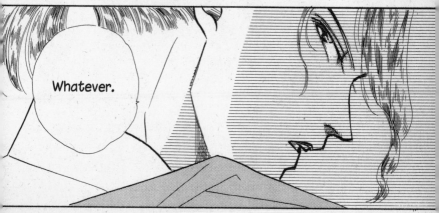

Whatever.

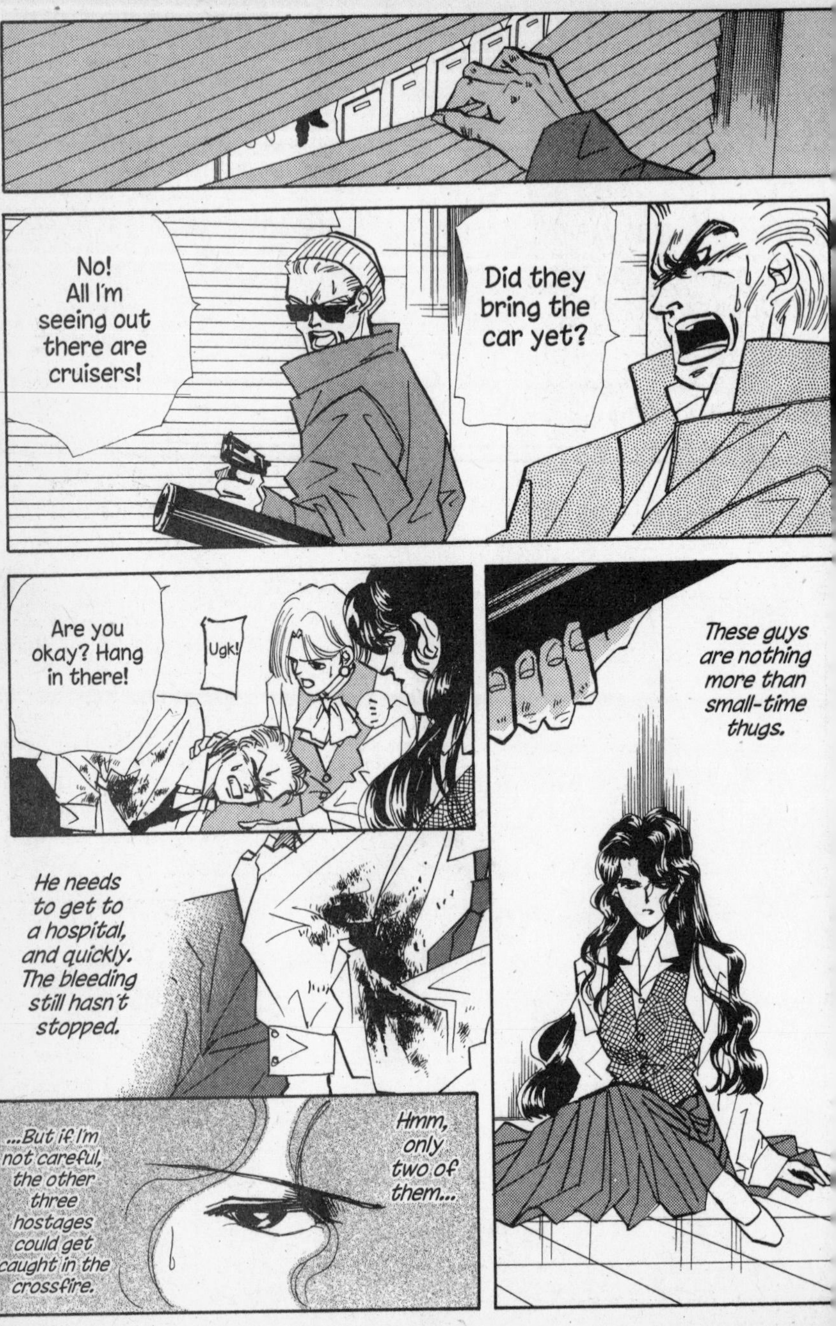
Did they bring the car yet?
No! All I'm seeing out there are cruisers!
These guys are nothing more than small-time thugs.
Are you okay? Hang in there!
Ugk!
He needs to get to a hospital, and quickly. The bleeding still hasn't stopped.
Hmm, only two of them...
...But if I'm not careful, the other three hostages could get caught in the crossfire.

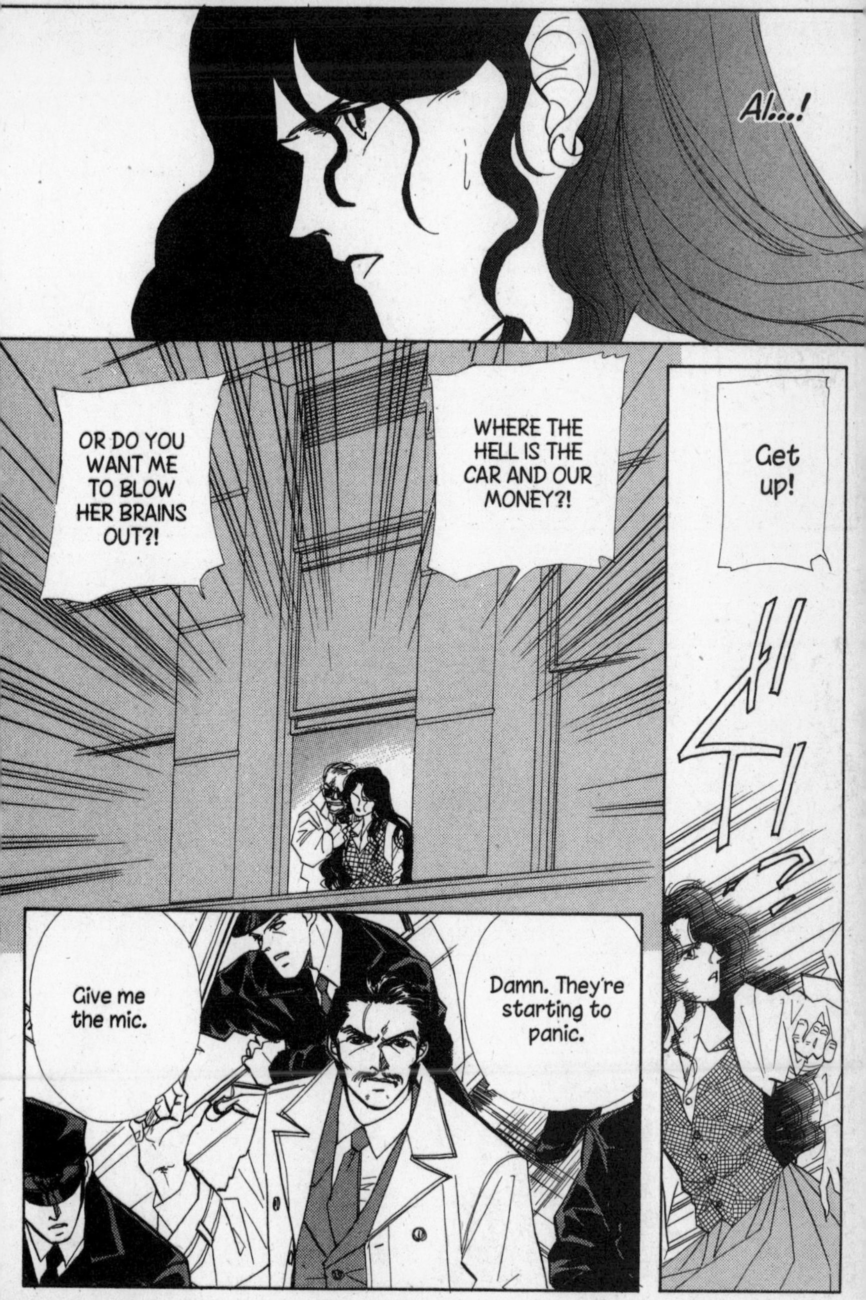
Al...!
Get up!
WHERE THE HELL IS THE CAR AND OUR MONEY?!
OR DO YOU WANT ME TO BLOW HER BRAINS OUT?!
Damn. They're starting to panic.
Give me the mic.

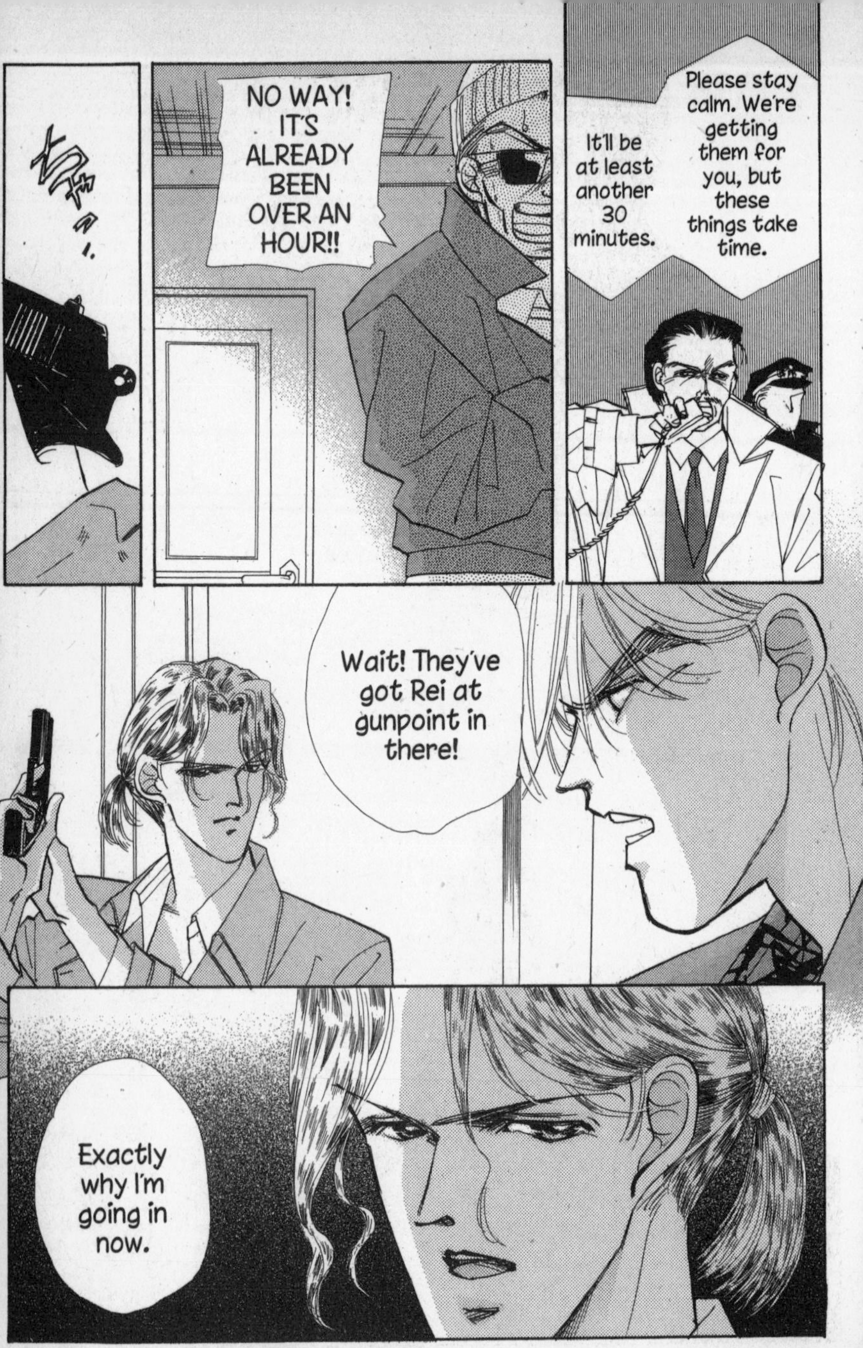
Please stay calm. We're getting them for you, but these things take time.
It'll be at least another 30 minutes.
NO WAY! IT'S ALREADY BEEN OVER AN HOUR!!
Wait! They've got Rei at gunpoint in there!
Exactly why I'm going in now.

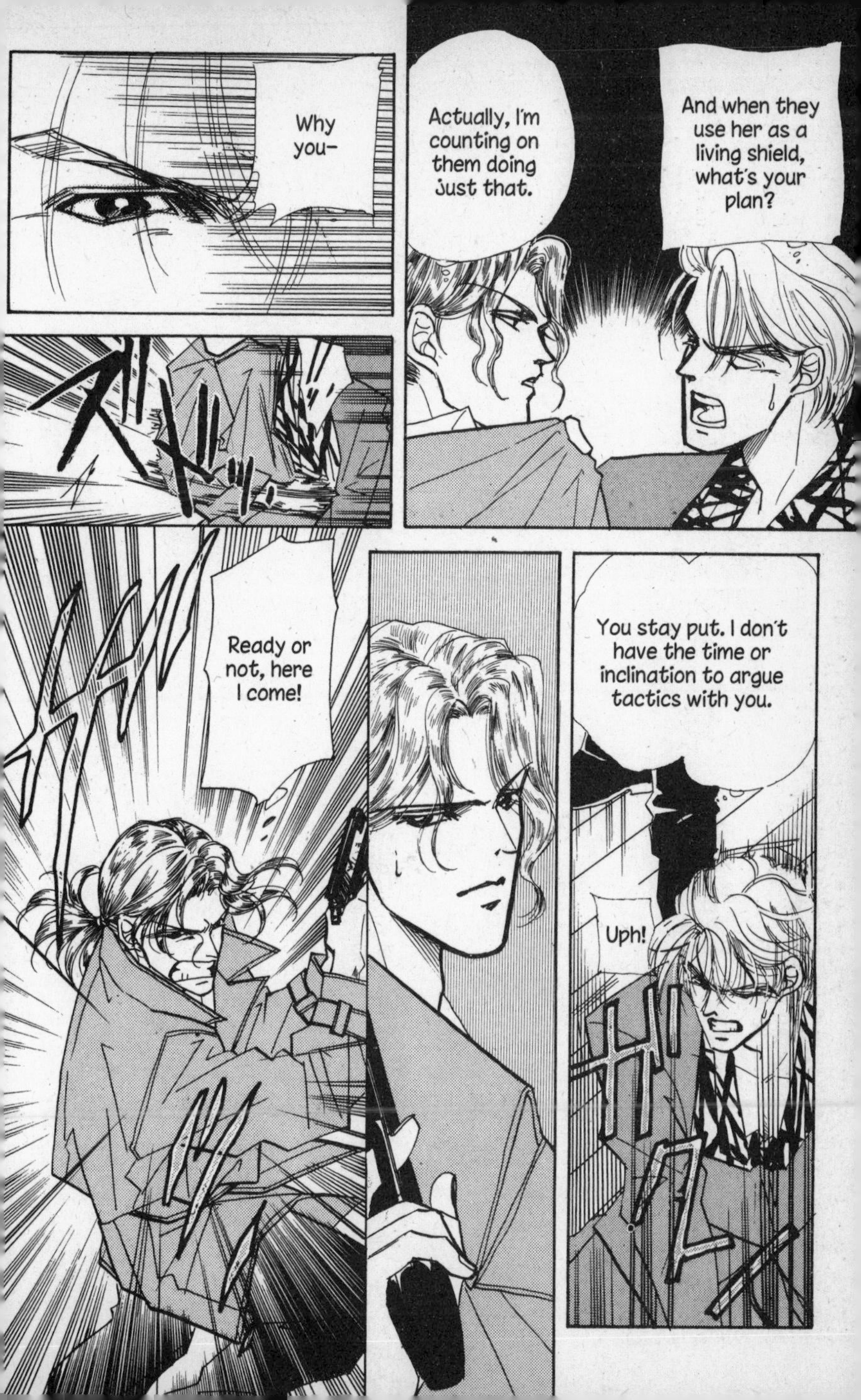
And when they use her as a living shield, what's your plan?
Actually, I'm counting on them doing just that.
Why you-
You stay put. I don't have the time or inclination to argue tactics with you.
Uph!
Ready or not, here I come!

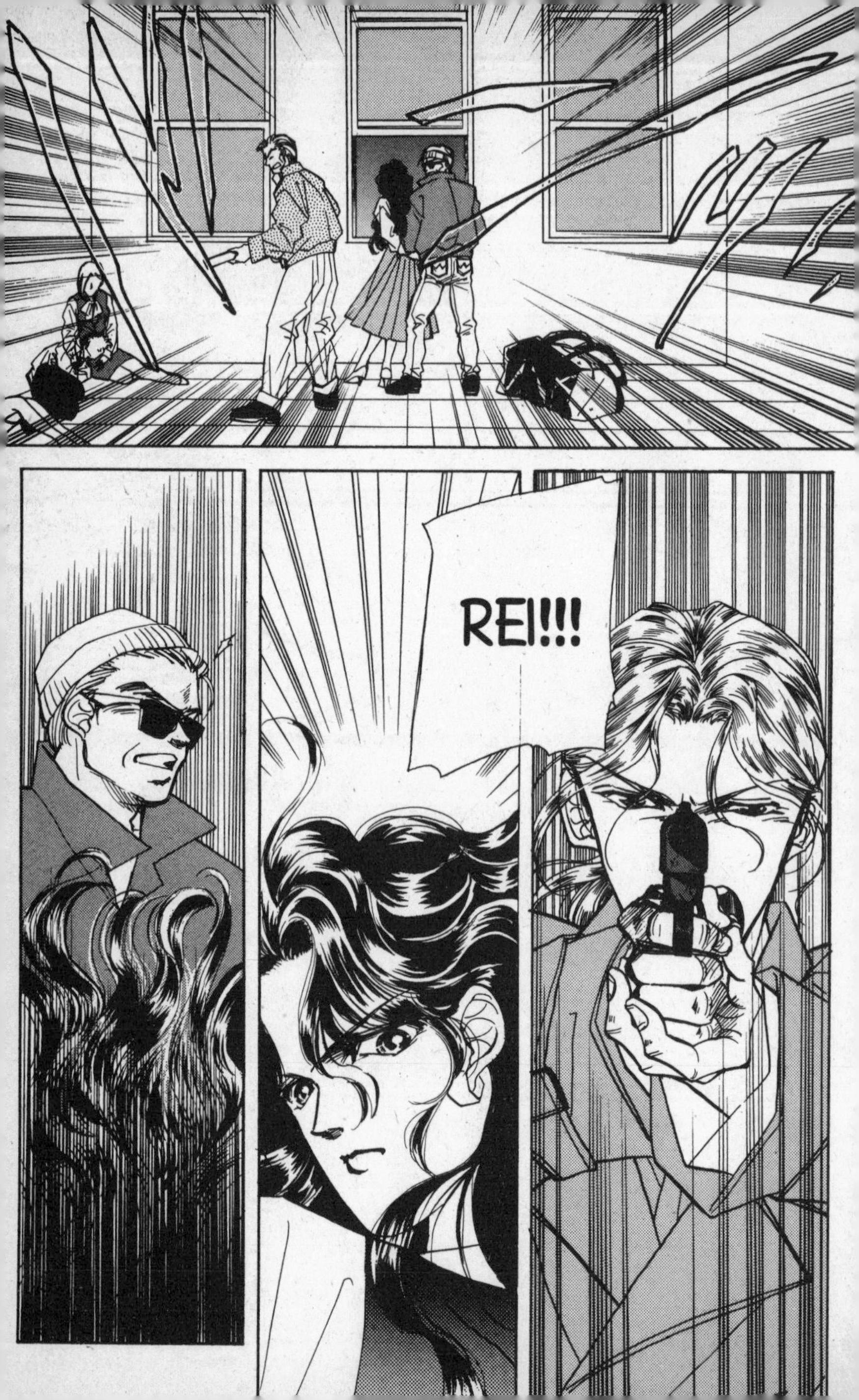
REI!!!

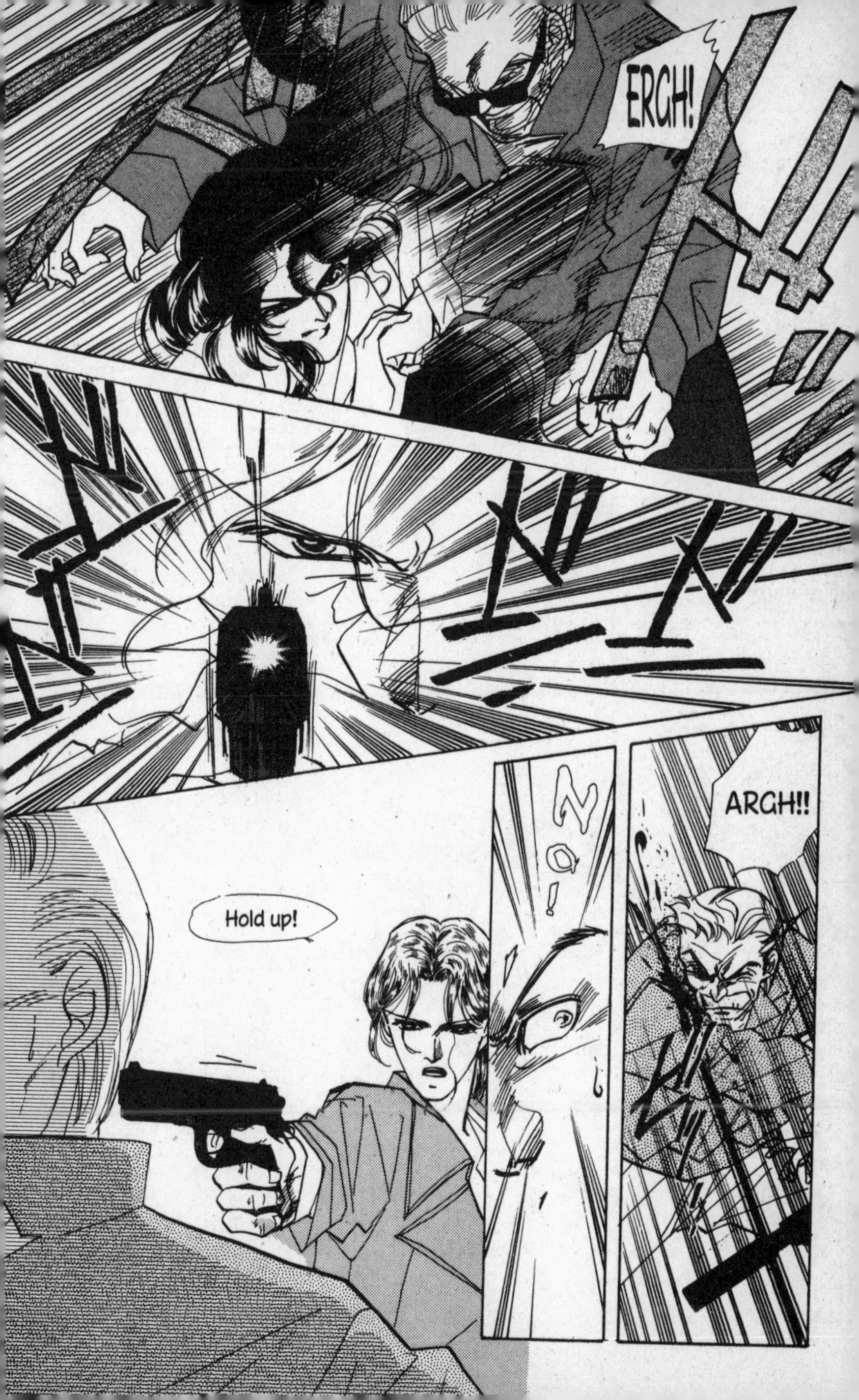
ERGH!
ARGH!!
Hold up!

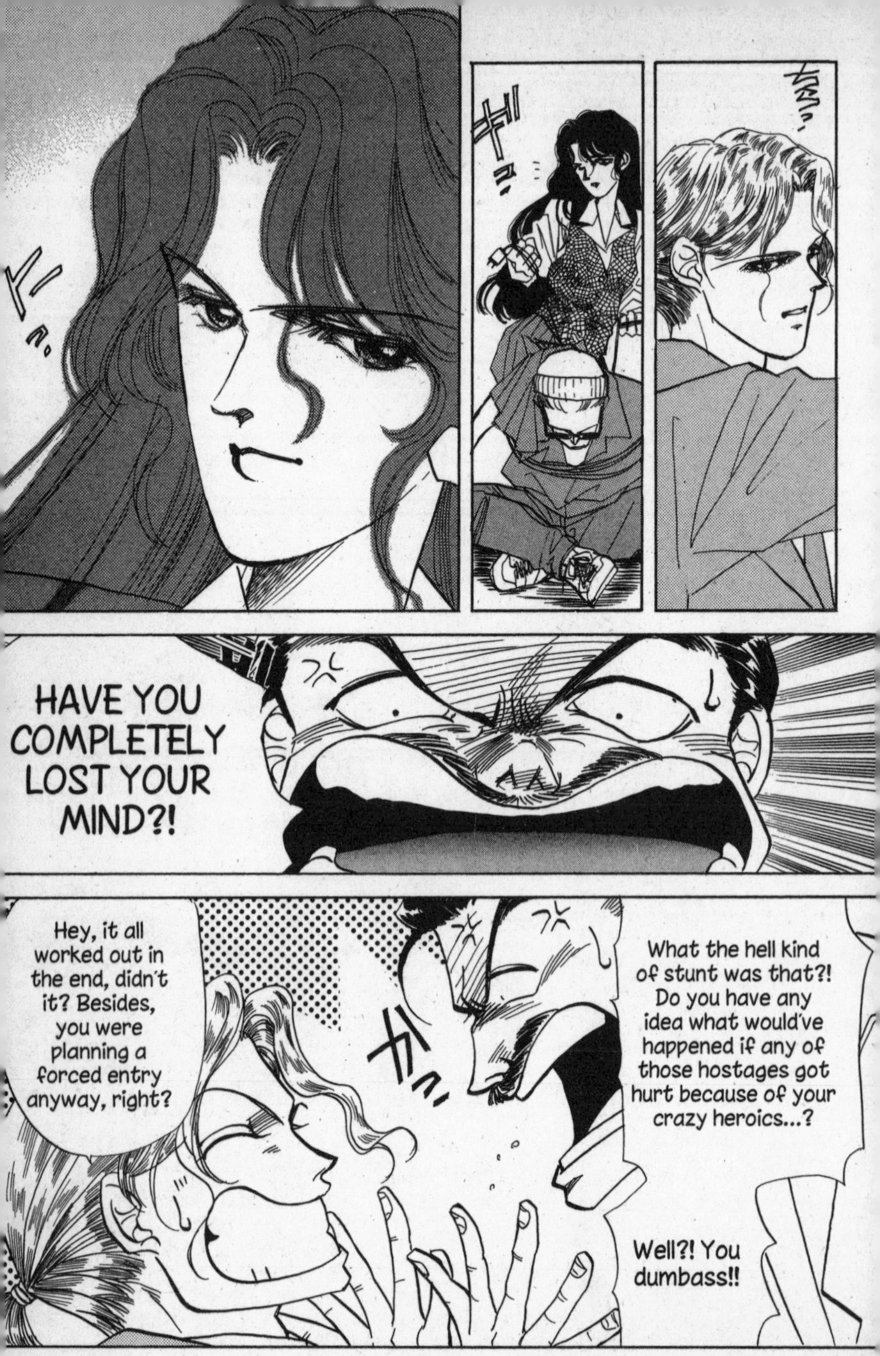
HAVE YOU COMPLETELY LOST YOUR MIND?!
What the hell kind of stunt was that?! Do you have any idea what would've happened if any of those hostages got hurt because of your crazy heroics...?
Well?! You dumbass!!
Hey, it all worked out in the end, didn't it? Besides, you were planning a forced entry anyway, right?

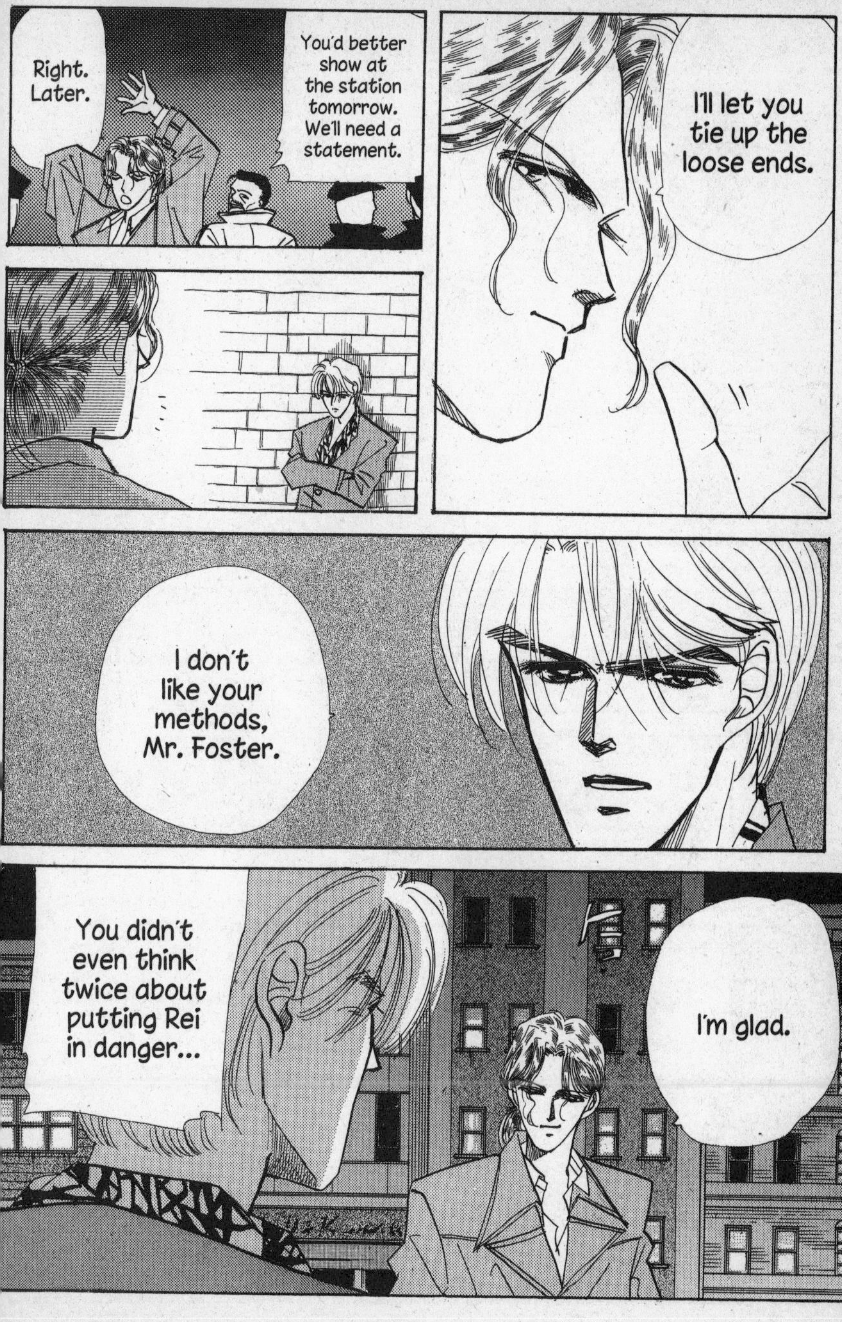
I'll let you tie up the loose ends.
You'd better show at the station tomorrow. We'll need a statement.
Right. Later.
I don't like your methods, Mr. Foster.
I'm glad.
You didn't even think twice about putting Rei in danger...

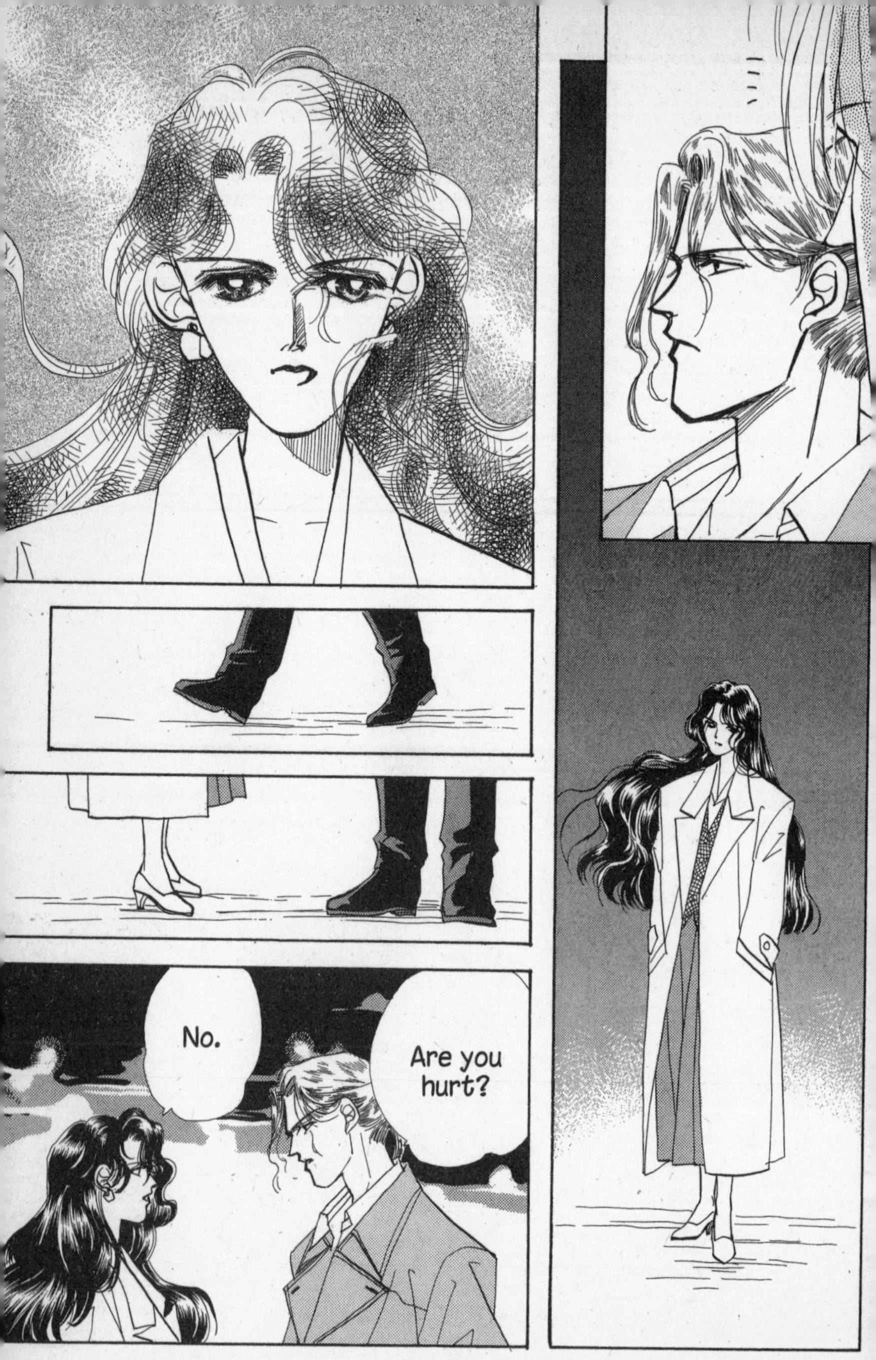
Are you hurt?
No.

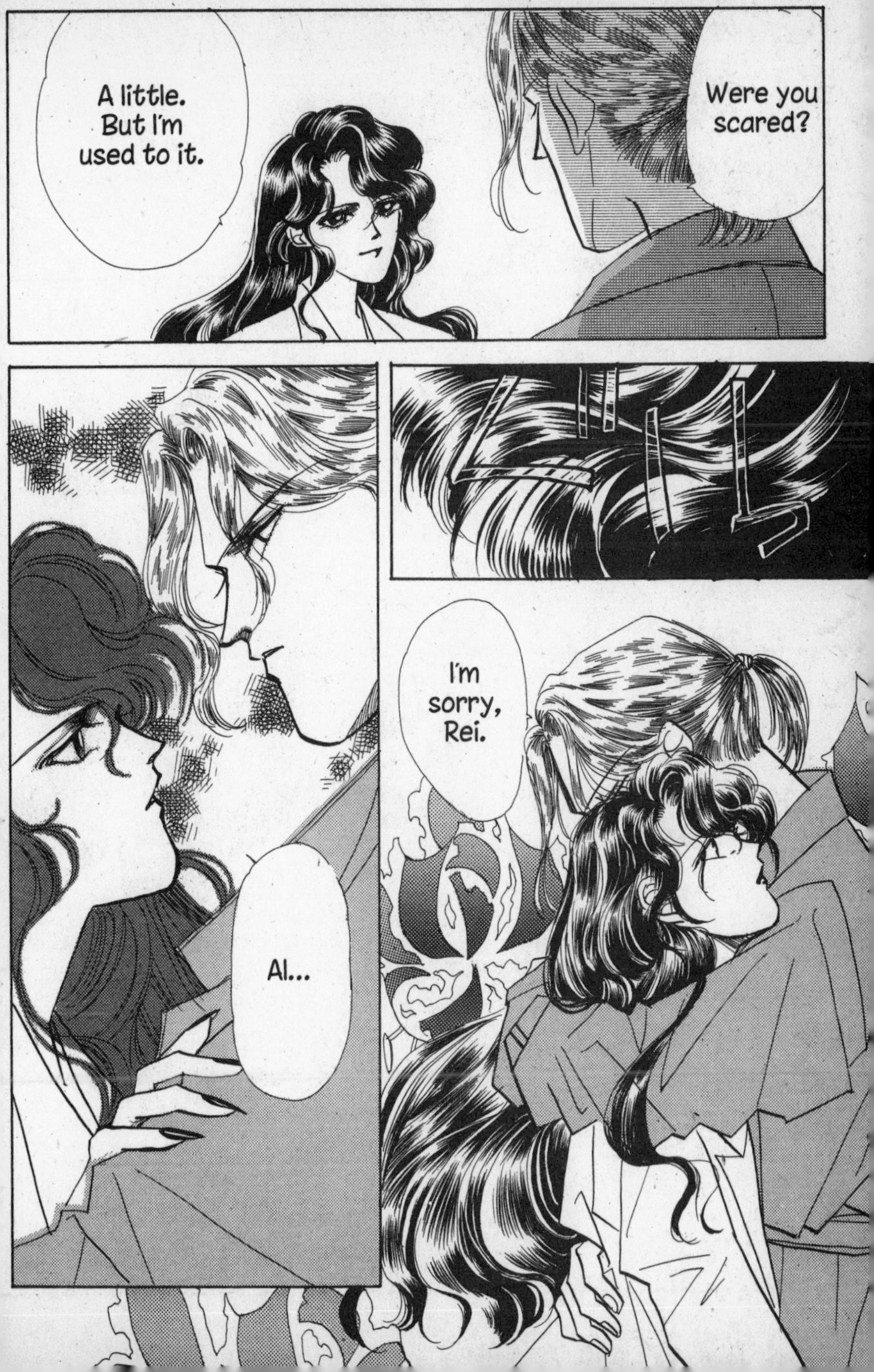
Were you scared?
A little. But I'm used to it.
I'm sorry, Rei.
Al...

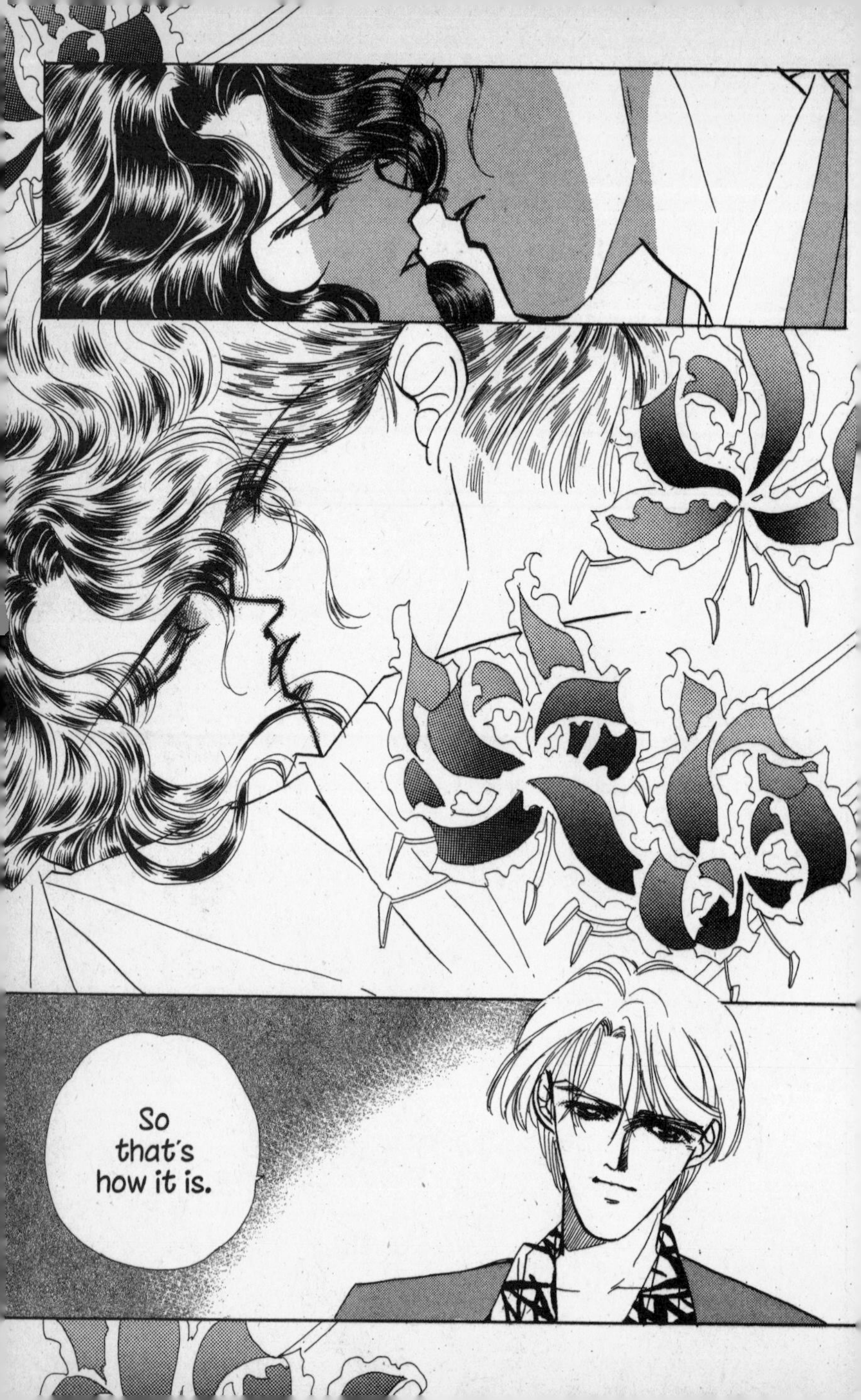
So that's how it is.

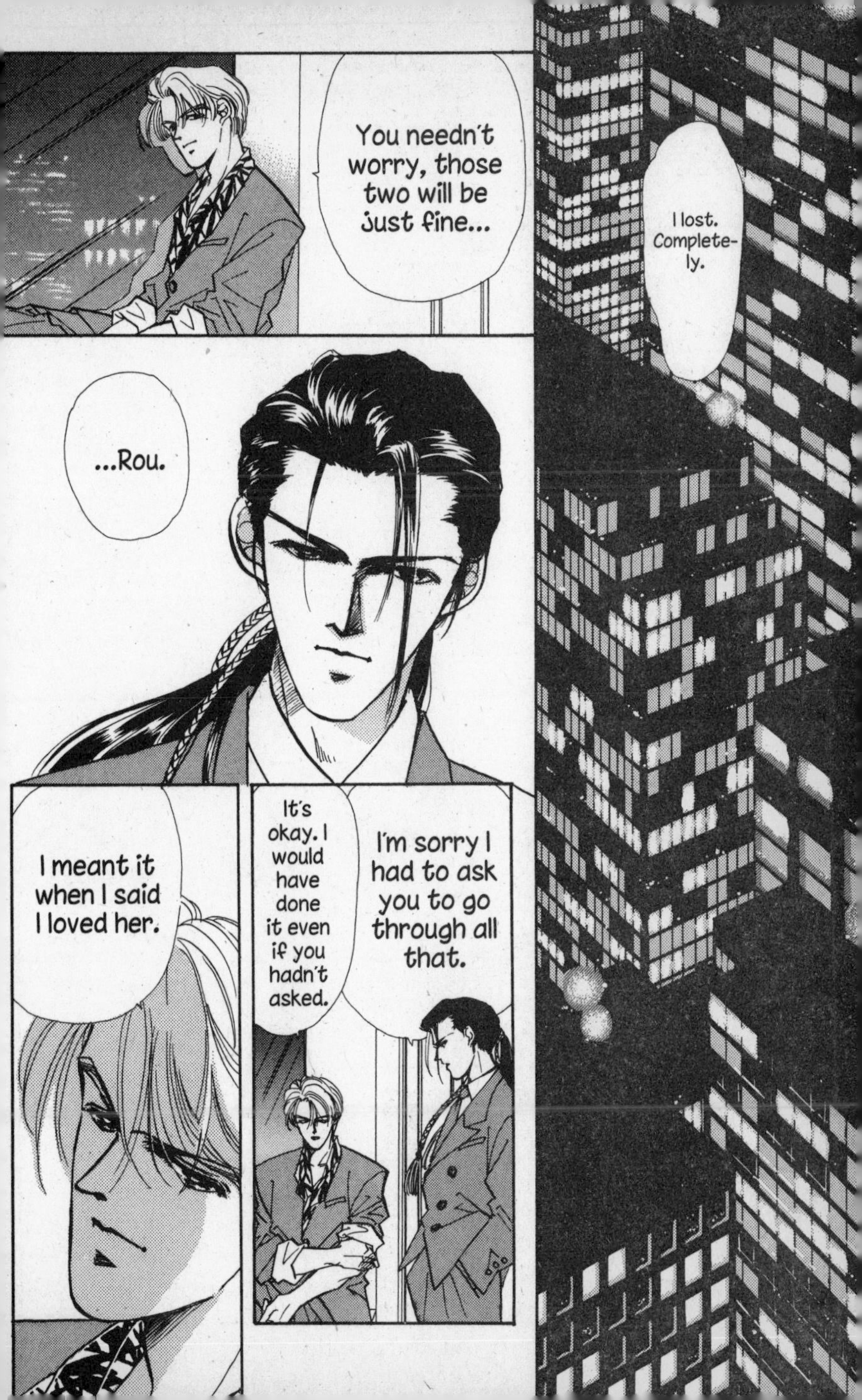
I lost. Completely.
You needn't worry, those two will be just fine...
...Rou.
I'm sorry I had to ask you to go through all that.
It's okay. I would have done it even if you hadn't asked.
I meant it when I said I loved her.

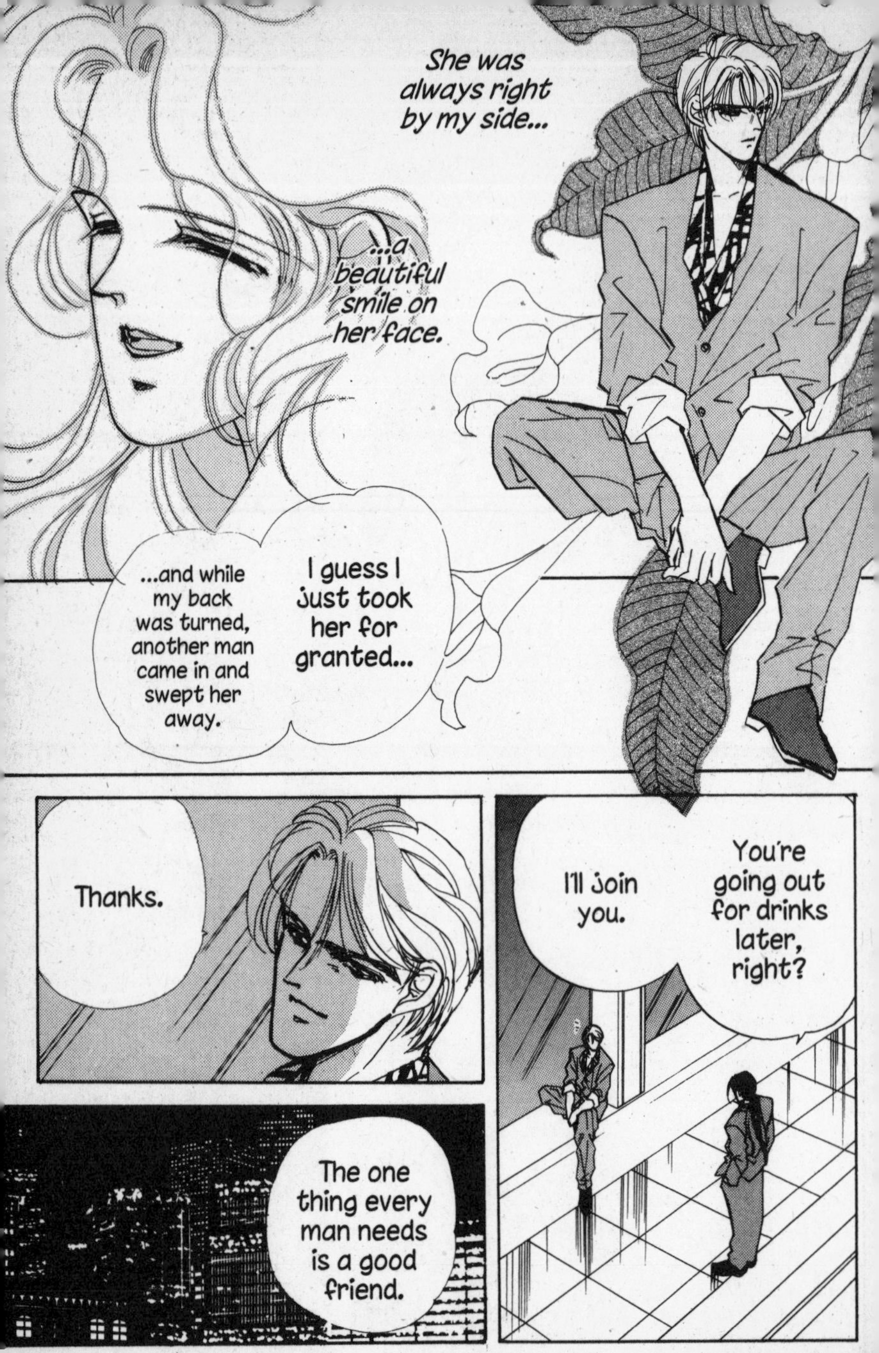
She was always right by my side...
...a beautiful smile on her face.
I guess I just took her for granted...
...and while my back was turned, another man came in and swept her away.
You're going out for drinks later, right?
I'll join you.
Thanks.
The one thing every man needs is a good friend.

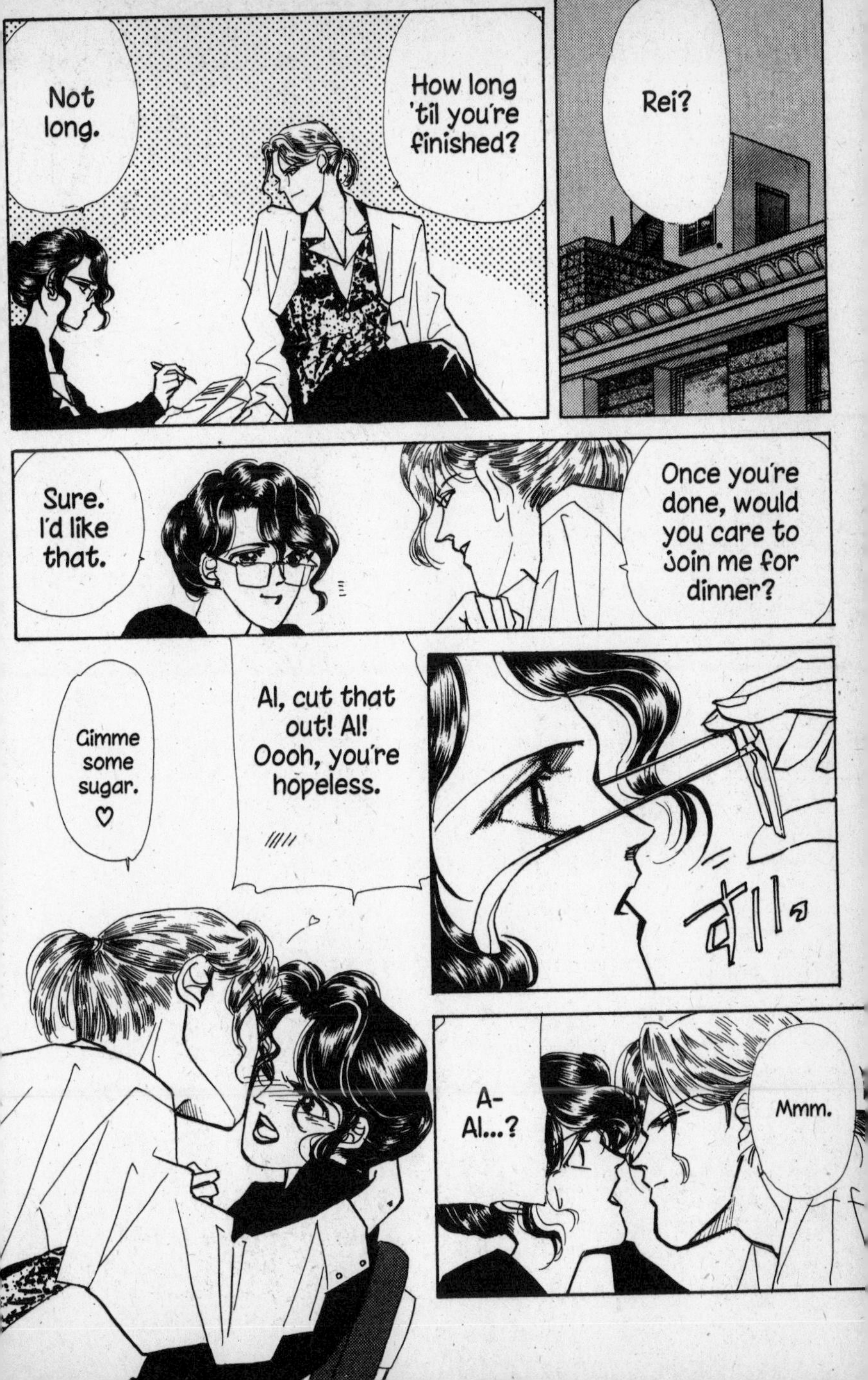
Rei?
How long 'til you're finished?
Not long.
Once you're done, would you care to join me for dinner?
Sure. I'd like that.
Mmm.
A- Al...?
Al, cut that out! Al! Oooh, you're hopeless.
Gimme some sugar. ♡

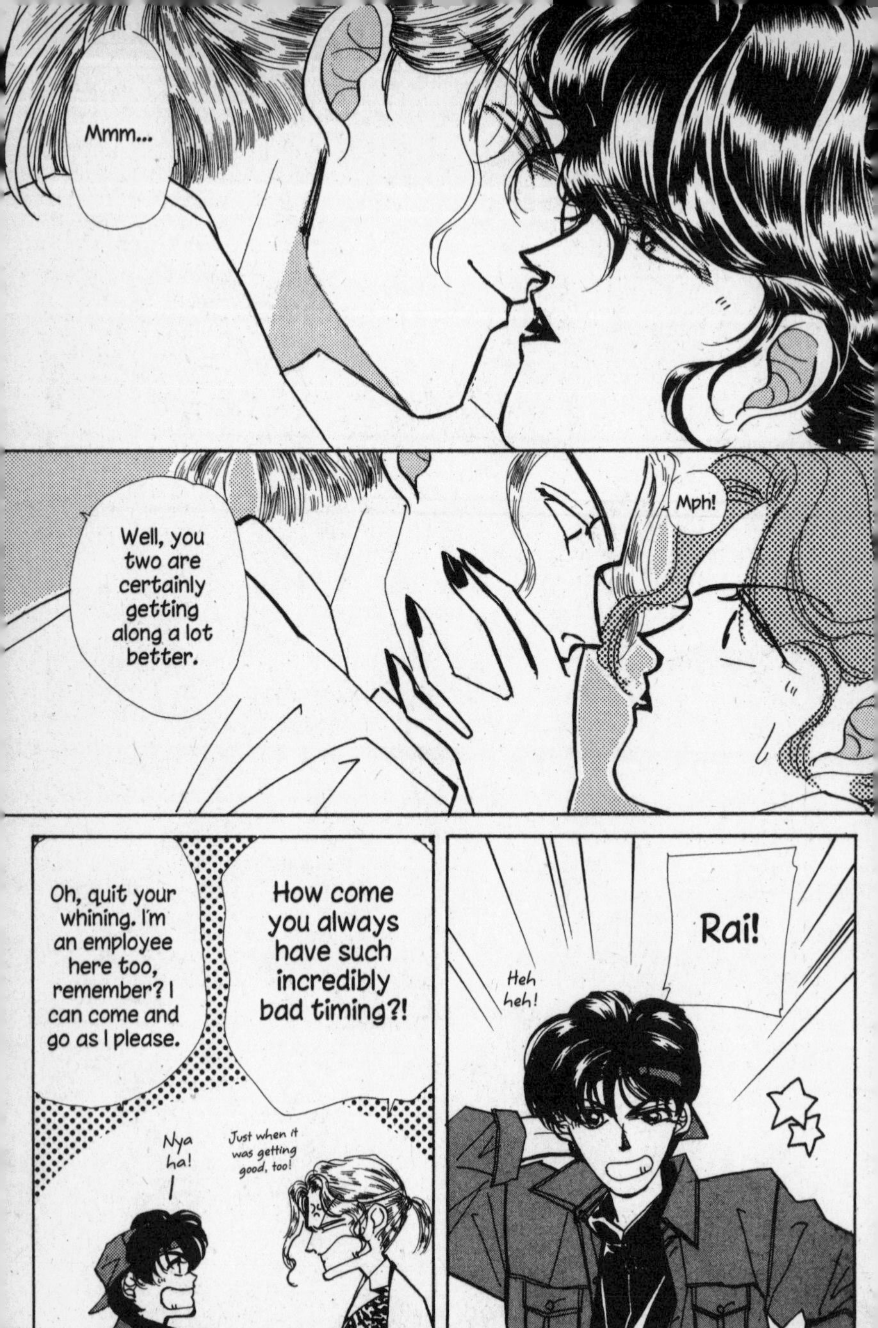
Mmm...
Mph!
Well, you two are certainly getting along a lot better.
Rai!
Heh heh!
How come you always have such incredibly bad timing?!
Oh, quit your whining. I'm an employee here too, remember? I can come and go as I please.
Just when it was getting good, too!
Nya ha!

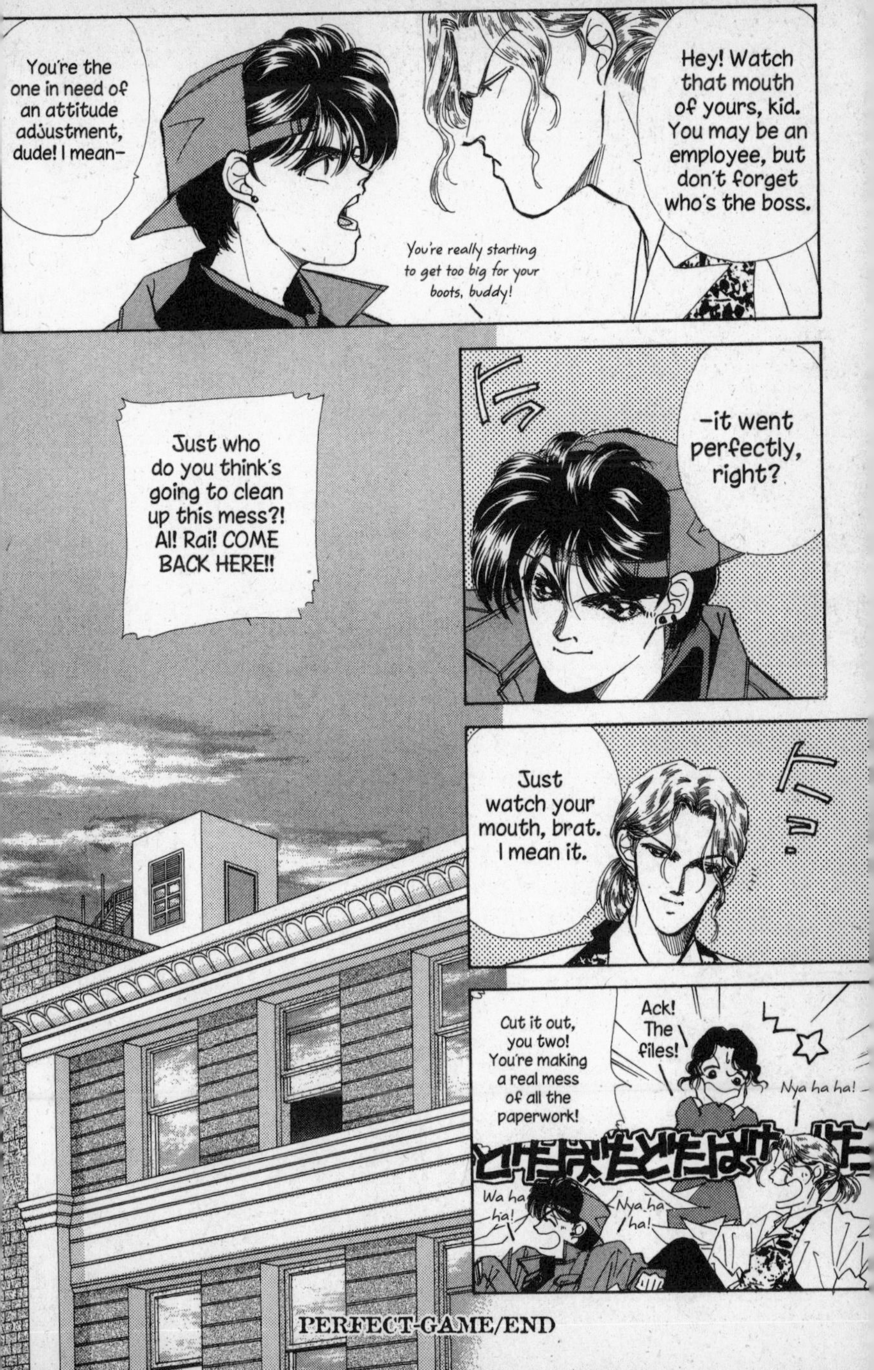
Hey! Watch that mouth of yours, kid. You may be an employee, but don't forget who's the boss.
You're really starting to get too big for your boots, buddy!
You're the one in need of an attitude adjustment, dude! I mean-
-it went perfectly, right?
Just watch your mouth, brat. I mean it.
Ack! The files!
Cut it out, you two! You're making a real mess of all the paperwork!
Nya ha ha!
Nya ha ha!
Wa ha ha!
Just who do you think's going to clean up this mess?! Al! Rai! COME BACK HERE!!
PERFECT-GAME/END

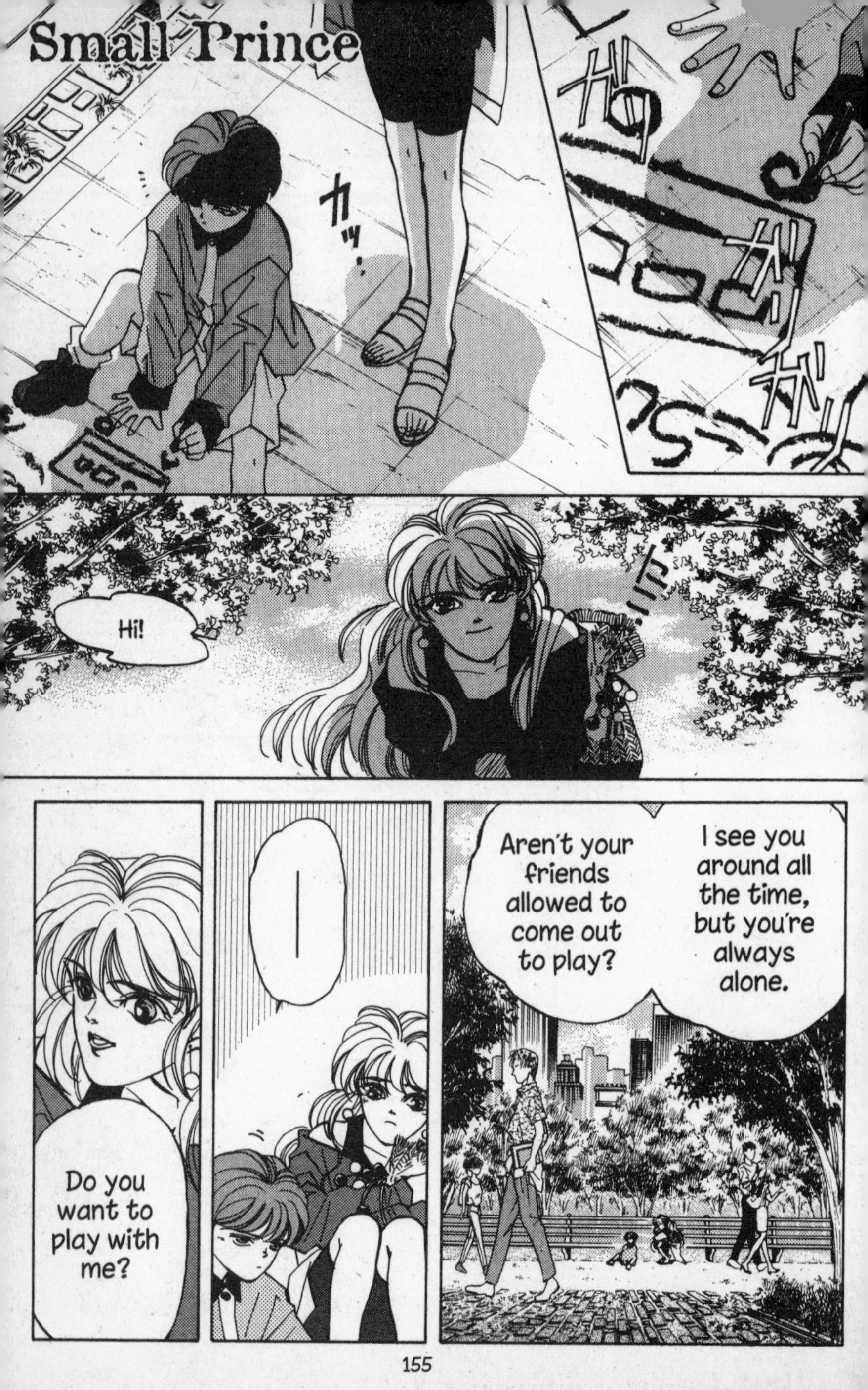
カッ
Hi!
I see you around all the time, but you're always alone.
Aren't your friends allowed to come out to play?
Do you want to play with me?

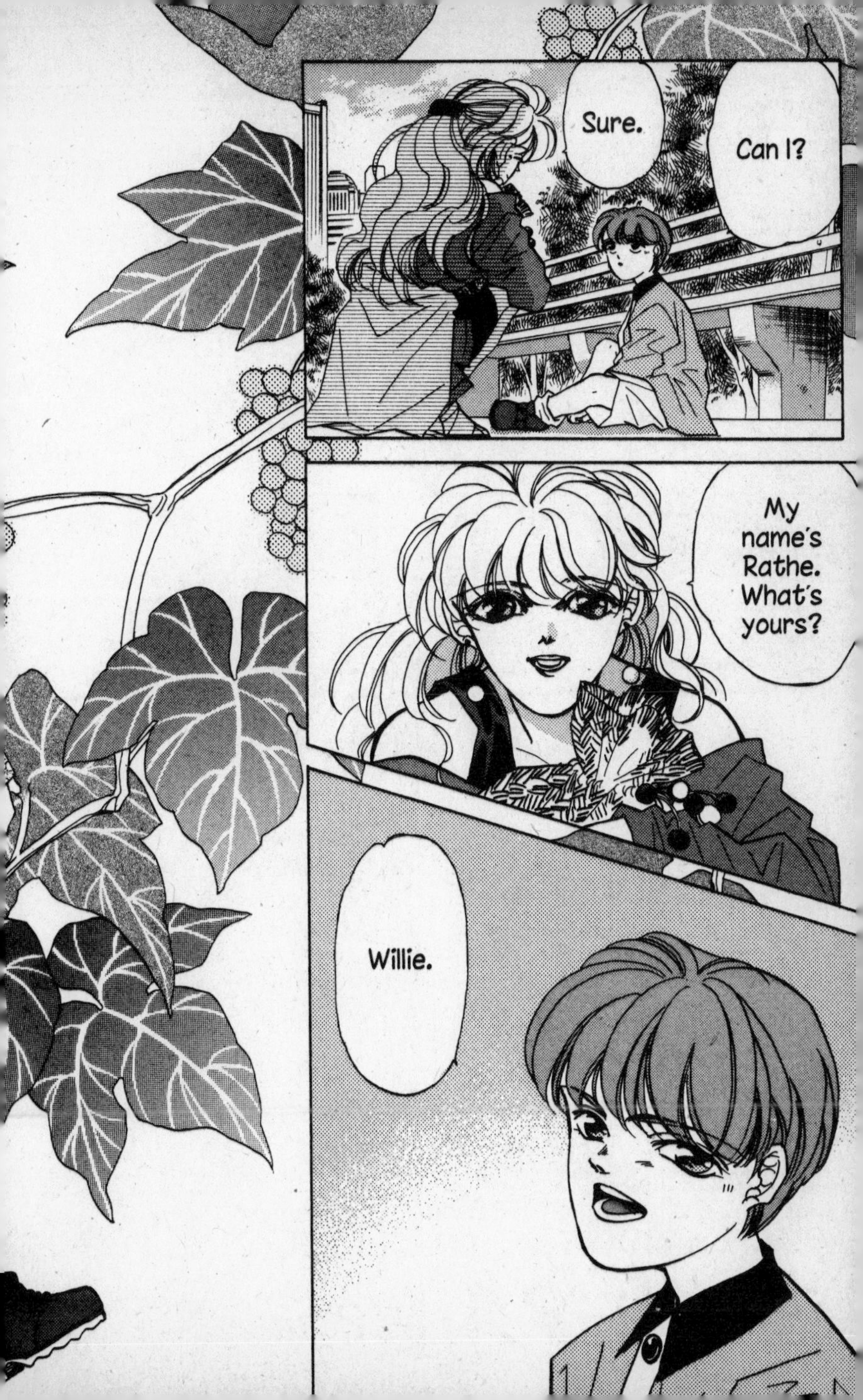
Can I?
Sure.
My name's Rathe. What's yours?
Willie.

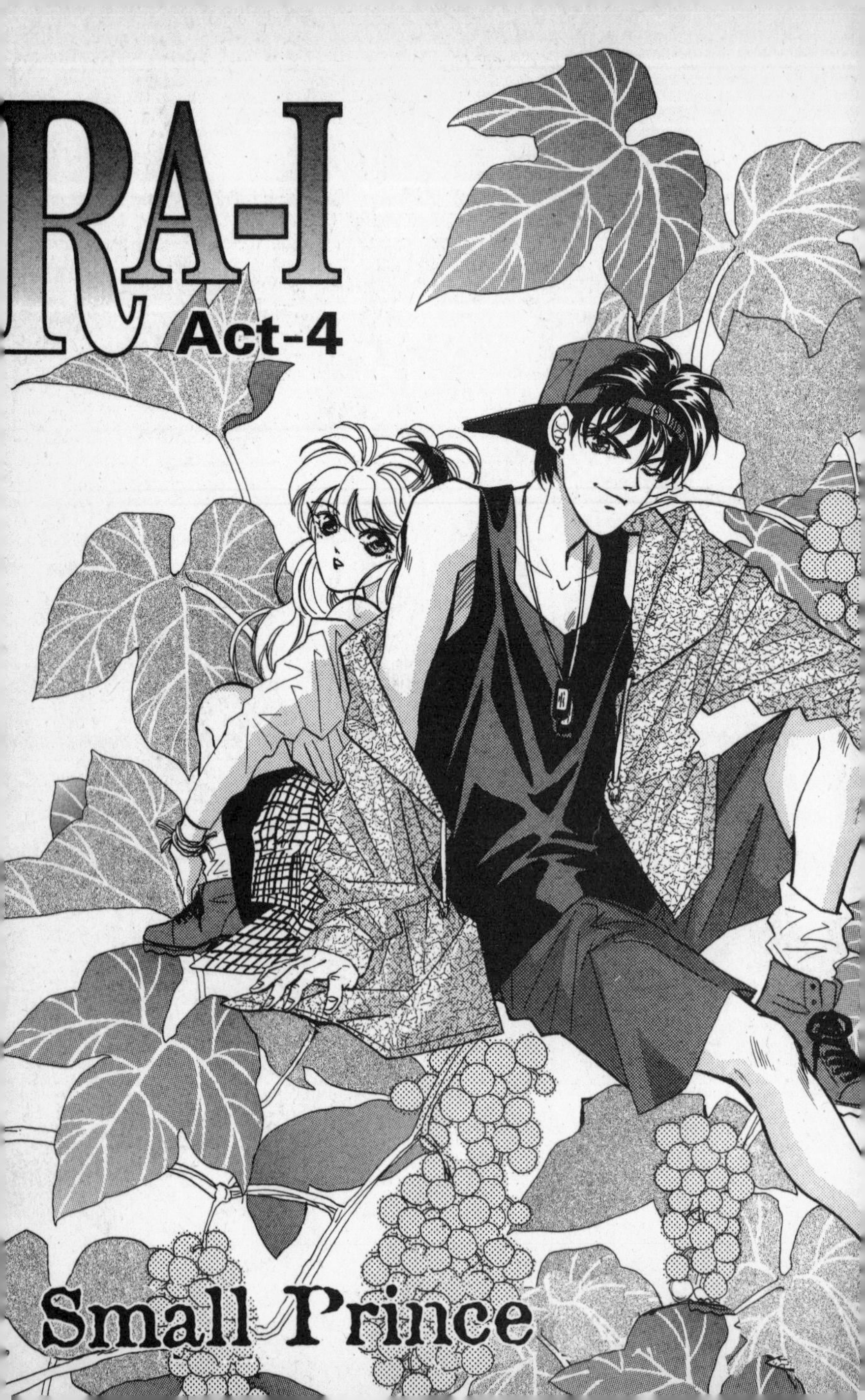
RA-I
Act-4
Small Prince

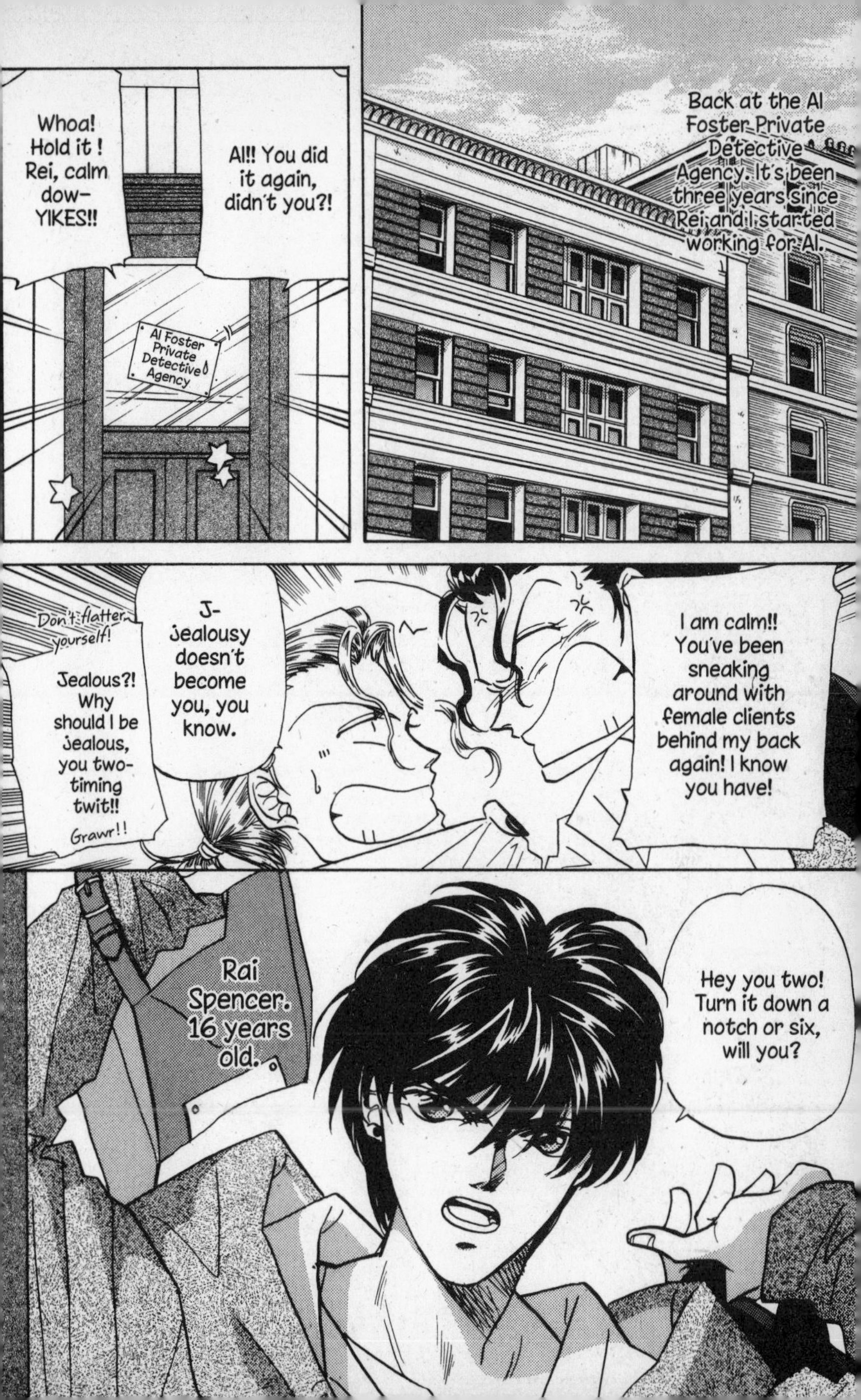
Back at the Al Foster Private Detective Agency. It's been three years since Rei and I started working for Al.
Al!! You did it again, didn't you?!
Whoa! Hold it ! Rei, calm dow— YIKES!!
Al Foster Private Detective Agency
I am calm!! You've been sneaking around with female clients behind my back again! I know you have!
J- jealousy doesn't become you, you know.
Don't flatter yourself!
Jealous?! Why should I be jealous, you two-timing twit!!
Grawr!!
Hey you two! Turn it down a notch or six, will you?
Rai Spencer. 16 years old.

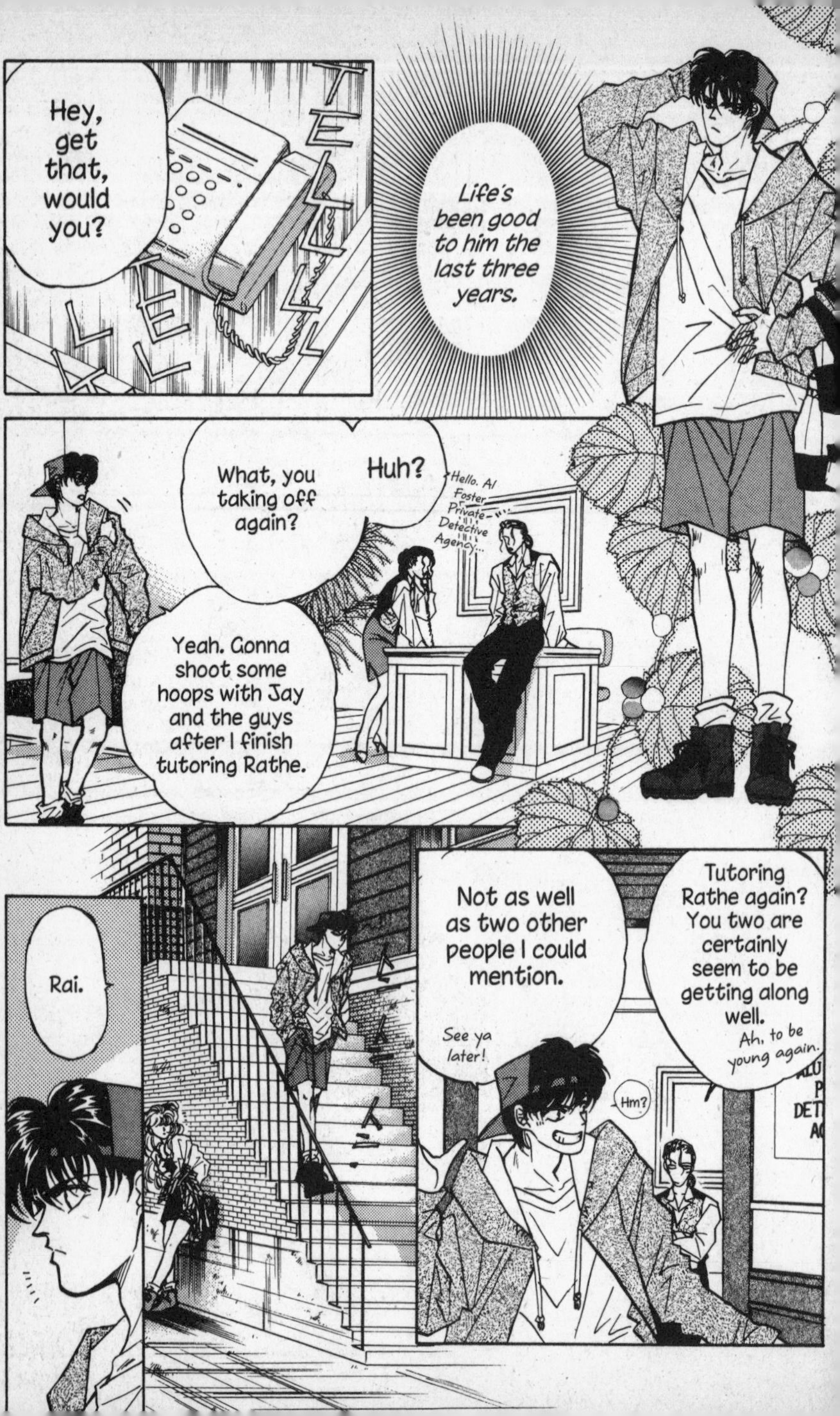
Life's been good to him the last three years.
Hey, get that, would you?
Huh?
Hello. Al Foster Private Detective Agency...
What, you taking off again?
Yeah. Gonna shoot some hoops with Jay and the guys after I finish tutoring Rathe.
Tutoring Rathe again? You two are certainly seem to be getting along well.
Ah, to be young again.
Not as well as two other people I could mention.
See ya later!
Hm?
Rai.

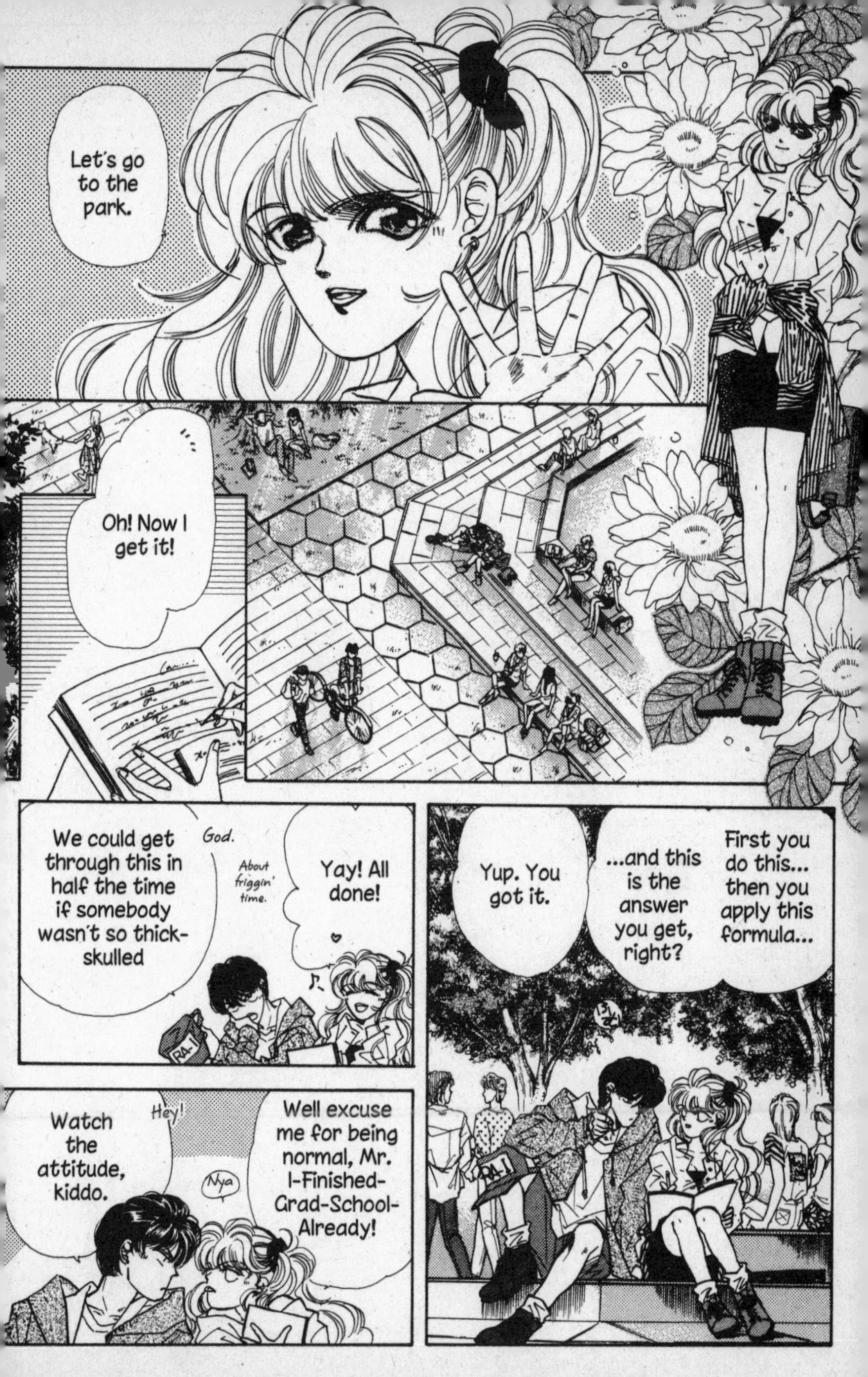
Let's go to the park.
Oh! Now I get it!
First you do this... then you apply this formula...
...and this is the answer you get, right?
Yup. You got it.
Yay! All done!
About friggin' time.
God.
We could get through this in half the time if somebody wasn't so thick-skulled
Well excuse me for being normal, Mr. I-Finished-Grad-School-Already!
Nya
Hey!
Watch the attitude, kiddo.

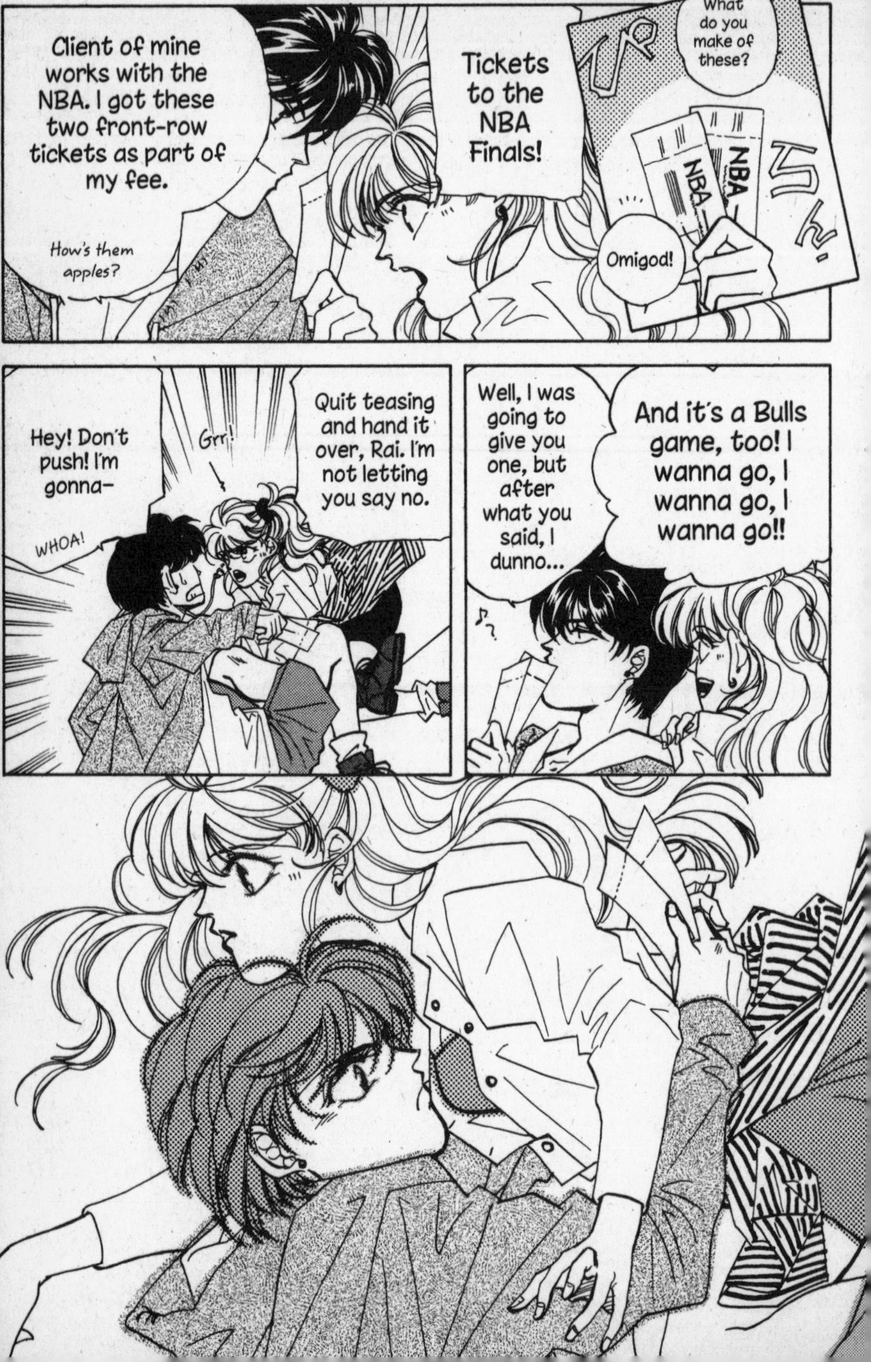
What do you make of these?
NBA
NBA
Omigod!
Tickets to the NBA Finals!
Client of mine works with the NBA. I got these two front-row tickets as part of my fee.
How's them apples?
And it's a Bulls game, too! I wanna go, I wanna go, I wanna go!!
Well, I was going to give you one, but after what you said, I dunno...
Quit teasing and hand it over, Rai. I'm not letting you say no.
Grr!
Hey! Don't push! I'm gonna-
WHOA!

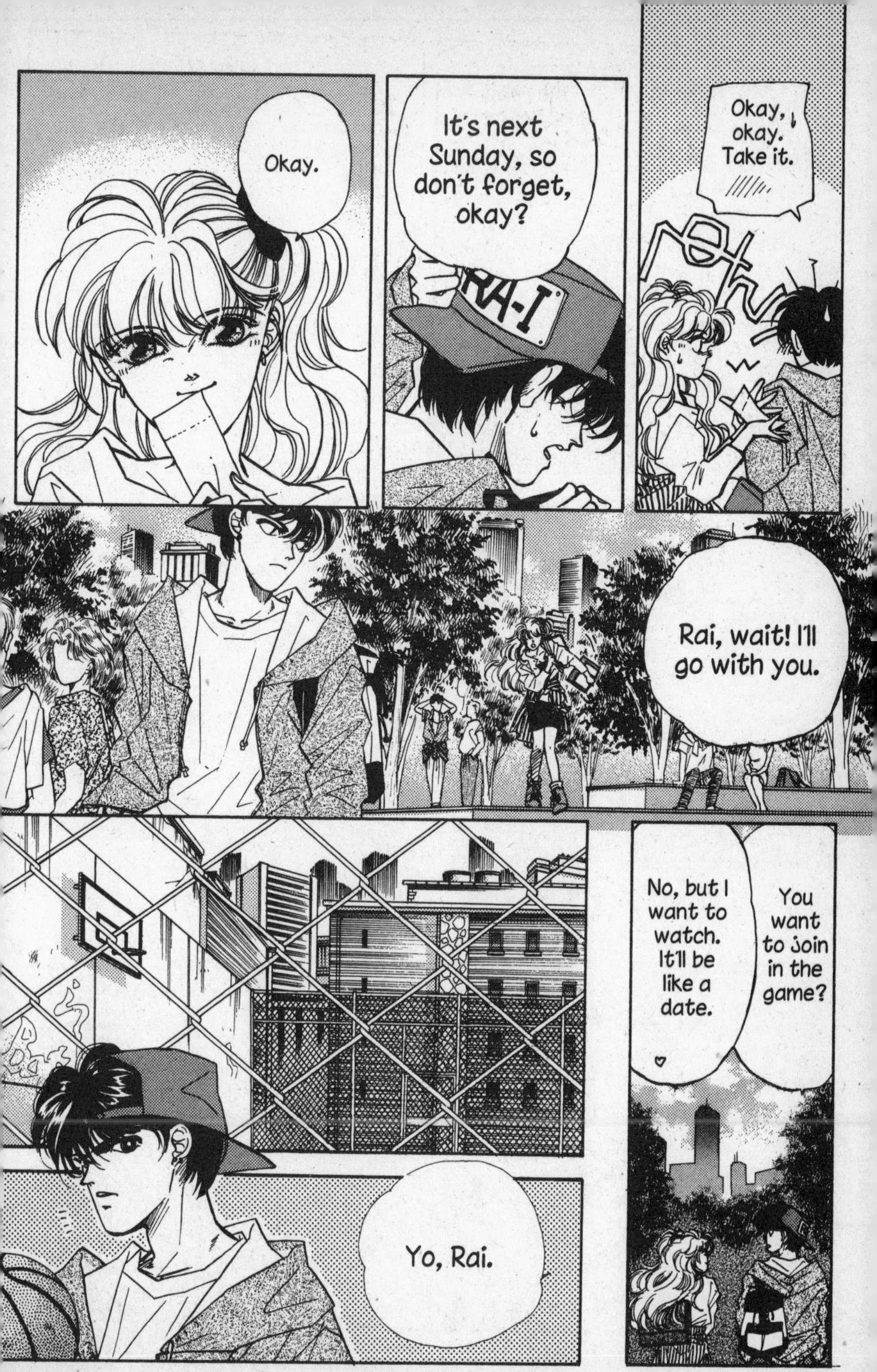
Okay, okay. Take it.
It's next Sunday, so don't forget, okay?
Okay.
Rai, wait! I'll go with you.
You want to join in the game?
No, but I want to watch. It'll be like a date.
Yo, Rai.

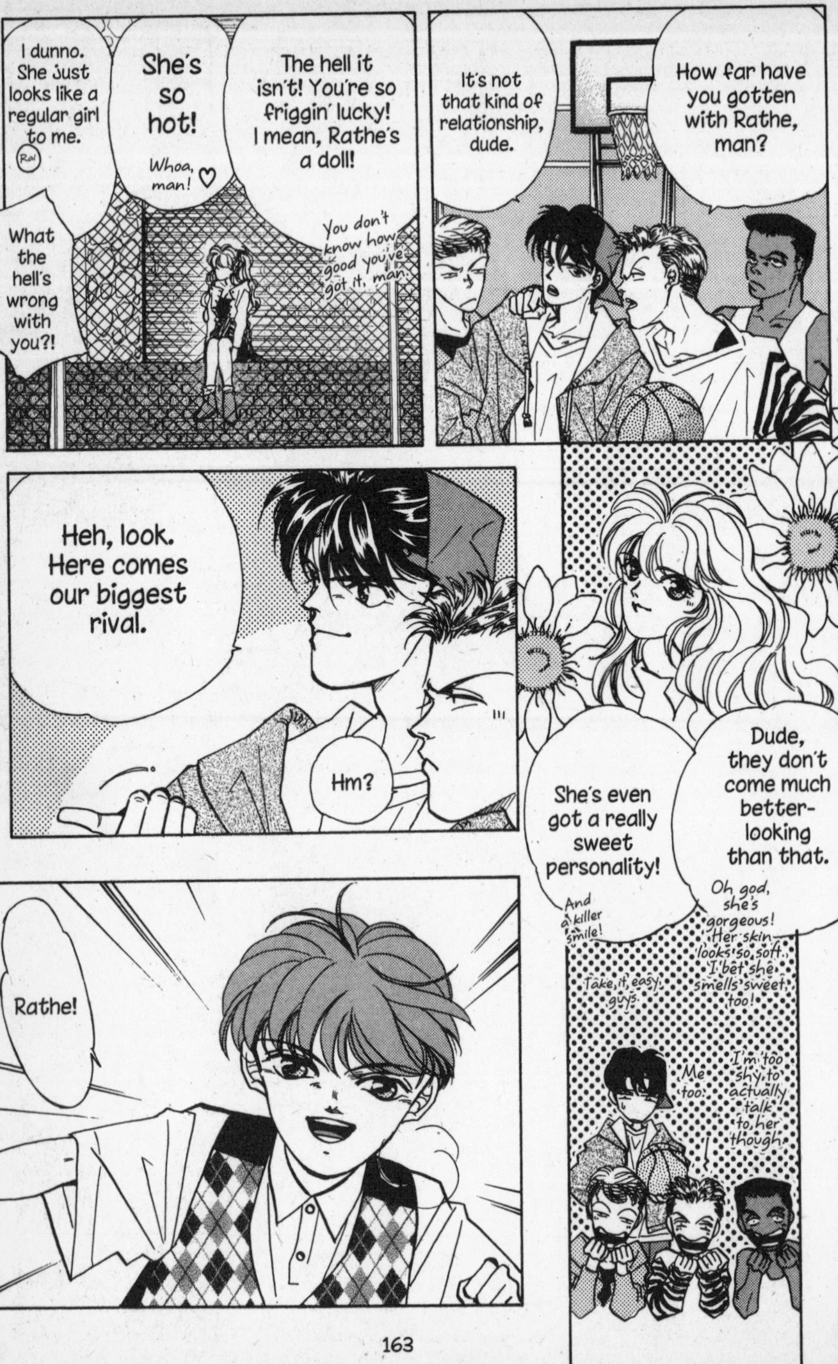
How far have you gotten with Rathe, man?
It's not that kind of relationship, dude.
The hell it isn't! You're so friggin' lucky! I mean, Rathe's a doll!
You don't know how good you've got it, man.
She's so hot!
Whoa, man! ♡
I dunno. She just looks like a regular girl to me.
Ral
What the hell's wrong with you?!
Dude, they don't come much better-looking than that.
She's even got a really sweet personality!
And a killer smile!
Oh god, she's gorgeous! Her skin looks so soft. I bet she smells sweet, too!
Take it easy, guys.
I'm too shy to actually talk to her though.
Me too.
Heh, look. Here comes our biggest rival.
Hm?
Rathe!

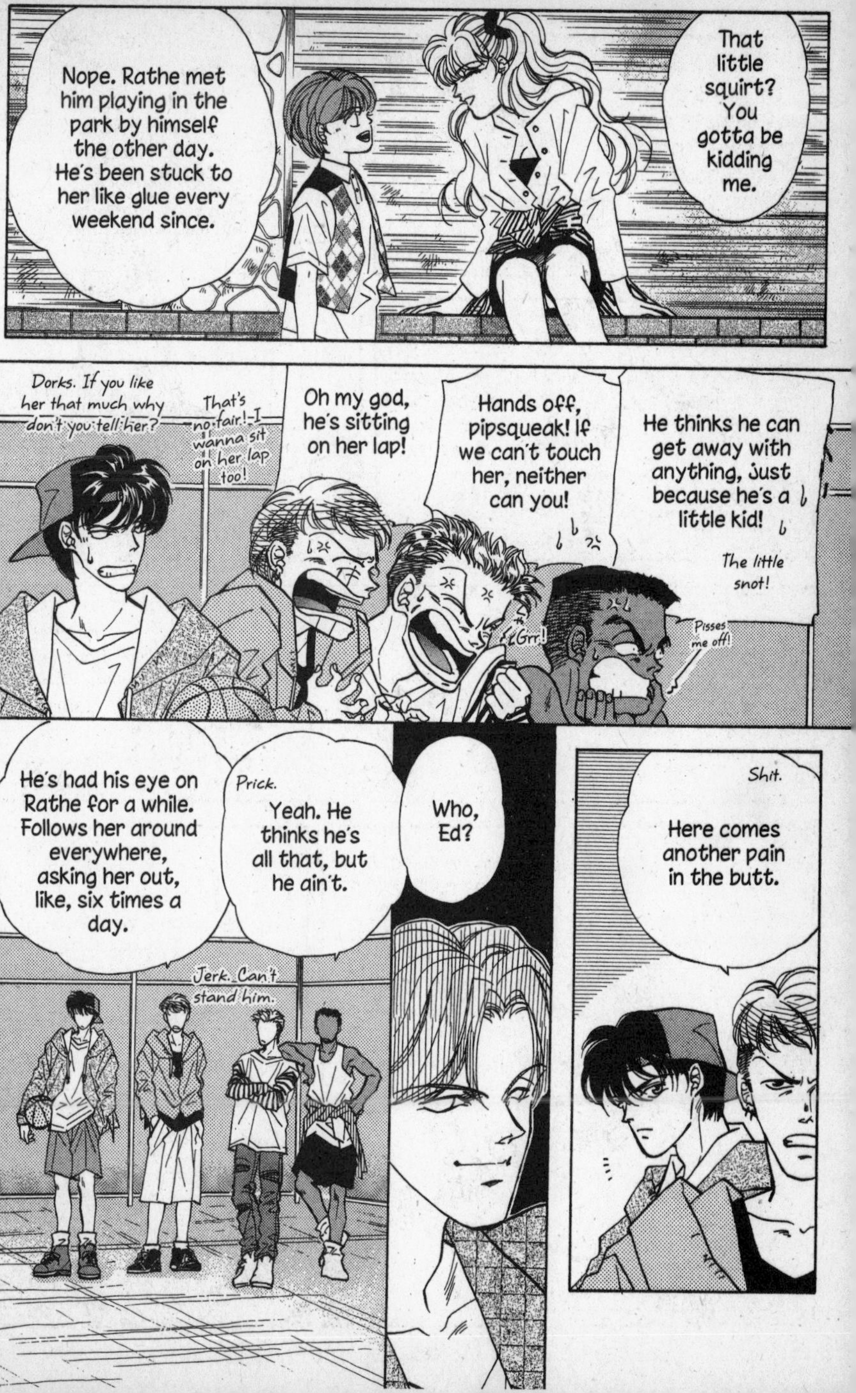
That little squirt? You gotta be kidding me.
Nope. Rathe met him playing in the park by himself the other day. He's been stuck to her like glue every weekend since.
He thinks he can get away with anything, just because he's a little kid!
The little snot!
Pisses me off!
Hands off, pipsqueak! If we can't touch her, neither can you!
Grr!
Oh my god, he's sitting on her lap!
That's no fair!-I wanna sit on her lap too!
Dorks. If you like her that much why don't you tell her?
Shit.
Here comes another pain in the butt.
Who, Ed?
Yeah. He thinks he's all that, but he ain't.
Prick.
He's had his eye on Rathe for a while. Follows her around everywhere, asking her out, like, six times a day.
Jerk. Can't stand him.

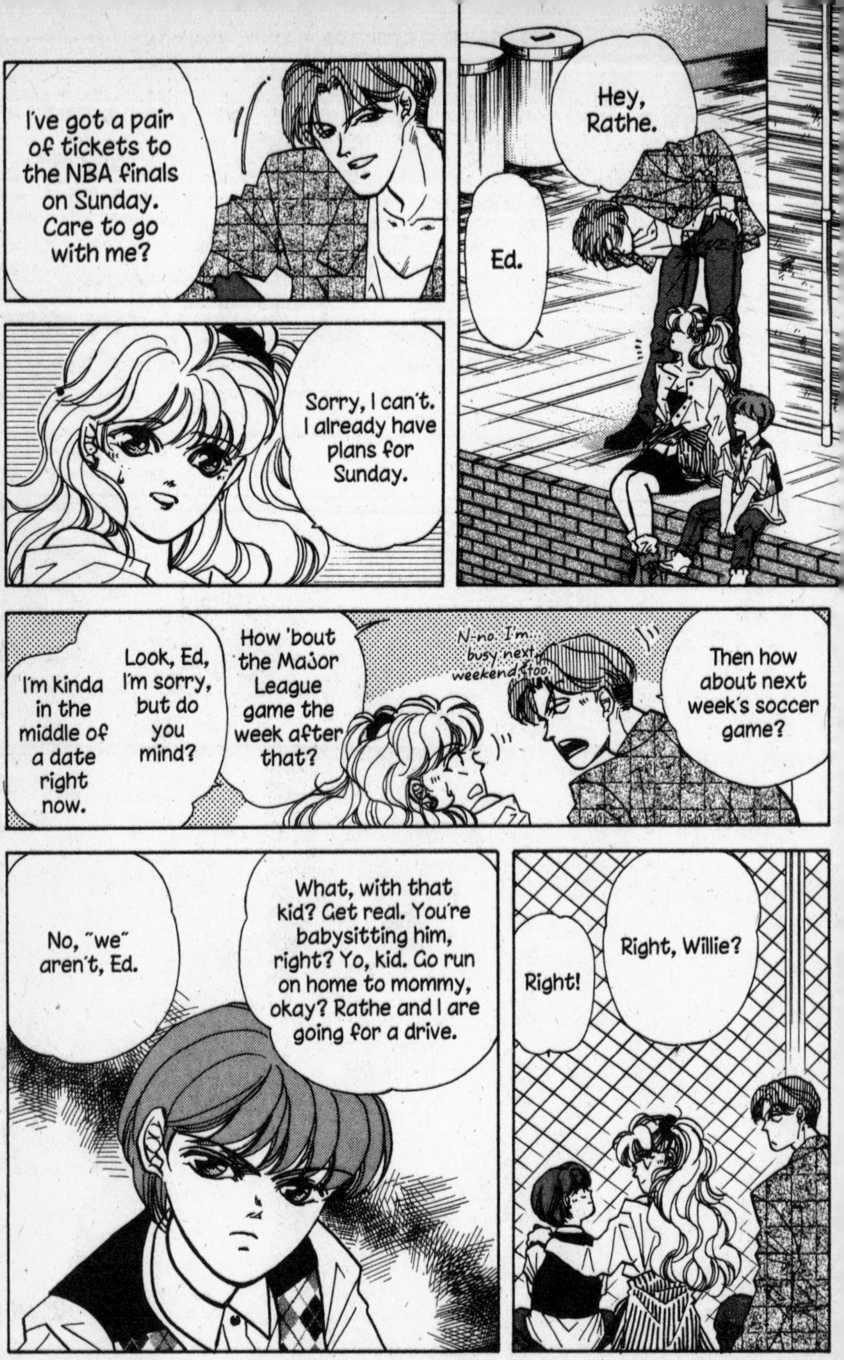
Hey, Rathe.
Ed.
I've got a pair of tickets to the NBA finals on Sunday. Care to go with me?
Sorry, I can't. I already have plans for Sunday.
Then how about next week's soccer game?
N-no I'm busy next weekend too.
How 'bout the Major League game the week after that?
Look, Ed, I'm sorry, but do you mind?
I'm kinda in the middle of a date right now.
Right, Willie?
Right!
What, with that kid? Get real. You're babysitting him, right? Yo, kid. Go run on home to mommy, okay? Rathe and I are going for a drive.
No, "we" aren't, Ed.

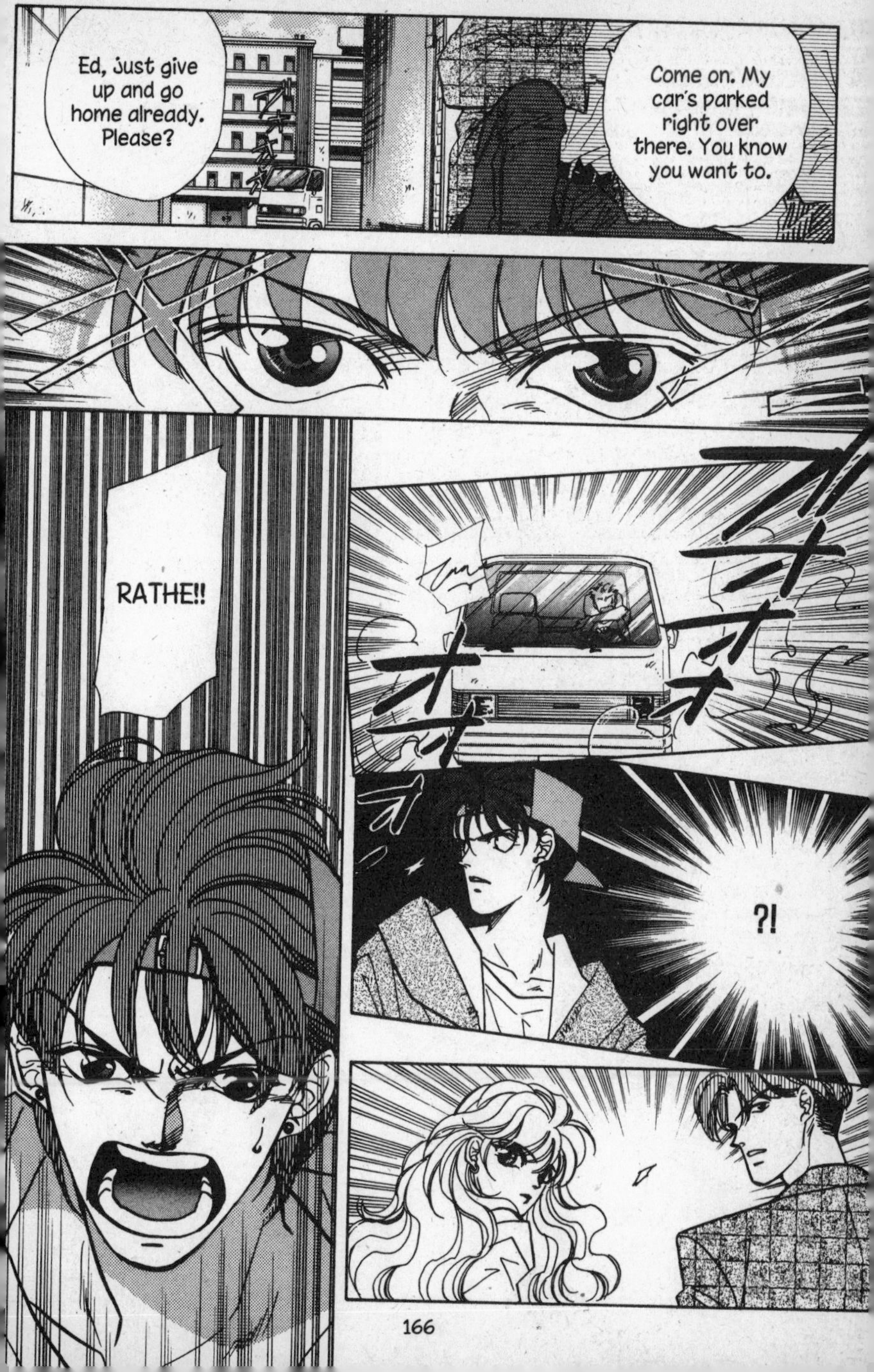
Come on. My car's parked right over there. You know you want to.
Ed, just give up and go home already. Please?
?!
RATHE!!

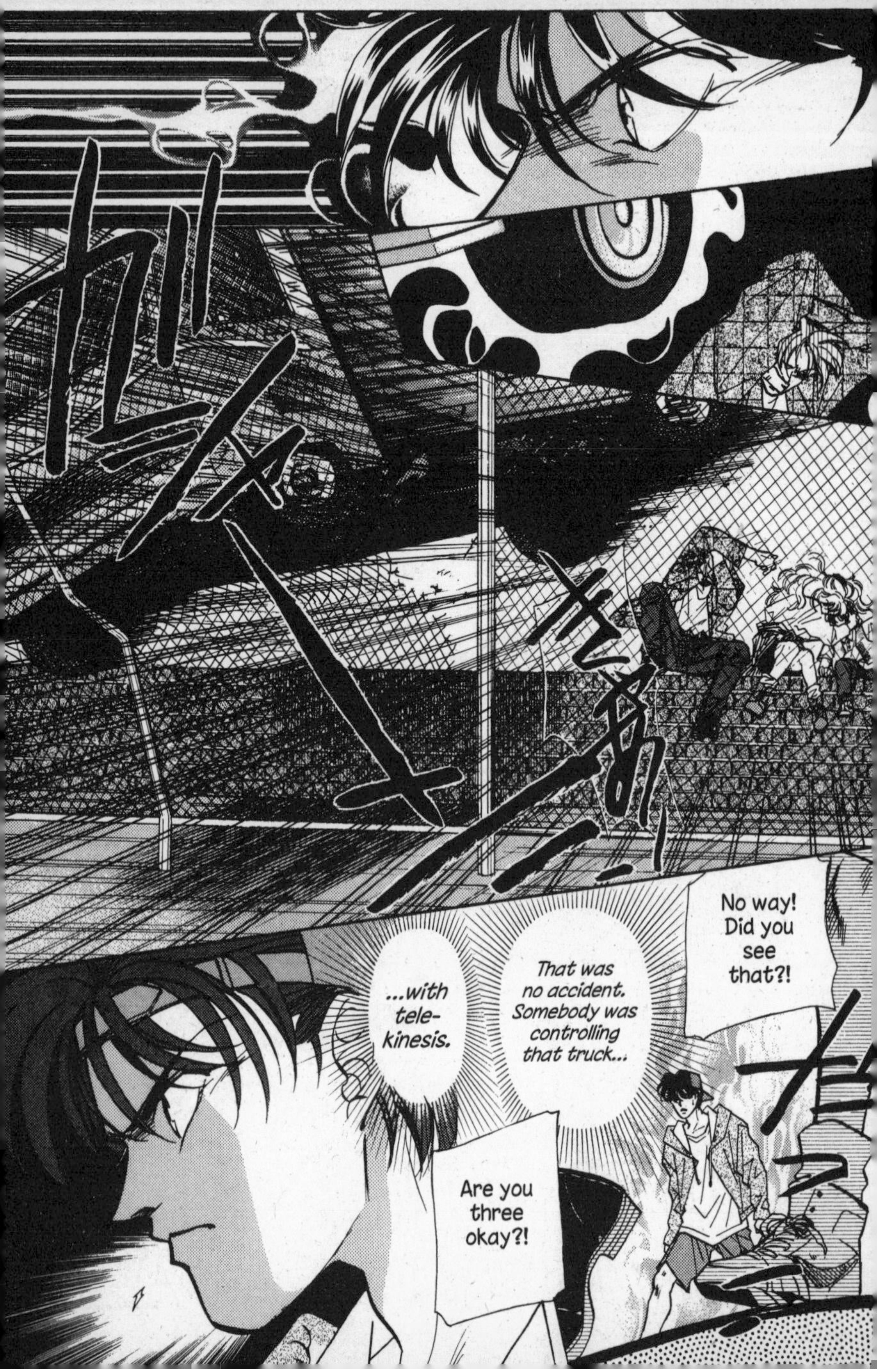
No way! Did you see that?!
That was no accident. Somebody was controlling that truck...
...with tele-kinesis.
Are you three okay?!

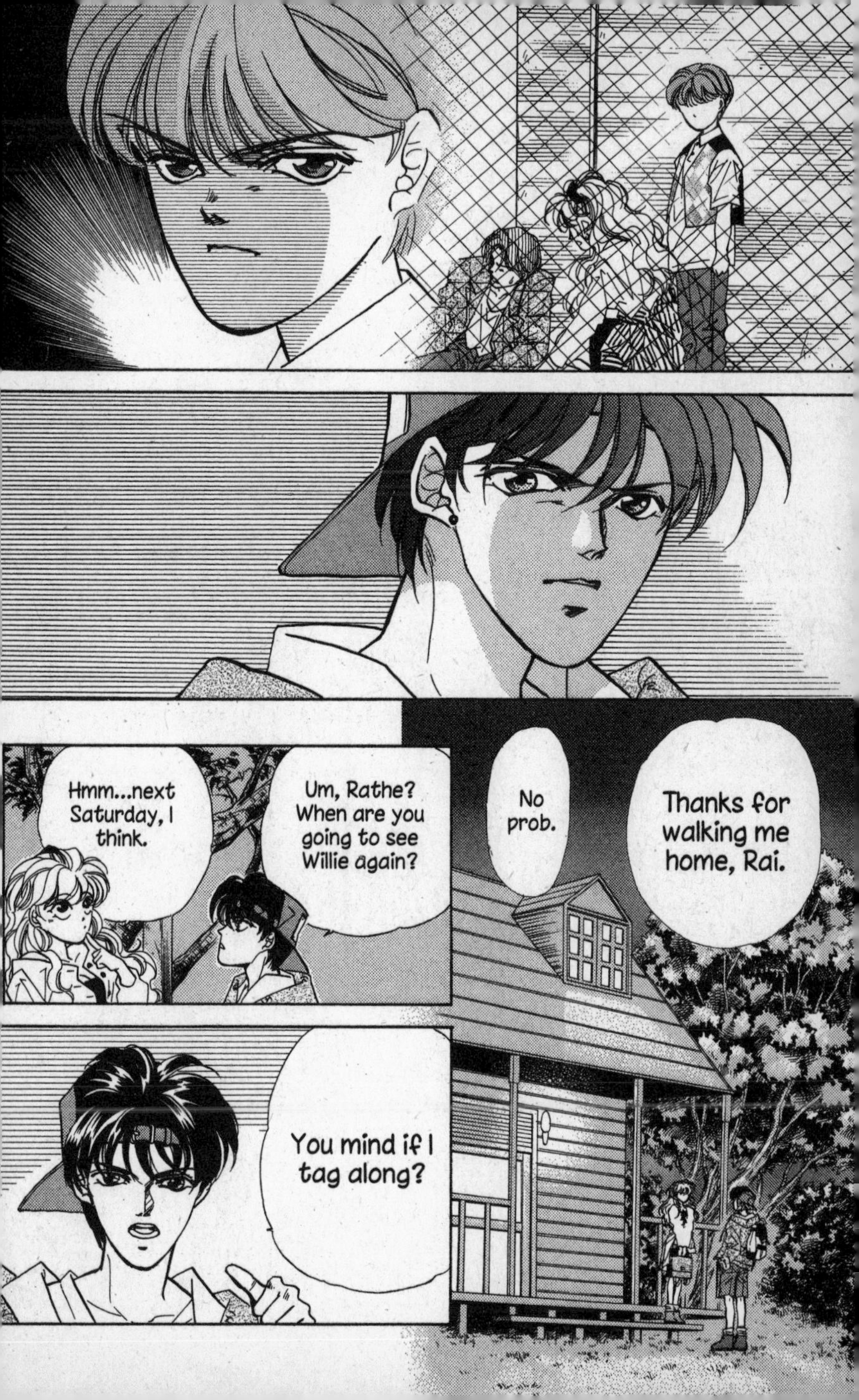
Thanks for walking me home, Rai.
No prob.
Um, Rathe? When are you going to see Willie again?
Hmm...next Saturday, I think.
You mind if I tag along?

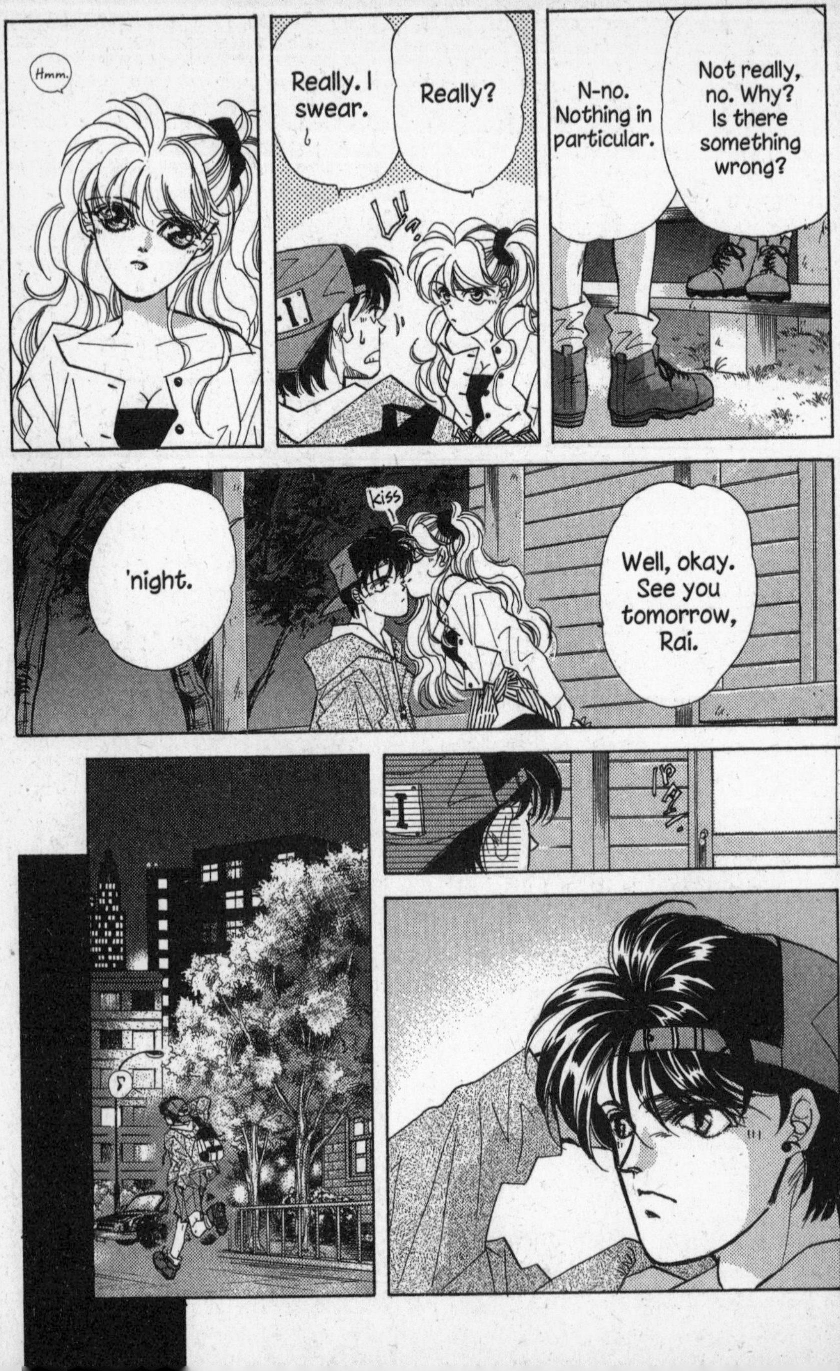
Not really, no. Why? Is there something wrong?
N-no. Nothing in particular.
Really?
Really. I swear.
Hmm.
Well, okay. See you tomorrow, Rai.
kiss
'night.

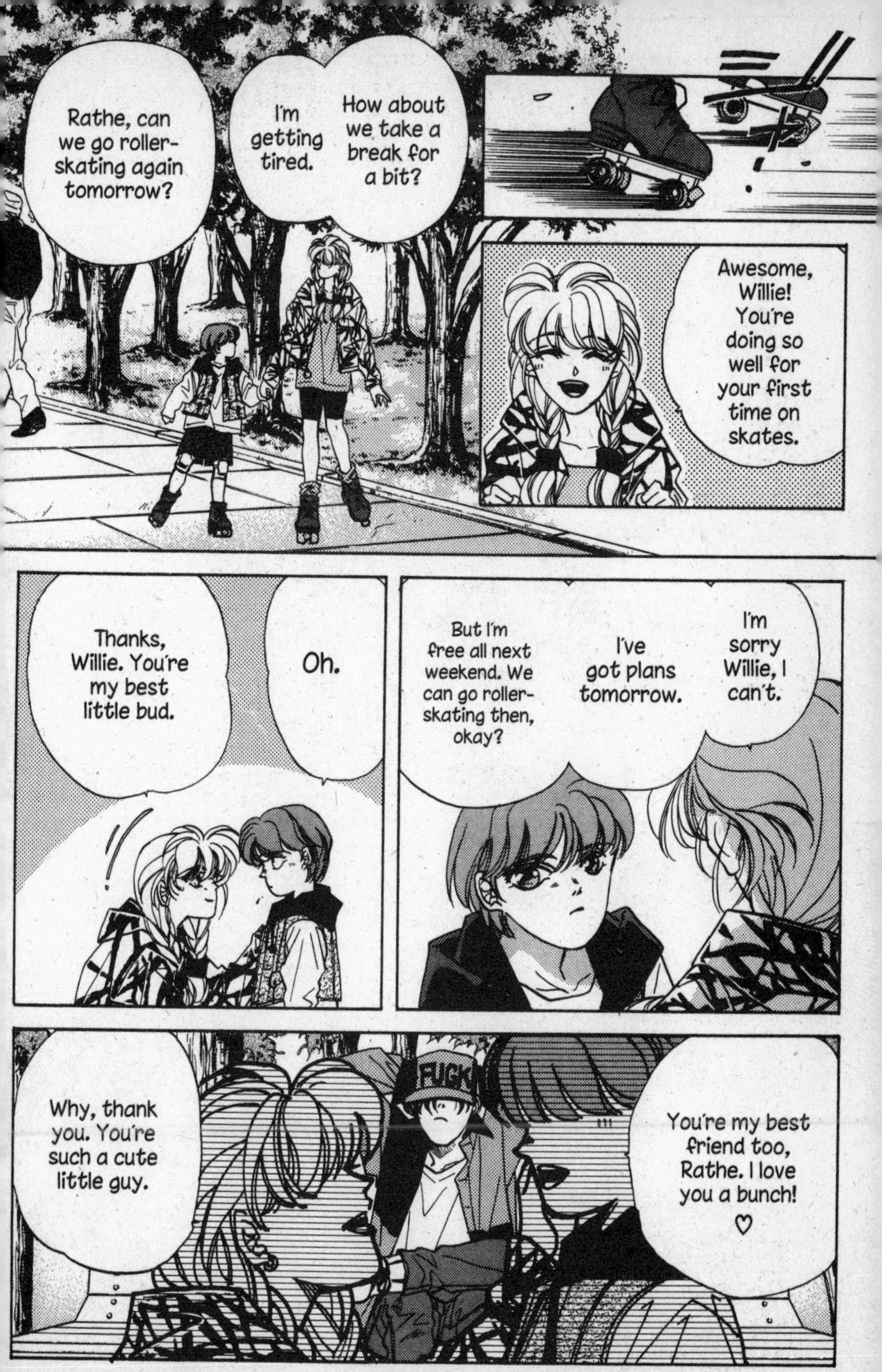
Awesome, Willie! You're doing so well for your first time on skates.
How about we take a break for a bit?
I'm getting tired.
Rathe, can we go roller-skating again tomorrow?
I'm sorry Willie, I can't.
I've got plans tomorrow.
But I'm free all next weekend. We can go roller-skating then, okay?
Oh.
Thanks, Willie. You're my best little bud.
You're my best friend too, Rathe. I love you a bunch! ♡
FUCK
Why, thank you. You're such a cute little guy.

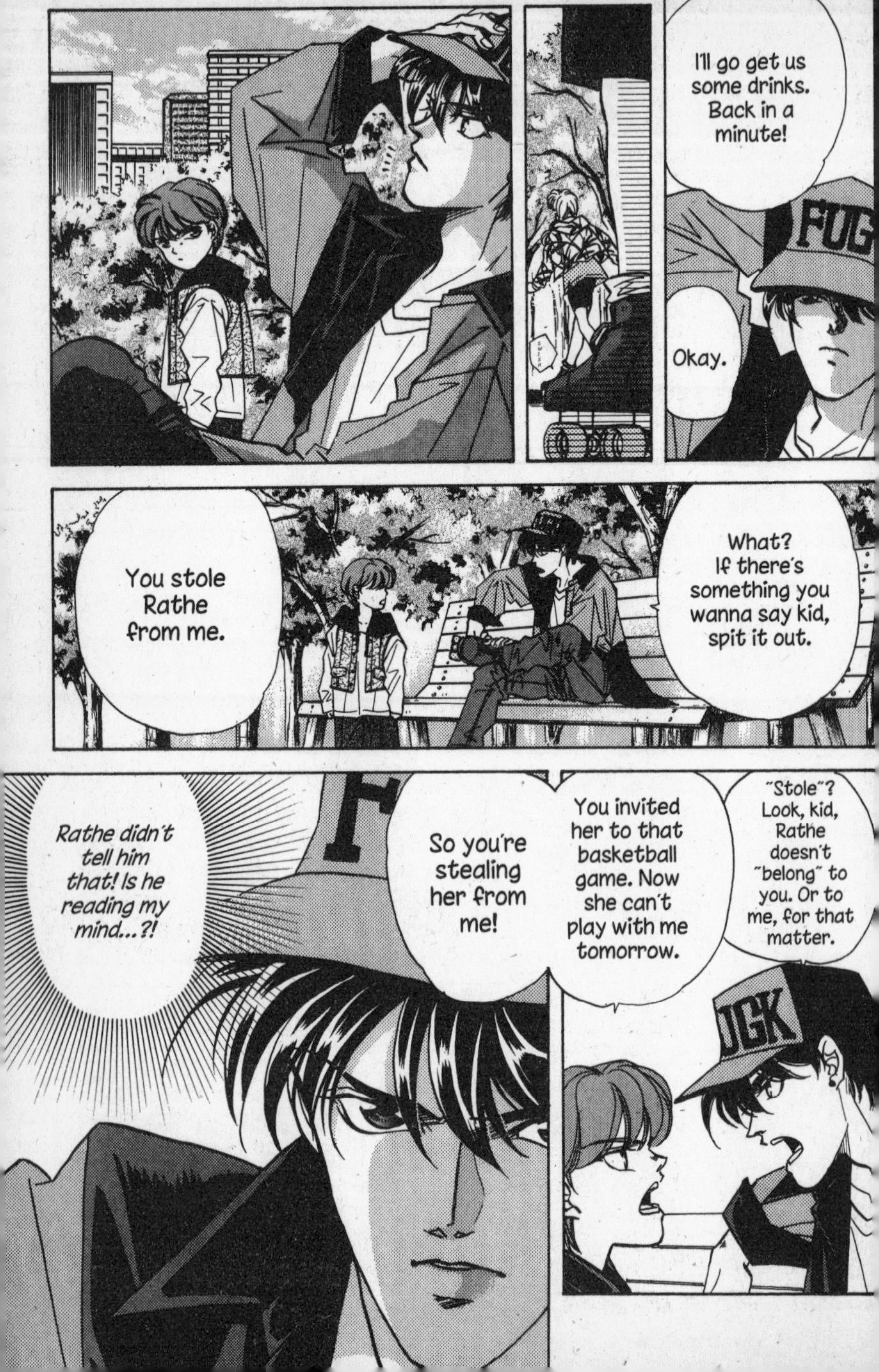
I'll go get us some drinks. Back in a minute!
Okay.
What? If there's something you wanna say kid, spit it out.
You stole Rathe from me.
"Stole"? Look, kid, Rathe doesn't "belong" to you. Or to me, for that matter.
You invited her to that basketball game. Now she can't play with me tomorrow.
So you're stealing her from me!
Rathe didn't tell him that! Is he reading my mind...?!

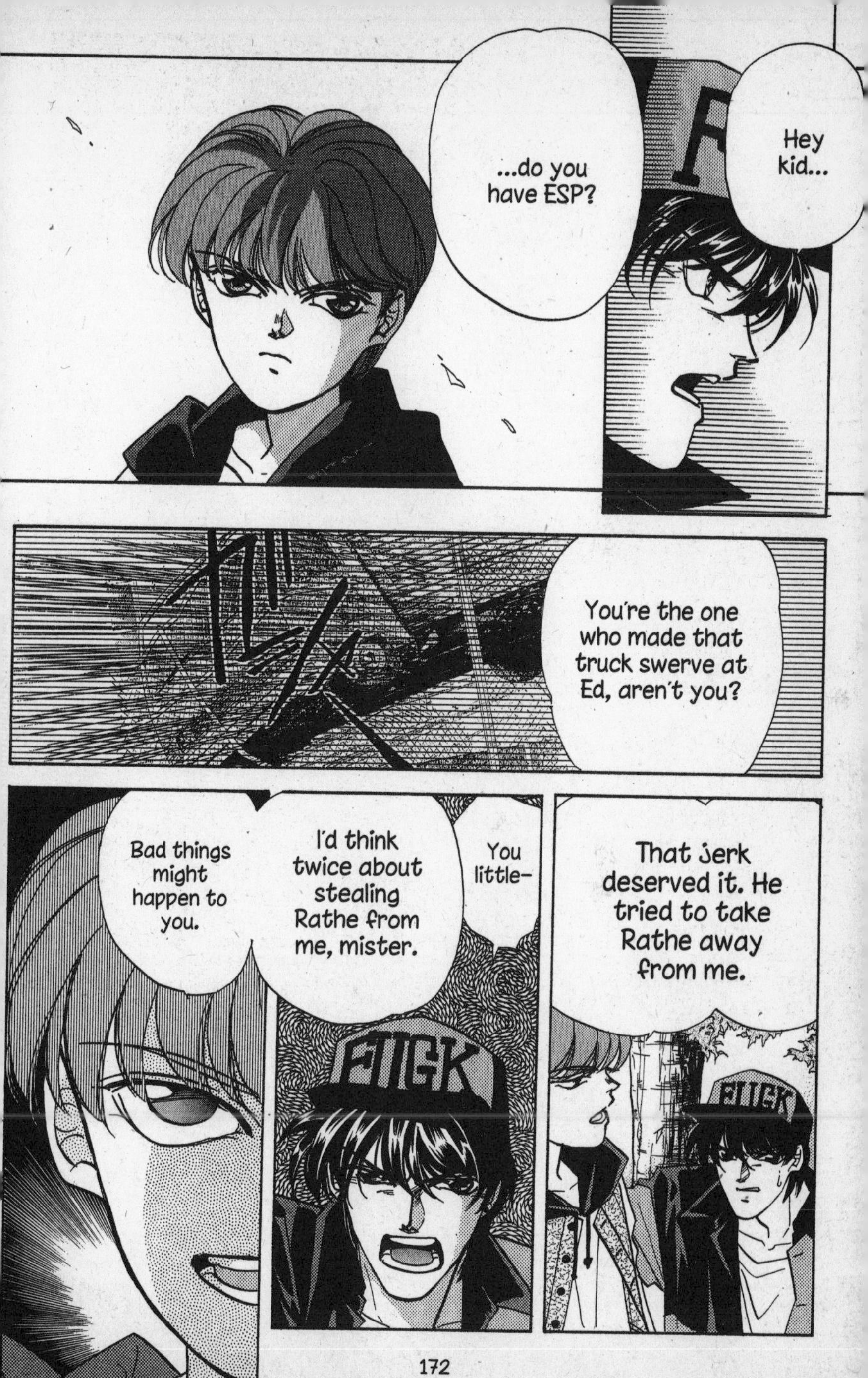
Hey kid...
...do you have ESP?
You're the one who made that truck swerve at Ed, aren't you?
That jerk deserved it. He tried to take Rathe away from me.
You little-
I'd think twice about stealing Rathe from me, mister.
Bad things might happen to you.

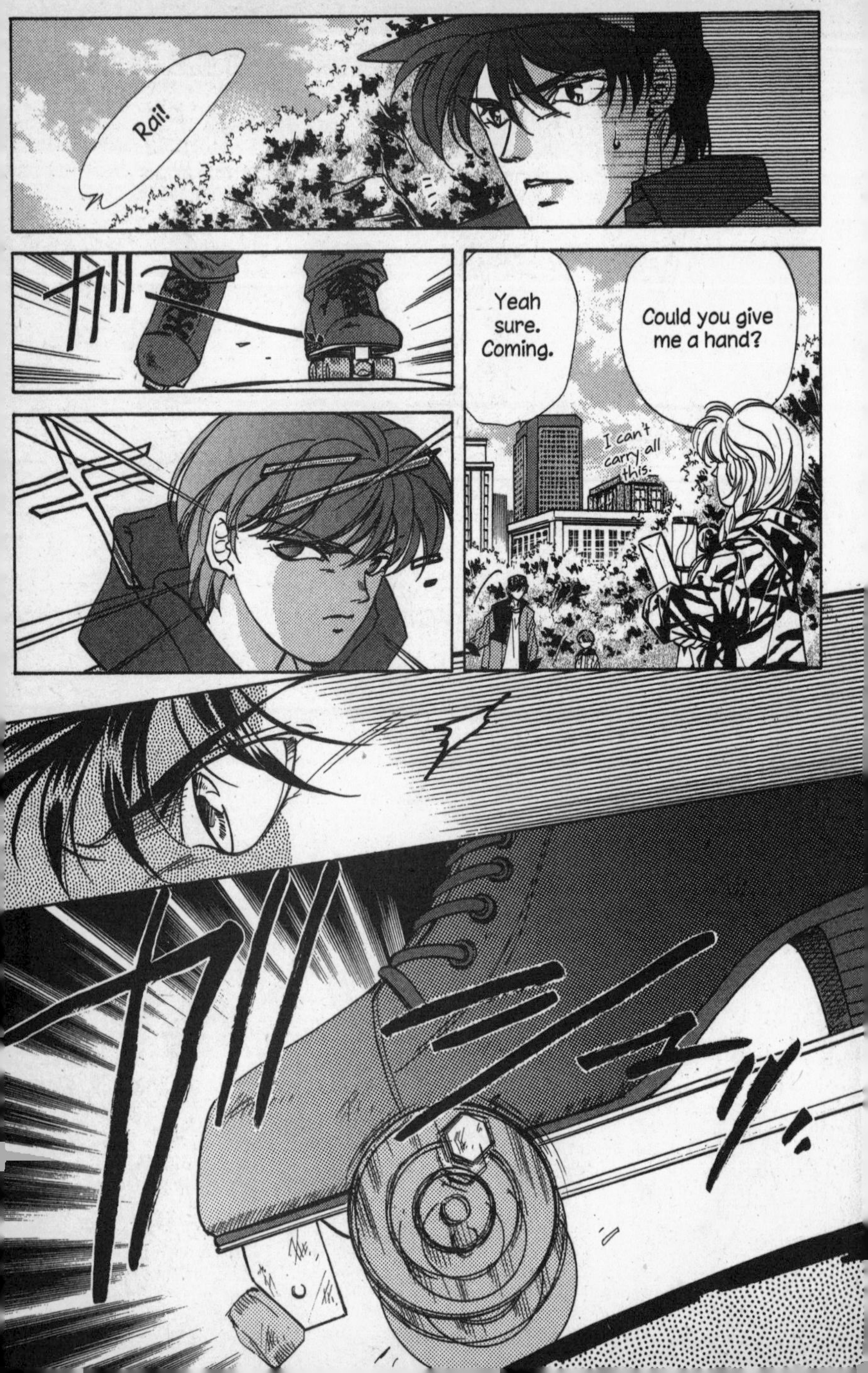
Rai!
Could you give me a hand?
Yeah sure. Coming.
I can't carry all this.

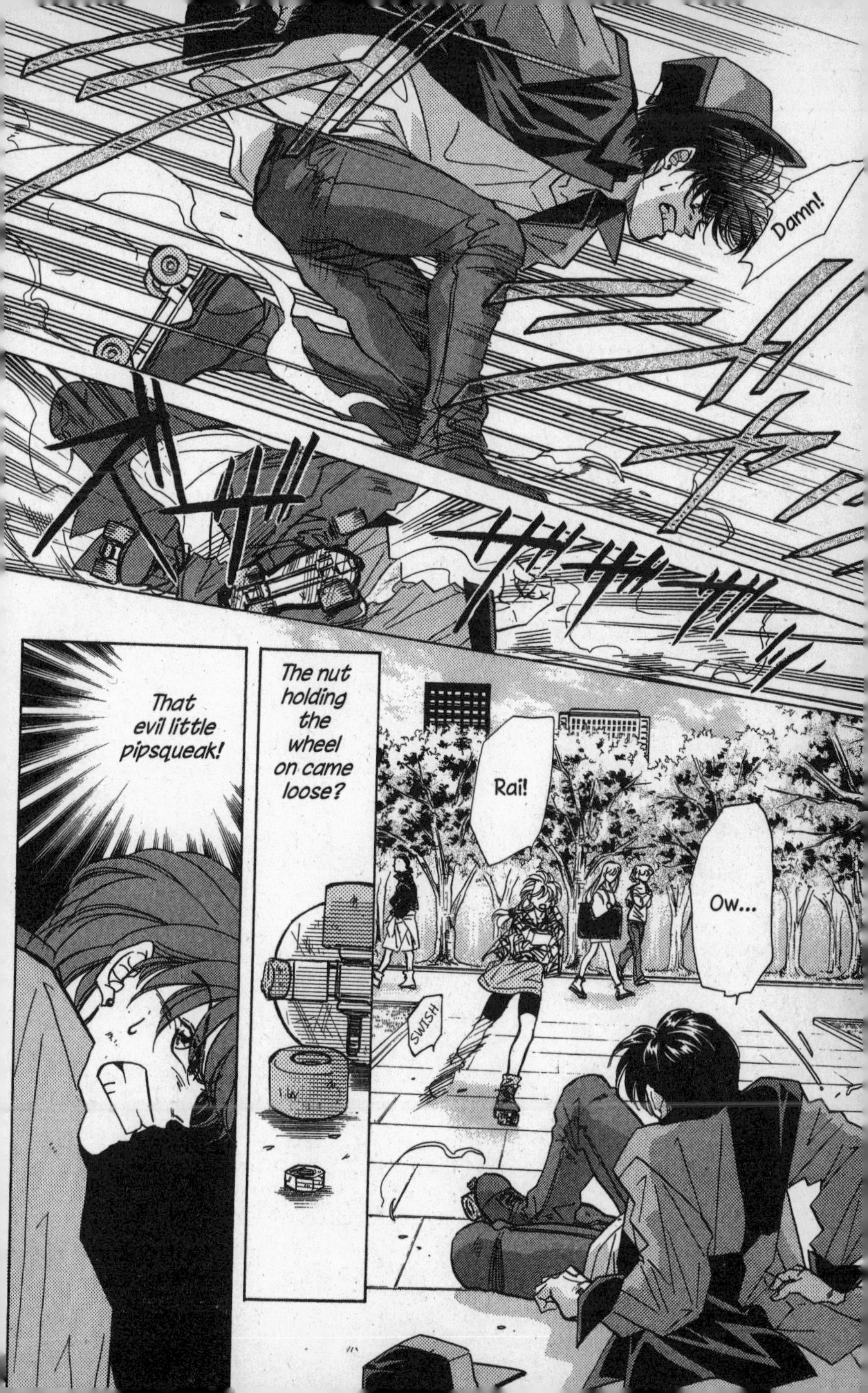
Damn!
Ow...
Rai!
SWISH
The nut holding the wheel on came loose?
That evil little pipsqueak!

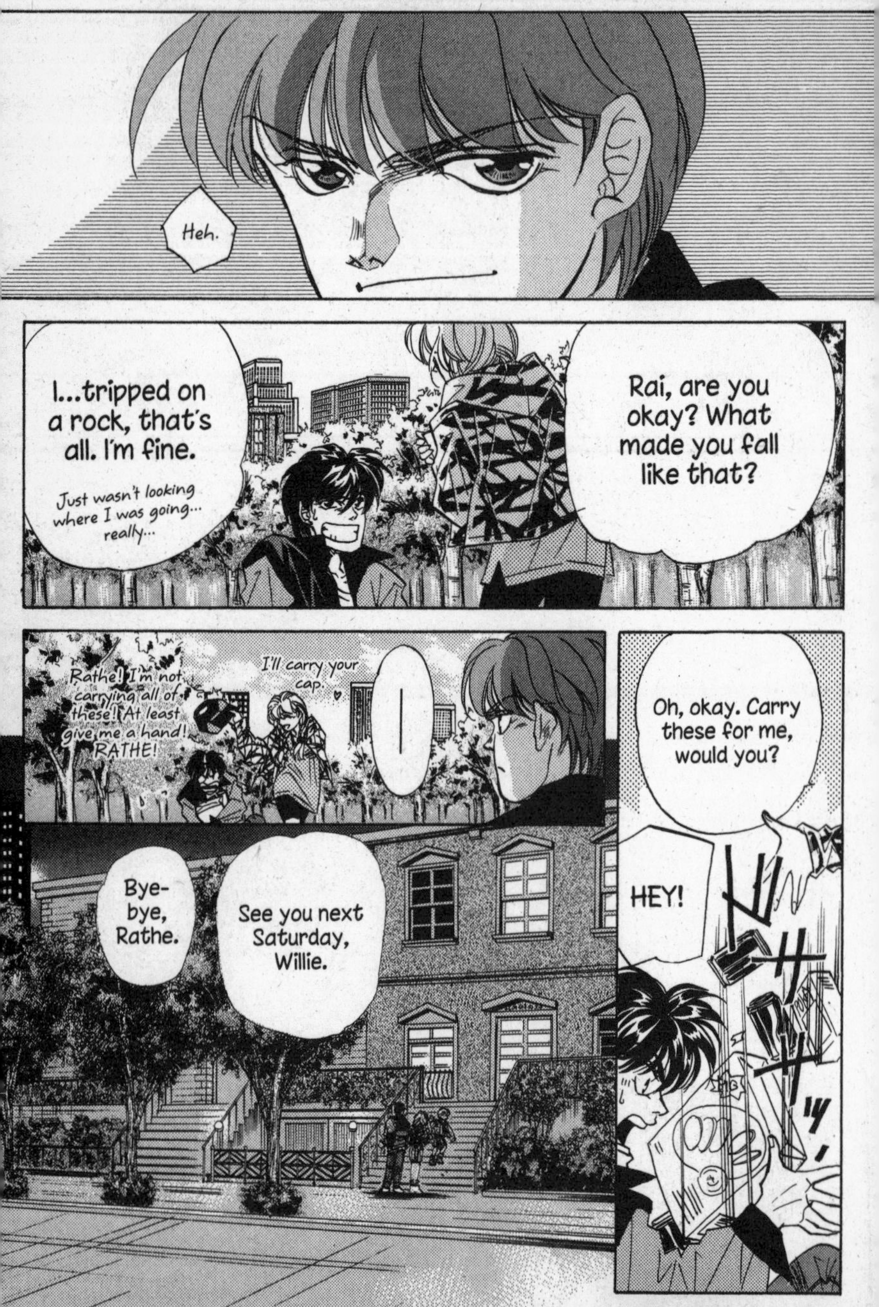
Heh.
Rai, are you okay? What made you fall like that?
I...tripped on a rock, that's all. I'm fine.
Just wasn't looking where I was going... really...
Oh, okay. Carry these for me, would you?
HEY!
I'll carry your cap.
Rathe! I'm not carrying all of these! At least give me a hand! RATHE!
See you next Saturday, Willie.
Bye-bye, Rathe.

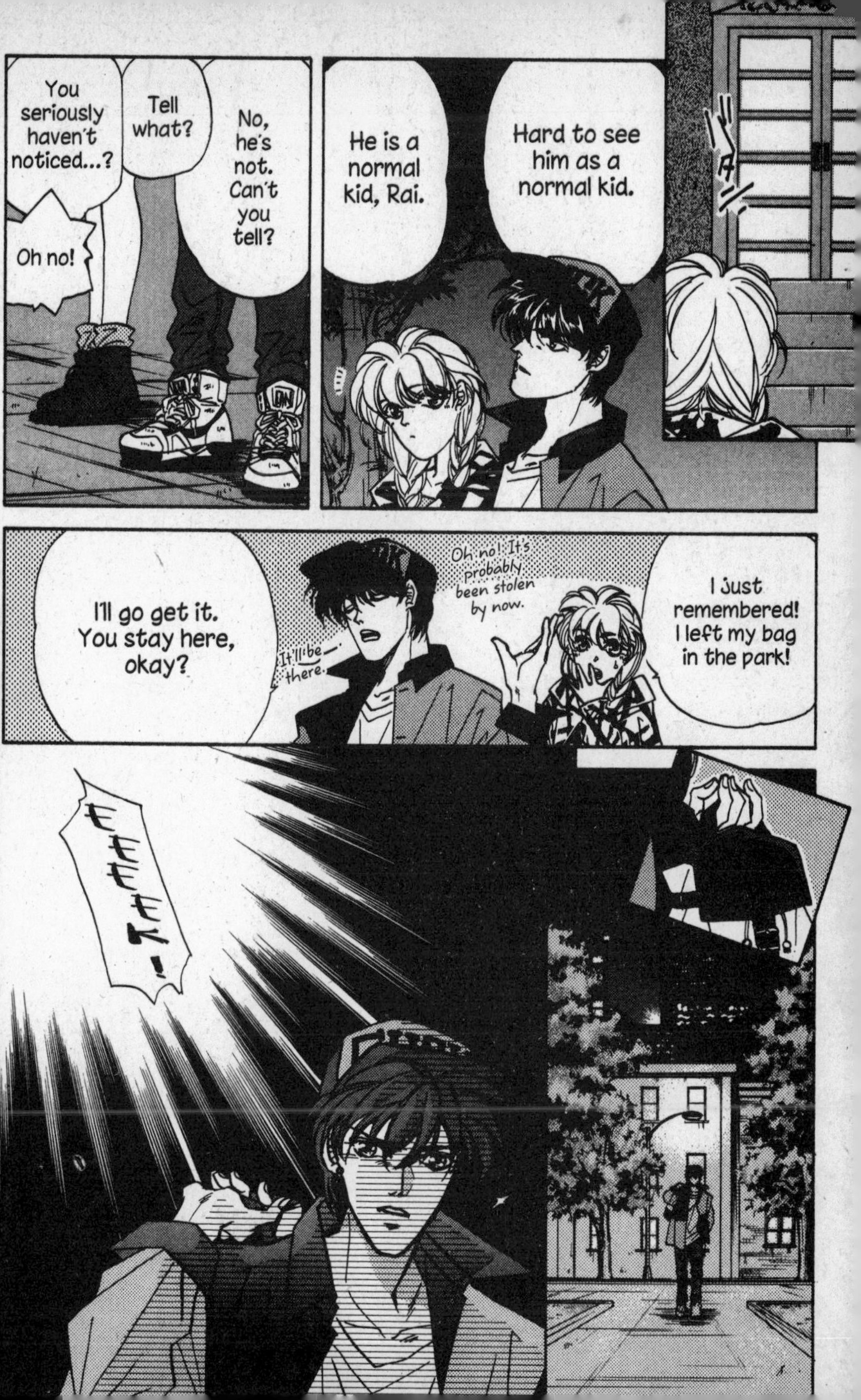
Hard to see him as a normal kid.
He is a normal kid, Rai.
No, he's not. Can't you tell?
Tell what?
You seriously haven't noticed...?
Oh no!
I just remembered! I left my bag in the park!
Oh no! It's probably been stolen by now.
It'll be— there.
I'll go get it. You stay here, okay?
EEEEEK!

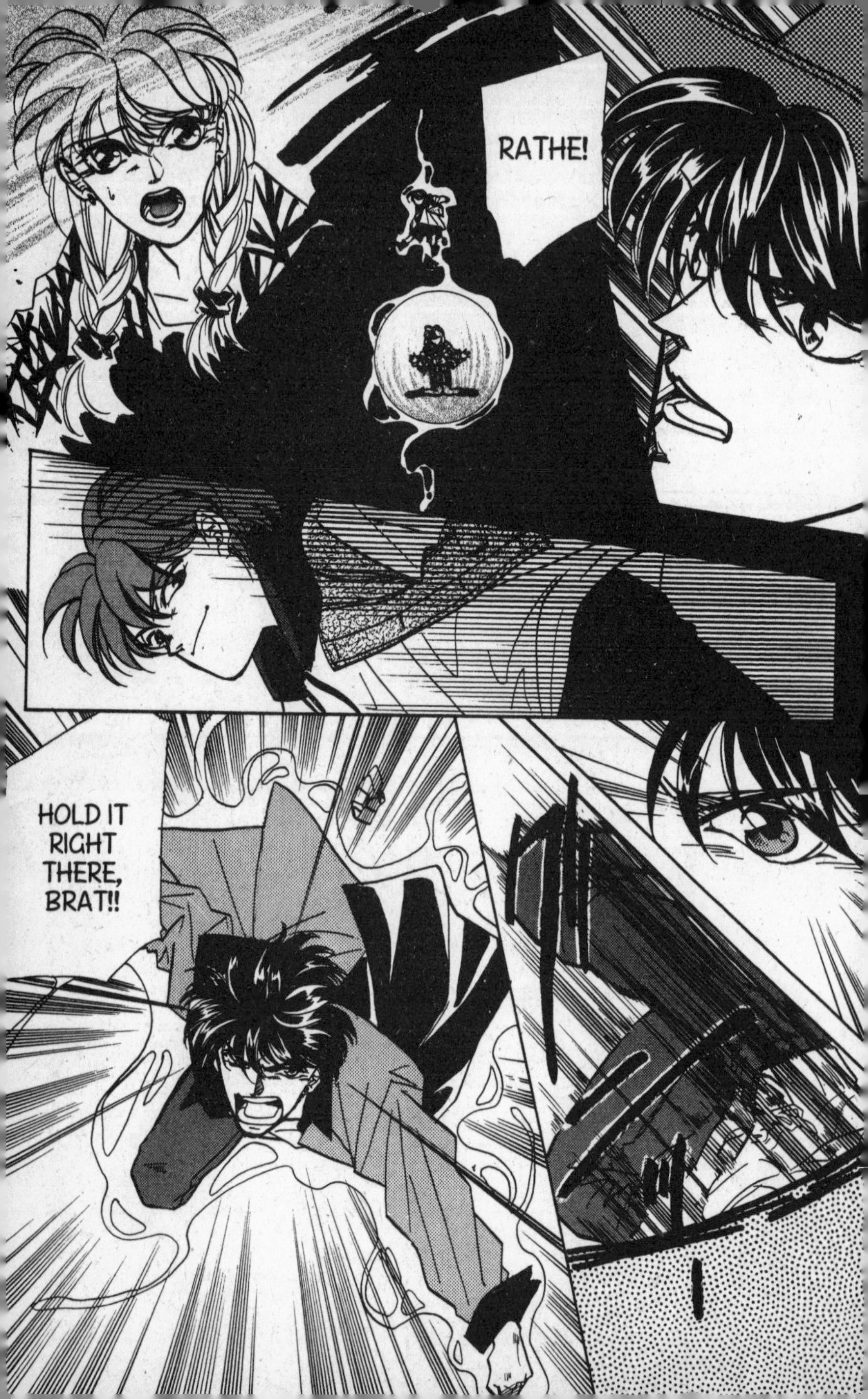
RATHE!
HOLD IT RIGHT THERE, BRAT!!

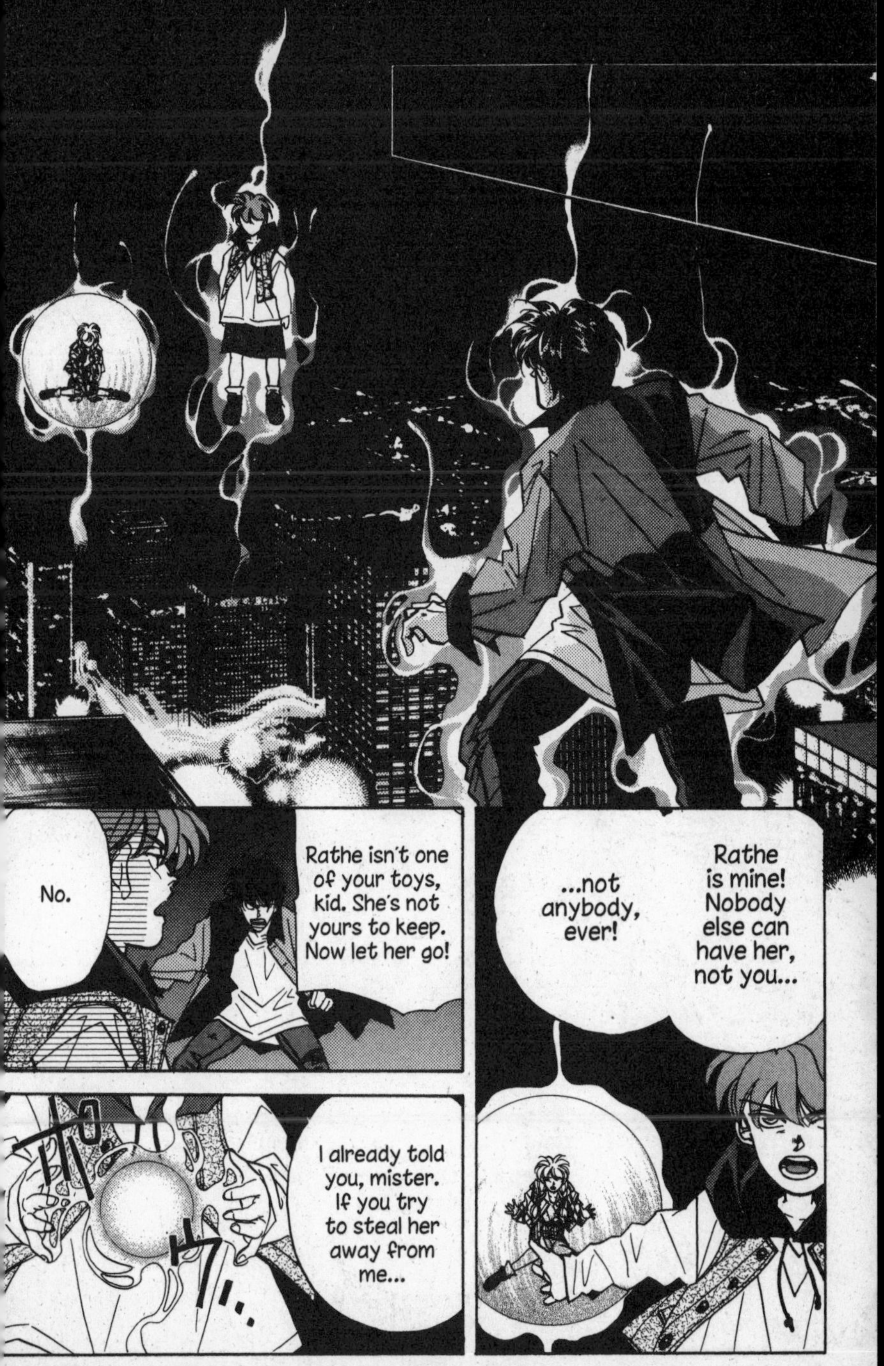
Rathe is mine! Nobody else can have her, not you...
...not anybody, ever!
Rathe isn't one of your toys, kid. She's not yours to keep. Now let her go!
No.
I already told you, mister. If you try to steal her away from me...

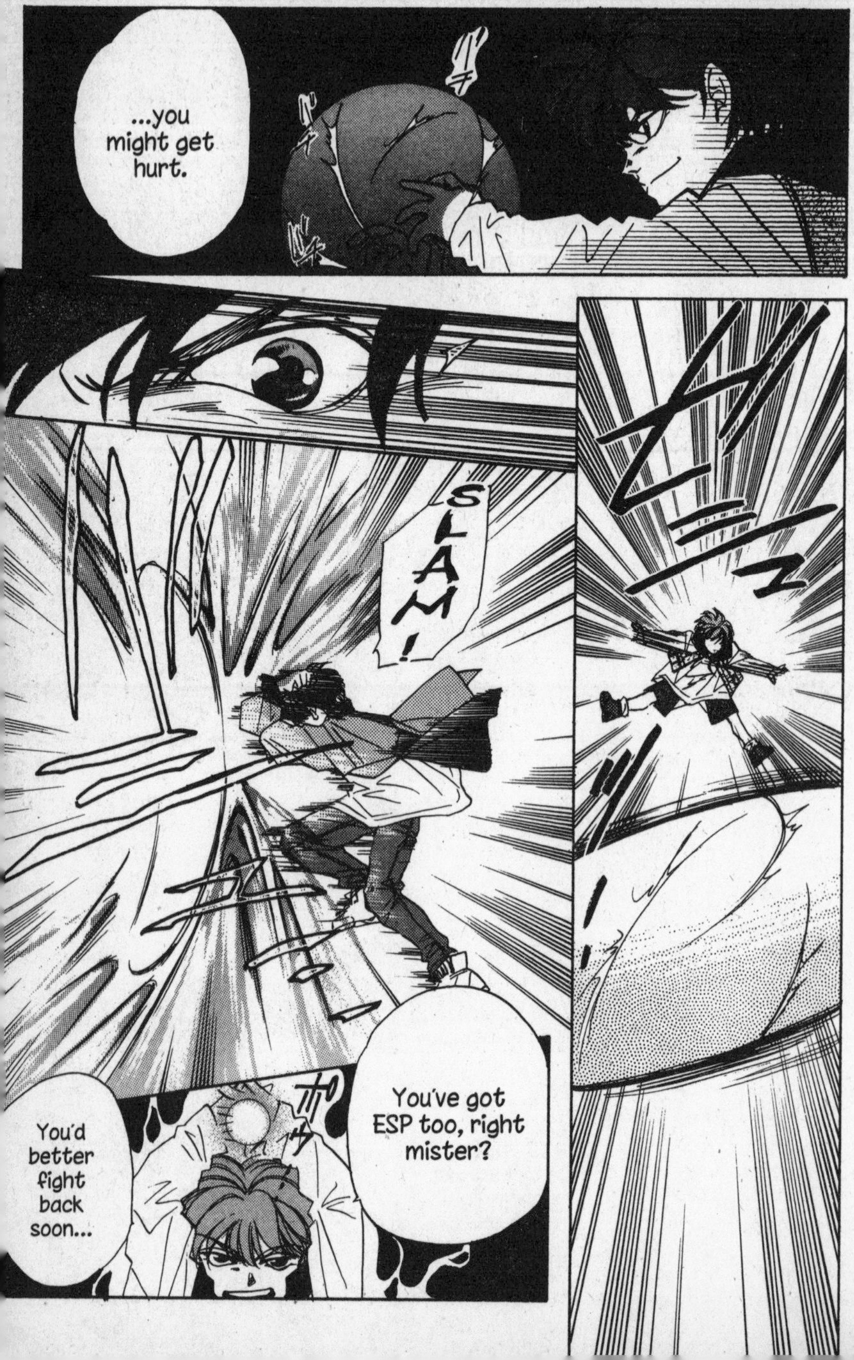
...you might get hurt.
SLAM!
You've got ESP too, right mister?
You'd better fight back soon...

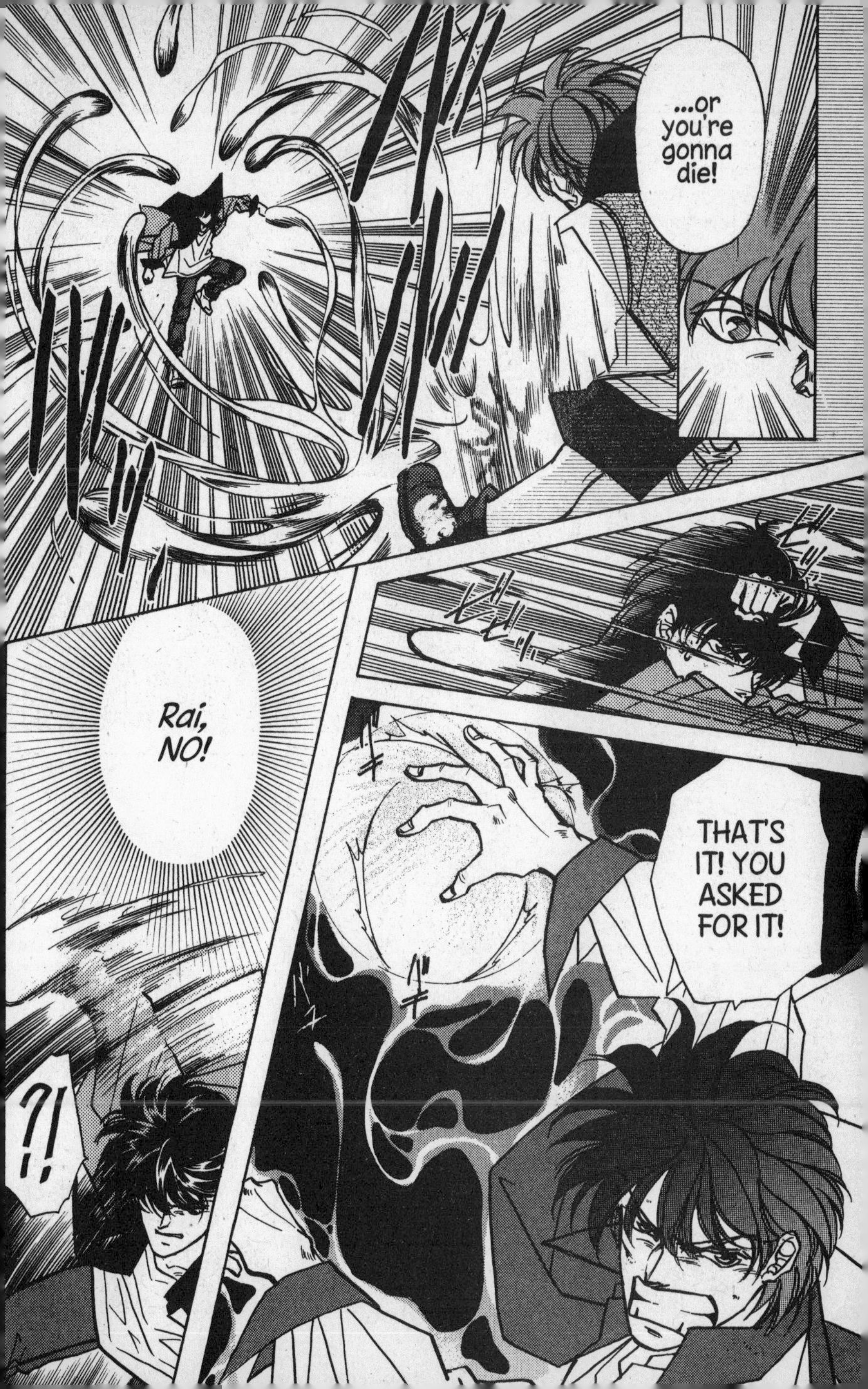
...or you're gonna die!
THAT'S IT! YOU ASKED FOR IT!
Rai, NO!
?!

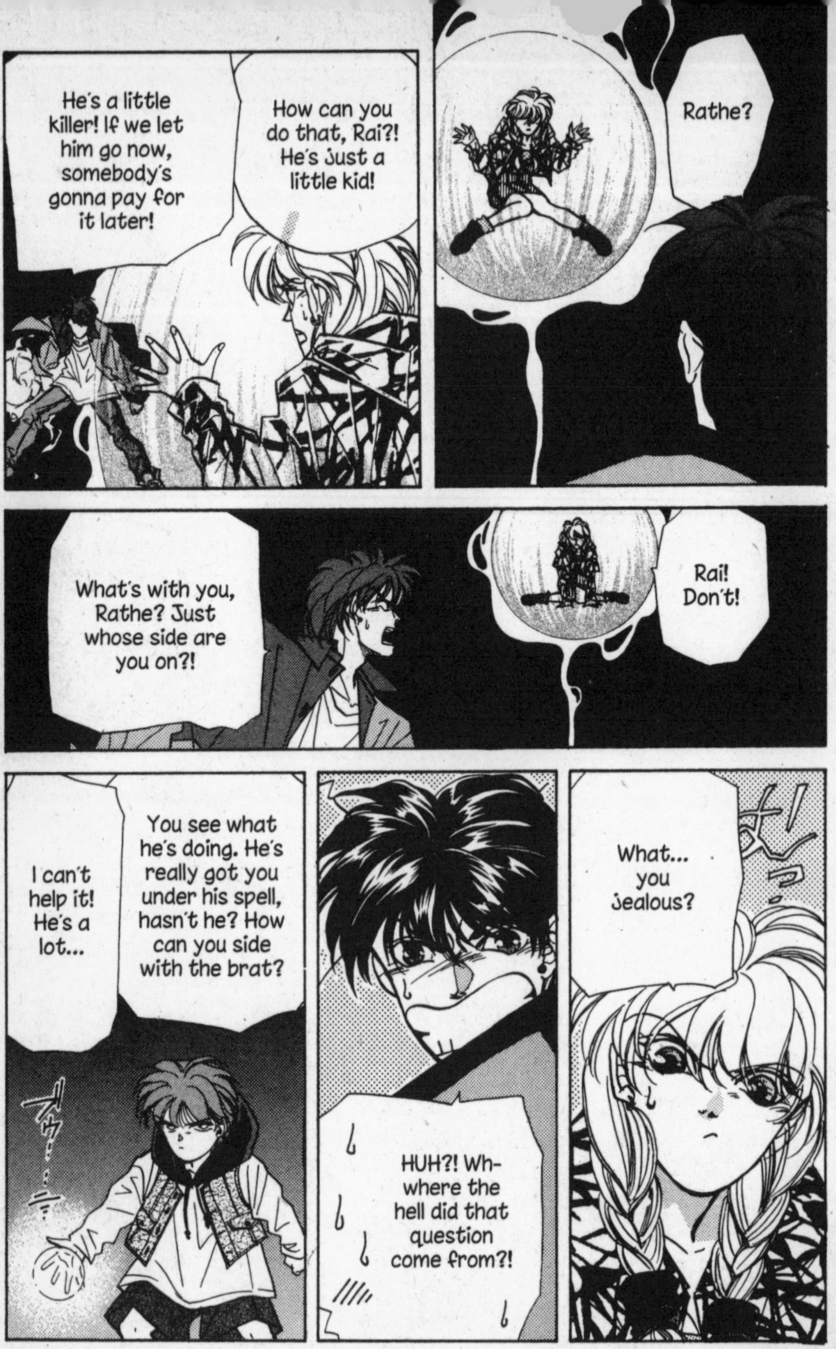
Rathe?
How can you do that, Rai?! He's just a little kid!
He's a little killer! If we let him go now, somebody's gonna pay for it later!
Rai! Don't!
What's with you, Rathe? Just whose side are you on?!
What... you jealous?
HUH?! Wh- where the hell did that question come from?!
You see what he's doing. He's really got you under his spell, hasn't he? How can you side with the brat?
I can't help it! He's a lot...

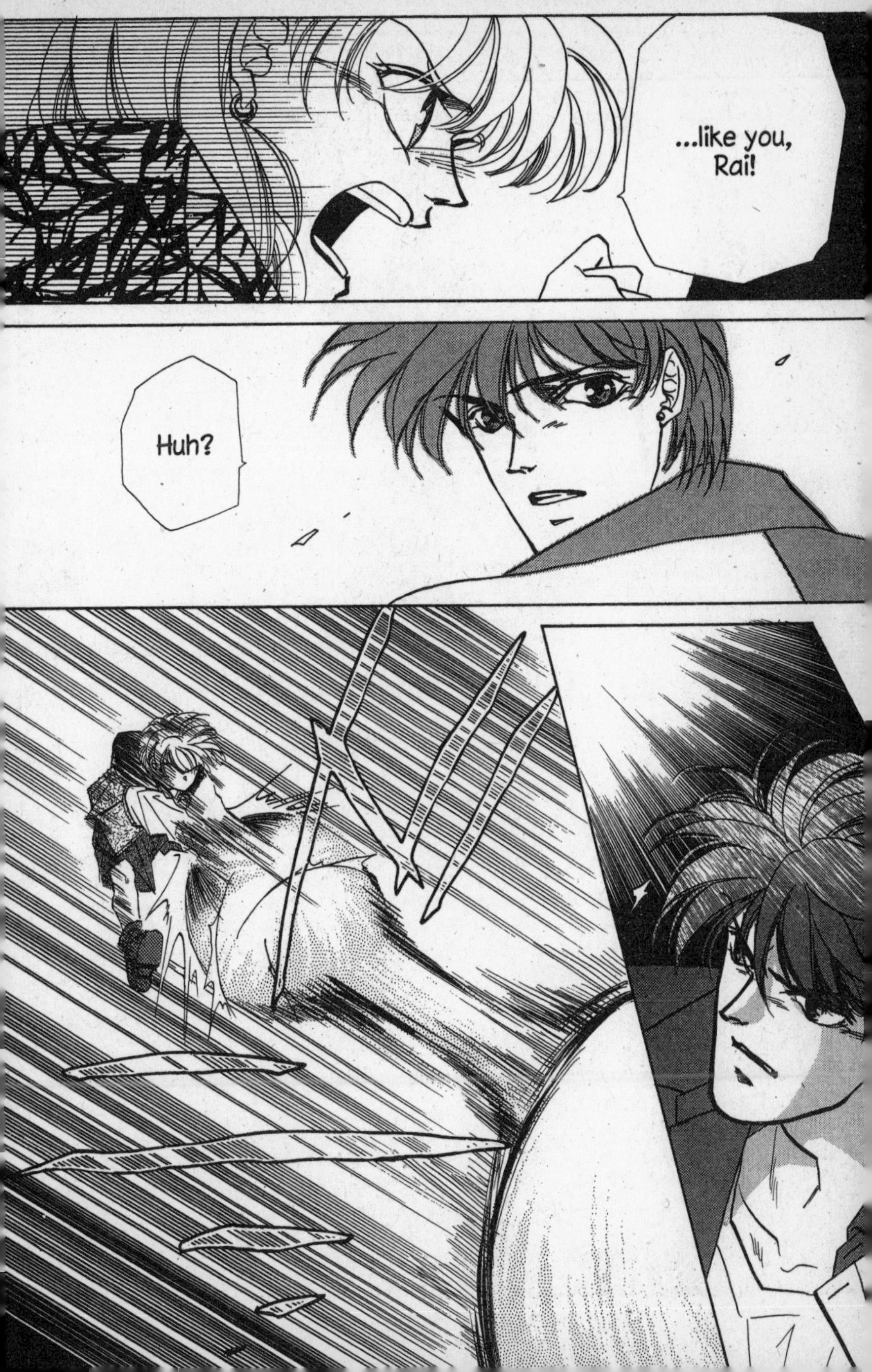
...like you, Rai!
Huh?

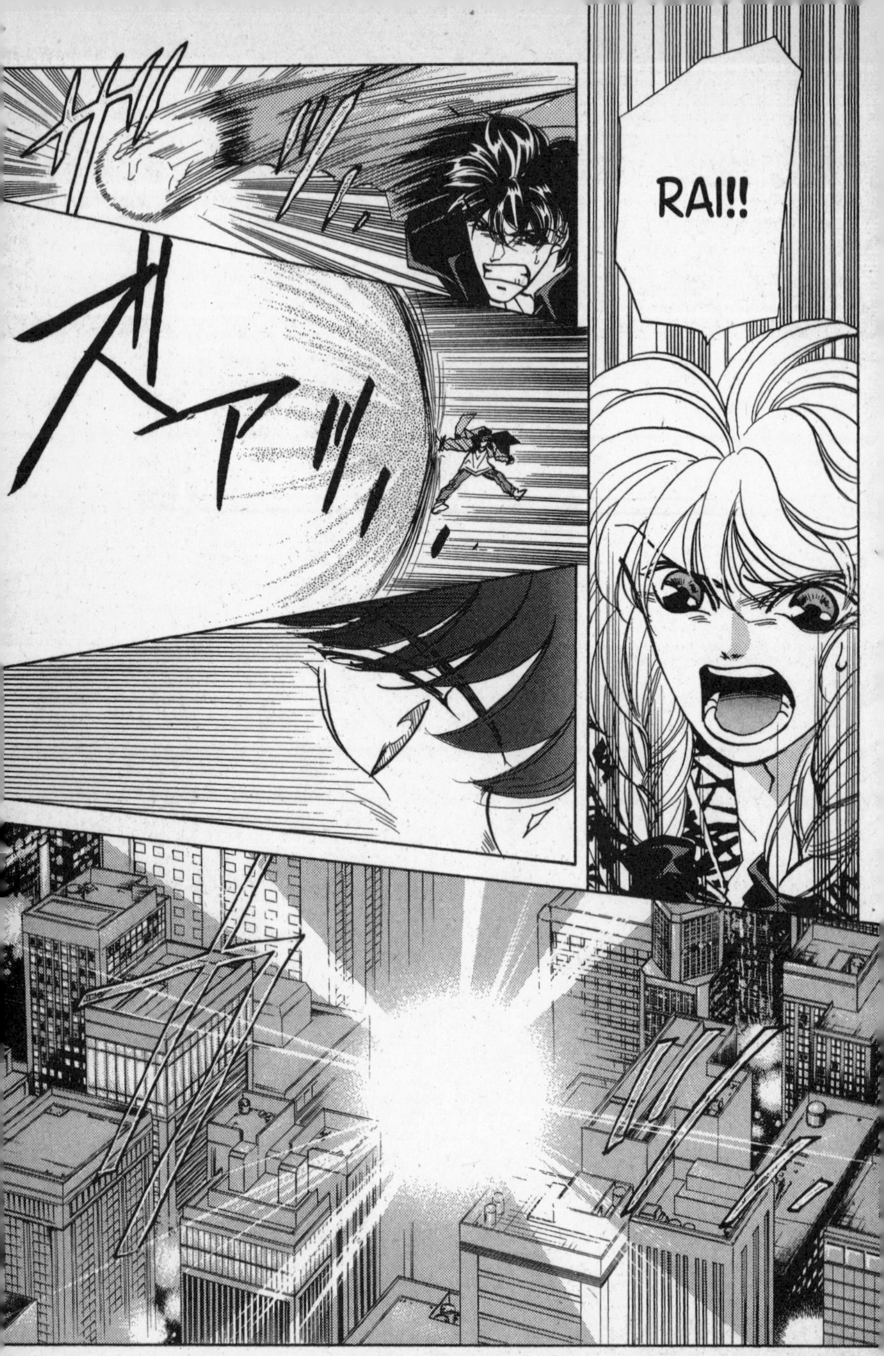
RAI!!

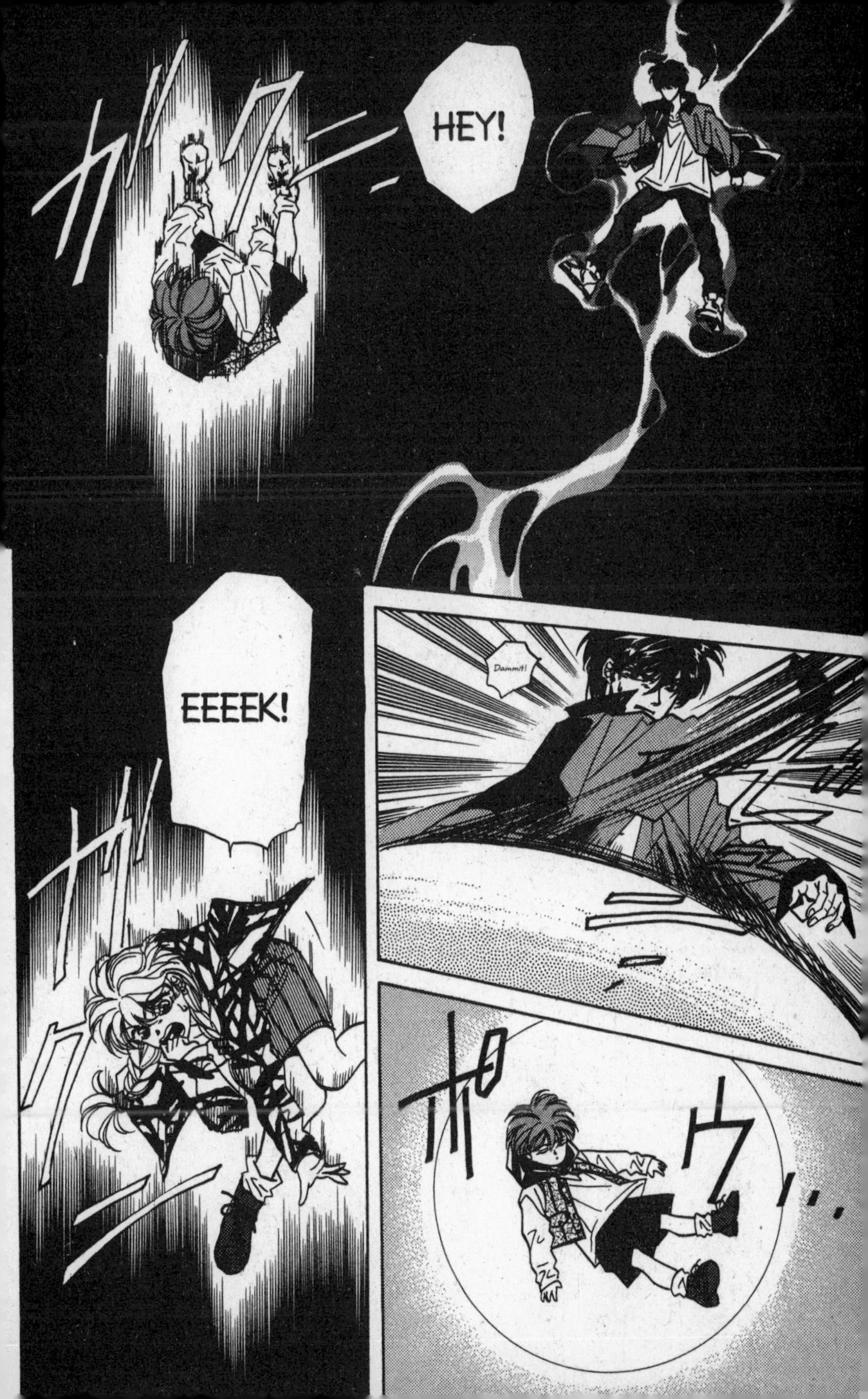
HEY!
Dammit!
EEEEK!

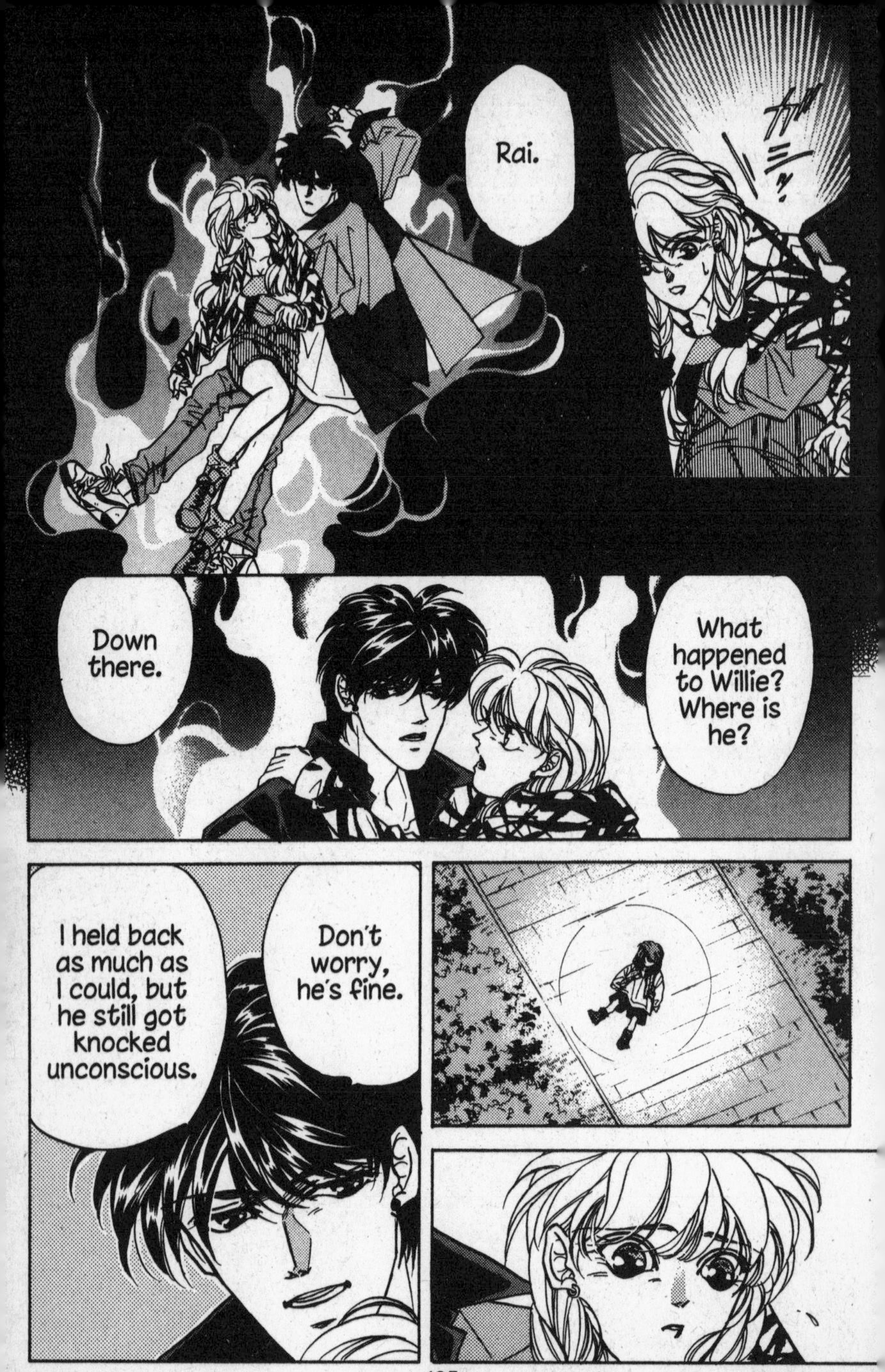
Rai.
What happened to Willie? Where is he?
Down there.
Don't worry, he's fine.
I held back as much as I could, but he still got knocked unconscious.

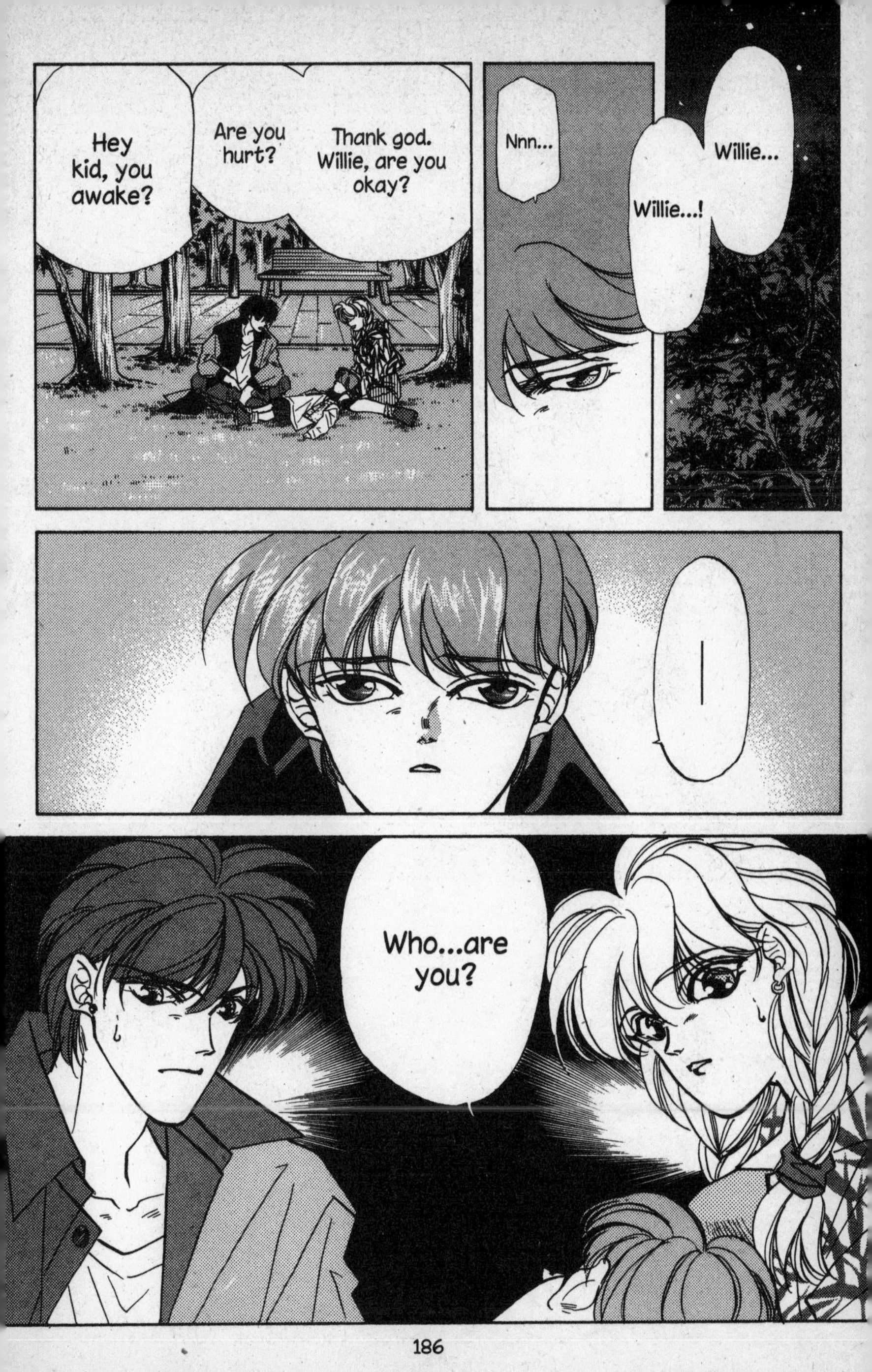
Willie...
Willie...!
Nnn...
Thank god. Willie, are you okay?
Are you hurt?
Hey kid, you awake?
Who...are you?

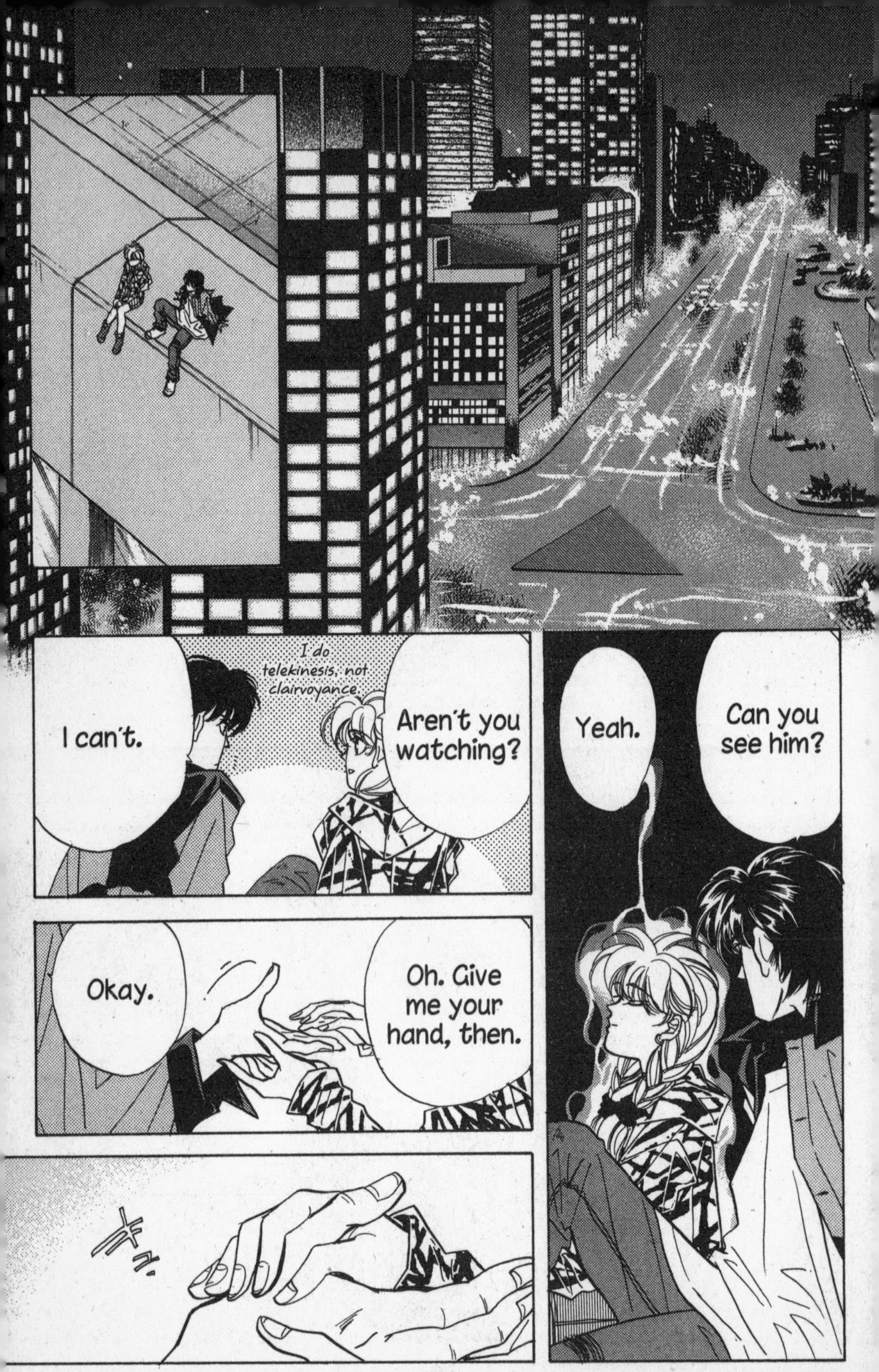
Can you see him?
Yeah.
Aren't you watching?
I do telekinesis, not clairvoyance.
I can't.
Oh. Give me your hand, then.
Okay.

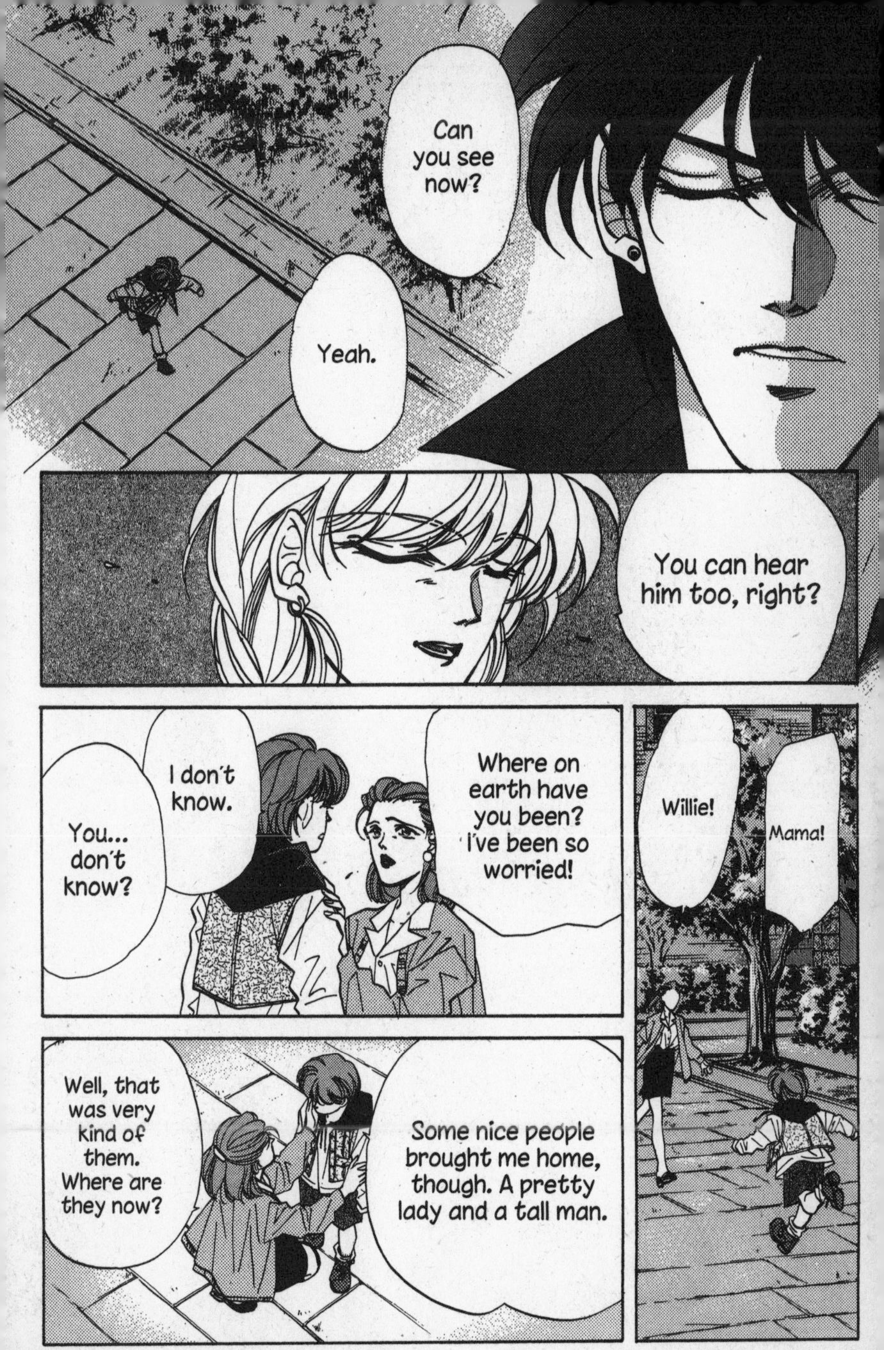
Can you see now?
Yeah.
You can hear him too, right?
Willie!
Mama!
Where on earth have you been? I've been so worried!
I don't know.
You... don't know?
Some nice people brought me home, though. A pretty lady and a tall man.
Well, that was very kind of them. Where are they now?

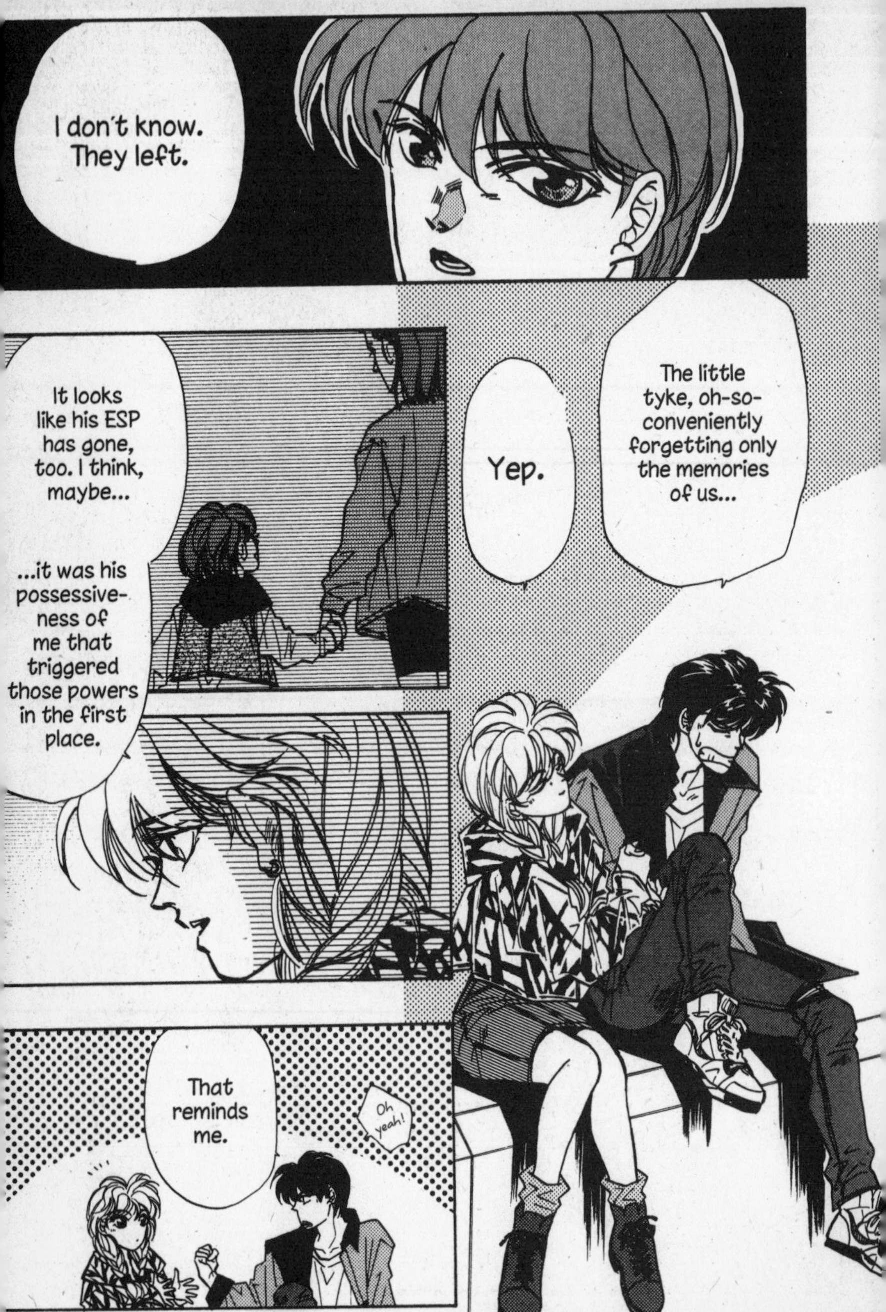

I don't know. They left.
The little tyke, oh-so-conveniently forgetting only the memories of us...
Yep.
It looks like his ESP has gone, too. I think, maybe...
...it was his possessive-ness of me that triggered those powers in the first place.
That reminds me.
Oh yeah!

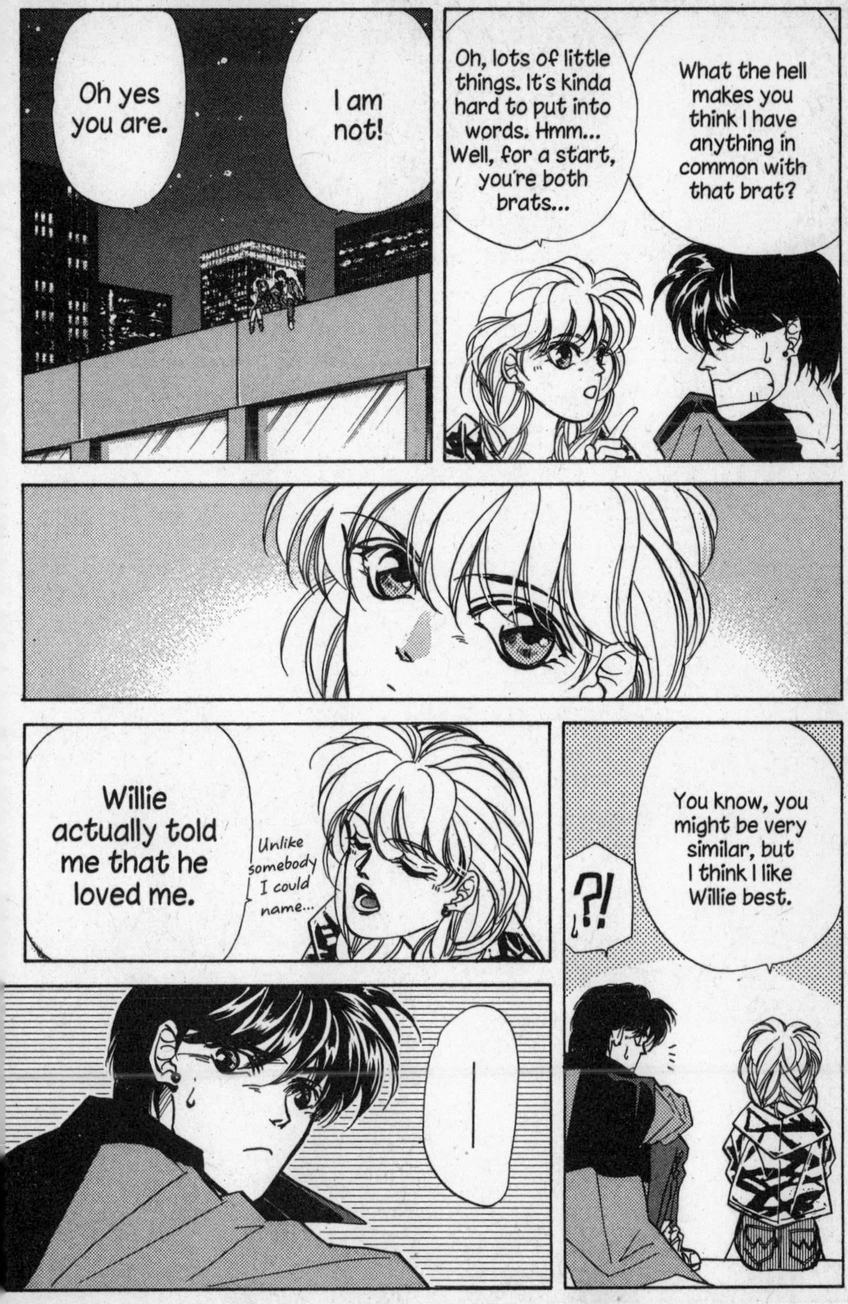
What the hell makes you think I have anything in common with that brat?
Oh, lots of little things. It's kinda hard to put into words. Hmm... Well, for a start, you're both brats...
I am not!
Oh yes you are.
You know, you might be very similar, but I think I like Willie best.
¿?!
Willie actually told me that he loved me.
Unlike somebody I could name...

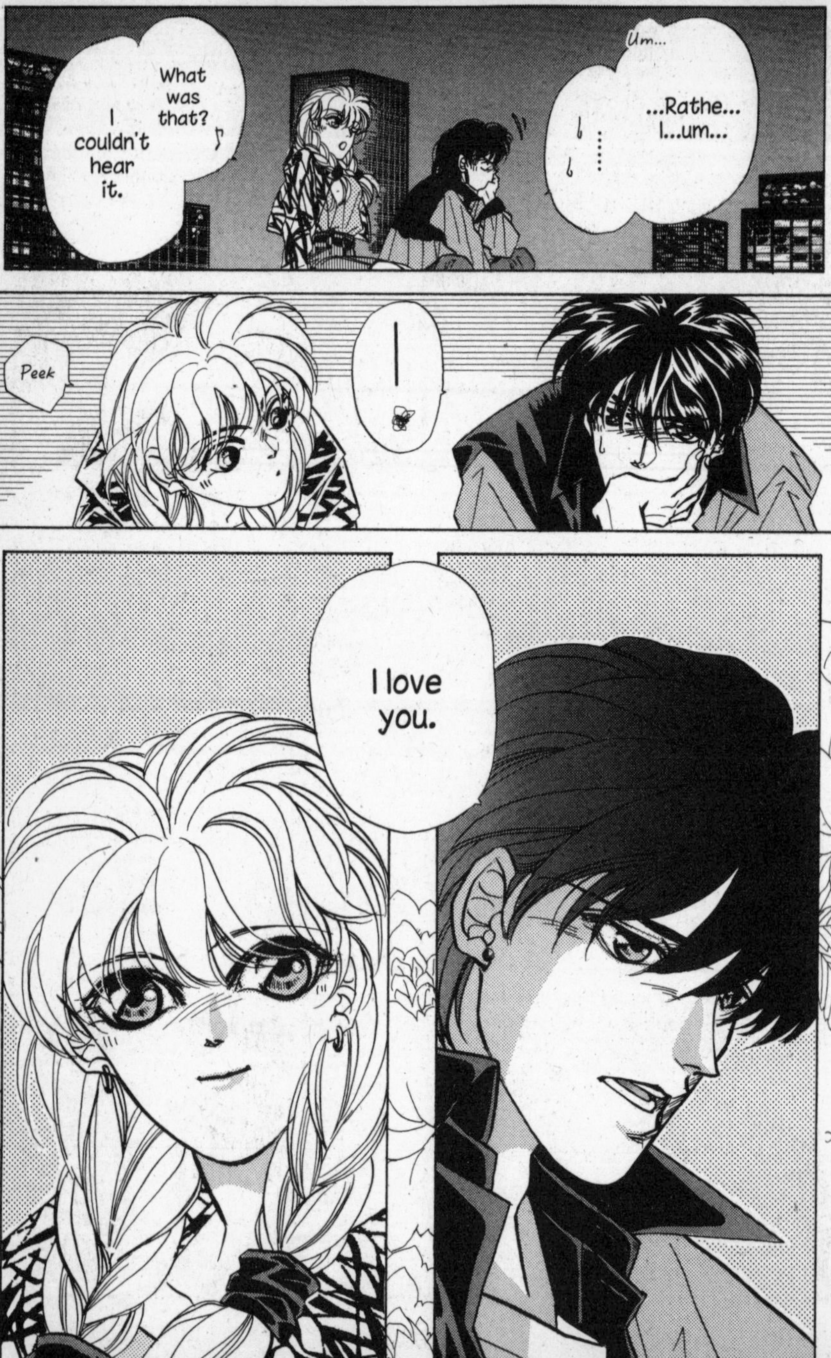
Um...
...Rathe... I...um...
What was that? I couldn't hear it.
I
Peek
I love you.

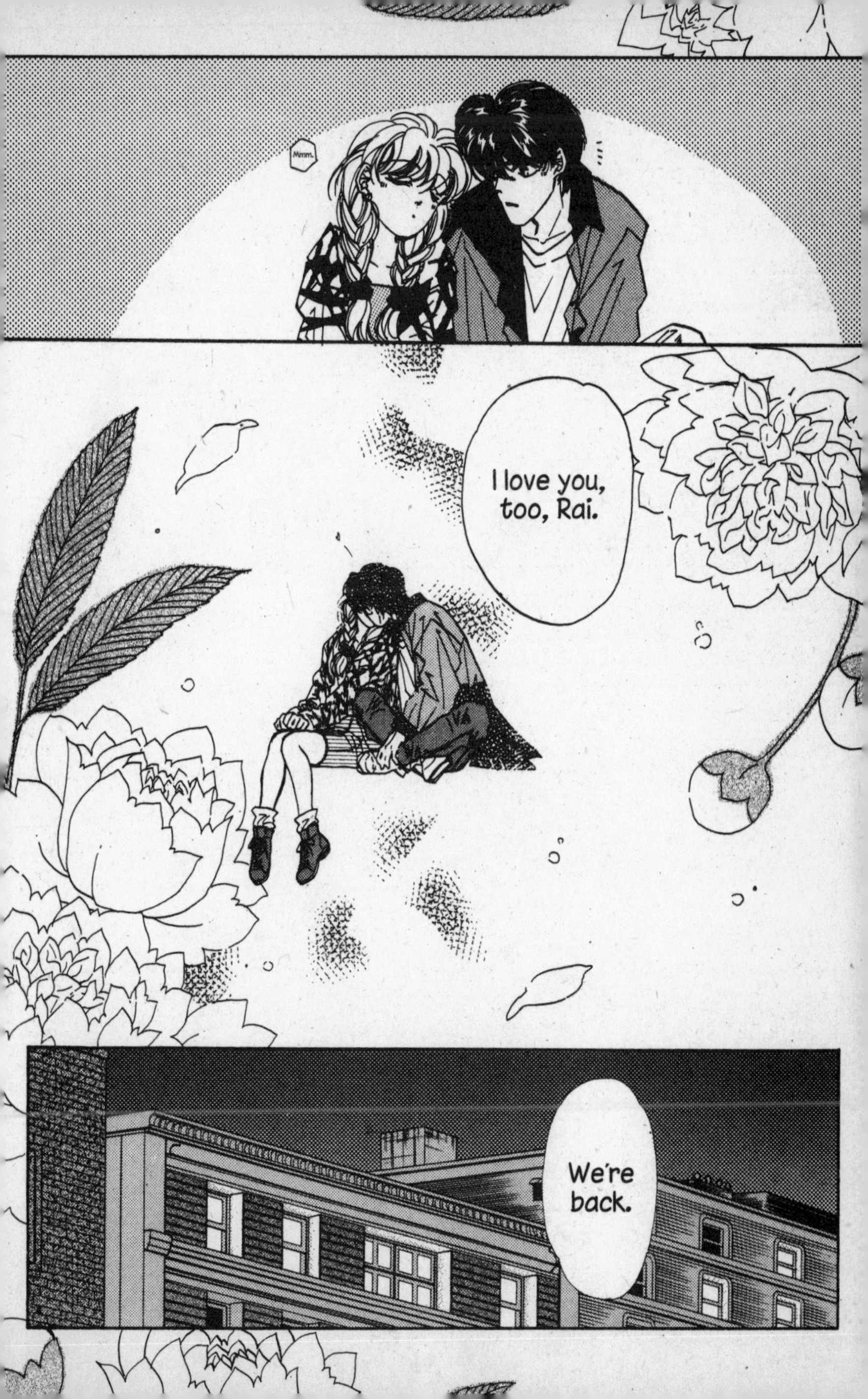
Mmm.
I love you, too, Rai.
We're back.

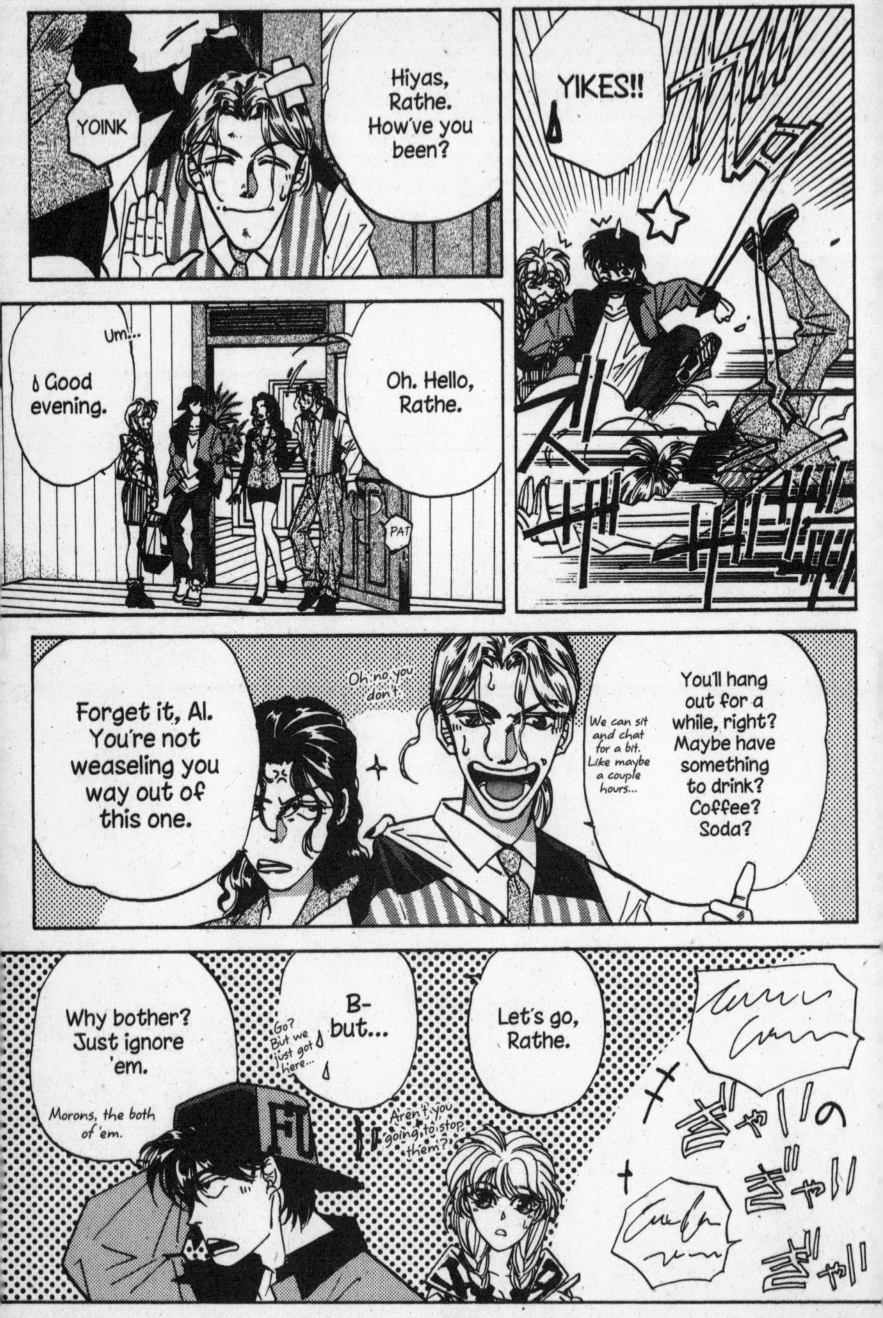
YIKES!!
Hiyas, Rathe. How've you been?
YOINK
Oh. Hello, Rathe.
Um... Good evening.
PAT
You'll hang out for a while, right? Maybe have something to drink? Coffee? Soda?
We can sit and chat for a bit. Like maybe a couple hours...
Oh no you don't.
Forget it, Al. You're not weaseling you way out of this one.
Let's go, Rathe.
B- but...
Go? But we just got here...
Aren't you going to stop them?
Why bother? Just ignore 'em.
Morons, the both of 'em.
ぎゃいの
ぎゃい
ぎゃい

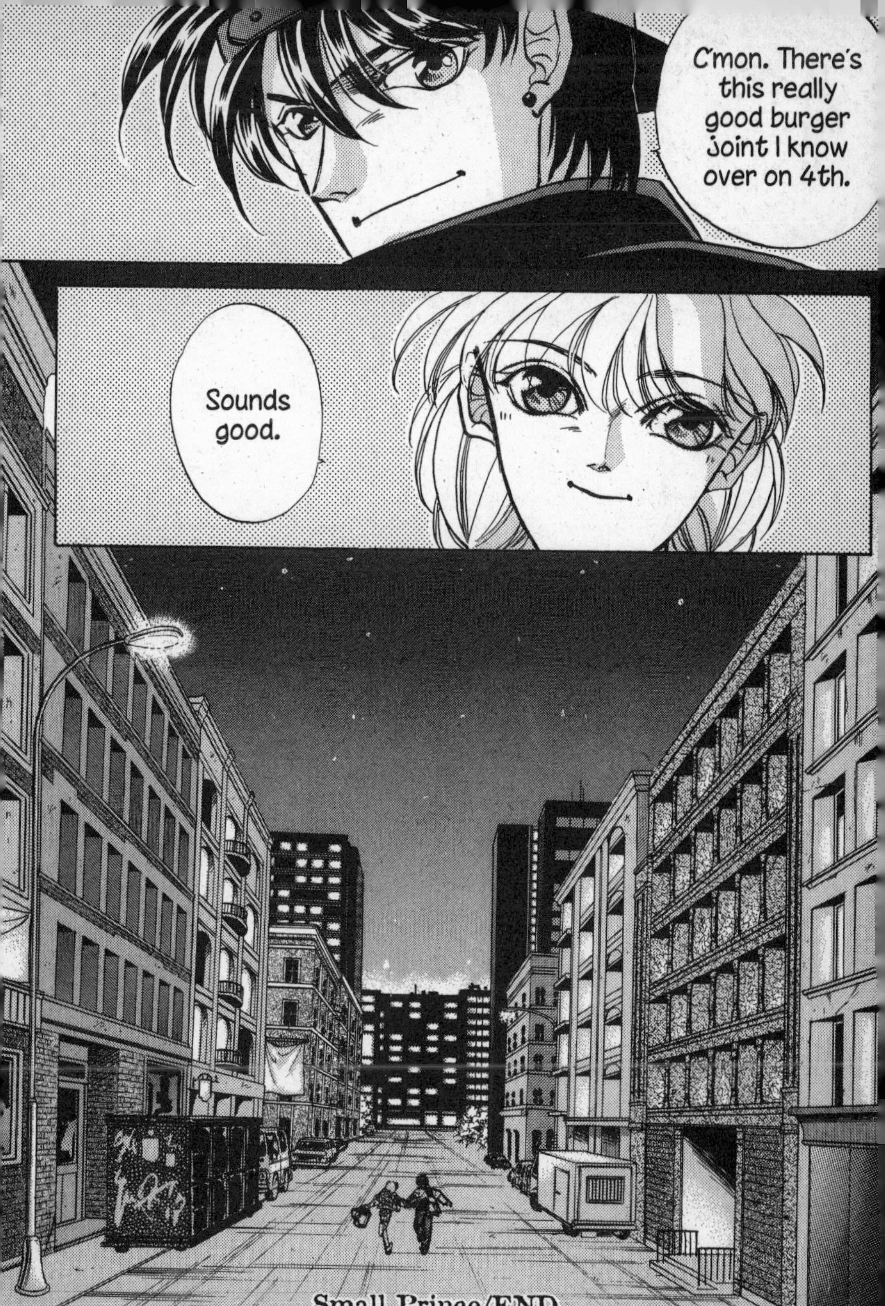
C'mon. There's this really good burger joint I know over on 4th.
Sounds good.
Small Prince/END

Free Talk.

by Matoh

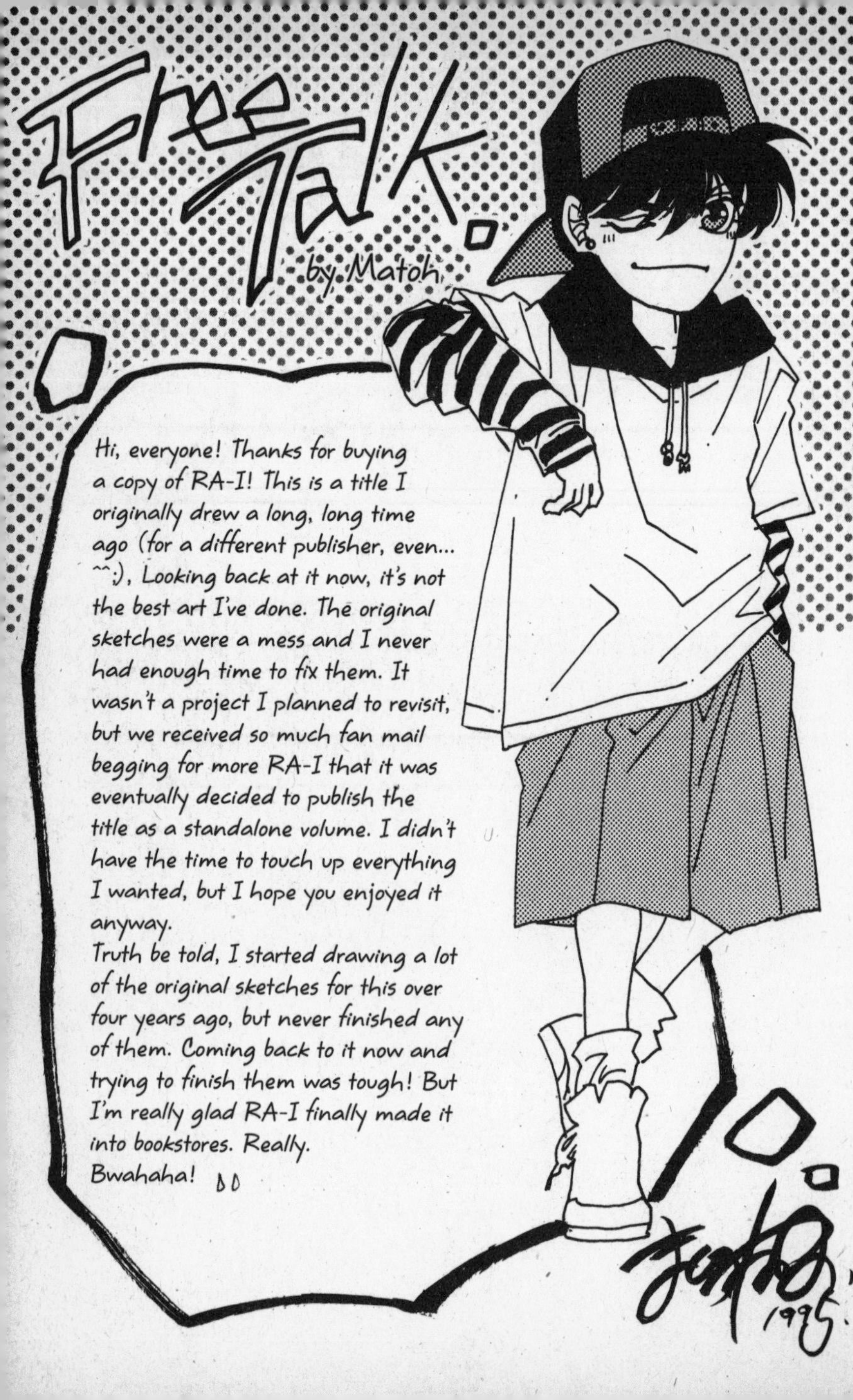

Hi, everyone! Thanks for buying a copy of RA-I! This is a title I originally drew a long, long time ago (for a different publisher, even... ^^;), Looking back at it now, it's not the best art I've done. The original sketches were a mess and I never had enough time to fix them. It wasn't a project I planned to revisit, but we received so much fan mail begging for more RA-I that it was eventually decided to publish the title as a standalone volume. I didn't have the time to touch up everything I wanted, but I hope you enjoyed it anyway.

Truth be told, I started drawing a lot of the original sketches for this over four years ago, but never finished any of them. Coming back to it now and trying to finish them was tough! But I'm really glad RA-I finally made it into bookstores. Really.

Bwahaha!

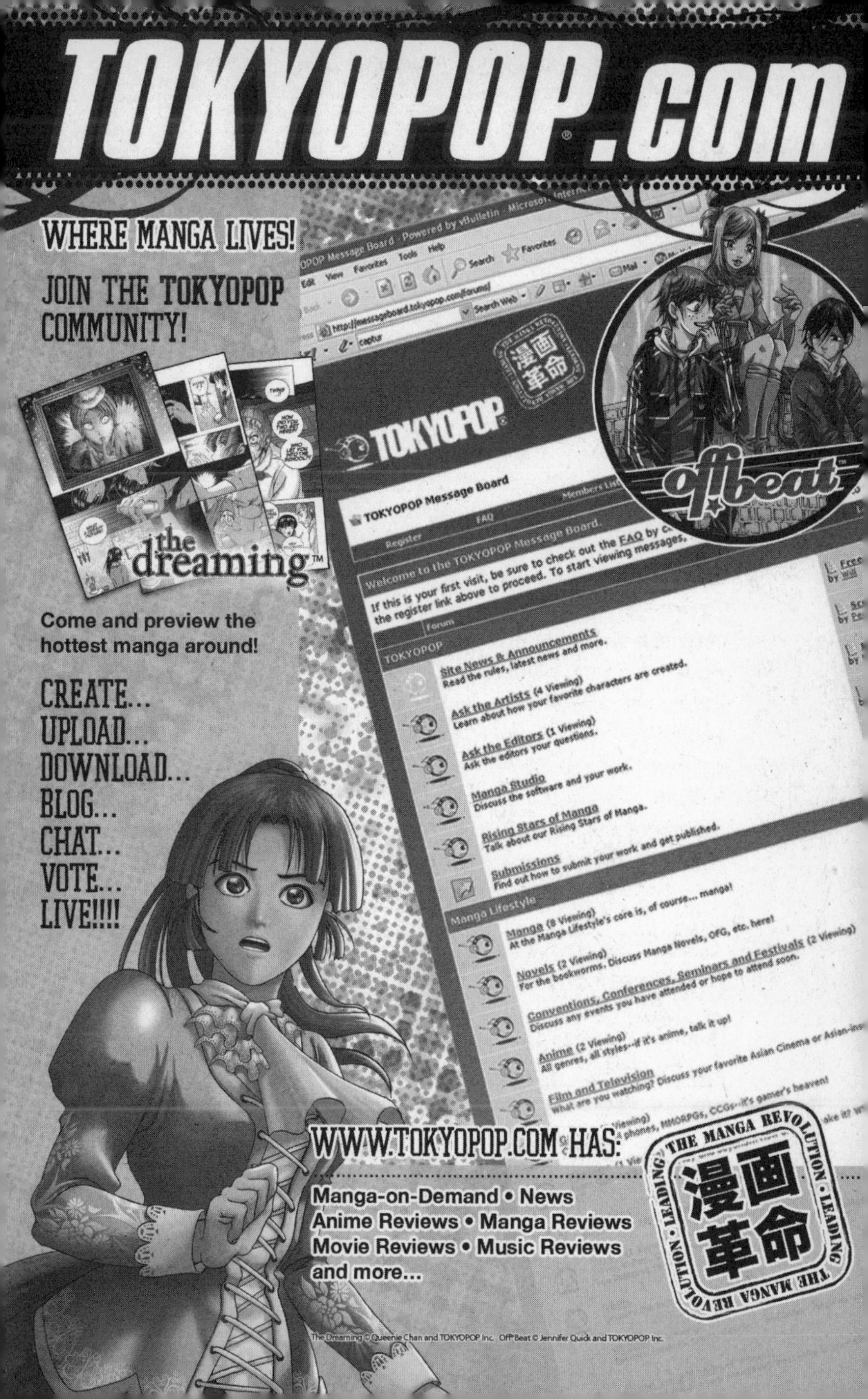
TOKYOPOP.com
WHERE MANGA LIVES!
JOIN THE TOKYOPOP COMMUNITY!
the dreaming
offbeat
Come and preview the hottest manga around!
CREATE...
UPLOAD...
DOWNLOAD...
BLOG...
CHAT...
VOTE...
LIVE!!!!
TOKYOPOP Message Board
Site News & Announcements
Ask the Artists
Ask the Editors
Manga Studio
Rising Stars of Manga
Submissions
Manga Lifestyle
WWW.TOKYOPOP.COM HAS:
Manga-on-Demand • News
Anime Reviews • Manga Reviews
Movie Reviews • Music Reviews
and more...
THE MANGA REVOLUTION • LEADING THE MANGA REVOLUTION • LEADING
漫画革命
The Dreaming © Queenie Chan and TOKYOPOP Inc. Off*Beat © Jennifer Quick and TOKYOPOP Inc.

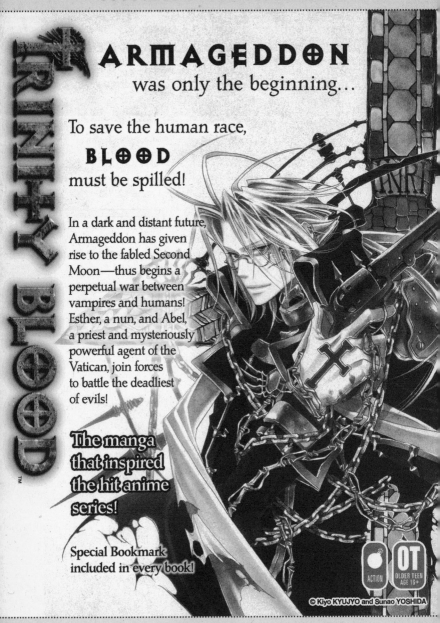

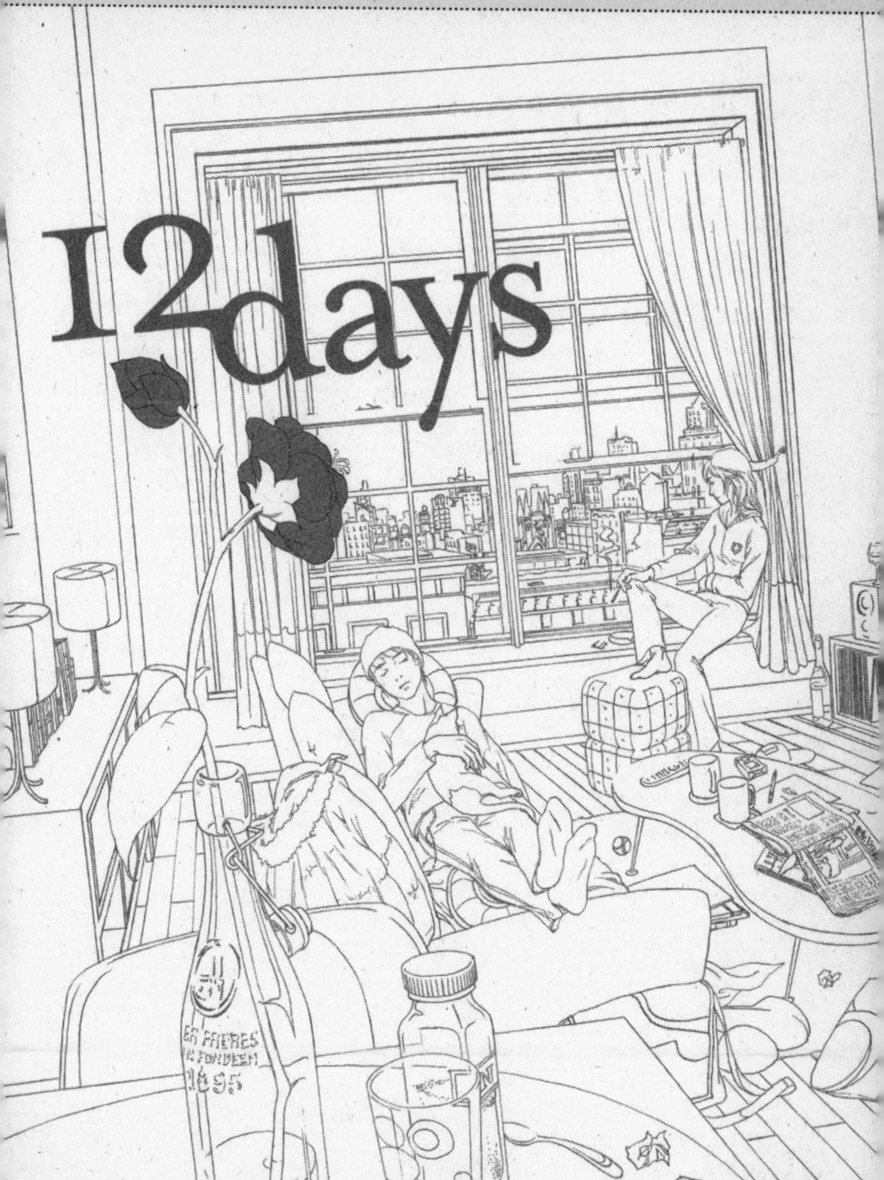
12days

How long would it take to get over...

losing the love of your life?

When Jackie's ex-lover Noah dies, she decides the quickest way to get over her is to hold a personal ritual with Noah's ashes. Jackie consumes the ashes in the form of smoothies for 12 days, hoping the pain will subside. But will that be enough?

From the internationally published illustrator June Kim.

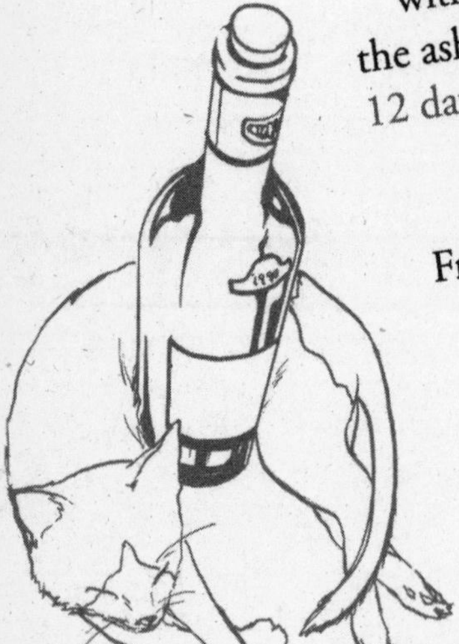

STOP!

This is the back of the book.
You wouldn't want to spoil a great ending!

This book is printed "manga-style," in the authentic Japanese right-to-left format. Since none of the artwork has been flipped or altered, readers get to experience the story just as the creator intended. You've been asking for it, so TOKYOPOP® delivered: authentic, hot-off-the-press, and far more fun!

DIRECTIONS

If this is your first time reading manga-style, here's a quick guide to help you understand how it works.

It's easy... just start in the top right panel and follow the numbers. Have fun, and look for more 100% authentic manga

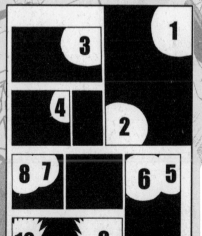

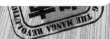